AI, Machine Learning, and Image Processing in Market Research and Branding

Md Faiz Ahmad
https://orcid.org/0000-0001-8002-6582
SRM University, Amaravati, India

Mudassir Rafi
King Khalid University, Saudi Arabia

Mohd Danish Kirmani
https://orcid.org/0000-0002-9641-8326
IILM University, Greater Noida, India

IGI Global
Scientific Publishing
Publishing Tomorrow's Research Today

Vice President of Editorial Melissa Wagner
Director of Acquisitions Mikaela Felty
Director of Book Development Jocelynn Hessler
Production Manager Mike Brehm
Cover Design Jose Rosado

Published in the United States of America by
IGI Global Scientific Publishing
701 East Chocolate Avenue
Hershey, PA, 17033, USA
Tel: 717-533-8845 | Fax: 717-533-7115
Website: https://www.igi-global.com E-mail: cust@igi-global.com

Library of Congress Cataloging-in-Publication Data

LCCN: 2025030716 (CIP Data Pending)
ISBN13: 979-8-3373-4506-2
Isbn13Softcover: 979-8-3373-4507-9
EISBN13: 979-8-3373-4508-6

British Cataloguing in Publication Data
A Cataloguing in Publication record for this book is available from the British Library.

Table of Contents

Detailed Table of Contents

This study examines the impact of artificial intelligence technologies in digital marketing storytelling to enhance brand engagement through personalized, dynamic content creation strategies. A descriptive research design was used along with purposive sampling to select 376 respondents from digital marketing consumers. The study analysed AI-driven storytelling frameworks to understand their application in creating adaptive marketing strategies across various digital media. AI-driven storytelling improves brand engagement by delivering personalized methods that adapt to individual consumer preferences. The technology enables real-time content optimization, resulting in higher engagement rates, improved customer retention, and enhanced brand loyalty. The effectiveness of AI-driven storytelling depends heavily on data quality, algorithm sophistication, and the balance between automation and human creativity.

With the development of advanced technologies that are reshaping our future, businesses around the globe are encompassing technologies within their business frameworks. One of the technologies that is reframing business practices is artificial intelligence (AI). Presently, AI has become an integral part of enterprise operations by driving innovation and competitiveness. It has also revolutionised businesses by improving their decision-making and operations, which has a positive impact on their performance and customer experiences. The present study aims to examine AI's future in enterprises by outlining the various dimensions of AI adoption in modern enterprises. Alongside, case studies of successful AI models of three tech giants (Google, Amazon, and Meta) are provided to further facilitate a practical understanding of the concepts that are underlying AI-driven enterprises. The study has managerial and practical implications, as it provides significant insights for the development and adoption of AI strategies for enterprises.

Brand equity ceases to exist as a fixed entity but as a dynamic and perceptual process which is influenced by visual interactions in real time. This chapter will discuss how generative AI, with the help of such devices as GANs, diffusion models, and computer vision, can be used to analyze brand sentiment in real-time via user-made images. This method combines emotion recognition, social media monitoring, and latent space modeling in order to capture brand perception by geography, culture, and time. In contrast to the traditional survey-based approach, the proposed AI-powered model will provide an in-depth understanding of how visuals influence brand associations, and emotional resonance. The chapter also covers ethical issues of automation and provides a framework of a hybrid human-AI solution to transparent and culturally aware brand analytics. Such an interdisciplinary synthesis will act as a strategic framework in which marketers, artificial intelligence coders, and scientists can gauge and manipulate brand equity in the visual digital age ethically.

The rise of Artificial Intelligence (AI) in market research and branding analytics is reshaping how organizations understand and engage consumers, offering advantages such as hyper-personalized campaigns, predictive brand positioning, and real-time sentiment analysis. Yet this transformation also raises major ethical concerns, including data privacy risks, algorithmic bias, opaque decision-making, and the erosion of consumer autonomy. This chapter examines these issues through a multidisciplinary lens, proposing a framework grounded in fairness, accountability, interpretability, and informed consent. Drawing on case studies and auditing failures, it shows how poorly designed or unregulated systems can damage brand integrity, foster mistrust, and produce discriminatory outcomes. The discussion highlights Explainable AI, bias detection, responsible governance, and user-centered design as essential for aligning innovation with ethics. Ultimately, it offers guidelines for building transparent, fair, and trustworthy brand–consumer relationships in the digital economy

The integration of Artificial Intelligence (AI), Machine Learning (ML), and image processing in marketing research and branding enables predictive analytics, hyper-personalisation, and real-time consumer engagement. However, these technologies raise ethical concerns over privacy, surveillance, consent, and behavioural manipulation. Personal and biometric data are often collected without user awareness, undermining autonomy. Risks include targeting based on inferred emotions, loss of agency, and algorithmic biases that may cause discrimination in segmentation and representation. The chapter also evaluates synthetic media, such as AI-generated influencers, for their impact on authenticity, trust, and perception. While legal frameworks like GDPR and CCPA exist, their limitations are noted. To address these challenges, the chapter proposes ethical frameworks stressing transparency, accountability, and interdisciplinary governance to foster fairness, trust, and societal benefit in AI-driven marketing.

AI-powered market research leverages diverse sources—transactions, surveys, browsing behavior, and more—to derive actionable insights that guide strategic decision-making. However, this data-intensive approach raises significant concerns regarding data privacy, a fundamental issue that must be rigorously addressed to maintain trust, ensure compliance with legal frameworks, and protect individual rights. Data privacy, broadly defined, refers to the handling, processing, storage, and sharing in ways safeguard prevent unauthorized access or misuse. In AI-driven market research, data privacy involves a complex interplay of ethical, technical, considerations influence, anonymized, encrypted, ultimately utilized. ensuring data privacy -powered market research need for detailed, high-quality data against privacy safeguards. AI algorithms thrive on detailed, granular data to detect subtle patterns

Preface

The emergence of technologies such as generative artificial intelligence (Gen AI), machine learning (ML) and image processing has transformed the marketing landscape. These technologies are changing the rules of the game and reshaping the marketing strategies *vis-à-vis* consumer engagement, brand management, market research and value delivering. As a result, the modern-day organizations are competing on the basis of speed, hyper-connectivity and the level of personalization provided to the consumers.

These emerging technologies have enabled the real-time consumer tracking and interactions, data driven decision making, and automated content generation. The contemporary marketers are using AI tools and analytics to predict consumer behaviour, map consumer journey and enhance brand value for the consumers. However, there are some concerns related to these technologies. These concerns are primarily related to privacy, unethical use, impact on health of the users, etc. This necessitates the proper understanding of how these emerging technologies can be responsibly and ethically integrated in the marketing strategies for an improved customer experience.

This book comprehensively examines the AI-driven disruptions in the marketing decisions led by branding and consumer engagement strategies. The book chapters explore the AI-driven disruptions in diverse contexts such as e-commerce, voice-assisted shopping, quick commerce markets, among others. The chapters also evaluate the ethical implications of AI-driven disruptions in marketing focusing on discriminatory targeting, intellectual property concerns, and the interpretability of algorithmic decision-making.

This edited book will contribute to improved understanding of the academics and researchers related to how the emerging technologies such as AI, machine learning and image processing can be leveraged in conducting market research and brand management. The book will also be a reference for the practitioners in their endevour to integrate AI tools effectively in the marketing framework. Further, the book will also act as a guide for the students to understand the future of marketing in the AI-driven world.

CHAPTER OVERVIEW

Chapter 1 explores GenAI's role in branding evolution from creative automation to real-time content personalization and integration into AR/VR environments. Case studies, including Coca-Cola's "Create Real Magic" and Canva's AI-driven design tools, demonstrate increased engagement, user participation, and operational efficiency. The chapter also addresses ethical concerns, copyright ambiguity, and the importance of human-AI collaboration. GenAI, when implemented responsibly, redefines branding with agility, creativity, and data-driven precision.

Chapter 2 explores the transformative role of computer vision in decoding and analyzing visual brand identity within today's visually driven marketplace. It highlights how AI-powered techniques such as logo detection, color palette extraction recognition enable marketers to objectively measure and manage the core visual elements that shape brand perception.

Chapter 3 explores the ways in which artificial intelligence is changing brand storytelling into a more dynamic and data-driven process for enhancing engagement and measuring brand equity. It looks at how AI helps generate personalized narratives and also measures emotional and behavioral reactions from consumers. The chapter discusses both the opportunities and challenges that come from blending computational tools with human creativity.

Chapter 4 examines the impact of artificial intelligence technologies in digital marketing storytelling to enhance brand engagement through personalized, dynamic content creation strategies. A descriptive research design was used along with purposive sampling to select 376 respondents from digital marketing consumers.

Chapter 5 aims to examine AI's future in enterprises by outlining the various dimensions of AI adoption in modern enterprises. Alongside, case studies of successful AI models of three tech giants (Google, Amazon, and Meta) are provided to further facilitate a practical understanding of the concepts that are underlying AI-driven enterprises.

Chapter 6 discusses how generative AI, with the help of such devices as GANs, diffusion models, and computer vision, can be used to analyze brand sentiment in real-time via user-made images. This method combines emotion recognition, social media monitoring, and latent space modeling in order to capture brand perception by geography, culture, and time.

Chapter 7 highlights Explainable AI, bias detection, responsible governance, and user-centered design as essential for aligning innovation with ethics. Ultimately, it offers guidelines for building transparent, fair, and trustworthy brand–consumer relationships in the digital economy

Chapter 8 proposes ethical frameworks stressing transparency, accountability, and interdisciplinary governance to foster fairness, trust, and societal benefit in AI-driven marketing.

The last chapter examines the growing role of AI-powered market research and the data privacy challenges it presents. Drawing on diverse data sources such as transactions, surveys, and digital behavior, AI systems enable deeper and more actionable market insights, but they also intensify concerns around the collection and use of sensitive information.

CONCLUSION

In conclusion, it can be stated that the rapid rise of GenAI will bring unprecedented disruptions in the marketing practices aimed at conducting marketing research, brand management and consumer engagement. The book not only explore the applications of AI in the marketing practices (such as personalization, consumer insights, predictive analytics) but it also highlights the ethical concerns and call for the responsible and transparent integration of AI in the marketing processes and practices.

The editors hope that the insights presented in this book will contribute to the advanced research, informed decision making, and building sustainable, responsible, and human-centric marketing ecosystems. The editors appreciate scholarly contributions of all the authors that strengthens academic discourse at a critical juncture of integration of emerging technologies with the marketing ecosystem.

Chapter 1

Generative Artificial Intelligence for Visual Branding and Creative Automation in Modern Marketing Ecosystems

R. N. Ravikumar
https://orcid.org/0009-0009-3705-1681
Marwadi University, Rajkot, India

S. Aarthi
https://orcid.org/0009-0006-9064-2091
Marwadi University, Rajkot, India

Valisher Sapayev
https://orcid.org/0000-0002-6751-5864
Mamun University, Khiva, Uzbekistan

Alijon Esanov
Termez University of Economics and Service, Termez, Uzbekistan

ABSTRACT

Generative AI (GenAI) is transforming visual branding by enabling automated creation of logos, packaging, advertising content, and social media assets. Leveraging models like GANs and diffusion models, tools such as DALL·E, Midjourney, and Canva's Magic Design facilitate personalized, high-quality visuals at scale. This chapter explores GenAI's role in branding evolution from creative automation to

DOI: 10.4018/979-8-3373-4506-2.ch001

real-time content personalization and integration into AR/VR environments. Case studies, including Coca-Cola's "Create Real Magic" and Canva's AI-driven design tools, demonstrate increased engagement, user participation, and operational efficiency. The chapter also addresses ethical concerns, copyright ambiguity, and the importance of human-AI collaboration. GenAI, when implemented responsibly, redefines branding with agility, creativity, and data-driven precision.

1. INTRODUCTION TO GENERATIVE AI IN BRANDING

The rapid advancement of the Generative AI (GenAI) is changing the branding and marketing plasm map because the level of innovation, customization, and automatization are on a new creative plane that has never been observed before. Unlike traditional approaches to design, which might be highly labour and skills-intensive and time-consuming, GenAI, through the aid of powerful models, such as Generative Adversarial Networks (GANs) and diffusion models, generates high-fidelity visual materials on its own and per brand aesthetics. The conceptualization and work on marketing and designing of logos, advertisement creatives, social media, and campaign collaterals can now be done with little or no manual input using DALL does not exist, the Midjourney, Runway ML, Adobe Firefly and many others (Cai, 2025a). The advance allows the brands to produce additional iterations, be creative and experiment in various forms and dynamically adjust the images to suit various audiences. It is not only a technical change but also a strategic change with GenAI in the branding processes in order to enable the hyper-personal content in such scales, never been heard of before. The branding shift in meaning, involving the transformation of identity to engagement, opens the field of engineered machine intelligence to co-creation with a co-creative partner, GenAI.

1.1. Evolution of Creative Automation in Marketing

Marketing automation has drastically changed on the creative side-at first, it was designed using templates, then it was made with the help of AI. First, automation industry was aimed at automation of repetitive operations such as email campaigns or banner automation. Nevertheless, the development of AI, mainly machine learning and natural language processing, enabled marketers to use smart tools to customize messages and the flow of content. The newest advancement fuelled by Generative AI has come in the world of a paradigm shift wherein machines are no longer there only to aid but ideate and even build. Compared to rule-based automation, GenAI will create original visual and textual work because it could learn based on significant data, and therefore the selected firm does not require any creative team to create standard information(Huang & Rust, 2021). This change enables brands to quickly respond to quickly moving consumer trends, create A/B variations at scale and develop the responsive creative ecosystems. This course of creative automation no longer runs toward signification, mechanical production parameters, and now heads towards changing human goals, which is data-driven design combining technology and story-telling, a paradigm shift in the digital era of branding. The Figure 1 illustrates the progressive stages of creative automation in marketing from template-based automation to AI-enhanced automation, followed by Generative AI ideation, data-driven design, and culminating in responsive creative ecosystems. The image reflects how the marketing process has evolved from static template usage toward dynamic, AI-driven, real-time content generation and iteration, emphasizing a continuous feedback loop fuelled by machine intelligence and human creativity.

Figure 1. Stages in the evolution of creative automation in marketing

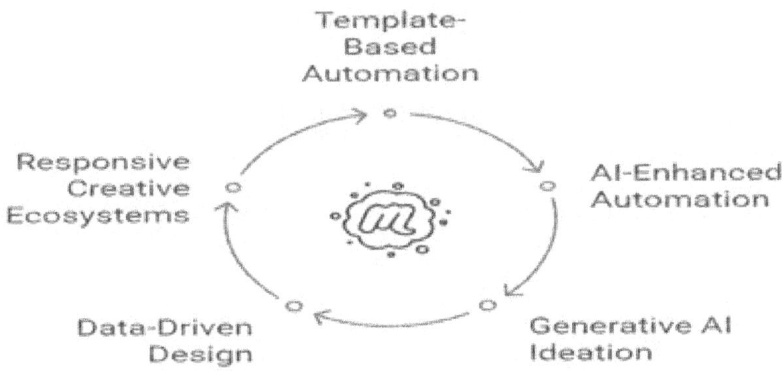

1.2. Role of Generative AI in Visual Identity and Content Strategy

Generative AI is actively involved in the redesign of the brand process of creating and expressing the visual element of identity. Previously, the visuals of a brand would be painted or drawn using stagnant instructions and it would take several weeks of design brain-storming. GenAI has come to disrupt this by making it possible to create logos, packaging, advertisement and campaign images in real time and based on branding. Like large data sets of images can train GenAI models to capture brand tonality, cultural implications and sentiment of the audience, which will eventually produce content that is both aesthetically pleasing and strategically right. This feature renders the content strategy a dynamic topic, the visuals altering on the premise of the performance, of the usage, contextual trends. GenAI also enables modular content creation, in which the marketing teams can build and dynamically customise assets to various platforms, groups and moods. Love, that is, provides brands with creative flexibility and enables them to seem consistent in terms of identity, and flexible in terms of expression, which is significant in the rapidly changing digital market (Iakovlev et al., 2023). The Figure 2 presents the five main capabilities of Generative AI to revolutionize creating visual identity of brands. Starting with the center, it outlines the ways in which GenAI would allow real time creation, brand tonality and cultural fit, dynamic content strategy, modular content creation, and creative flexibility. Every capability is identified by a distinctive icon and color-coded path, which is used to demonstrate the interdimensional advantages of applying GenAI tools in visual branding. This characterization highlights the fact that AI can enable brands to create more flexible, contextually aware and culturally relevant visual content on an expedited basis and with enhanced strategic value.

Figure 2. Key capabilities of generative AI in brand visuals

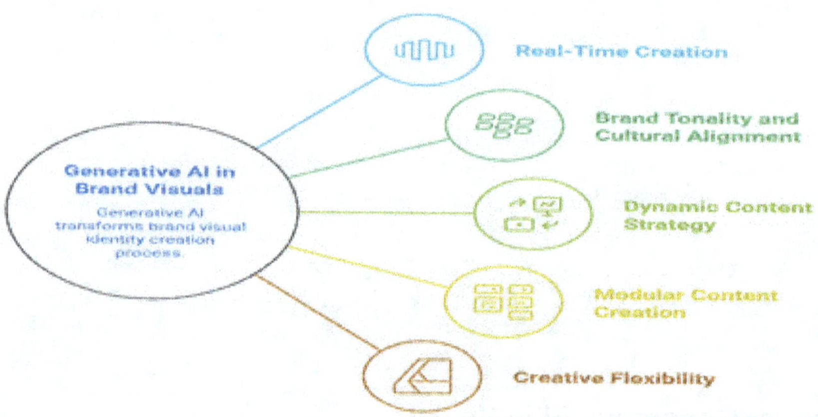

1.3 Literature Review

The sources supporting the idea of Generative Artificial Intelligence in branding and marketing point out the fact that the time of traditional, human-oriented creative processes has passed, and the hybrid ecosystems in which machine intelligence and human judgment co-exists have come to existence (Hoppe, 2018). The initial studies on marketing automation were aimed at the efficiency benefits of rule-based marketing automation and template-based content generation, focusing on scalability of operations instead of creativity (Prabagar et al., 2025). As machine learning, especially deep learning advanced, researchers started to acknowledge the role of AI as an enabler of both decisions and creativity, which can produce original visual and textual results. Recent research points out that the visual branding has been radically transformed with GANs and diffusion-based models because they allow rapid ideation, high-volume variation, and more contextual generation of content that fits brand aesthetics (Aarthi et al., 2025). It has always been reported in the literature that these technologies facilitate real-time personalization, multichannel adaptation, data-driven experimentation, and, consequently, increased engagement and responsiveness in dynamic marketing settings.

Meanwhile, scholars urge against a technocentric perspective, pointing out that creative automation may be exposed to risks associated with dilution of brands, loss of authenticity, and over-standardization unless human supervision is reduced to a minimal level. New work is defining AI generative as an assistant to designers instead of a substitute, and emphasizes the relevance of human-in-the-loop models in order to maintain strategic intent, cultural sensitivity and emotional appeal (Murár et al., 2024). The aspect of ethics has also become prominent with the studies talking about amplification of bias, imbalance in representation, ambiguity in intellectual property, and the problem of transparency as related to synthetic media. Governance wise, the literature highlights that there should be organizational policies, ethical principles and quality-control to make sure they are deployed responsibly (Ravikumar & Aarthi, 2025). In the recent years conceptual contributions have tried to incorporate generative AI into larger branding and technology adoption models, by connecting creative automation to brand identity theories, consumer trust theories and diffusion of innovation theories. Nevertheless, in spite of increasing conceptual clarity, the literature has significant gaps, especially in empirical confirmation, longitudinal testing of brand impact and cross-industrial and cross-cultural comparative analysis (Theurer et al., 2018). All in all, the current body of knowledge makes generative AI a revolution in visual branding, but at the same time, underlines that its value in the long term depends on the healthy balance of its use, ethical responsibility, and strategic direction of its core values.

2. TECHNICAL FOUNDATIONS OF GENERATIVE AI

Technical nature of Generative AI relies on a series of more sophisticated machine learning architectures capable of generating new content based on what the model was trained on and is highly similar to it. Generative Adversarial Networks (GANs) and diffusion models are two of the most influential ones. GANs are a type of neural network introduced back in 2014 by Ian Goodfellow and essentially comprise two neural networks a generator and a discriminator and operate together in an opposition manner (Shukla, 2024). The generator generates images, and discriminator checks their validity. The generator, through repeated training is enhanced to generate more realistic outputs that resemble that of the real-world data generating photorealistic images and stylized images among other creative resources.

Diffusion models instead operate by applying large amounts of noise to training data gradually, and learning to undo the noise to generate images. Such models, including the ones integrated in DALL·E 2 and in Stable Diffusion, have been successful in producing very detailed and coherent imagery based on textual descriptors. The other major attributes are the transformer architectures with prompt learning and CLIP (Contrastive Language is Image Pretraining) models that connect texts to image attribute and allow fine-tuned control of the content creation. Availability of large datasets and high-performance computing infrastructure enables one to use these models at scale and at various tasks. These types of models do not simply perform stylistic patterns learning but also acquire context and cultural clues-so they are ideal models of branding where tone and relevance are other influential factors (Gual-Ort\'\i et al., 2025). These are the technology fundamentals that marketers and designers ought to know as they seek to adopt GenAI in the creation team of their content and art design. The table 1 contrasts the main features of Generative Adversarial Networks (GANs) and Diffusion Models like architecture, quality of output, time spent on training, and compatibility with branding applications. It assists the readers to know the technical potentials and compatibility of each model type to the creative design context. Figure 3 below illustrates two major Generative AI models GANs and Diffusion Models and their operations. Generators and Discriminators are used in GANs to generate realistic images, whereas diffusion models such as DALL·E 2 and Stable Diffusion are used to produce detailed images. They both result in effective branding applications including logos, advertisements and visual content development.

Table 1. Comparison of generative AI models used in visual branding

Feature	GANs (Generative Adversarial Networks)	Diffusion Models
Architecture	Generator vs. Discriminator	Noise addition and denoising (reverse process)
Output Quality	High (may contain artifacts)	Ultra-high, photorealistic
Training Time	Faster but less stable	Slower but more stable
Prompt-based Generation	Limited	Highly effective
Use in Branding	Logo variants, style mimicry	Concept visuals, ad creatives, thematic imagery
Popular Tools	StyleGAN, BigGAN	DALL·E 2, Stable Diffusion, Midjourney

Figure 3. Generative AI model architectures and their role in branding

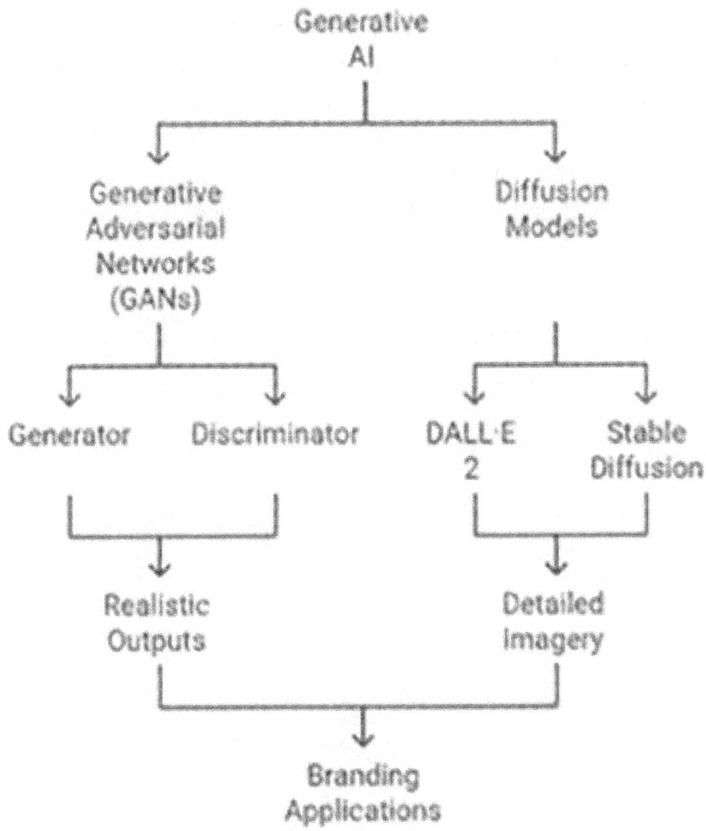

2.1. Overview of Generative Adversarial Networks (GANs) and Diffusion Models

The two biggest Generative AI innovations are Generative Adversarial Networks (GANs) and diffusion models. First developed in 2014 more recent, GANs also work in a two-model framework: a generator that synthesizes content, and a discriminator that trains to judge how realistic it is. With time, the generator develops the ability to render the outputs that cannot be distinguished from real ones, allowing to create realistic pictures, stylized images, and even animated videos (He et al., 2023). GANs find particular application in branding to create novel iterations of logos, style transfers and synthetic product mock-ups.

The newer and more popular architecture would be diffusion models. What they do is that they slowly inject random noise on input data and are then taught to undo the noise. The outcome is the possibility to create extraordinarily detailed, subtle images based off of pure noise steered typically through text cues. Such models as DALL·E 2 and Stable Diffusion have taken this process one step further by generating visual outputs that are consistent with language inputs, thus suitable to produce responsive and contextual visual output (Peng, 2024). The combination of these models composes the technological backbone of the AI-augmented visual branding innovation. The Figure 4 compares Generative Adversarial Networks and Diffusion Models, highlighting their distinct mechanisms GANs' two-model framework vs. diffusion's noise-based process. Both models are pivotal in branding applications, enabling realistic and detailed image generation.

Figure 4. Comparison of GANs and diffusion models in branding

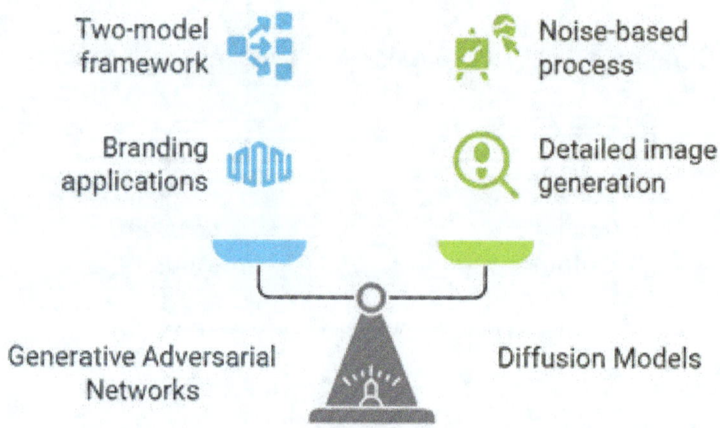

2.2. Key Tools and Platforms: DALL·E, Midjourney, Runway ML, Adobe Firefly

The marketers, designers, and content creators have been presented to some of the most sophisticated tools that have provided Generative AI. Among them, OpenAI has created DALL·E that uses diffusion to generate renowned images using natural language prompts. It is particularly useful in regard to abstract brand concept and advertising imagining, mood boards, and ideation. Its artistic and aesthetic slant has won the affections of the artistic folk because of its capacity to produce style and imagery that has an emotional appeal (Bagga & Kaur, 2025a). When a branding needs to utilize visual expressions during a campaign or social media content which is in need of artistic touch then it is applied.

Runway ML is an easy-to-use outlet that comprises various generative frameworks, such as text to image, video editing, and real-time editing. It features a no-code interface that allows non-technical users to create as well as manipulate brand assets. Adobe Firefly, a part of the Adobe Creative Cloud, brings AI close to professional designing processes (Cai, 2025b). Users can perform such operations like the generation of variations of content, extension of images, and the implementation of stylish changes with preservation of brand consistency. Content production can be dynamic and not require hundreds of designers to come up with brand creative; these platforms democratize creativity and make brand storytelling in a large amount of quantity and quality possible.

3. APPLICATIONS OF GENAI IN VISUAL BRANDING

Generative AI is transforming the visuality of any brand by automating the creative process and creating new high-efficiency creative workflows in design, advertising, and consumer engagement. It can no longer be used as a prototype or a concept art as its uses are now being applied in real production of big brands and marketing companies (Limantara, 2024). This is one of its major applications in generative AI logos where tools such as Looka or Tailor Brands employ the tool of GenAI, creating different logo variations that match brand tone, target audience, and industry appropriateness. This brings democracy to design where startups and small businesses can now be served with quality branding assets even where they do not have a dedicated design team. The other important use is in the design of packages and visualization of products. Generative models can be used in the creation of several visual prototypes applied to A/B Testing, regional packaging or especially limited-edition designs, all within the context of brand aesthetics and customer segmentation.

The ad creative production and social media assets are also done dynamically through GenAI. By creating contextually relevant branded visuals; brands are able to create visuals suited to different mediums, moods as well as audience demographics (Yuan, 2024). AI is even capable of generating variant sets in performance marketing to optimize on creative assets on a real-time basis depending on the engagement metrics. When it comes to the content specifically related to the campaign, GenAI will assist in facilitating visual stories, animated storytelling, and themed images in harmony with the brand. It facilitates quick ideation and scalability at the same time assuring quality and consistency (Babadoğan, 2024a). After all, GenAI can enable brands to scale creativity, individualize their interactions and streamline content delivery making it the co-creative partner in the contemporary visual branding. Table 2 outlines specific branding applications enabled by Generative AI such as logo creation, packaging visualization, social media content generation, and thematic storytelling along with examples and tools used. It serves as a quick reference for marketers exploring how GenAI can enhance their brand asset development.

Table 2. Key use cases of GenAI in visual branding

Application Area	Description	Common Tools Used	Benefit to Brands
Logo Design	Generates multiple stylistically aligned logo options	Looka, Adobe Firefly	Faster ideation, accessible for non-designers
Packaging Design	Visualizes product packaging in various formats and styles	Canva, Runway ML	Localization, A/B testing, rapid prototyping
Social Media Creatives	Platform-specific content in various moods or styles	Midjourney, Jasper Art	Increased engagement, rapid variant testing
Campaign Themes	Generates visuals based on moodboards or narratives	DALL·E, Firefly	Cohesive storytelling, brand tone matching

3.1. AI-Generated Logos, Icons, and Packaging Designs

Generative AI has made the generation of brand-defining assets like logos, icons and packaging design far easier and faster. The GAN and diffusion model-powered tools can generate many high-quality variations of the design produced on prompts, sketches, or reference images. Services such as Looka, Brandmark, and Adobe Firefly offer the possibilities to have specified style, industry, and tone as according to brand personality and core values, providing automatically generated logos, and icons. In packaging design, GenAI plays the role in visualizing product aesthetics displayed in various formats, colours and ethnic motifs (Davtyan, 2024). These systems, through training on large amounts of consumer products data and market tendencies, come up with on-brand packaging concepts that are pushed to a certain demographic group or territories. This is because it involves a fast ideation process, which cur curbs the need to have large teams of designers, and allows brands to scale their visual A/B testing. Using only a minimum prompt symbol to full-blown, culturally informed package design, GenAI boosts efficiency and creative possibilities - helping brands take creative brand assets to market, fast and cheap.

3.2. Visual Storytelling and Thematic Brand Imagery

In addition to logos and packaging, Generative AI enables visual storytelling creation which is all about creating a theme based on imagery to convey brand values, feelings, and identity. Tools such as Midjourney and Runway ML enable marketers to create campaign visuals that are all-encompassing visually, emotionally, and contextually by turning textual prompt into highly emotive visuals. To give an example, a fashion brand might have created campaign images with lifestyle looks in various cultures and seasons, but in the visual tone of the brand. On the same note, FMCG brands are creatively able to map out the customer journeys or the use-cases of their products in an art style that strikes a chord within their audiences (Farseev et al., 2018). It allows creating more consistent visual themes not only in any online environment but also in advertisements and Augmented Reality (AR) campaigns. Theme-based brand images made with the assistance of AI will be able to adjust in accordance with the latest trends, user-data, or campaign intent and be dynamic. GenAI makes storytelling an expandable task, in which plots are not finalized but can change depending on audience reactions, and the images can no longer be considered unchangeable as they become dynamic and data-based.

4. DYNAMIC CONTENT CREATION FOR MARKETING CAMPAIGNS

Generative AI can be used to create dynamic content - the automated composition of a wide range of marketing material that is targeted, high impact and that responds to the audience behaviors, preferences and platforms in real time. Conventional marketing efforts commonly count on pre-considered unmoving designs, which may easily end up being rapid and redundant or obsolete by various age groups and touchpoints. GenAI solves this by making brands able to create variants of content in large numbers in a fraction of a second (Gilbert, 2024). As an illustration, one campaign idea can be translated into various styles, languages, emotional moods, or visual types with the help of AI such as Adobe Firefly, Runway ML, or Jasper Art. Such a buffer comes in handy when working with performance marketing when A/B testing of the visual aspect of marketing on other platforms (Facebook, Instagram, Google Ads) requires constant experimenting and improving.

Besides, with GenAI, it is possible to scale personalization. Depending on the location, browsing history, or trends, brands can customize visuals to concrete user profiles, such as a change in colour, background or position of a product. This increases the interaction rates and conversions because the user feels more personal and closer (Havale et al., 2025). Generative AI also provides real-time creative modification, so once a marketer noticed the campaign analytics or dynamically changing market conditions, they can make real-time adjustments without having to revisit the design team. This accelerates time to market and gives marketing teams more flexibility and control of creative decision making. GenAI reshapes the very limits of creative production by reinventing the conception and execution of marketing assets, turning campaigns into adaptive, individually tailored, and data-driven to an unprecedented degree. The table 3 highlights how GenAI supports multichannel content adaptation, A/B testing, and real-time personalization. It includes key metrics like engagement rate improvement, time savings, and use across marketing platforms (e.g., Instagram, YouTube, Google Ads).

Table 3. AI-enabled content personalization and ad variant strategies

Strategy	Description	AI Role	Resulting Impact
Multichannel Variant Creation	Generates content for various platforms and formats	Auto-resizing and tone adaptation	Campaign consistency, time efficiency
Real-Time Personalization	Tailors visuals based on consumer data (location, preference, behavior)	Adaptive image generation	Higher engagement, relevance
A/B Creative Testing	Auto-generates multiple ad variations	Visual element variation (color, copy, CTA)	Optimized ad performance
Creative Refresh Automation	Replaces low-performing assets in real-time	Data-driven visual optimization	Improved CTR and reduced fatigue

4.1. Multichannel Ad Variants and A/B Testing at Scale

Generative AI grants marketers the ability to generate multichannel ad variants at an incredibly high scale that allows marketers to create massive A/B test experiments across ad platforms such as Google, Meta, YouTube, and programmatic display networks. In the traditional form, creating platform-optimized ad creatives, which are the creatives that are size, tone, audience and placement optimized, have to be made through a manual process of design and iteration. Using GenAI tools, marketers get a chance to create dozens or even hundreds of ad variations based on one campaign brief (Hemalatha, 2023). The variants may vary by colour scheme, typefaces, background context, characters and their presence, mood, or even product placement, and give marketers an idea of what content appeal the most to which segment. As an example, a visual of the advertisement of a drink can be auto-generated with the tropical motivators in the coastal lands and warm, indoor sceneries in the colder locations. Creative optimization, too, is automated with AI-driven tools by taking the steps of retiring poorly-performing images, and amplifying top-performing ones in real time, when integrated with ad performance dashboards (Huynh et al., 2021). Such a data-driven and scalable model of generating content decreases ad fatigue and magnifies returns on investments as well as lessens the learning cycles in digital marketing.

4.2. Real-Time Personalization of Visual Content Using Consumer Data

One legacy application of GenAI in marketing is real-time visual personalization, such that brand content is changed on the fly based on personal data about a consumer. AI systems can change backgrounds, language, colours or what products to feature, according to location, demographics, behavioural patterns, or even emotional tone as inferred by reactivity to past interactions that are integrated through Customer Data Platforms (CDPs). As an example, a fashion retailer can display winter clothes visuals to the users of colder locations and summer clothes to the users of warmer climates, all this can be done using DA generated from AI. Likewise, when a user is viewing an advertisement of a product, the colour scheme can be customized to accommodate past history of views or Facebook favourites. Such an amount of hyper-personalization increases customer interest, and now the viewer will feel noticed and understood (Koswara, 2025). It also increases the number of click-throughs and conversion, since users react better to contextually relevant content. By automating this, GenAI gives brands the opportunity to reduce production bottlenecks and increase speed to market, which subsequently allows them to generate scale-at-will custom content that unpredictably affects brand consistency and degree of creative work.

5. INTEGRATING GENAI INTO CREATIVE WORKFLOWS

In order to take full advantage of the potential of Generative AI, the organizations need to integrate generative AI into the current creative workflow in a strategic manner. GenAI should not take over the role of human creativity but act as an auxiliary tool of co-creation, which supports ideation, saves time and routine, and speeds up content generation departmentally (Kubovics, 2024). The integration itself usually starts on the conceptualization level and the visuals created by AI can be employed as the moodboards and earlier drafts or conceptual variations. They allow the faster brainstorming process on the part of designers and marketers and enable them to test ideas with stakeholders. This makes the creative approval processes leaner, and the whole process is sped up since feedback can be obtained sooner and iteration can happen faster.

During the production process, GenAI is integrated in design programs or linked by API with, e.g., Adobe Creative Cloud, Canva, or Figma. Through the same interface, marketers are able to create platform-specific materials on the fly, adapt imagery to localize experiences, and create real-time campaign resources. GenAI is also used at the distribution and optimization phases together with marketing automation tools (e.g., HubSpot, Salesforce, or Meta Ads Manager). In this case, visual material is dynamically set, depending on the campaign results, the A/B tests and customer activity data (Massoudi et al., 2023). Organizations use quality control systems to make them consistent since the quality control involves the participation of creative directors and brand managers in checking the AI generated outputs. What is good about this mixed model is that it will have speed and scale at a point of intersection of brand identity. Using GenAI as a key component in the creative process enables a brand to enter a more implicit, information-driven, collaborative content universe, in which an idea can be taken to execution more quickly than it has ever been before (Moharam & Tawalbeh, 2025). The Figure 5 illustrates how Generative AI can be embedded across three key stages of the creative workflow Conceptualization, Production, and Distribution & Optimization. It highlights the AI's role in ideation, design automation, campaign execution, and performance-driven content refinement.

Figure 5. Integrating generative AI into creative workflows

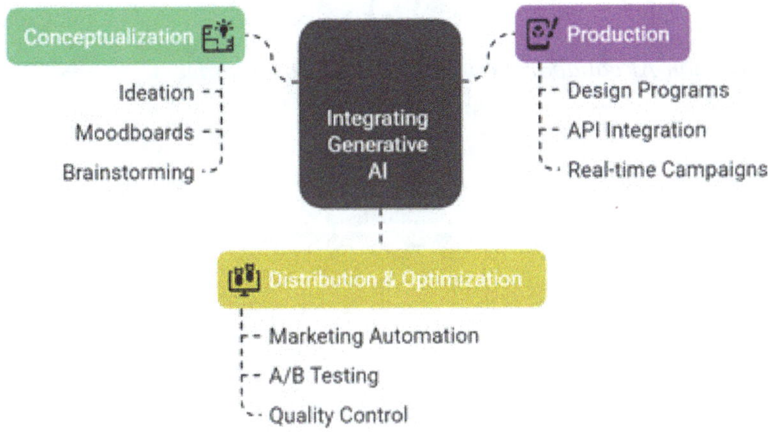

5.1. Human-AI Collaboration in Brand Design Pipelines

Generative AI does not seek to usurp human creativity, but it is an ally, whose capabilities increase the speed and efficiency of design. AI may be regarded as a creative partner in the modern brand design channel, which is capable of providing rapid visual advice, generate design alternatives, and assist in the brand directions through iteration. A lot of visual interpretations of the information given by designers in their prompt or quick-drawn sketches, scribbled style pointers, or even rough designs are produced by GenAI models (Raut et al., 2024). As an illustration, brand strategists can use Midjourney or Adobe Firefly to design the moodboards or the theme of the campaigns that are later refined by hand. This is time-saving and reduces the load on the brain during a brainstorming process. Human control is however needed. Creative directors are the ones that give the nod to the potential designs and they are certain that they are within the cultural framework, and they are brand-transparent and morally correct. It is up to the human designers to then be the curators, editors and strategic thinkers who ensure that the technology is not a dilution of brand identity but rather a supplement of it (National, 2025). It is the collaborative process that endows the power to work fast without the need to lose creativity or any emotional appeal to allow the marketing teams the autonomy to focus on strategic storytelling. Figure 6 depicts the repeatable process of branding using Generative AI which begins with AI generated images, which are then refined by humans, approved to a certain consistency, and finally a strategic account is given to them. It puts emphasis on the co-creative cycle in which technology and human creativity contribute to every step of brand designing.

Figure 6. Human-AI collaboration in the brand design process

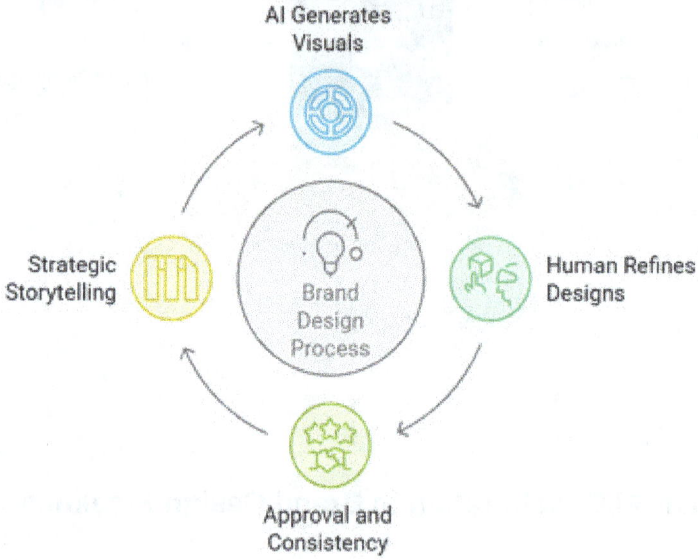

5.2. Automating Visual Asset Generation in Marketing Automation Systems

Generative AI can be applied to marketing automation systems: they can be used to create personalized content in real-time where customers interact. Marketing tools such as Salesforce Marketing Cloud, HubSpot and Adobe Experience Manager now have AI enhanced content modules which have the ability to auto-create, modify, and publish visuals depending on user information and campaign results. An example is, upon product launch, GenAI is able to create custom ad creatives (e.g.: Instagram story, YouTube thumbnail, banner ad, etc.), platform-optimized and an audience-segment (each audience segment) is practically generated automatically (Verma, 2025). These images are formed by using available brand materials or word descriptions and handed through automated processes with limited human interaction. As GenAI has access to campaign analytics, brands can make sure that the creative work is always better matched, that the content that is not popular can be substituted, or that the resources can be configured to accommodate and fit the new activity of the user. This reduces the time delays between performance intelligence and creative update to allow the marketing more flexibility and response rates (H. Wang et al., 2024). The possibility to automate the creation of visual assets transforms the marketing process into a closed machine that produces a feedback, creates and delivers the content in a single step which can be scaled and ultimately assists in producing personalization, efficiency and scale of creative throughput.

6. CHALLENGES, ETHICS, AND GOVERNANCE

Although Generative AI is a treasure trove of branding and marketing opportunities, it has also posed various challenges, ethical concerns, and regulations and rules that should be actively addressed by companies. One of the most significant challenges is ambiguity to the Intellectual Property (IP) and copyrighting. The AI-generated visuals are often trained on publicly available datasets, which may include the work which is copyrighted or have various styles. This raises the issue of the proprietorship, originality and even the liability in case of legal standoff especially when it comes to designs that are somehow related to the already existing brand property (Figoli et al., 2022). Brand inconsistency is another major issue that should be addressed. Although GenAI may create an infinite number of visual variations, to be certain that all the outputs are successful adhering to the branding, tone, insensitivities and so on will need excellent quality measures and human oversight. When uncontrolled, this may result in such problems as divided up brand identities or apposite conditionings publishing-related to brand names.

Ethically, concern with bias and representation of AI generated content has been on the increase. The trained models on non-diverse datasets further normalize the stereotypes or do not reflect some cultures, ages, or communities in such a way that they undermine inclusivity in brand messages. On top of these, the loss of human creativity poses both philosophical and business-related dilemma (Guerra-Tamez et al., 2024). What might happen as human designers continue to focus on the process of content generation is that there may be a situation where the individuals may become too reliant on the output of the machine and as a result, the level of original thought may decline. In order to steer clear of these problems, organizations are expected to introduce AI governance systems such as open policy measures, audit logs, responsible utilization controls, and innovative confirmation points (Gual-Ort\'\i et al., 2025). GenAI responsibility adoption implies disrupting a balance between innovation, responsibility, and compliance with human-based values on branding. The table 4 shows possible challenges such as copyright infringement, brand inconsistency, bias, and authenticity problems and remedies such as human control and transparency policies, ethical datasets, and transparency policies.

Table 4. Risks and ethical considerations in AI-generated branding

Risk Area	Description	Example Scenario	Mitigation Strategy
Copyright Ambiguity	AI-generated content may reflect copyrighted styles or works	Logo closely resembles existing brand	Use vetted datasets, add human review
Brand Inconsistency	Outputs may stray from defined visual identity	Mismatched colour or tone in campaign assets	Prompt engineering, style guides
Bias and Representation	Lack of diversity in training data may skew results	Images lack gender/race balance	Inclusive datasets, regular audits
Loss of Authenticity	Over-automation may dilute human creativity	Over-reliance on templates for storytelling	Keep human-in-the-loop in final approval

6.1. Copyright, Originality, and Brand Consistency Risks

The issue of copyright and originality is one of the most burning issues of Generative AI in branding. Because most of the generative models are used on amassed, openly scraped datasets, their content can touch upon or repetitively recreate aligned works without planning it. This is a major legal hazard to brands particularly when it comes to using the AI generated visuals in public campaigns or the packaging of the products. Besides, GenAI instruments may produce the works that violate well-developed brand rules without appropriate imaginative guidance (Wang, 2024). Even a slight variation in colour, typography, tone or symbolism will blur a brand identity as time goes by. The AI does not have, unlike human designers, the implicit knowledge of culture specifics, emotional intent and the perspective of the brand. Brands need to implement AI usage policies to curb against the above risks, retain humanized oversight through final-approval, and adopt guardrails through brand style libraries and immediate engineering templates. It is vital to combine the use of AI in a controlled creative environment that will provide legal security and coherence in design.

6.2. Ethical Considerations and Bias in AI-Generated Visuals

Generative AI models are representative of what they have been trained of and this inadvertently results in biases and ethical lapse in visual branding. When training data is not diverse, or poorly representative of cultural groups, generated visuals will likely encourage stereotyping, prejudice against some groups, or the promotion of exclusionary norms (Babadoğan, 2024b). As an example, AI will revert to a certain gender role as well as body and racial types based on the overrepresented trends in data logs. This may create exclusive marketing content that is not able to communicate effectively with the global community or with multicultural world.

Moreover, it poses moral issues of authenticity and manipulation with the fact that it is possible to create photorealistic people and environments. The AI-synthetics can lessen the clarity in real and fake pictures hence denting the confidence that exists between brands and consumers. In order to resolve these problems, organizations will be required to implement ethical principles into design, train AI models based on a diverse and inclusive dataset, and require interdisciplinary teams, such as ethicists, designers, and legal experts, in the implementation of AI (Friatin, 2025). A consortium of AI-generated content that upholds an accountability system and consumer trust in a GenAI-driven branding ecosystem can be achieved through transparent means of labelling AI generated content as well as through a system of constant audits.

7. CASE STUDIES: REAL-WORLD DEPLOYMENTS OF GENERATIVE AI IN BRANDING

Generative AI has already produced an immense wave of influences in branding by the large campaigns and commonly utilized tools. The Coca-Cola campaign, Create Real Magic is also a historic one, wherein Coca-Cola collaborated with OpenAI to enable people all over the world to create Coca-Cola art with products such as DALL 39 E and ChatGPT (Ip, 2023). More than encouraging the creativity of users, this project facilitated the enhancement of the brand engagement process by allowing consumers to be a part of the designing process in a style where a boundary between an audience and a creator is not distinct.

In the same manner, Canva Magic Design has dissolved the elitism of small companies branding. With the help of AI, Canva allows a non-designer to make a professional logo, brand kit, and marketing asset that fits their industry, tone and audience in mere iterations or uploaded text and images (Varsha P. S. et al., 2021). All of these case studies show how GenAI can empower not only multi-national companies but small businesses as well, facilitating creativity, removing the boundaries of design and transforming the future of visual branding by using co-creation, access, and personalized generation of content.

7.1 Coca-Cola's Use of DALL·E for "Create Real Magic" Campaign (2023)

In 2023, the company rolled out its pioneering campaign, Create Real Magic, a worldwide initiative in the context of which Coca-Cola implemented OpenAI technologies in the branding used by consumers (DALL·E and GPT-4). This was among the first occasions when such a large global brand has given the ability to ordinary users to co-create visual content with state-of-the-art generative AI tools (Kotapati, 2025). The campaign allowed users to create exclusive digital paintings on the theme of Coca-Cola, which were created with the help of their AI, featuring such traditional elements of the brand identity as the contour bottle, polar bears, red ribbon, and the classic Spencerian script. The game achieved excellent international coverage as people generated over 120,000 original works of art within only a few weeks of launch and in more than 100 countries. The percentage of people who created content and shared it in social media amounted to about 30, and it increased organic reach and brand engagement significantly (Kubovics, 2025). The metrics of its digital activity such as likes, shares, and comments on Coca-Cola main social media platforms have increased by 5% during the campaign period. In addition, the campaign was able to align with 6% quarter-over-quarter sales in the Q2 2023 period, in part because of an increase in consumer interaction.

In order to enhance the influence further, Coca-Cola displayed some pieces of user-made art on huge digital screens in Times Square, New York and Piccadilly Square, London, again, stressing the idea of creativity and civic imagination. The campaign was also a brand transformation experiment in AI. Internally, the Coca-Cola embarked on deeper exploration of the use of generative AI and experimented with dynamic asset generation, real-time ad variation and AI-assisted storytelling to be used in future campaigns (Tao et al., 2025). Overall, the campaign entitled "Create Real Magic" did not only establish Coca-Cola as a leader in using AI technology in branding but also depicted how GenAI can be used to achieve 30% increased participation rate, 5-6% higher engagement and sales rates, and a high level of perception of innovative and inclusive brand. The Figure 7 illustrates the key performance outcomes of Coca-Cola's 2023 generative AI-powered branding initiative, "Create Real Magic." The bar chart compares three core metrics: user participation (30%), engagement increase on social media platforms (5%), and quarter-over-quarter sales growth (6%). The data demonstrates how incorporating Generative AI tools like DALL·E and GPT-4 not only boosted global user engagement but also contributed to tangible improvements in marketing performance and brand innovation.

Figure 7. Impact metrics of Coca-Cola's "create real magic" campaign (2023)

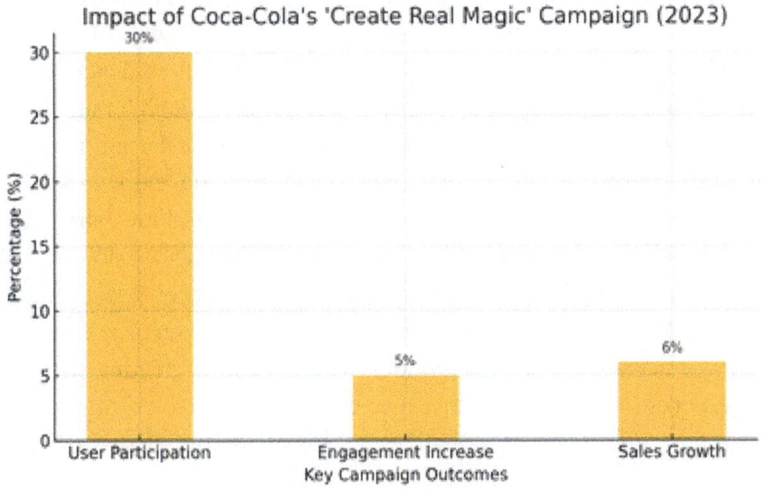

7.2 Canva's Magic Design Tool for Small Business Branding

Canva introduced Magic Design, an AI component in its design service that uses artificial intelligence to enable small companies and non-designers to design professional-quality branding materials in 2023. The tool uses the power of generative AI that, on a few parameters, automatically generates visually regular logos, marketing materials, and brand packages. Magic Design had popularity based on small business communities, especially new businesspeople, teachers and advertisers who did not learn how to design it. In small business segment and within the first six months of its launch, Canva had recorded a 42% growth in design interactions by its users. More than 65% of users of Magic Design tool managed to create not only logos but also secondary templates that could be used on social media, presentations, and business cards and prove its efficiency as a complete branding tool (Du Plessis, 2025). Magic Design also brought the average design cycle down to 35%, and users can produce polished visual materials in less than 10 minutes as the manual templates require at least 15-20 minutes to create.

About 28% of the users stated that they used the AI-generated designs with no additional manual adjustments, which demonstrates that AI results are quite consistent with user demands. When it comes to adoption, Canva has increased its number of users by 18% annually, and during the close of 2023, it is expected to have more than 135 million monthly active users. It was Magic Design that was deemed to drive such growth, especially the new markets and the SMB segment. This tool has not only allowed Canva to be present in the enterprise and educational areas where simplicity of use is supremely vital and where consistency with and within the brand has become a key business requirement (Reed et al., 2025). It is evident that by automating basically all design work and making it accessible enough for anyone to use it, the Magic Design feature of Canva demonstrates the practical usability of GenAI in branding due to allowing any business, small or large, to develop, prototype, and distribute the branded material in a pace, precision, and overall low barrier to skill. The Figure 8 highlights the measurable outcomes of Canva's AI-powered Magic Design feature. Following its launch, design interaction grew by 42%, with 65% of users creating full brand kits beyond logos. The average design time decreased by 35%, and 28% of users used designs without manual edits, indicating strong alignment with user needs. Canva's user base also grew by 18%, driven largely by small businesses and non-designers adopting the tool for accessible, scalable branding.

Figure 8. Canva magic design performance metrics (2023)

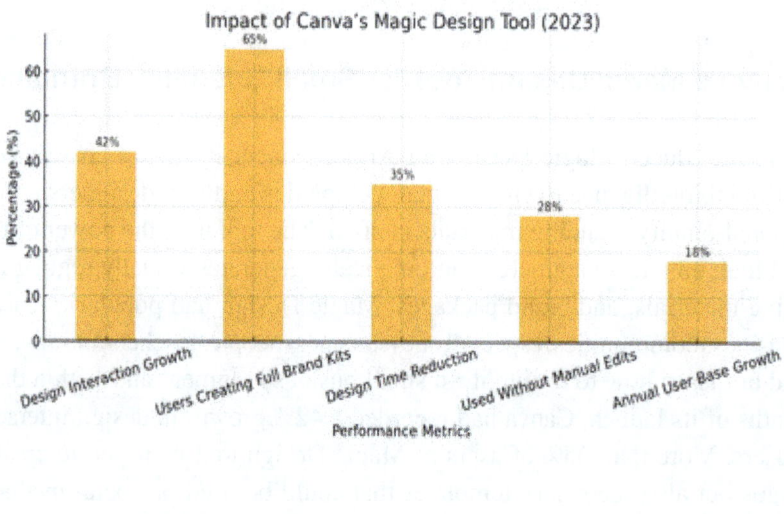

8. FUTURE OUTLOOK AND STRATEGIC RECOMMENDATIONS

A more personalized future of Generative AI in visual branding is more real-time content creation and seamless lead through the marketing systems. GenAI models will keep becoming context- and multimodal, so that over time the brands will keep using AI to deliver the most personalized experiences, which will adapt to the behaviour, preferences and mood of each user. The regulations of creativity will be altered by the new technologies such as prompt engineering, synthetic media regulation, and AI human co-creating systems (Vasantdada et al., 2025). On the strategic level, organizations should invest in hybrid workflow (the introduction of automation with and without AI filters) and personal control over their brands. The emergence of moral and multi-diversified datasets, the formation of AI use control and training AI-knowledgeable inventive teams will be crucial. More to the point, contrary to replacement, creative augmentation with the assistance of AI ensures credibility and sustainable believability (Limantara, 2024b). Through aligning marketing aspirations with GenAI potential, the brands will keep up with the speed, innovation and cultural fit, which can only be realized by unlocking options of scalable creativity on the discourse of the digital consumers in the AI-drived marketplace.

8.1. Emerging Trends: Generative AI in AR/VR and 3D Branding

Generative AI is emerging as the main focus of branding developments in immersive spaces, especially Augmented Reality (AR), Virtual Reality (VR), and 3D interfaces, as the separation between the physical and digital continues to merge. Companies are now using GenAI to generate not merely unanimously defined, but also interactive, spatial, and dynamic content (in real-time). Among the most prominent are AI-produced 3D assets the model of a product, an avatar, a setting, which can be rendered in real-time to be used in a virtual shop, metaverse, or an AR mask (Çelik & Akagün Ergin, 2025). As an example, GenAI can transform a small cosmetics brand into a large one by taking a photo of any product and generating a 3D product preview or even a virtual try-on with no time wasted on the design process and taking into account that the product will be customized to the skin tone or the lighting of a specific user. The personalization factor increases conversion rates in AR shopping by using the product placements generated by AI in the form of scenes.

Generative models in VR allow designing narrative-based branded spaces where users can engage in content in a game environment. GenAI can also promote adaptive storytelling, in which the images change according to the user activity or the state of his emotions. Furthermore, entities are considering AI-edited concept fashion and goods to be applied to online-only wearables and collectibles, two of the most important elements in NFT-based rewards schemes and game-based activities. Adoption is going to pick up: it is projected that more than 40% of the marketing-driven AR/VR content will incorporate in some way GenAI by the year 2024. Nevertheless, such change requires technical support, moral moderation and fluent design in 3 motion narration (Bagga & Kaur, 2025b). GenAI is the key to the future of visual branding because it will gradually move towards multi-sensory, real-time experiences. Innovative brands need to initiate creative pipelines containing AI-generated 3D content, so that they can differentiate themselves in the immersive digital ecosystem, the space where presence, interaction and personalisation meet. The Figure 9 visualizes projected adoption and impact percentages for GenAI in immersive branding use cases. Categories include AR shopping conversion boosts (35%), AI-powered 3D product previews (45%), VR narrative environments (50%), NFT-based digital fashion (30%), and overall GenAI use in AR/VR by 2024 (40%) highlighting how GenAI is reshaping the future of interactive, personalized brand experiences.

Figure 9. Adoption trends of generative AI in AR/VR and 3D branding

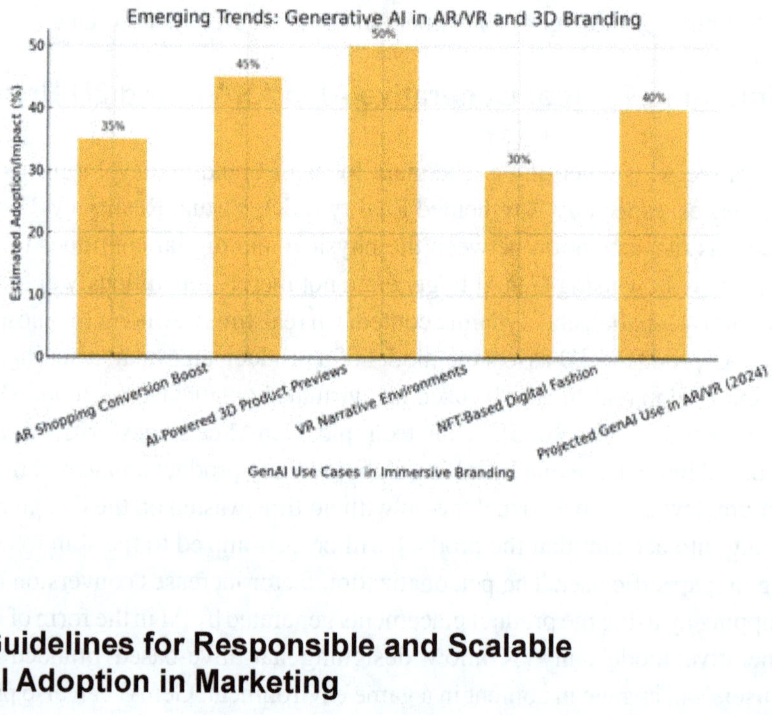

8.2. Guidelines for Responsible and Scalable GenAI Adoption in Marketing

Generative AI can make its way to marketing, and to guarantee sustainable and responsible application, brands need to integrate structured and ethical frameworks. In the absence of control, the potentially problematic nature of AI-generated content might surface in the form of the violations of copyright legislation, inconsistency of brands, cultural insensitivity, and loss of audience confidence (Al Balushi et al., 2024). To initiate scalable adoption, AI usage policies must be in place. Organizations ought to stipulate the conditions of usage of GenAI tools, who is responsible in outputs, and what are the quality control processes. This involves educating creative groups about timely engineering, other moral quick design, and the model constraints. Second, brands need to spend resources in inclusive dataset and bias reduction methods. Making a wide range of duties and based on a variety of historical data is important in avoiding stereotypes or exclusion, given that AI learns by being taught with historical data. AI created imagery must be subject to frequent auditing of impartiality and cultural precision. An important model is a hybrid one that entails automation but with human supervision.

Although GenAI can save production time, the end should be approved only by the creative directors or brand managers and checked in terms of the tone, context and brand values. Third, the element of transparency is critical (Guo, 2025). The brands ought to disclaim AI-generated scenarios in which cases brand is fitting to do it in a sensitive i.e. social advocacy or health-related advertising. The open usage creates a trusting relationship and separates the real and false impressions. And the final point is that there should be feedback loops in an organization (Kirkby et al., 2023). To be continuously moving and adapting to the changing brand stories, AI systems should be able to learn through the data on campaign performance, as well as creative assessments and customer impressions. Promoting creativity upon large scales and preserving authenticity by developing ethical, collaborative, and flexible GenAI pipelines is possible. It is not a matter of becoming efficient, but rather of being responsible with innovations in the sense that GenAI accelerates their creativity without losing track and finding themselves instead grounded in trust, equity, and strategy alignment.

9. CONCLUSION

Even the fact that Generative AI is penetrating the branding and the marketing industry is a sign of a paradigm shift that can alter the manner in which brands think, create and publish the visual work. Generative AI does not design, they are a co-creator of brand communication and therefore are more agile, personal, and novel in what they can accomplish as found out in this chapter. AI, be it in the form of DALL·E and Midjourney or a more practical tool such as Canva Magic Design or Adobe Firefly, is even easier to use than ever to produce content, regardless of being a large company or a small business. That allows generating top-notch logos, ad creatives, packaging, and thematic brand visuals with high precision, appropriate channel, target market, and user behavior. Some of the real-life applications like the campaign by Coca-Cola, Create Real Magic, point to the role of GenAI to increase user engagement, co-creation, and increase on its sales.

Central to such a change has been strong models such as GANs and diffusion systems which are being trained on enormous visual atlases to produce human-like and stylistically consistent images. They do not just work much faster at content production, but they also allow real time customization and dynamic and adaptive stories, a major characteristic of the multi-platform, time-sensitive world of branding in 2018. However, the notion of terms of copyright, moral appropriateness, cultural issues, and brand identity is also a matter of concern regarding the increased presence of GenAI. Without stringent restrictions, the uncontrolled use of AI can lead to the following outcomes: the legal ambiguity, bias in outcomes, the violation of a brand identity. Therefore, there is a need to strike a balance; a mix of AI that is fast and scalable and that that has human oversight and ethical means of designing AI.

Some new applications, such as AI-created content to the AR/VR environment, real-time 3D branding, and AI-based experiential marketing, will expand the creative possibilities of brands even further into the future. Organizations should establish responsible AI pipelines to make sure that they remain innovative and at the same time enable authenticity and trust to guide their lives. In conclusion, it is possible to note that Generative AI presents a good opportunity to think about another way of visual branding in the digital-first world. By placing GenAI in the right context through creative processes, ethical concerns and partnership between machines and people, brands can achieve at scale dynamic, personalized and emotionally effective experiences. Machines will not fail to play its role in future of branding, but it will be determined by how the human being will use it: in a responsible and creative manner.

REFERENCES

Aarthi, S., Ravikumar, R. N., & Pardaev, J. (2025). Synergizing multimodal generative AI and blockchain for the future of digital media. In *Advances in Computational Intelligence and Robotics* (pp. 1–34). IGI Global Scientific Publishing. DOI: 10.4018/979-8-3373-1504-1.ch001

Al Balushi, M. K., Soliman, M., Al Hosni, M. S., & Al Mamari, A. (2024). Artificial Intelligence and Destination Branding. In Advances in Hospitality, Tourism, and the Services Industry (pp. 141–164). IGI Global. DOI: 10.4018/979-8-3693-6700-1.ch006

Babadoğan, B. (2024b). Exploring the role of AI in automating content marketing: Unlocking opportunities and navigating challenges. *Next Frontier For Life Sciences and AI*, *8*(1), 67. DOI: 10.62802/gkj6f352

Bagga, P., & Kaur, J. (2025b). Understanding artificial intelligence and its impact on branding. In Advances in Marketing, Customer Relationship Management, and E-Services (pp. 231–258). IGI Global. DOI: 10.4018/979-8-3693-9461-8.ch009

Cai, Y. (2025b). Innovative design and development of brand visual system under the background of Artificial Intelligence-assisted visual communication design. In *Research Square.*

Çelik, T., & Akagün Ergin, E. (2025). AI-driven design exploration: Utilizing brand logos as an inspiration source for architectural design. *Artificial Intelligence for Engineering Design, Analysis and Manufacturing*, *39*(e5), e5. DOI: 10.1017/S0890060425000046

Davtyan, N. (2024). AI in consumer behavior analysis and digital marketing: A strategic approach. The Integration of AI and Technology in Modern Business, 61–70.

Du Plessis, C. (2025). Ethical requirements for generative AI in brand content creation: A qualitative comparative analysis. *Frontiers in Communication*, *10*, 10. DOI: 10.3389/fcomm.2025.1523077

Farseev, A., Lepikhin, K., Schwartz, H., Ang, E. K., & Powar, K. (2018). SoMin.ai. *Proceedings of the 26th ACM International Conference On*, 1234–1236.

Figoli, F. A., Rampino, L., & Mattioli, F. (2022). Ai in the design process: Training the human-Ai collaboration. DS 117: Proceedings of the 24th International Conference on Engineering and Product Design Education (E&PDE 2022), London South Bank University in London, UK. 8th - 9th 2022.

Friatin, L. Y. (2025). Revolutionizing writing: The impact of technology on enhancing students' writing skills. [Journal of Applied Linguistics and Literacy]. *JALL, 9*(1), 87. DOI: 10.25157/jall.v9i1.17963

Gilbert, M. A. (2024). Disrupting marketing. In Advances in Marketing, Customer Relationship Management, and E-Services (pp. 21–56). IGI Global. Gual-Ort\'\i, J., Juan-Verdoy, P., Amat-Cózar, J., & Mart\'\inez-Moya, J. A. (2025). Exploring the role of Artificial Intelligence in brand image creation. In Research Square. DOI: 10.4018/979-8-3693-4361-6.ch002

Guerra-Tamez, C. R., Kraul Flores, K., Serna-Mendiburu, G. M., Chavelas Robles, D., & Ibarra Cortés, J. (2024). Decoding Gen Z: AI's influence on brand trust and purchasing behavior. *Frontiers in Artificial Intelligence, 7*, 1323512. DOI: 10.3389/frai.2024.1323512

Guo, E. (2025). Redefining exclusivity: The role of generative AI in luxury brand strategies. Advances in Economics. *Management and Political Sciences, 165*(1), 80–85.

Havale, D. S., Raut, N., Anute, N., Ahluwalia, G. K., Kalshetti, P., & Selvakumar, P. (2025). Ethical challenges and bias in AI marketing. In *Advances in Computational Intelligence and Robotics* (pp. 27–54). IGI Global.

He, H., Zhao, S., Xi, Y., & Ho, J. C. (2023). MedDiff: Generating electronic health records using accelerated denoising diffusion model.

Hemalatha, A. (2023). *AI-driven marketing: Leveraging Artificial Intelligence for Enhanced Customer Engagement*. Jupiter Publications Consortium. DOI: 10.47715/JPC.B.978-93-91303-61-7

Hoppe, D. (2018). Linking employer branding and internal branding: Establishing perceived employer brand image as an antecedent of favourable employee brand attitudes and behaviours. *Journal of Product and Brand Management, 27*(4), 452–467. DOI: 10.1108/JPBM-12-2016-1374

Huang, M.-H., & Rust, R. T. (2021). A strategic framework for artificial intelligence in marketing. *Journal of the Academy of Marketing Science, 49*(1), 30–50. DOI: 10.1007/s11747-020-00749-9

Huynh, T., Nguyen, H. D., Zelinka, I., Nguyen, K. V., Pham, V. T., & Hoang, S. N. (2021). ADVO: A system to manage influencer marketing campaigns on social networks. *Applied Sciences (Basel, Switzerland), 11*(14), 6497. DOI: 10.3390/app11146497

Iakovlev, I., Kremleva, E., & Guzanov, R. (2023). Enterprise automation using artificial intelligence: Methods, technologies and prospects. E3S Web Conf., 460, 4007.

Ip, K. (2023). Revolutionising content recommendation: The impact of AI in marketing. Journal of AI. *Robotics & Workplace Automation*, *2*(4), 382. DOI: 10.69554/AMHI2323

Kirkby, A., Baumgarth, C., & Henseler, J. (2023). To disclose or not disclose, is no longer the question – effect of AI-disclosed brand voice on brand authenticity and attitude. *Journal of Product and Brand Management*, *32*(7), 1108–1122. DOI: 10.1108/JPBM-02-2022-3864

Koswara, A. (2025). The intersection of generative AI and applied linguistics in modern marketing & Advertising practices. LinguaEducare. *Journal of English and Linguistic Studies*, *2*(1), 19–28.

Kotapati, S. P. (2025). Artificial Intelligence in Scalable Content Creation for Micro-influencer Marketing Agencies. *Asian J. Res. Com. Sci.*, *18*(6), 215–222. DOI: 10.9734/ajrcos/2025/v18i6692

Kubovics, M. (2024). Innovative Content Production in Marketing Communication Through AI. *Proc. Eur. Conf. Entrep. Innov.*, *19*(1), 377–383. DOI: 10.34190/ecie.19.1.2877

Kubovics, M. (2025). AI in the creation of Marketing Communication content. *INTERANTIONAL JOURNAL OF SCIENTIFIC RESEARCH IN ENGINEERING AND*, *09*(04), 1–9. DOI: 10.55041/IJSREM42613

Limantara, Q. R. (2024). Exploring the role of Generative Artificial Intelligence in crafting brand experiences: Insights from selected case studies. *International Journal of Creative Multimedia*, *5*(2), 88–100. DOI: 10.33093/ijcm.2024.5.2.6

Massoudi, A. H., Birdawod, H. Q., & Raewf, M. B. (2023). Personal Digital Marketing Influence on Successful Marketing Campaign in Today's Digital Age. *Cihan U Erbil J H SOC SCI*, *7*(1), 158–165. DOI: 10.24086/cuejhss.v7n1y2023.pp158-165

Moharam, M. M. R., & Tawalbeh, A. (2025). The role of gen AI in enhancing creativity and efficiency in content marketing creation: Scoping review and future insights. *Ijirss*, *8*(1), 2804–2814. DOI: 10.53894/ijirss.v8i1.5060

Murár, P., Kubovics, M., & Jurišová, V. (2024). The impact of brand-voice integration and artificial Intelligence on social media marketing. *Communication Today*, 50–63. DOI: 10.34135/communicationtoday.2024.Vol.15.No.1.4

Peng, Y. (2024). A comparative analysis between GAN and Diffusion Models in image generation. *Transactions on Computer Science and Intelligent Systems*, *5*, 189–195. DOI: 10.62051/0f1va465

Prabagar, S., Mothkur, R., Swetha, C. B., Kurian, A., Pavithra, K., & Aarthi, S. (2025). Generative AI for inclusive special education. In *Advances in Computational Intelligence and Robotics* (pp. 205–236). IGI Global Scientific Publishing., DOI: 10.4018/979-8-3373-3745-6.ch008

Raut, S., Chandel, A., & Mittal, S. (2024). Enhancing marketing and brand communication with AI-driven content creation. In Advances in Marketing, Customer Relationship Management, and E-Services (pp. 139–172). IGI Global.

Ravikumar, R. N., & Aarthi, S. (2025). AI-driven governance. In *Advances in Computational Intelligence and Robotics* (pp. 343–372). IGI Global Scientific Publishing. DOI: 10.4018/979-8-3373-3760-9.ch012

Reed, C., Wynn, M., & Bown, R. (2025). Artificial intelligence in digital marketing: Towards an analytical framework for revealing and mitigating bias. *Big Data and Cognitive Computing*, *9*(2), 40. DOI: 10.3390/bdcc9020040

Shukla, A. (2024). Innovative ways of utilizing generative AI for graphical big data analysis. *J Arti Inte & Cloud Comp*, *3*(1), 1–3. DOI: 10.47363/JAICC/2024(3)222

Tao, M., Li, X., Alam, F., Yan, Y., & Chau, T. (2025). Unveiling the impact of AI technological anxiety on the marketers' intention to adopt Generative AI. *Journal of Global Information Management*, *33*(1), 1–22. DOI: 10.4018/JGIM.372177

Theurer, C. P., Tumasjan, A., Welpe, I. M., & Lievens, F. (2018). Employer branding: A brand equity-based literature review and research agenda. *International Journal of Management Reviews*, *20*(1), 155–179. DOI: 10.1111/ijmr.12121

Varsha, P. S., Akter, S., Kumar, A., Gochhait, S., & Patagundi, B. (2021). The impact of artificial intelligence on branding. *Journal of Global Information Management*, *29*(4), 221–246. DOI: 10.4018/JGIM.20210701.oa10

Verma, A. (2025). Social Media Marketing. In Marketing in a Digital World: Strategies, Evolution and Global Impact (pp. 179–205). BENTHAM SCIENCE PUBLISHERS. DOI: 10.2174/9789815305456125010009

Wang, H., Du, Q., Wang, Y., Xu, H., Wei, Z., & Wang, X. (2024). GPro: Generative AI-empowered toolkit for promoter design. *Bioinformatics (Oxford, England)*, *40*(3), btae123. DOI: 10.1093/bioinformatics/btae123

Wang, Y. (2024). KOL strategy under the empowerment of AI: A new chapter in brand marketing. Advances in Economics. *Management and Political Sciences, 113*(1), 116–122.

Yuan, P. (2024). A research on the dynamization effect of brand visual identity design: Mediated by digital information smart media. *Journal of Information Systems Engineering & Management, 9*(1), 24153. DOI: 10.55267/iadt.07.14078

KEY TERMS AND DEFINITIONS

A/B Testing: A comparative evaluation method in which two or more content variants are tested to determine which version performs more effectively against defined metrics.

AI-Assisted Design: The application of artificial intelligence to automate or enhance stages of the design process, including the generation of layouts, logos, illustrations, or other visual assets.

Brand Consistency: The maintenance of uniform visual identity, tone, and messaging across all communication channels to support brand recognition and audience trust.

Creative Automation: The use of AI-driven tools and software to streamline and accelerate creative production processes, reducing manual workload while increasing scalability.

Diffusion Models: A class of generative models that produce data by learning to reverse a noise-injection process, widely used in advanced image synthesis systems such as DALL·E 2 and Stable Diffusion.

Ethical AI Use: The responsible design, deployment, and governance of AI technologies, emphasizing fairness, bias mitigation, transparency, accountability, and societal impact.

GAN (Generative Adversarial Network): A neural network architecture consisting of two competing components a generator and a discriminator that iteratively improve the realism of synthetically generated content.

Generative AI (GenAI): A branch of artificial intelligence focused on creating new content such as images, text, audio, or video by learning patterns from large-scale datasets.

Human-in-the-Loop (HITL): A design and governance approach that ensures continued human oversight and intervention in AI systems to maintain quality control, ethical alignment, and decision accountability.

Prompt Engineering: The practice of designing and refining textual inputs to effectively guide generative AI models toward producing specific, high-quality outputs.

Real-Time Personalization: The dynamic customization of content for individual users based on behavioral data, preferences, or contextual signals, typically enabled through AI-driven analytics.

Synthetic Media: Visual, audio, or video content that is artificially generated by AI systems rather than recorded or captured from the physical world.

Chapter 2
Decoding Visual Brand Identity Through Computer Vision:
AI-Driven Insights for Modern Branding

Md Mehedi Hasan Emon
https://orcid.org/0000-0002-6224-9552
American International University-Bangladesh, Bangladesh

Tahsina Khan
https://orcid.org/0000-0001-8032-3376
Bangladesh University of Professionals, Bangladesh

ABSTRACT

This chapter explores the transformative role of computer vision in decoding and analyzing visual brand identity within today's visually driven marketplace. It highlights how AI-powered techniques such as logo detection, color palette extraction recognition enable marketers to objectively measure and manage the core visual elements that shape brand perception. By integrating machine learning and image processing, brands can achieve greater consistency, track competitive positioning, and better understand consumer responses across digital platforms. The chapter also addresses key challenges including data variability, cultural nuances, and ethical considerations, while exploring future directions like multimodal AI and real-time brand monitoring. Through a blend of theoretical insights and practical case studies, this work offers a comprehensive perspective on how AI-driven visual analysis is

DOI: 10.4018/979-8-3373-4506-2.ch002

redefining branding strategies, providing valuable implications for academics and marketing professionals aiming to leverage emerging technologies to strengthen brand identity and engagement.

INTRODUCTION

An identity of the brand is not a product of the slogans or the mission statement anymore in the context of contemporary marketing, yet is more visual, immediate and digitally mediated. The growing popularity of image-based platforms and trends in the consumption of media have exacerbated the need to develop brands that can effectively communicate in a consistent and successful manner through the assistance of visual content. The chapter is a detailed analysis of how a somewhat new area like artificial intelligence, especially the computer vision, is transforming the way we visualize, understand, and interpret the visual brand identity. The chapter starts with the contextualization of the importance of visual brand identity in the present hypercompetitive market in which visual components of logos, color scheme, typography, and other visual components create a familiar image of a brand to the consumer influenced by the consumer psychology. In doing so, it places computer vision in context of a powerful instrument of analysis that provides scientific precision to an area that was previously considered an artistic and subject field. It goes on to conceptual discussion on the crucial aspects of the visual brand identity which are logos, colors, typefaces, imagery and graphic expressions and their communicative and symbolic roles. The chapter describes how these elements are incorporated in the formation of values of the brands, competitive differentiation and eliciting the intended consumer responses.

The third section discusses computer vision technology in the analysis of brands. It contains some of the most important processes such as image recognition, feature extraction and image segmentation which introduces machine vision systems to others who might not have been conversant with machine vision. The processes enable automatic recognition and cognition of brand images on a broad platform and situations. According to this argument, the chapter then proceeds to conduct a comprehensive discussion of the AI techniques that may be applied to the visual brand. It discusses the methods of logo-detection and logo-classification, color palette extraction and analysis algorithms, typography and design Carlism recognitions. These techniques are synthesized in the chapter together with branding objectives thereby bridging the disconnect between technical capacity and marketing utility. In showing how the chapter is applied, the chapter provides case studies and applications, which shows how the AI-based computer vision can be applied to measure brand consistency across channel, visual strategy and competitor comparisons, and consumer reaction towards visual branding. The discussion is based on practical examples and demonstrations on the real situations in marketing and reveals the practical benefits of these new technologies. The chapter, however, does not overlook the problems and limitations of having computer vision in branding. It is among the most significant articles which bring up the problem of data quality, variability and lack of clarity of visual styles, and the contextual peculiarities that AI models cannot necessarily pick. In this case, the authors emphasize the importance of the accuracy of algorithms and human intuition. On the outlook, the chapter recognizes the prospects of the field that would have involved the aspect of multimodal AI, the integration of sight with natural language processing, to facilitate brand perception analysis. It also fancies the surfacing of real time brand monitoring in which dynamic response may be undertaken to observe visual branding performance in the online space. The conclusion of the chapter will include the synthesis of the key findings and the reflection of the implications of the findings to the academic research and marketing practice. It argues that computer vision in ethical and care approach could offer a ground-breaking method of decoding visual brand identity, a methodology which integrates creative branding with empiricism, and convention and technological innovation. Finally, this chapter makes scholars, practitioners, and technologists think anew about visual branding as something that is computational to investigate rather than art.

DIGITAL BRANDING THROUGH VISUAL IDENTITY AND COMPUTER VISION

Visual brand identity has emerged as the most perennial, immediate brand communication due to the ever-changing digital ecosystem of information overload, discrete consumers, and discrete platforms. The turns and twists of a logotype or the vibes and dispositions behind a color scheme, brands these days are not what they say but what they ought to see. The necessity of establishing a visual brand image has been drastically enhanced in the world where digital images, video snips, and posts on social networks become the main means of communication with the brands. Visual cues, not only of aesthetic value, have turned into a strategic dimension of trustworthiness, distinction, and cultural relevance and feeling (Shukla et al., 2023). The brand image was traditionally created through slogans, mascots, and strategic stories but the visual component of identity has been slowly ascending to the leading role due to excessive prevalence of visual media sources such as Instagram, YouTube, Tik Tok, and Pinterest. Under such circumstances the identification of a particular brand through recognition to the eye as fast and retentively as possible may signify success of a brand. Visual identity can be defined as a mental short handing- it sets the expectation of the consumer, affects the way he or she feels, and can be used to enable the consumer to make direct decisions when faced by a saturated market. In fact, it has also been discovered that the creation of visual cues takes less than few milliseconds and it is also a major contributor to consumer attitude and behavior (Overgoor et al., 2022). The semiotic aspects of the visual branding encompass logos, colors, typography, graphic motifs, layout pattern, and styles of photography, which in a normal usage form a cohesive identity on the cross-channel and multi touch points. Communicative power is present in all these factors. The plain logo can be interpreted as a sign of contemporariness and simplicity and the font full of serifs may make one think of the old and the old-fashioned. Similarly, color psychology demonstrates that blue color may have been linked with the quality of trust, and red may appear as something urgent or passionate (Ahlawat & Swami, 2024). Thus, the visual identity is not decorative but is based on the perception of consumers and brand positioning. Nonetheless, managing visual brand identity on a large scale is becoming increasingly harder. As the brands operate in the global markets and the numerous online platforms, the visual format and impact are not only a logistic, but also a strategic concern to ensure. Old methods of visual auditing and implementation of brand guidelines, that were previously sufficient, are overwhelmed by speed and volume of the digital materials. The game-changing solution, in this case, is artificial intelligence (AI) in the form of computer vision.

One of the branches of AI is computer vision that allows computers to perceive and work with visual data. Initially, computer vision was developed to accomplish such tasks as facial recognition and autonomous navigation, but this time round it is being recycled in marketing and brand analysis. The analysis of brand images in great quantities of data and in different digital situations can be automated through the application of algorithms that can recognize, label and isolate features of images and videos and utilize computer vision (Nanne et al., 2020). It is an effective brand manager and a marketing tool because it can identify logos in the content created by users, extract prominent color palettes on product packaging, or even quantify typography on social media posts. The effects of computer vision utilization in brand analysis are numerous. Firstly, it achieves objectivity in a subjective and interpretive domain that is traditional. Computer vision provides scalable, data-driven solutions as to visualization of brand images and performance of these images in the online environment, as opposed to relying on subjective opinion and discussions of a small sample group. The above can be the example of AI models, which may evaluate the consistency of visual resources of a brand in cross-market applications or user generated content by the brand rules (Hauser et al., 2023; Khan & Hasan Emon, 2024). Second, brand identification monitoring is possible in real-time due to computer vision. With the age of viral content and direct brand presence, it is relevant that firms ought to detect brand presentation anomalies and respond to them. Organizations can prevent abuse, monitor sentiment-driven visual content and dynamically adjust campaigns by continually monitoring brand visuals on online ecosystems. The fashion industry is another good example where visual branding is critical in identity creation. Following fashionable trends on visuals, application of logos in influencer posts and trends among competition can now be tracked using the intelligence in fashion houses (Alanadoly et al., 2024). Third, and, most significantly, AI enables brands to understand the perception of the consumers with respect to their visual identity. To match some visual products with consumer engagement and consumer emotion, it is possible to analyze the visual interactions, i.e., likes, shares, comments, or even eye-tracking data using computer vision tools (Nanne et al., 2020). This will enable better tailoring of visual content to target tastes, culture or emerging trends of aesthetics to the market. Despite all the developments mentioned, one more thing that deserves to be noted is that there are no restrictions as far as the use of computer vision in branding is concerned. Visual identity is situational and culturally based and may require implicit understanding, which cannot be provided by the currently used AI methods. As an example, the color or design theme can be used in different cultures with different symbolic meaning. Besides, the ethical considerations of surveillance, data and algorithmic bias in use of computer vision matters should be factored during the correlation of the tools in the consumer facing world. Nevertheless, the intersection of AI and branding is a sign that demonstrates that the concept of visual identity will be radically changed with its conceptualization and management. Brand visuals have ceased to be the domain of the creative director or graphic designer, and they are currently quantifiable and optimizable in the data-driven marketing strategy. Computer vision does not exist to replace the human creative aspects of humans; it only can provide marketers with more empirical evidence that can be utilized to produce more touching and powerful visual tales.

Figure 1. AI and computer vision in brand analysis workflow

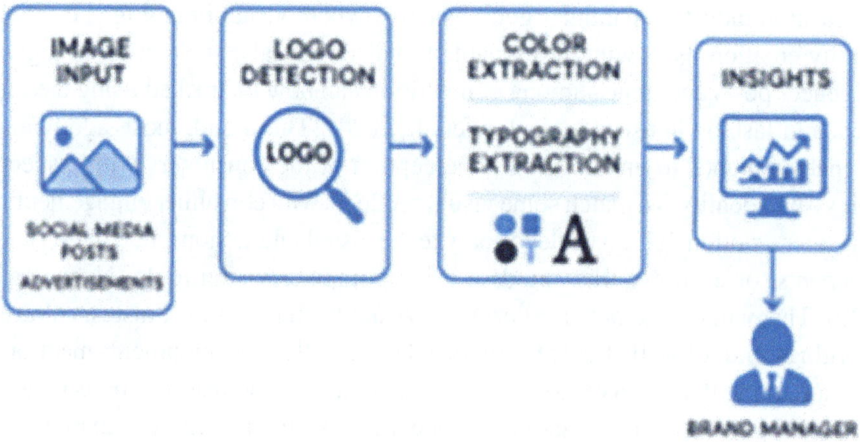

This figure presents a chronological cycle of AI and computer vision technologies, in terms of how they perceive and process brand images. The input of the system is the image (or a group of images) using social media posts or advertisements as a prototype and undergoes processes of logo recognition, color recognition and typography recognition. The information is then computed, and such information is turned into actionable data which will eventually be applied by the brand manager in making data driven decisions regarding the brand. Figure 1 shows the entire technical process and has focused more on what AI brings to the table in relation to scaling up analysis of the brand as well as objective measurements.

CORE ELEMENTS OF VISUAL IDENTITY

In the digital world, when brands are becoming increasingly atomized, where the short attention span is the norm, and where there is an ongoing need to compete, the value of a coordinated visual brand identity has never been so central to strategic marketing. The visual part of the branding can give the first and most memorable image of the brand although verbal communication is significant. The image of visual identity, which is selected and combined to create the outer appearance of a brand, assists in shaping consumer emotions and attitude and the recognition, loyalty, and emotional engagement, is called visual brand identity. Becoming more data-driven and performance-oriented, the element components of visual identity cannot be considered in the aesthetic or artistic perspective only but also be evaluated in the context of their strategic utility and consistency through touchpoints. Essentially, visual brand identity is a Construct of semiotic elements, a system of signs and symbols that express the character values and positioning of the brand. These components cannot be described as accidental; they are planned to be communicatively consistent and psychologically sound. Visual identity of a brand does not simply act as a visual appeal to sight, but it generates meaning, develops trust, and distanced themselves to a greater cultural narrative (Waqas et al., 2021).

Logos: Emblems of Recognition and Trust

One of the most recognizable aspects of the visual identity is the logo, a graphical symbol that recaps the identity of a brand in a simplistic, easily recognizable manner. There is a two-fold role of logos: they offer the visual cues of brand memory, and they are the indicators of confidence in the consumer decision making processes. The articles prove that consumers are more likely to develop emotional and cognitive associations with logos over time and associate with a specific experience, promise, and reputation (Shukla et al., 2023). Also, the aspects of logo design, such as the propinquity of symmetry, curvature, and color, represent an element of psychology. To take an example, symmetrical logos may be regarded as more credible, the angular ones may be associated with power and energy (Huang et al., 2021). The recent hypercharge growth of the brand content in various screens and online platforms has brought forth new demands on the logos to be scalable and even flexible. It has led to the creation of so-called responsive logos, easily identifiable, although they vary in magnitude depending on the circumstances, which is made significantly easier with the assistance of AI-based design and testing (Caires, 2025).

Color Palette: Evoking Emotion and Identity

Color is the most relevant aspect of emotional register of a brand. The psychological effects of color do not belong to the new literature in the marketing world. Warm colors (reds, oranges) may ensure that a person gets excited and, as a result, consequential, whereas cool colors (blues, greens) may ensure that a person gets relaxed and trusting (Qian et al., 2024). Interestingly, even colors do carry a culturally specific connotation. In western cultures, white is normally connoted with purity but in most of the Asian cultures, it can be described as dying. Hence, emotional intentions should not be alone to justify the choice of the color scheme of a brand, but also the cultural background. A particular color - Tiffany Blue - is so closely associated with such brands that the color is seen to be a signifier to the brand name, Tiffany Co. The computer vision technologies have allowed marketers to look at the frequency of use of these hues that identify a brand on platforms and across geographies, and it offers an empirical base on which the wholeness of a brand can be judged (Balmer, 2023).

Typography: Conveying Voice and Personality

Typography has ceased to be a functional element of written communication- it is a subtle and at the same time a powerful manifestation of brand voice and personality. Serif fonts may be seen to be official, traditional and authoritative as compared to the sans-serif fonts which may be seen to be contemporary, brief and accommodative (Mogaji, 2021). The readability and less obvious, tone of communication will be established by typefaces weight, spacing and rhythm. The font chosen is very compatible with the rest of the graphics and makes a brand more coherent. To further demonstrate it, the fonts that the company uses, these are non-serif, clean fonts, are included in the minimalist design that makes the company create an image of a sophisticated and modern-thinking company. The New York Times, on the other hand, does not abandon its traditional serif type font, which recalls it of the history and sobriety of paper. Typography can be measured quantitatively as it is conducted currently, whereby with the assistance of the AI-driven font recognition and sentiment analysis, one can assess consumer perception in various digital media (Luo et al., 2024).

Graphical Patterns and Iconography: Shaping Aesthetic Coherence

Visual identity, as a supplement to logos and typography is also attained in respect of repetitive patterns, icons, and design motifs. The supporting actors to the bigger visual story are the elements and increase thematic coherence and brand recognizability. As a case in point, the human connection and warmer in the brand promise can be observed already in soft and natural shapes of the web and app interface of Airbnb. Similarly, we also have dynamic, fluid graphics that are applied by brands like Spotify to show the personalization and motion, which are the most essential features of their graphics. Such repeated patterns can be recognized and grouped by using computer vision technologies which deal with millions of visual resources altogether. Machine learning models can isolate the characteristics such as shapes, textures, color overlays, etc., and as a result, identify whether the design language in a brand is being applied consistently across channels, which is an important characteristic that brand managers need in that they have to manage several market campaigns (Bertão et al., 2025).

Layout Tendencies and Composition: Establishing Visual Grammar

Visual brand identity also includes compositional logic, which is the arrangement of images and text, negative space, grid systems, content hierarchies. These are the working components of the visual grammar of the brand, such that different components would be operating in unison and to attract the viewer in a productive manner. The systematized use of space constitutes order, professionalism, and focus, the systematized use of space can consist of creativity, disruption or playfulness, and the disorganized or experimental use of space can constitute the same. The layout coherence proves to be a sensitive operation as the consumer browses through brand contents using web interfaces, mobile screens, email newsletters, and AR/VR worlds. The recent research states that brand trust and consumer engagement have a strong positive relationship with perceived visual coherence (Kim et al., 2025). AI technology will be able to read scale layout patterns and identify anomalies or deviations and suggest optimizations to enhance performance of a brand.

The Need for Consistency and Cross-Platform Adaptability

A beautiful brand image in visual form must be capable of balancing stability and plasticity. On the one hand, platforms of media are consistent making it easy to memorize and credible. On the contrary, digital spaces demand flexible visual resources, i.e. the ones that expand and reform their shape without becoming anything different. One of them is that a YouTube banner, an Instagram story, and a mobile app interface must be designed visually and follow the requirements of the format. AI-assisted computer vision is an essential component of the audit of such a balance. Algorithms can show abnormalities in visual representation of the brands through the visual representation of brands in channels in large quantities, identify its strengths, and suggest ways of optimizing it through providing data-driven recommendations (Castañeda-García et al., 2020). This technology intervention transforms the brand management practice into an initially focused responsive work to an evidence-based proactive work.

COMPUTER VISION FOR BRAND ANALYSIS

A computer vision has brought something of a paradigm shift in the marketing world and a fresh dimension of studying the visual identity has acquired a new dimension through the brand managers and the researchers. Based on the convergence of machine learning, neural network structure, and image processing, computer vision in fact enables machine to extract and understand visual information in digital images and moving pictures, with quality and speed (Sharma et al., 2021). Specifically, the technology has potential in brand identity analysis, where consistency, recognizability, and consumer experience of visuals are considered important factors. In the problem of branding, computer vision technologies are not a technical instrument, or even a paradigm shift in the way visual meaning is quantified and operationalized. They allow brand practitioners to cease using subjective and manual interpretations and instead scalable and data-based evaluation of brand visuals on a large scale and a variety of digital contexts. Since platforms are becoming more image-oriented, Instagram, Tik Tok, YouTube and even e-commerce platforms, through their visual exchanges, it is becoming invaluable as a strategic tool to be able to track and study the visual aspects of the brand.

Figure 2. Key computer vision techniques for visual brand analysis

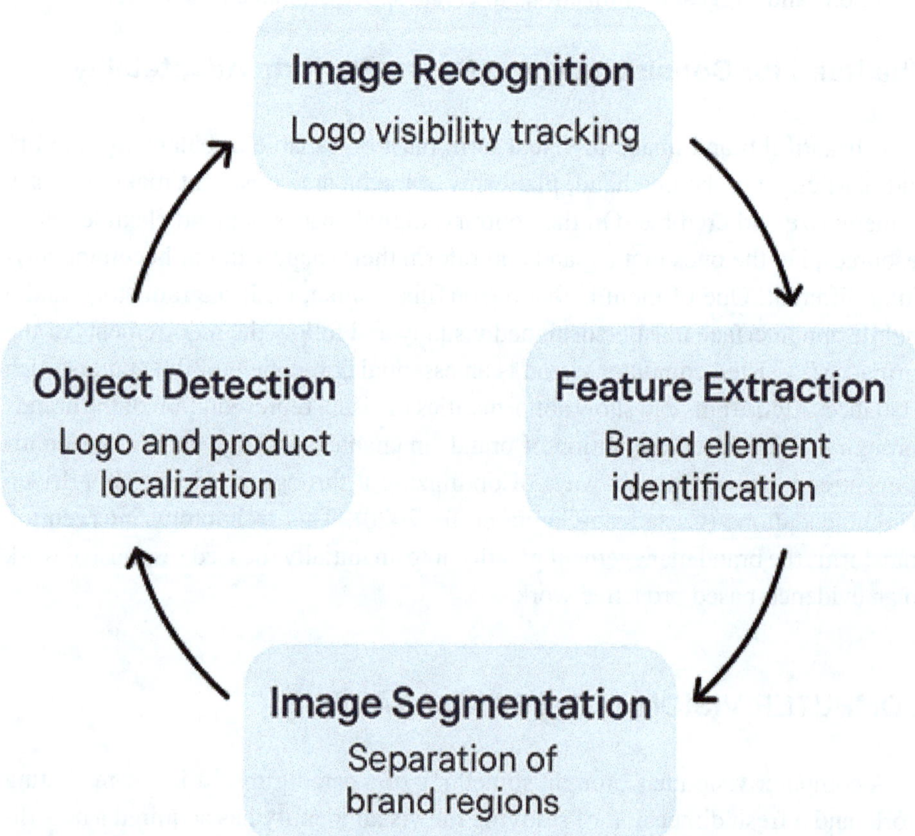

Figure 2 shows the simplest computer vision steps that are applied in the visual brand analysis. The concept map isolates four methods, which are linked, such as Image Recognition (a method of tracking the presence of logos), Feature Extraction (seeing the brand elements), Image Segmentation (who can isolate individual brand areas in a photograph), and Object Detection (seeing logos and branded commodities). The following strategies can be embraced simultaneously to investigate brand visibility, positioning and identity through the digital media.

Image Recognition: Understanding and Identifying Brand Elements

The type of computer vision application in branding is image recognition since the machines identify and classify the visual objects in the images. Image-finding algorithms, known as convolutional neural networks (CNNs) algorithms have greatly contributed to the science by imitating the visual processing of spatial hierarchies by humans (Zhao et al., 2024). These CNNs are also trained on large volumes of labeled images to recognize objects such as logos, products and brand packaging and mascots. Branding Image recognition is particularly beneficial in monitoring the presence of the image or products in various mediums like the user-created image in the social media or the rival advertisement. The use of trained image recognition models can be implemented by responsible companies to identify when their logos were used in unauthorized regions or even scan whether the logo can be found in influencer posts. These capabilities are already commercialized with solutions like Google Cloud Vision or Amazon Recognition that might be applied in advertisement performance audit, and protection of intellectual property (Singh & Arora, 2024). Another significant part of the brand equity measurement of visual sphere is image recognition. They can infer the salience of a brand and exposure by consumers as they scrutinize the place and frequency of visual property of a brand, and occasions of occurrence. This empirical character provides more robust background of brand visibility judgment as compared to the traditional survey-based measurements.

Feature Extraction: Quantifying the Elements of Design

Extracting certain visual characteristics in an image, which can be lines, edges, colors, and textures that define the composition and look of an image, is called feature extraction. These properties are what one derives more sophisticated classification tasks and makes complicated comparisons between different brand images. To study brand identity, it is possible to observe the logos, the elements of typography, the palettes of colors, and other design features and disaggregate them under the assistance of feature extraction. To provide an example, the key points can be generated by the feature detectors of SIFT (Scale-Invariant Feature Transform) or HOG (Histogram of Oriented Gradients) to provide the key points that would be the same in a brand icon even in the presence of various scale or lighting (Dixit et al., 2023). This is necessary to ensure that the visual properties of a brand are experienced even when it is subjected to a new environment; crop, resized and fitted in the noisy backgrounds. Moreover, the high-level abstraction and semantic meaning of brand imagery through the deep feature extraction of CNN layers, in particular, intermediate layers of a pretrained model i.e. ResNet or VGGNet, is applicable. It is possible that the following features can be clustered, compared, and analyzed to reveal stylistic uniformity or deviation within and between brand portfolios (Wu et al., 2019). As an illustration, an enterprise can compare the characteristics of the new packaging designs generated with the current visual language and retain the style the same.

Image Segmentation: Isolating Brand-Specific Visual Regions

Image segmentation that divides an image into semantically significant segments is another very important computer vision technique. With a high degree of accuracy, it can be used to isolate brand-relevant components e.g. logos on clothing in a fashion shoot or product images in shelf pictures or branded material in composite advertisements. This is very useful, particularly where the visuals of the brand are incorporated in a complex background that is typically the case with social media messages or in urban adverts. The semantic segmentation models are U-Net, Mask R-CNN or DeepLab, ones that are based on improved CNN models in order to label each individual pixel in the image and, thus, distinguish between foreground and background or various objects within a scene (Hamatta et al., 2025). Branding applications can be done with these tools that are able to divide visual contents into branded and non-branded content and that also examine images and videos in detail in terms of brand location, size and prominence. Image segmentation has also been used in contextual analysis of visuals that allows the marketers to be aware of how their brand assets relate to other visuals. One of them is that a logo can be involved in influencer posts around certain products (e.g., food, luxury cars, sportswear) and this may be valuable to inform the strategy partnerships and positioning.

Object Detection: Locating and Classifying Visual Brand Elements

The image recognition and image segmentation are extensions of object detection, which can detect the position of objects in a picture along with their nature. It creates bounding boxes of objects of interest and classifies them concurrently.

Faster R-CNN, YOLO (You Only Look Once), and SSD (Single Shot Multi Box Detector) are the most popular object detection models and each one is inclined to be accurate or fast (Balakrishna & Mustapha, 2023). In brand identification, object detectors provide the ability to automatically localize logos, products or brand components in different visual scenes. It enables the marketers to scrutinize visual eminence, the magnitude and nature of the focal position of a logo (e.g. Is it huge or petite, etc.) and visual context (what is about the brand assets). Such measurements provide specific insights regarding the effectiveness of the visuals of the brand that are applied in campaigns or occur naturally in the content of consumers. In addition, competitor analysis can be affiliated to object detection that entails identification and benchmarking of the visual assets of the competitors in common media contexts. This allows the companies to track the market trends, visual differentiation, and opportunity of visual repositioning (Karjalainen & Snelders, 2010).

Real-Time and Scalable Analysis of Brand Visuals

Scalability and real time analysis are the unique characteristics of computer vision as compared to the old method of processing visual information. The AI-based applications can scan the pictures or video frames of thousands of images within a few seconds- not only have the right information but also in time. An example is that sports marketing can implement real-time logo identification in live-streamed content to direct sponsorship strategies and automated package scans on retailer websites can be implemented to implement a visual policy. Besides, when used in combination with geotagging, sentiment analysis, or click-through measures, computer vision outcomes could be related to broader trends in consumer behavior. The results of such a multi-dimensional analysis open new possibilities to understand how the visual brand identity influences consumer perception and experience in digital ecosystems (Almeida & Lelis, 2024).

AI METHODS FOR VISUAL BRAND ANALYSIS

The sophistication of artificial intelligence (AI) and computer vision has shown new possibilities of automatizing the finesse of the visual analyzing brand parts. The machine learning algorithms and image processing techniques of extracting and quantifying the primary components of visual identity is an inseparable attribute to visual identity as individual brands proceed to create a continuous and persuasive presence on the increasingly more diverse and dynamic online platforms. This section establishes additional AI-driven solutions to logos, color scheme, font, and design lines, which are fundamental to the way brands determine themselves visually.

Figure 3. AI workflow for visual brand element analysis

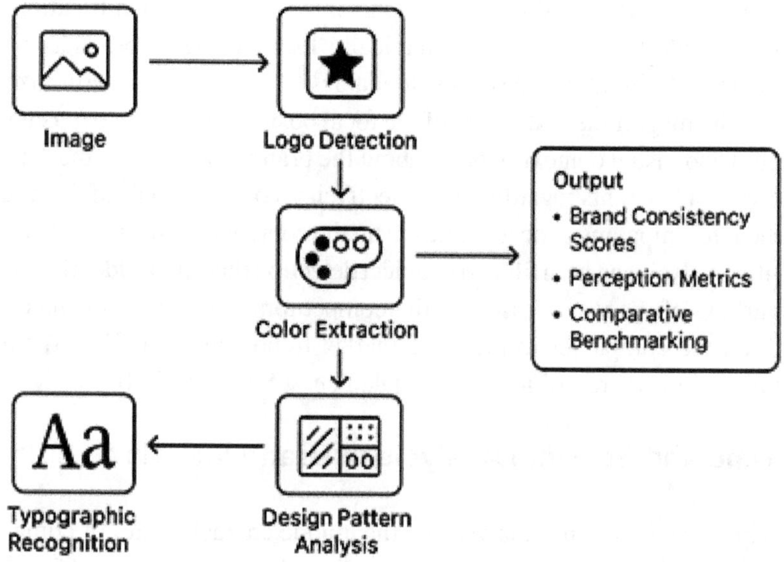

The next workflow is known as an AI-based workflow which must be utilized in the analysis of the visual facets of the brand. The images will be typed into the system and will be redirected to the big modules that will be carried out upon the selection of the logo, the choice of the color, recognition of the typography and the analysis of the pattern. Brand consistency scores, perception measures and comparative benchmarking will emerge as the last deliverable. The abstract conceptualization of how single computer vision tasks are combined into one structure to assess brand strategies is a good example provided in Figure 3.

Logo Detection and Classification: Precision in Brand Presence

The most recognized instance of brand identity is Logos which has been widely researched in AI with the aim of automating the process of recognizing and categorizing them in real-life images. The current digital content including social media posts, video frames, advertisements, or even product images are too huge and diverse to use the manual auditing procedures. AI works around this problem by applying deep convolutional neural networks (CNNs), which can identify the logos in complex visual images of any size, orientation, half presence, or distortion of the background. YOLO (You Only Look Once), Faster R-CNN, and SSD (Single Shot Detector) are also the most popular object detectors that are used to identify logos due to their accuracy and the efficiency of the computational methods (Yadav et al., 2023). This is typically trained on large and annotated datasets containing thousands of images of logos of numerous brands so that they can learn a distinctive set of logo features and variation. Upon identification, the classification models will make identified logo a match to a given brand entity. Influencer marketing the two-step model is required in these applications to track the use of illegal logos in user-generated content, or to evaluate the brand presence. To explain this, Hughes et al., (2019) demonstrated that the penetration of brands and the engagement of users on such platforms as Instagram can be introduced in a practical form with the assistance of the large-scale logo detection. The few-shot learning techniques are also applied in more recent developments, which identify novel or rare logos with sparse labelling information and extend the usefulness of AI in the high-turnover brand books. In addition, it has a real-time logo recognition feature, that helps a brand to keep track of live feeds or the current social media trends and offers unparalleled flexibility of the reputation management and marketing mix.

Color Palette Extraction and Analysis: Quantifying Brand Emotion

Colors have high roles in emotion and cultural meaning and therefore are the center of visual branding tactics. With the help of AI, the extraction and analysis of the color palette in images can occur in a systematic way, which will make it quantitative data on how brands use color to form identity and influence the psyche of consumers. This is done by initially converting images in the normal RGB color space into color models that are perceptually uniform, such as the HSV (Hue, Saturation, Value) or the CIELAB (Lab) which are better desensitized to human color vision (Chaki & Dey, 2021). The AI next implements clustering algorithms to the color space (e.g. k-means, DBSCAN, or Gaussian Mixture Models), to subdivide the color space into dominant and secondary colors, and to subdivide a visual asset into accent colors (Isohanni, 2024). The automatic extraction permits comparisons of color application among a huge array of brand images, and the shared themes or desired variations are revealed. As an example, one can track change in palette based on the time of the year, i.e. warmer colors in a holiday campaign or more subdued colors in sustainability communication and check how these changes align with marketing objectives (George, 2025). Also, AI is used in cross-cultural research to understand how the color of the brand may be modified to the sensibilities of the region to avoid the threat of being misinterpreted or culturally insensitive. Color analysis is also facilitated by competitive benchmarking. The areas of gaps or clusters in the visual aesthetics of the market can be seen by plotting schemes of competitor colors in a multidimensional space, which potentially can be used to form decisions to be repositioned or comply with category standards. Such a combination of the psychology of color and the recognition abilities of AI, consequently, increases the ability of marketers to become tactical in their application of color to narrate their brand stories.

Typography and Design Pattern Recognition: Decoding Brand Voice and Aesthetic

Typography is a highly significant aspect of brand identity, which is not very researched. Its analysis is a problem to automate since the font styles, as well as typographic presentation, are complex, especially in highly stylized or artistic cases. The traditional OCR (Optical Character Recognition) devices are good with standard fonts and printed text and do not work with decorative typeface or script typeface and experimental typeface, which are typical in branding. More modern transformer-based architecture, such as TrOCR or Vision Transformers (ViT) have made better results in font recognition, combining feature extraction on an image with sequence modeling, and thus including both a visual and contextual representation (Atienza, 2021). These models are effective to determine typography in the noisy background or distorted format, as is the case in the real-world marketing materials. Besides defining font families and font styles, the pattern of design, including repetitive motif and other compositional elements, as well as symmetry, negative space, alignment and texture, may be defined with the assistance of AI-based methods. The level of symmetry or balance in a logo or layout, which can be measured through feature detection using a geometric reasoning as an example, can provide objective values of visual harmony or tension (Orth et al., 2020). These granular insights can be applied to find out the level of visuality of a brand against the personality traits that they are trying to capture i.e. modernity, luxury or approachability. To take a specific instance, the brands that are interested in depicting innovation may intentionally introduce asymmetry and moving patterns that may be identified and analyzed by AI and assist in monitoring brand development and innovation metrics.

Integrating Multi-Level Visual Analysis for Holistic Brand Evaluation

The actual power of AI in visual brand analysis lies in the fact that such techniques are stacked into numerous layers. Using the example, a more detailed brand audit can be found on the frequency of logo recognition, the color palette that is not changing, and the similarity of typography applied throughout the digital interfaces. These features can be combined by the machine learning models and ranked on brand consistency, detect anomalies, and report these against established rules (Kazi et al., 2025). Moreover, AI-powered dashboards with visualization services may enable the brand manager to explore visually interactive exploration and draw insights on visual data, competitor landscapes, and make corrections on the campaigns. These kinds of data-driven models will make the brand management process based, rather than a creative-oriented activity, which can be quantified and held responsible.

APPLICATIONS AND CASE INSIGHTS

The application of AI-related computer vision technologies in the field of branding is no longer a distant future, but the novel reality pursued by numerous companies that work in different spheres. Technology also enables the brands to programmatically decode and measure images with depth and frequency never seen before, completely changing the measurement of brand consistency, competitive positioning and consumer perception. In this section, some of the applications and real-life case examples that prove the power and the potential of the AI-based visual brand analysis will be discussed.

Measuring Brand Consistency: Safeguarding Visual Integrity at Scale

The pillar of successful branding is the sign of brand consistency that will help in increasing consumer awareness and credibility. However, as the brands expand their operations in numerous digital platforms and increasingly rely on decentralized production of content both via regional marketing offices and via influencer agreements, it becomes challenging to maintain visual integrity. The computer vision with AI would offer the solution that would robotize the process of tracking the brand elements in the significant and varied collections of images. One of the companies that has managed to apply AI-powered logo recognition to scan its iconic red-white bottle image has been the Coca-Cola, as part of its global campaigns, it has been scanning the image of the bottle with the assistance of AI. Through convolutional neural network models that detect the trends of the Coca-Cola logo and the color schemes, the firm tracks the application of visual codes in line with the example of the social network and online advertising and packaging in stores (Zheng & Huang, 2022). These surveillance systems are automated to detect anomalies such as use of incorrect color tint or improperly placed logo that would have otherwise not been noticed and would report a potential threat to brand equity. The specified solution, in turn, will also benefit the time analysis, with a company such as Coca-Cola being capable of tracing the changes in the visual identity as the duration of the campaign in question unfolds, and of gauging the success of the rebranding efforts in question. The objective measure of the consistency of the logo positioning, color, and typography would enable the company to determine whether it meets the brand standards or not to increase the governance within the highly complex global marketing ecosystem. Similarly, FMCG and retail companies apply AI-based audits of visuals to ensure that the product is produced to look the same in the e-store, where the difference in the picture can cause individuals to lose confidence in the products (Emon, 2025; Singh et al., 2025). Computer vision can be scaled hence such organizations can process tens of thousands of images in a day, something that cannot be done using the manual review.

Competitor Visual Analysis: Mapping the Competitive Landscape Through AI

Besides inner consistency, AI also enables a more subtle analysis of the competitors since it provides the brands with the possibility to carry out a visual analysis of identities within the industry in a more organized way. Competitive benchmarking is a strategic undertaking that is very important and traditionally s/he was relied on the labor-intensive research on market, surveys or anecdotal. To enhance this process, computer vision is used to analyze advertisement, packaging and computerized material of the competitors to generate measurable visual information such as color scheme, logo prominence, design patterns. An example of this application can be such luxury fashion houses as Gucci and Louis Vuitton. These brands scan the posts and advertisements of competitors with AI software, extract logic in the positioning of the logos, use of colors, and visual storytelling (Juska, 2021; Khan & Hasan Emon, 2024). As an example, the frequency and positioning of logos in the digital campaigns used by rivals will make Gucci conclude any alterations in visual prominence strategies, which will presuppose the new tendencies in the expression of competitors brands. Color analytics can also give the luxury firms a glimpse into the trends in the palette at the moment: whether to switch to a more natural color scheme or to introduce more metallic details that will help to keep abreast with the newly-developed consumer preferences or the change of the season (Khan et al., 2024; Kohrs, 2021). With these, brands alter their visual campaigns to remain different yet be culturally and aesthetically feasible. The companies in consumer electronics employ visual benchmarking with AI, which monitors the progress of competitors in their packaging and product design discussion and apply it in its research and marketing (Pascucci et al., 2023). Such sustained visual market intelligence allows companies to forecast their competitor moves, new designs take shorter times, and brand narratives to expect the market.

Consumer Perception Studies: Unpacking Visual Engagement and Emotional Response

Probably the most radical application of computer vision might be the application to research consumer behavior. It is critically important in the development of a powerful brand-experience that the extent of perception and reaction to visual aspects of the brand by the consumer, other than self-reported preference. The AI does this through multimodal data fusion, which includes image analysis and eye-tracking, sentiment analysis, and social media monitoring to build detailed consumer attention and emotion model building. To demonstrate this, one of the studies by Sharakhina et al., (2024), has integrated AI-based logo recognition with eye-tracking data to investigate the distribution of visual attention on brand elements of internet advertisements by consumers. The findings showed that there was strong effect on length of gaze and brand recognition by some logo placements and differences in color contrasts. These intuitions allowed the marketers to use the ad layouts to the maximum to get the greatest consumer engagement. In social media, computer vision is a technology used by the brands to scan user-generated content (UGC) in which the products have been featured in. By identifying the logos and color scheme of the thousands of photos posted to consumers, the sentiment analysis of the captions and comments posted, the companies will have the overall picture of brand sentiment as seen with the eyes and words (Peng et al., 2024). This is a real-time feedback process, which informs creative direction, community management and crisis response. Brands in automotive industry have applied multimodal analysis to gauge the consumer emotional response of products and events. The visual attention patterns that AI models determined through wearable sensors and image-related effect through online forums and photo shares showed minor factors that lead to emotional response concerning the elements of design and promotional images.

Case Study: PepsiCo's AI-Powered Brand Monitoring System

The case study of PepsiCo is intriguing as it shows the way that AI can be operationalized to track the progress of the brand in its entirety. Having a huge portfolio size and covering numerous markets, PepsiCo implemented a computer vision platform, and it involved logo recognition, color recognition, and package recognition to track brand usage throughout the globe (Kesavan et al., 2024). The system constantly expedites search in the social media, retail websites and advertising channels, providing the marketing personnel of PepsiCo with dashboards displaying visual consistency scores, rival positioning and consumer interest indicators. When these discrepancies occur, e.g., when using an old version of a logo in a regional campaign, the platform contains alerts and the amendment can be done within a short amount of time. Besides that, there are the possibilities of tailoring visual branding to specific audience groups by analyzing the color preferences in the region and consumer response, which enable the localized, yet standardized branding campaigns of PepsiCo. The fact-based strategy mentioned is an excellent illustration of the effectiveness of AI in streamlining brand governance and enabling agility and shortening time to market.

Emerging Trends: From Static Images to Dynamic Visual Ecosystems

As the AI technologies evolve, their application to the visual analysis of the brand is integrated increasingly, and it is not confined to the mere image material but also covers video content, augmented reality (AR), and virtual reality (VR) space. More and more brands are considering visual representation in live videos, interactive advertisements, and immersive and applying real-time logo observation and visual integrity (Baele et al., 2023). These dynamic applications open new dimensions of what we understand about brand engagement wherein the visual identity interacts with the user behavior in multifaceted relations. One case in point is the esports sponsorships where the AI must evaluate the visibility of the logo and its location performance when broadcasting a live event, the data that will guide the investment decision and the creative decisions. In addition, computer vision and NLP, which incorporates both visual and written sentiment, serve to further interpret a multimodal brand communication with a view of developing better insights into the consumer (Emon & Khan, 2025).

CHALLENGES AND CONSTRAINTS

Despite the existence of enormous opportunities associated with the inclusion of the computer vision into the process of brand analysis, the latter is also accompanied by a complex set of challenges and limitations that scientists and practitioners will need to contend with. These issues are related to technical, methodological, and ethical layers of either of which influence the credibility, impartiality, and relevance of AI-based insights in branding. Such limitations should be known to ensure that the field is effective and well promoted.

Data Quality and Diversity: The Foundation of Model Performance

The quality and representativeness of data that it is trained and tested on can ensure the effectiveness of any AI system. It is particularly severe in the example of computer vision in branding. Brands convey their visual image with the help of the rainbow of styles, media types, and solutions, including high-resolution print advertisements, social media posts which are created by the users via smartphones. This heterogeneity is what introduces noise and variability that may significantly reduce the accuracy of the model (Ramalli, 2024). In fact, concept detectors previously trained on mostly high-quality, studio photographs might not work as well with blurred, partially distorted or manipulated logos on social media. Similarly, color extraction algorithms can be misled by the lighting environment, artefacts of image compression, color distortions caused by various display devices, and so on (Fang et al., 2021). This variability too needs much preprocessing, augmentation and normalization to offer, which is again complicated and may be biased. The issue of the visual styles is also diverse. Global brands shape their visual cues to local audiences, which encompass culturally-mediated color, pattern, and typography that can widely differ in comparison to the global ones (Emon & Khan, 2024). Lack of access to such variation will either cause AI models to be misclassified or reduce them to too simplistic, something that successful brand management can do without.

Contextual Nuance and Semantics: Beyond Pixels to Meaning

Computer vision proves to be very effective in identifying shapes, colors and patterns but it is basically weak in identifying the contextual and cultural contexts of the visual brand elements. One such situation is that something that in one culture may be perceived as an indication of trust may have entirely different meanings in another culture (Dey et al., 2021). The existing models, predominantly trained only on visual features, do not have the capability of incorporating such semantic and cultural context into a entire without extra sources of multimodal information. This weakness will be represented in analysis of logos or design motifs which are meditated with culturally charged symbols or allusions. Without complimentary linguistic, historical or ethnographical details, AI can provide superficial or false meaning. This is a critical problem in relation to global branding and any slight culture-related mistake can lead to consumer backlash or brand dilution (Yari et al., 2020). A hybrid of computer vision and NLP and knowledge graphs known as multimodal AI is potentially able to fill this gap. However, these systems require big, edited data and complex integration solutions, not solutions, but topics of active research.

Annotation Challenges: The Bottleneck of Supervised Learning

Most computer vision models are built on supervised learning and need huge amounts of data with fine-grain annotations, e.g. bounding boxes around logos, color chunks or font groups. These annotated datasets are notoriously very difficult to create and costly, as well as subject to human error and bias. A lack of objectivity in annotation can also arise because of subjective interpretations of the right positioning of logos or color palette when the branding guideline is loose or evolving. Annotator cultural background, and expertise also influence the quality of labeling and might bias model training results. The unavailability of high quality and varied datasets, on which the model can be implemented to differentiate between brands, further limits generalizability of models. To work around all these, semi-supervised, unsupervised and self-supervised forms of learning are also gaining popularity where models are trained with unlabeled or partially labelled data. Although, these methods are likely to compromise some accuracy and interpretability which may be a viable tradeoff when applying these methods in commercial applications where high accuracy is required.

Ethical Concerns: Surveillance, Manipulation, and Transparency

Along with the technical barriers, there is also a moral side to the subject of computer vision analysis of a brand that needs to be discussed carefully. One of the burning questions is to which extent such endless monitoring of brand images, especially in the user-created content, goes into the surveillance territory, at the cost of consumer privacy (Shaban, 2024). Firms and influencers should balance the act of gathering valuable data and taking personal privacy. Moreover, manipulation is questioned by the fact that AI is applied to study and forecast emotional responses of consumers relying on visual images. The information obtained via computer vision might be utilized to create hyper-targeted, psychologically appealing branding messages, which capitalize on lack of knowledge or susceptibility and augment the dread of carrying out unlawful marketing conduct (Dulloo & Struweg, 2025). One more significant issue is the transparency of AI models development and deployment. The deepest learning models are black-box hard attempts to comprehend how specific brand features are considered or even detected is the fact that they attempt to understand how these factors are implemented. This kind of obscurity can lead to the breakdown of trust between stakeholders such as marketing departments and customers among them and among others, due to inability to hold anyone accountable, based on errors or biased outcomes. It is a necessity that the integration of marketers, ethicists, computer scientists, and legal experts initiate guidelines and frames within the context of which AI could be ethically applied in branding. Such structures should be concerned with equality, openness and sensitivity to cultural differences.

FUTURE TRENDS AND RESEARCH DIRECTIONS

As the development of artificial intelligence increases more rapidly than ever, the sphere of visual brand analysis is on the brink of the radical changes that are bound to result in better perception of brand image and consumer interaction. Going further than the visual examination of specific images, the direction to take in the future is multifaceted integrations of multimodal AI, real-time systems, and interdisciplinary designs that bring technology and humanistic insights together. This section will describe these emerging trends and give a summary of future areas of potential academic and practical studies.

Multimodal AI: Bridging Vision and Language for Richer Brand Narratives

The traditional uses of computer vision in branding have concentrated on extraction and quantification of visual brand character such as logos, colors and typography. However, branding is by its very definition a multiprotection comprising not just the visual content but the textual descriptions, including captions, hashtags, reviews, and social media commentary, which determine consumer interpretation and affect. One of the important directions in the future of brand analysis is computer vision along with natural language processing (NLP). The multimodal AI systems can be interpreted through the processing of images and text (in relation to images) to form a general perception of brand communication. To provide an example, the post about the product on Instagram may include a picture, a description of the usage of the product, and comments with the emotion of the user. With the assistance of a collective process of understanding such modalities, AI can not only observe what is introduced into our visuals, but also how it is introduced and remembered by people (Wen & Laporte, 2025). This deeper interpretation assists a marketer in finding such subtext as irony, humor, or cultural reference that cannot be easily seen. The most recent transformer designs, such as CLIP (Contrastive Language-Image Pre-training), can learn this cross-modal understanding population by being trained to predict the image-text combination (Samayamantri et al., 2024). Application of such models to branding allows the researcher to map the agreement or discrepancy among the visual identity and verbal message which is a sophisticated tool of brand integrity assessment and reputation management. Additionally, multimodal AI can get a chance to work on sentiment analysis, which is directly related to visuals, and comprehend the impact of some design choices on consumer moods. To provide an example, a color palette or development of a logo can be associated with more positive or negative textual feedback to inform an adaptive branding mechanism (César et al., 2025).

Figure 4. Framework of multimodal AI in visual brand analysis

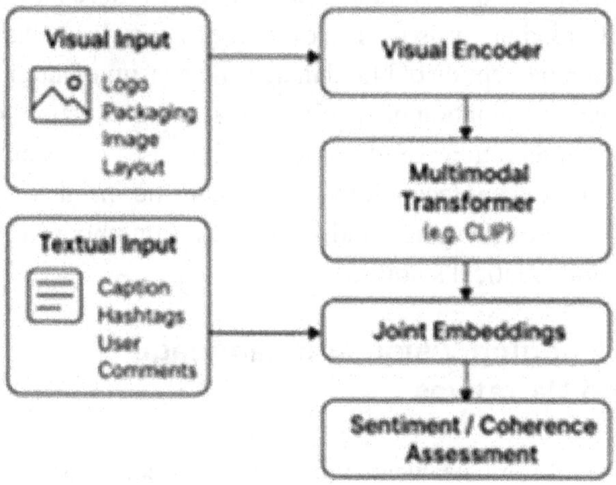

The visual brand analysis provides multimodal AI application, which is explained with the help of such figures. It would consist of two parallel streams of inputs, one of which (the visual one) would be fed through a visual encoder (logo, graphics on the packaging and layout) and the other one (textual one) would be fed through a textual one (captions, hashtags, and the comments left by the users). The two of these forms of data are combined with the assistance of a Multimodal Transformer (e.g., CLIP) and the result is computed into a set of joint embeddings, which are then forwarded to two modules to be examined in the perception of sentiment and coherence. To see a more detailed view of the brand perception, it is necessary to change to multimodal integrated analysis, which is presented in figure 4.

Real-Time Visual Brand Monitoring: From Static Images to Dynamic Ecosystems

The advent of the live streaming, augmented reality (AR) and virtual reality (VR) platforms is redefining the operations of the consumers who need real-time monitoring of the visual brand identity. These dynamic environments allow the flow of visual information, which is constant in comparison to more classic, fixed sets of image data where the elements of the brand are being presented temporarily and in different locations. Brands are also starting to implement and deploy low-weight computer vision models that are capable of processing video feeds or AR interactions in real time with low latency due to the development of edge computing and streaming analytics (Basole et al., 2024). The capability allows the companies to track the logo action of live events, such as sport event streaming or the influencer stream, assessing the advertisement efficiency and keeping the brand values in real-time. The intellectual property is also enhanced in respect of real-time tracking of the illegal use of logos or misrepresentation of brands. Online auctions or social networks could be utilized by fashion companies to identify the pictures of counterfeit products within several seconds (Divea & Surjit, 2022). However, real time analysis presents limitations in terms of computing power, motion blur/occlusion and contextual data fusion within a short period of time. The ongoing study is underway towards the optimization of model structures and utilizing 5G connectivity to defeat these bottlenecks.

Longitudinal Studies: Mapping Brand Evolution and Business Impact

Though AI-based visual analysis provides a glimpse into the current brand identity, a vital direction to follow in the future is that of a longitudinal, systematic approach to study visual forms of brand elements in terms of their evolutional change over the years and its correlation with the business performance. This is a step that goes further to analyze the analysis to deduce causal correlations and predictive patterns. Using logos or color scheme or typeface changes as an example, using years of product releases, promotions, or rebranding, a person can identify the effect that the visual change has had on the consumer perception, market share, or financial performance (Hanna et al., 2021). The successful implementation of AI-based tools into business analytics and consumer research enables analyzing the success of the brand strategy in its entirety. Such longitudinal information is also useful in terms of the trends and cycles of visual branding which can provide an insight into the future of aesthetics and cultural shifts. The brands which anticipate those changes and react to them make sure that they are relevant and competitive. The requirement to engage in interdisciplinary research to integrate AI practices with the study of semiotics, which is the study of signs and symbols, and consumer psychology are some of the academic imperatives. The information on what is changed and why it is cognitively and emotionally appealing to the consumers creates a new theoretical approach to branding science (Mora Cortez et al., 2022).

Towards an Integrated Discipline: Visual Brand Science

The intersection of AI, semiotics, marketing, and psychology creates a new subject of research which can be referred to as visual brand science. It is a synthesizing discipline that would be methodical regarding learning about the role of visual elements as communicative actions to mediate brand meaning and to establish consumer behavior by computational rigor. It is a discipline whereby AI would be used as a measuring tool, but also to test the hypothesis concerning visual symbolism, cultural semiotics, as well as emotional resonance at the scale. Using the example of the color meaning, it might be explored how these semiotic meanings of color can change based on the demographic population or how typography impacts perceived brand personality using big data interpolated by AI. Such a set up would also encourage collaboration of the technologists, marketing researchers, and humanities researchers, forming a more holistic view of comprehension of phenomena relevant to branding and informing the ethical component of AI application.

CONCLUSION

This chapter discusses the interactive relationship between visual brand identity and transformational attributes of computer vision and artificial intelligence (AI). As marketing continues to evolve within the context of the visual saturation of the digital world, these visual aspects of a brand of logos, color, typography and design motifs have never played an important role as much. They are powerful semiotic signs that distinguish brands together with evoking emotional appeal, passing values and shaping the impressions of the consumer. As AI-based computer vision technologies come into existence, the analysis, quantification and optimization of such visual assets are introduced with a chance that is hardly preceded in the conventional methods, and on a scale and accuracy such as never experienced. The chapter has provided a breakdown of the visual language of brands understanding through AI by describing some of the most significant computer vision technologies, such as image recognition, feature extraction, and segmentation. The application of the advanced techniques, i.e. the automatic logo recognition, the color palette recognition, and the typography recognition, is used to underline the practical significance of the machine learning models in the interpretation of the nuances creating a visual image of a brand.

As can be seen in real-life situations and research, AI-based visual analysis is already changing the industry of brand management. Regardless of whether it is brand consistency measurement with disjointed digital sources to competitive visual benchmarking research and consumer perception research, computer vision gives marketers objective and data-driven information, which can be applied to create more consistent and practical branding strategies. These devices help in detecting anomalies, tracking brand performance and adapting to the evolving market dynamics, which ultimately would increase consumer interaction and competition practice. Nevertheless, despite this, which is potentially a bright spot of branding and AI, there are very grave obstacles. The issue of data quality, variability of brand expression and cultural symbolism situationless negative implications of existing AI systems. Ethical issues that complicate the use of these technologies are privacy, transparency, and manipulation. Such limitations should be known to embrace responsibility and remain innovative. In the future, the next step is the integration of multimodal AI (computer vision and natural language processing), which can lead to more contextual and deep information about the brand. The brands will be able to respond instantaneously to the visual conditions, and this will be made possible by the immediate market conditions and consumer interaction visual monitoring with the innovative edge computing and streaming analytics. Besides, the emergence of interdisciplinary research models is present and is likely to improve theoretical backgrounds and practical interventions of visual brand science. The repercussions are tremendous in the marketing-branding. Companies working with AI in visual analysis can leave subjective and manual brand evaluation behind and embrace the empirically and scalable-based approaches that are far closer to consumer realities. This is an ability to make technology a lot easier to participate in dynamic brand governance, competitive positioning that is more competitive, and whose consumer conversation is more meaningful through visual storytelling. At the same time, marketing experts must create a vital sense of the negative aspects of AI and its ethics. The formula that works is the blend of techno savvy and cultural sensitivity, creativity and strategic thinking to blend in. Whether branding is moving into a future where AI enables it to be enhanced or whether the opportunities of AI are being used by the brands to provide the brands with authenticity, relevance, and resonance in an increasingly visual world, is a question that is subject to discussion.

REFERENCES

Ahlawat, R., & Swami, P. (2024). *The Right Color Attracts the Right Customer.*, DOI: 10.4018/979-8-3693-4236-7.ch017

Alanadoly, A. B., Sidhu, S. K., & Richards-Carpenter, N. (2024). *AI Landscape in Fashion: Insights on Transforming Design, Supply Chains, Marketing, and Consumer Experiences* (pp. 417–439). DOI: 10.1007/978-3-031-71052-0_16

Almeida, S., & Lelis, C. (2024). *Implications of New Media in Brands' Visual Identities: A Systematic Literature Review* (pp. 809–825). DOI: 10.1007/978-3-031-47281-7_66

Atienza, R. (2021). *Vision Transformer for Fast and Efficient Scene Text Recognition.*, DOI: 10.1007/978-3-030-86549-8_21

Baele, S. J., Brace, L., & Coan, T. G. (2023). Uncovering the Far-Right Online Ecosystem: An Analytical Framework and Research Agenda. *Studies in Conflict and Terrorism, 46*(9), 1599–1623. DOI: 10.1080/1057610X.2020.1862895

Balakrishna, S., & Mustapha, A. A. (2023). Progress in multi-object detection models: A comprehensive survey. *Multimedia Tools and Applications, 82*(15), 22405–22439. DOI: 10.1007/s11042-022-14131-0

Balmer, J. M. T. (2023). Design, corporate brand design, and corporate heritage brand design: What are they? what of them? *Journal of Brand Management, 30*(2), 97–115. DOI: 10.1057/s41262-023-00314-z

Basole, R. C., Park, H., & Seuss, C. D. (2024). Complex business ecosystem intelligence using AI-powered visual analytics. *Decision Support Systems, 178*, 114133. DOI: 10.1016/j.dss.2023.114133

Bertão, R. A., Yeoun, M.-H., & Joo, J. (2025). A blind spot in AI-powered logo makers: Visual design principles. *Visual Communication, 24*(1), 222–250. DOI: 10.1177/14703572231155593

Caires, C. S. (2025). *From Words to Icons.* Advancements in Prompting Text-to-Image Models for Logo Design with Artificial Intelligence., DOI: 10.1007/978-3-031-76156-0_12

Castañeda-García, J. A., Frías-Jamilena, D. M., Del Barrio-García, S., & Rodríguez-Molina, M. A. (2020). The Effect of Message Consistency and Destination-Positioning Brand Strategy Type on Consumer-Based Destination Brand Equity. *Journal of Travel Research, 59*(8), 1447–1463. DOI: 10.1177/0047287519881506

César, I., Pereira, I., Rodrigues, F., Miguéis, V., Nicola, S., & Madureira, A. (2025). Exploring multimodal learning applications in marketing: A critical perspective. *International Journal of Hybrid Intelligent Systems*, *21*(1), 29–46. DOI: 10.3233/HIS-240018

Chaki, J., & Dey, N. (2021). *Introduction to Image Color Feature*., DOI: 10.1007/978-981-15-5761-3_1

Dey, A. U., Ghosh, S. K., Valveny, E., & Harit, G. (2021). Beyond visual semantics: Exploring the role of scene text in image understanding. *Pattern Recognition Letters*, *149*, 164–171. DOI: 10.1016/j.patrec.2021.06.011

Divea, K., & Surjit, R. (2022). *Blockchain Utility by Pioneers in Fashion and Apparel Industry*., DOI: 10.1007/978-981-19-6569-2_4

Dixit, U. D., Shirdhonkar, M. S., & Sinha, G. R. (2023). Automatic logo detection from document image using HOG features. *Multimedia Tools and Applications*, *82*(1), 863–878. DOI: 10.1007/s11042-022-13300-5

Dulloo, R., & Struweg, I. (2025). The Rise of Experience Economy and Marketing 5.0. In *Leveraging AI-Powered Marketing in the Experience-Driven Economy* (pp. 1–38). IGI Global., DOI: 10.4018/979-8-3693-9561-5.ch001

Emon, M. M. H. (2025). The Mediating Role of Supply Chain Responsiveness in the Relationship Between Key Supply Chain Drivers and Performance: Evidence from the FMCG Industry. *Brazilian Journal of Operations & Production Management*, *22*(1), 2580. DOI: 10.14488/BJOPM.2580.2025

Emon, M. M. H., & Khan, T. (2024). A Systematic Literature Review on Sustainability Integration and Marketing Intelligence in the Era of Artificial Intelligence. *Review of Business and Economics Studies*, *12*(4), 6–28. DOI: 10.26794/2308-944X-2024-12-4-6-28

Emon, M. M. H., & Khan, T. (2025). The mediating role of attitude towards the technology in shaping artificial intelligence usage among professionals. *Telematics and Informatics Reports*, *17*, 100188. DOI: 10.1016/j.teler.2025.100188

Fang, H., Chen, D., Huang, Q., Zhang, J., Ma, Z., Zhang, W., & Yu, N. (2021). Deep Template-Based Watermarking. *IEEE Transactions on Circuits and Systems for Video Technology*, *31*(4), 1436–1451. DOI: 10.1109/TCSVT.2020.3009349

George, R. (2025). Tourism and Hospitality Product-Offerings, Branding, and Pricing. In *Marketing Tourism and Hospitality* (pp. 225–255). Springer Nature Switzerland., DOI: 10.1007/978-3-031-65983-6_8

Hamatta, H. S. A., Deepika, C. L. N., Rjoub, G., Kassaymeh, S., Manikandan, R., Suman, S. K., & Bhagyalakshmi, L. (2025). Integration of Deep Learning and Image Segmentation in Computational Modeling for Improved Biospeckle Image Analysis. *SN Computer Science*, *6*(4), 350. DOI: 10.1007/s42979-025-03872-y

Hanna, S., Rowley, J., & Keegan, B. (2021). Place and Destination Branding: A Review and Conceptual Mapping of the Domain. *European Management Review*, *18*(2), 105–117. DOI: 10.1111/emre.12433

Hauser, J. R., Li, Z., & Mao, C. (2023). *Artificial Intelligence and User-Generated Data Are Transforming How Firms Come to Understand Customer Needs.*, DOI: 10.1108/S1548-643520230000020007

Huang, H., Cai, Y., & Xu, L. (2021). Stability or instability: The impact of brand concepts on logo design preferences. *Journal of Brand Management*, *28*(5), 465–480. DOI: 10.1057/s41262-021-00238-6

Hughes, C., Swaminathan, V., & Brooks, G. (2019). Driving Brand Engagement Through Online Social Influencers: An Empirical Investigation of Sponsored Blogging Campaigns. *Journal of Marketing*, *83*(5), 78–96. DOI: 10.1177/0022242919854374

Isohanni, J. (2024). Recognising small colour changes with unsupervised learning, comparison of methods. *Advances in Computational Intelligence*, *4*(2), 6. DOI: 10.1007/s43674-024-00073-7

Juska, J. M. (2021). *Integrated Marketing Communication*. Routledge., DOI: 10.4324/9780367443382

Karjalainen, T.-M., & Snelders, D. (2010). Designing Visual Recognition for the Brand. *Journal of Product Innovation Management*, *27*(1), 6–22. DOI: 10.1111/j.1540-5885.2009.00696.x

Kazi, K. S. L., Shinde, S. S., Nerkar, P. M., Kazi, S. S., & Kazi, V. S. (2025). *Machine Learning for Brand Protection.*, DOI: 10.4018/979-8-3693-7041-4.ch007

Kesavan, V., Polisetty, A., & Dash, G. (2024). *The Application of AI in Transitioning Business Houses Towards New Product Development Process.*, DOI: 10.4018/979-8-3693-9122-8.ch017

Khan, T., Emon, M. M. H., & Rahman, S. (2024). Marketing Strategy Innovation via AI Adoption: A Study on Bangladeshi SMEs in the Context of Industry 5.0. *2024 6th International Conference on Sustainable Technologies for Industry 5.0 (STI)*, 1–6. DOI: 10.1109/STI64222.2024.10951050

Khan, T., & Hasan Emon, M. M. (2024). Determinants of AI Image Generator Adoption Among Marketing Agencies: The Mediating Effects of Perceived Usefulness. *2024 IEEE 3rd International Conference on Robotics, Automation, Artificial-Intelligence and Internet-of-Things (RAAICON)*, 177–182. DOI: 10.1109/RAAICON64172.2024.10928548

Kim, J., Kim, M., & Lee, S.-M. (2025). Unlocking Trust Dynamics: An Exploration of Playfulness, Expertise, and Consumer Behavior in Virtual Influencer Marketing. *International Journal of Human-Computer Interaction, 41*(1), 378–390. DOI: 10.1080/10447318.2023.2300018

Kohrs, K. (2021). The language of luxury fashion advertising: Technology of the self and spectacle. *Journal of Fashion Marketing and Management, 25*(2), 257–273. DOI: 10.1108/JFMM-02-2020-0029

Luo, L., Liu, L., Zheng, Y., & Chen, J. (2024). Visual information and appearance: The impact of visual attributes of user-generated photos on review helpfulness. *Telematics and Informatics, 92*, 102164. DOI: 10.1016/j.tele.2024.102164

Mogaji, E. (2021). Brand Identity. In *Brand Management* (pp. 85–122). Springer International Publishing., DOI: 10.1007/978-3-030-66119-9_5

Mora Cortez, R., Ghosh Dastidar, A., Cortez, R. M., & Dastidar, A. G. (2022). A longitudinal study of B2B customer engagement in LinkedIn: The role of brand personality. *Journal of Business Research, 145*, 92–105. DOI: 10.1016/j.jbusres.2022.02.086

Nanne, A. J., Antheunis, M. L., Van Der Lee, C. G., Postma, E. O., Wubben, S., & Van Noort, G. (2020). The Use of Computer Vision to Analyze Brand-Related User Generated Image Content. *Journal of Interactive Marketing, 50*(1), 156–167. DOI: 10.1016/j.intmar.2019.09.003

Orth, U. R., Nickel, K., Böhm, R., & Röwe, K. (2020). Agreement by design: The effect of visual harmony on responses to surveys. *Journal of Consumer Behaviour, 19*(2), 196–207. DOI: 10.1002/cb.1804

Overgoor, G., Rand, W., van Dolen, W., & Mazloom, M. (2022). Simplicity is not key: Understanding firm-generated social media images and consumer liking. *International Journal of Research in Marketing, 39*(3), 639–655. DOI: 10.1016/j.ijresmar.2021.12.005

Pascucci, F., Savelli, E., & Gistri, G. (2023). How digital technologies reshape marketing: evidence from a qualitative investigation. *Italian Journal of Marketing*. DOI: 10.1007/s43039-023-00063-6

Peng, Y., Lock, I., & Ali Salah, A. (2024). Automated Visual Analysis for the Study of Social Media Effects: Opportunities, Approaches, and Challenges. *Communication Methods and Measures*, *18*(2), 163–185. DOI: 10.1080/19312458.2023.2277956

Qian, S., Lu, Y., Peng, Y., Shen, C., & Xu, H. (2024). Convergence or divergence? A cross-platform analysis of climate change visual content categories, features, and social media engagement on Twitter and Instagram. *Public Relations Review*, *50*(2), 102454. DOI: 10.1016/j.pubrev.2024.102454

Ramalli, E. (2024). Data Quality, Data Diversity and Data Provenance. *Ethical Perspectives*, •••, 39–48. DOI: 10.1007/978-3-031-52962-7_4

Samayamantri, L. S., Singhal, S., Krishnamurthy, O., & Regin, R. (2024). *AI-Driven Multimodal Approaches to Human Behavior Analysis*., DOI: 10.4018/979-8-3693-3739-4.ch025

Shaban, A. (2024). Digital Rights, Digital Representation, and Digital Justice—Towards Digital Democracy and Freedom of Expression. In *Digital Geographies—Theory, Space, and Communities* (pp. 765–899). Springer Nature Singapore. DOI: 10.1007/978-981-97-4734-4_7

Sharakhina, L., Ilyina, I., Kaplun, D., Teor, T., & Kulibanova, V. (2024). AI technologies in the analysis of visual advertising messages: Survey and application. *Journal of Marketing Analytics*, *12*(4), 1066–1089. DOI: 10.1057/s41270-023-00255-1

Sharma, V., Gupta, M., Kumar, A., & Mishra, D. (2021). Video Processing Using Deep Learning Techniques: A Systematic Literature Review. *IEEE Access : Practical Innovations, Open Solutions*, *9*, 139489–139507. DOI: 10.1109/ACCESS.2021.3118541

Shukla, M., Misra, R., & Singh, D. (2023). Exploring relationship among semiotic product packaging, brand experience dimensions, brand trust and purchase intentions in an Asian emerging market. *Asia Pacific Journal of Marketing and Logistics*, *35*(2), 249–265. DOI: 10.1108/APJML-10-2021-0718

Singh, D., & Arora, D. (2024). *Cloud-Based Object Detection Model Using Amazon Rekognition*., DOI: 10.1007/978-981-99-9811-1_13

Singh, D., Sharma, A., Singh, R. K., & Rana, P. S. (2025). Artificial intelligence enabled supply chain resilience: insights from FMCG industry. *Journal of Global Operations and Strategic Sourcing*. DOI: 10.1108/JGOSS-02-2024-0017

Waqas, M., Hamzah, Z. L., & Mohd Salleh, N. A. (2021). Customer experience with the branded content: A social media perspective. *Online Information Review*, *45*(5), 964–982. DOI: 10.1108/OIR-10-2019-0333

Wen, Y., & Laporte, S. (2025). Experiential Narratives in Marketing: A Comparison of Generative AI and Human Content. *Journal of Public Policy & Marketing*, *44*(3), 392–410. DOI: 10.1177/07439156241297973

Wu, Z., Shen, C., & van den Hengel, A. (2019). Wider or Deeper: Revisiting the ResNet Model for Visual Recognition. *Pattern Recognition*, *90*, 119–133. DOI: 10.1016/j.patcog.2019.01.006

Yadav, S. P., Jindal, M., Rani, P., de Albuquerque, V. H. C., dos Santos Nascimento, C., & Kumar, M. (2023). An improved deep learning-based optimal object detection system from images. *Multimedia Tools and Applications*, *83*(10), 30045–30072. DOI: 10.1007/s11042-023-16736-5

Yari, N., Lankut, E., Alon, I., & Richter, N. F. (2020). Cultural intelligence, global mindset, and cross-cultural competencies: A systematic review using bibliometric methods. *European Journal of International Management*, *14*(2), 210. DOI: 10.1504/EJIM.2020.105567

Zhao, X., Wang, L., Zhang, Y., Han, X., Deveci, M., & Parmar, M. (2024). A review of convolutional neural networks in computer vision. *Artificial Intelligence Review*, *57*(4), 99. DOI: 10.1007/s10462-024-10721-6

Zheng, H., & Huang, L. (2022). Owned Social Media Advertising: Cannibalization and Competition. *Journal of Interactive Marketing*, *57*(3), 442–456. DOI: 10.1177/10949968221095555

KEY TERMS AND DEFINITIONS

Brand Consistency: To what extent are the visual and message-related elements of a brand homogenous and consistent across platforms and touchpoints.

Color Palette Extraction: The ways to identify and break down the most common and secondary colors used in the brand image to study and quantify the use of colors.

Computer Vision: A subfield of artificial intelligence, which enables the machines to read and process visual information about images or videos to mimic human visual processing.

Image Segmentation: It is the procedure of breaking down an image to extract meaningful pieces to isolate a given visual object, e.g. remove a logo off the background.

Logo Detection: The identification and monitoring of brand logos as pictures or videos by means of AI algorithms.

Multimodal AI: An advanced AI solution, which is a synthesis of other forms of data to provide more comprehensive and context-sensitive analysis i.e. images and text.

Typography Recognition: Artificial intelligence and image recognition to determine and classify fonts and other graphics features of brand image.

Visual Brand Identity: The total collections of visualized elements such as logos, colors, typography and pattern of designs constituting the brand image in the market.

Chapter 3
Narrative Intelligence: Leveraging AI in Storytelling and Content Creation for Brand Engagement and Equity Measurement

Zerin Tasnim
https://orcid.org/0000-0002-5705-1648
North South University, Bangladesh

Md Mahdi Hasan Ahid
https://orcid.org/0009-0008-2304-5283
American International University-Bangladesh, Bangladesh

Md. Adnan Rahman
https://orcid.org/0000-0003-3378-0958
Uttara University, Bangladesh

Mohammad Mofasserul Islam
https://orcid.org/0000-0002-1717-4467
International University of Business Agriculture and Technology, Bangladesh

Md. Nafis Fuad
https://orcid.org/0009-0000-4406-7440
American International University-Bangladesh, Bangladesh

Abu Bakar Abdul Hamid
https://orcid.org/0009-0007-5177-8145
Infrastructure University Kuala Lumpur, Malaysia

ABSTRACT

This chapter explores the ways in which artificial intelligence is changing brand storytelling into a more dynamic and data-driven process for enhancing engagement and measuring brand equity. It looks at how AI helps generate personalized narratives and also measures emotional and behavioral reactions from consumers. The chapter discusses both the opportunities and challenges that come from blending computational tools with human creativity. Using theoretical frameworks, real-world case studies, and ethical reflections, it shows how brands can use AI to create

DOI: 10.4018/979-8-3373-4506-2.ch003

authentic and culturally aware stories, while carefully assessing their effectiveness. The argument is made for a hybrid approach where human insights work alongside algorithmic precision, aiming to develop brand communication strategies that are emotionally meaningful and ethically sound building trust, loyalty, and lasting brand value in a marketing world that is becoming increasingly personalized.

INTRODUCTION

The intersection of artificial intelligence (AI) and branding is one of the most radical changes in contemporary marketing, not only in the mechanics of communication, but also in the philosophical backgrounds that the brands establish and sustain when it comes to their relationships with consumers. It has never been more important to be able to cut through the noise and deliver compelling and meaningful stories in a world that is defined by a flood of information and fragmented attention, where people are bombarded with thousands of brand messages per day (Ke et al., 2023). It is here that the narrative generation and content personalization opportunities offered by AI have become an important tool that allows brands to create a variety of stories that appeal to certain audiences without sacrificing a unified brand image on a larger scale. Traditionally, storytelling has taken a central place in branding strategies due to its exclusive capacity for inducing emotions, generating trust, and creating loyalty. In the classic marketing literature, psychological processes of telling the story, such as narrative transportation and identification are highlighted and enable more cognitive and emotional interaction with brand messages (Kang et al., 2020). The processes play a role in developing perceptions of brand authenticity and credibility qualities that consumers are placing more importance on in a world dominated by doubt in corporate messaging (Paul & Nikolaev, 2021). But conventional storytelling is dependent on the intuition and imagination of human marketers that whilst it cannot be replaced in various aspects is bound to scale, speed, and consistency (Emon & Khan, 2025a).

The recent technological progress, especially in generative language models like GPT-4, diffusion-based image generators, and advanced computer vision systems, has made storytelling not as limited by human ability. Such AI devices are capable of producing original texts and visual content based on brand stories, which can be tailored in real time based on different cultural factors, psycho-graphic factors, and situational factors (Berger et al., 2020; Emon & Khan, 2025b). As an example, AI-based platforms can dynamically tune a brand tone and message to various social media platforms so that it is relevant, but brand coherence is not affected. Such responsiveness is a radical break with the old one-size-fits-all approaches to campaigns and an indication that we are entering the era of hyper-personalized, context-driven narrative. Besides, the assimilation of AI to storytelling is not only a question of efficiency and novelty, but it changes the strategic calculus of brand communication fundamentally (Khan & Hasan Emon, 2024). Brands can now access, compute and analyze large volumes of consumer interaction data with embedded analytics and turn qualitative dimensions of storytelling like emotional resonance into quantifiable data. With the help of sentiment analysis and emotional AI, marketers can discover what stories bring positive emotions, generate engagement, and, most importantly, lead to the long-term brand equity (Kumar et al., 2024). Those metrics give an opportunity to constantly improve brand material, based on empirical evidence, not relying solely on intuition, which constitutes a feedback loop in which the stories are constantly improved due to real-time consumer feedback. The difference between the present wave of AI-driven narrative intelligence and the previous content automation attempts is in the complexity of algorithms and the scope of data it may gather. Unlike the previous methods of personalization which were based on simple rule-based frameworks or fixed segmentation (Khan et al., 2024), the current models of AI are trained based on behavioral, demographic, and contextual information. The ability to develop stories that not only capture but predict a change in consumer preferences, societal trends, and cultural nuances is made possible through this learning ability (Verganti et al., 2020). Practically, it enables an international brand to retain its coherent identity whilst addressing the local markets with the authentic voice, which has been a long-term ban of international marketers. In addition, when AI and branding collide, serious questions are also posed regarding the essence of creativity, authenticity, and trust of consumers. It has been observed by scholars that even though AI may produce content that seems to be creative, it is produced using statistical recognition patterns, but not human-like intuition or intentionality (Berber Sardinha, 2024; Emon, 2025b).

The difference raises the question of what is considered an authentic brand storytelling in a digital world that is becoming increasingly filled with algorithmic pieces. Is it possible that a story, which was created by a machine, is still authentic? Does awareness of the consumer of the AI involvement increase or decrease the trust the consumer has on the brand? These are not questions that are mere scholarly inquiries, they are the fundamental questions of morality and brand-to-consumer relationships that will shape the future of AI implementation in marketing. The other crucial aspect of the AI-led storytelling is its possibility to democratize creative processes. Whereas high-quality, personalized storytelling used to be the domain of the brands that had large resources, AI allows nowadays smaller companies and new brands to play on a more equal footing (Wu et al., 2024). AI has the potential to create more diversity in the content created and shared by brands and in the narrative of the brands and voices itself, which is beneficial to the overall marketing ecosystem. Nevertheless, this democratization should be counterbalanced with the danger of homogenization because regular exposure to the same AI tools and training sets may unintentionally cause the convergence of the style and theme of different brands. The significance of AI in the estimation of brand equity also matters, which has traditionally used indirect proxies, including market share or consumer surveys. The AI-based analytics of today can break down unstructured data of customer reviews, social media discussions, and user-generated content and extract subtle aspects of consumer sentiment and activity (Khan et al., 2024). When these insights are mapped to already-established frameworks of brand equity, the organizations will be able to create more dynamic and responsive brand-health tracking models. This is a major step forward as compared to the previous brand equity measures that were carried out in a reactive manner and not proactively. Regardless of these opportunities, there are no challenges of integration of AI in storytelling. Issues related to the privacy of data, the bias of algorithms, and the ethical usage of consumer information are looming large. Consumers are becoming more conscious and sensitive of the ways their data is used to inform brand messages and any failure in transparency or consent may be disastrous to their reputation. Besides, algorithmic bias, which is caused by biased training data or improper model development, can lead to stories that reinforce stereotypes or marginalize the major audience groups. These issues highlight the importance of educational moral systems and administrative systems to inform the usage of AI in narrative strategies. The convergence of AI and brand storytelling marks the beginning of a new era in marketing: a place where innovativeness and algorithms can both exist and develop, allowing them to create more meaningful, more applicable, and more empirically based stories. The focus of this chapter is to open this intersection and examine the technological, strategic, measurement, and ethical possibilities that characterize AI-powered storytelling. Due to the analysis of the theoretical basis and practical implications, it provides a broad vision of how brands can use AI to not only better engage consumers but also create sustainable and authentic relationships that increase long-term brand equity.

THEORETICAL FOUNDATIONS

Brand engagement and brand equity are two constructs that are interdependent but different in concept that are the conceptual foundation of AI-powered brand storytelling. The knowledge of these Constructs, as well as their overlap with the narrative patterns, is critical to understanding the opportunities and constraints of using artificial intelligence to communicate about a brand. The concept of brand engagement has been characterized in the marketing literature as a measure of cognitive, emotional, and behavioral commitment that customers make to a brand (Santos et al., 2022). Engagement, in contrast to transactional interactions, is a more psychologically involved action and occurs in the form of content sharing, product recommendation, or brand communities (Bowden & Mirzaei, 2021). This engagement is essential since active consumers will tend to become brand loyalists, form better brand associations as well as be brand promoters; all of which have a direct impact on the competitive advantage of a firm (Christofi et al., 2020). On the other hand, brand equity is defined as a difference in effect on consumer reaction towards brand marketing effort occasioned by brand knowledge (Alvarado-Karste & Guzmán, 2020). This construct summarizes the abstract value that a brand brings to a product that creates a perception of quality, trusting, and purchase intentions. According to Khan et al. (2024), brand equity was argued to have a number of dimensions including brand awareness, perceived quality, brand associations and brand loyalty, which has a different contribution to the overall value of a brand in the market. It is becoming clear that the strength of brand equity is a key factor to drive firm performance, strength in periods of economic recalls, and price premium capabilities (Hussain et al., 2020).

Story telling is central to both brand engagement and brand equity. According to the narrative paradigm, human beings interpret the world by means of stories; we interpret information better when it is obtained in narrative forms since stories give the context, emotional appeal and meaning (Thomas & Grigsby, 2024). Marketing research has proven on numerous occasions that narrative can establish the sense of creation of immersion, a phenomenon called narrative transportation, in which the audience becomes immersed in a story and displays less counter-arguing, greater emotional reactions, and more positive attitudes (Emon, 2025b; Thomas & Grigsby, 2024). This is the immersive process, which is the basis of successful brand communication as it not only attaches the attention but also enables internalization of brand values and messages. Traditionally, the development of such narratives was in the domain of human creators (testers), marketers, copywriters, designers, who develop stories based on the cultural background, brand heritage and customer feedback. With the emergence of generative AI technologies, however, there is a major shift in this process. Large language transformers and diffusion-based visual generators are now able to generate text and images autonomously and in accordance with brand specifications and preferences (Daneshfar et al., 2024). This implies that AI can be used to expand the presence of brand stories, which is consistent across markets but can be customized at a scale and speed previously unattainable. Theoretically speaking, the infiltration of the AI into the storytelling process adds significant layers to brand engagement models. It was suggested by Emon & Khan (2024) that a framework should view engagement as an iterative process that is dynamic and modified by brand-related stimuli and moderated by personal consumer traits. Narratives of AI can be highly influential stimuli, designed in real-time and according to the context of the consumer, and, therefore, may serve to increase the level of engagement and its levels. As an example, customized stories depending on the browsing or buying habits can increase relevance, which is one of the most important antecedents of engagement found in the marketing literature (Bowden & Mirzaei, 2021; Khan et al., 2025).

Additionally, the concept of brand experience, which focuses on sensory, affective, intellectual, and behavioral aspects, can help shed more light on how AI-generated stories can influence consumer-brand relationships. Multimodal descriptions Multimodal descriptions allow a brand to develop multimodal objects that capture both visual and verbal cues. The AI tools that combine NLP with computer vision help a brand to achieve this. When combined in a unified manner, the brands can create more enriching and memorable experiences, which will play a role in engaging as well as equity (Khan & Hasan Emon, 2024; Taheri et al., 2024). Overall, the CBBE model by Keller is most applicable to conceptualizing the effect of AI-generated narratives on brand strength on the measurement side. Khan et al. (2024) argues that the CBBE pyramid comprises four stages that are ascending, namely brand salience, brand performance and imagery, consumer judgments and feelings, and brand resonance. AI-generated storytelling could be more salient, creating exposure and memorable content because of personalization, reinforce performance and imagery by providing stories that resonate with preferred brand identifications and influence judgments and emotions by creating emotionally anecdotal narratives. AI can make every step higher and, in turn, increase the brand equity hierarchy. It is also essential to focus on the theoretical perspective of persuasion, in particular, the elaboration likelihood model (ELM), in which the individual processing of persuasive messages occurs along the central or peripheral routes based on his or her motivation and ability. Personalization, which is driven by AI, can make messages more relevant, which promotes central processing where consumers think deeply about brand messages. The result of this higher form of processing is more long lasting attitude changes which increases engagement as well as equity (Emon, 2025a; Vredenburg et al., 2020).

The topicality of the social identity theory in the interpretation of AI-driven narratives is also noted in the emerging scholarship. Consumers tend to identify themselves and identify with social group through brands (Appel et al., 2020). Using social media interactions and other user-created content, AI can create stories that appeal to the identities and aspirations of certain segments and create a sense of belonging that will improve brand relationships. This individualized identity reinforcement is found to enhance the level of engagement as well as loyalty (Khamaj & Ali, 2024). Nonetheless, it should be cautious when applying AI to theoretical models. Although AI may improve relevance and personalization, overuse of algorithmic personalization will result in the formation of the echo chamber or filter bubble and deny the chance to encounter a range of views and may be harmful to long-term engagement because it reduces the sense of novelty and surprise. Also, predictive abilities of AI should be counterbalanced by the consumer attitudes towards authenticity that is a pivotal predictor of brand trust. Research has revealed that the consumers appreciate brand communication transparency and can respond adversely when they find the content to be manipulative or unnatural (Heinberg et al., 2021). The theoretical premises of brand engagement and brand equity provide a solid model of interpreting the consequences of AI-generated storytelling. We can place the abilities of AI in the context of some already-known notions like narrative transportation, customer-based brand equity, brand experience, and social identity to value both the possibilities that AI offers in terms of improving the engagement, as well as the possible traps when implemented recklessly. As more brands start exploring AI-driven stories, it will be necessary to base them on theory to utilize the potential of AI and still maintain the level of authenticity and emotional appeal that are still the staples of successful storytelling.

Figure 1. Theoretical foundations of AI-driven brand storytelling

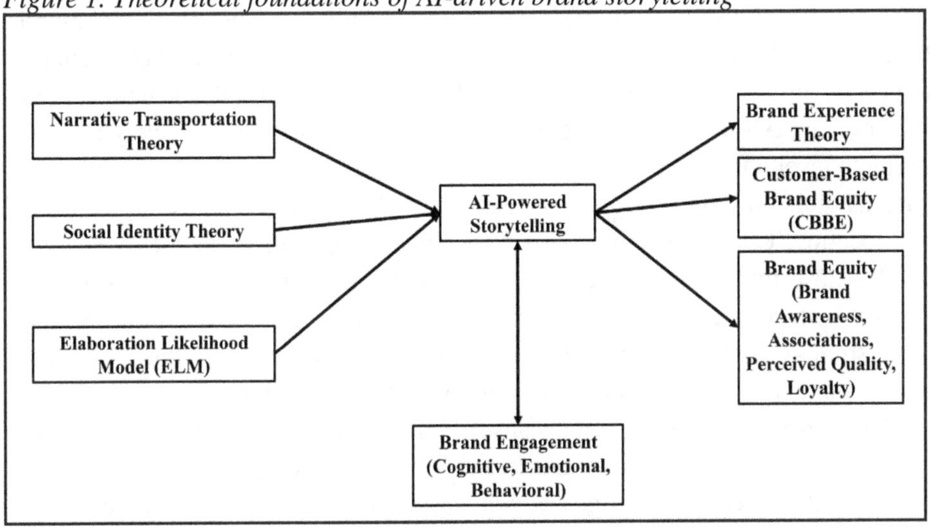

AI IN CONTENT CREATION

Creation of content is the most dominant AI aspect that is transforming the marketing industry. In the not-so-distant past, the development of meaningful brand stories relied on creative efforts that were time-consuming and required the services of a team of copywriters, a team of designers, a team of videographers, as well as a team of strategists. Although this manual system could create rich culturally driven content that emotionally appealed to consumers, it could not compete with the demands of the modern hyper-connected consumer who demanded constant, personal communication. In the context of generative AI technologies, especially LLMs such as GPT-4 and diffusion-based image generators, the platform has altered the latter significantly by providing brands with the opportunity to create high-quality personalized content at scale and speed never previously seen (Emon & Khan, 2025a; Ray, 2023). NLG is one of the best applications of AI in content generation and is a complex algorithm developed to generate text that is close to that written by humans. NLG tools can be used to create the social media posts, product descriptions, web copy, newsletters, and even chatbot conversations, which change their tone and style in response to audience traits or contextual conditions (Lemos et al., 2024). As an illustration, a fashion store can use AI to write product descriptions that are trendy with the Gen Z audience and comfort with practicality with older consumers without losing brand voice. This feature of modeling subtle changes in tone is a breakthrough as opposed to conventional templated copy, which does not always appeal to different groups of the audience. The other revolution is the ability of AI to personalize in real-time and has taken stagnant marketing content to new dynamic responsive stories. Using behavioral, contextual, and demographic information, AI-driven content engines can customize message delivery at an individual level adapting images, text, and calls to action depending on information such as their browsing history, purchasing patterns, and even weather conditions and location (Campbell et al., 2020). This type of personalization goes beyond the level of inserting names and creates an individualized approach to the story that gives it a sense of closeness and immediacy between the brand and the consumer. Such strategy conforms to the current consumer preference toward more valuable and contextually sensitive interactions with the brands (Campbell et al., 2020).

The feedback loop that arises because of reintroducing content performance data into generative models is a key element in AI-enabled personalization. In contrast to the fixed marketing campaigns, which are designed, initiated, and measured after the event, AI-supported content creation follows a cyclic process of creation, measurement, and optimization. The metrics of engagement (e.g., the rate of clicking through, the rate of sentiment, dwell time, and conversion rates) are returned to AI systems, which learn what kind of narratives are popular among various segments. This mechanism contributes to adaptive storytelling, in which brand stories are updated on almost a real-time basis to suit shifting consumer behavior or external circumstances such as social movements or economic changes (Gilbert, 2024). Besides written information, the generative AI has changed the visual narrative. It is possible to create impressive images, animations or even video clips that are aesthetically aligned to a brand, which can be quickly prototyped and created, with the usage of diffusion models and GANs (generative adversarial networks). As an example, the 2023 Create Real Magic campaign of Coca-Cola allowed using DALL·E to invite the audience to create AI-generated artworks inspired by the logos and themes of the brand, transforming passive viewers into active collaborators and showing how AI might be used as a tool of participatory marketing (Bijsterveld, 2023). The examples of such initiatives demonstrate that AI-generated imagery can be used to further improve the level of engagement by allowing consumers to co-write brand histories. In addition to that, AI has not only influenced the creation of content in terms of its speed of production or customization, but also localization. One of the eternal dilemmas that brands with global presence must deal with is how to be consistent and be culturally relevant at the same time. Although classic localization presupposes the services of groups of translators and cultural advisors, AI models trained on multilingual and culturally diverse datasets can modify the material to reflect the specifics of the place, its traditions, and aesthetics, without distorting the brand essence (Haleem et al., 2022). This localized content capability without brand DNA-thinning will be especially useful in fast-paced sectors like fashion, entertainment, and technology where time-to-market may be the key to competitive advantage. The strategic implications of the AI-enabled content-creation cannot be underestimated. First, it dramatically saves time and resources devoted to production and enables the brands to implement campaigns in a shorter time span and with fewer resources. Second, it provides uniformity in communication between channels and touchpoints, which is essential in brand integrity upholding amidst omnichannel marketing settings. Third, AI-created content could be used in agile marketing, as brands can rapidly change the story to respond to a crisis, competitor action or new customer trends without undergoing long creative processes. These functionalities align with the contemporary trends in marketing obsessions of speed, flexibility, and customer-centeredness. However, these opportunities are also accompanied by some significant challenges. The first one is that, when trained on similar data, AI may generate generic or homogenized content, which causes convergence in style within the brands (Yang et al., 2020). To address this risk, brands need to spend on fine-tuning AI models using proprietary data and brand unique guidelines to make sure that outputs are differentiated and authentic. The other issue is creative authenticity: consumers are becoming more interested in transparency and will be unwilling to consume what they consider insincere or too artificial. Brands that do not discuss their application of AI in their message run the risk of losing trust, especially digitally literate consumers, who are aware of the problem of algorithmic manipulation and authenticity. In addition, even though AI is better than humans in assessing information and creating variations of the existing themes, AI is deficient in lived experience, emotional intuition, and cultural sensitivity that human creativeness possesses. Such attributes are all that is needed to do a breakthrough, culturally relevant campaign, one that goes against the grain or redefines a category. In this way, numerous professionals insist on combining AI with human creativity instead of substituting it (Sánchez-Aguayo et al., 2022). Within this model, AI will execute monotonous and data-heavy chores like drafting, personalization, and optimization and leave human creatives to think about macro-level strategy, ideation and subtle narratives. Lastly, the AI-enabled content creation needs to be ethically preempted (Du & Xie, 2021).. The algorithms which promote personalization are based on consumer data and one is left wondering on matters of privacy, consent and protection of data. The collection and use of data to create and deliver tailored narratives by brands is becoming a topic of growing concern among regulators and consumers alike, and clear practices and sound data management are the key to sustainable application of AI in content creation (Pedersen & Ritter, 2024). These brands also need to overcome the biases in the AI training data, that can either support the stereotype accidentally or omit the voices of marginalized groups unless audited and fixed. The development of AI-based content creation is the next crucial step in brand storytelling, with its offering, more opportunities have never existed to customize, make better the localization, and react to the customer. However, the strategic advantages should be weighed against intelligent management which makes brand communication to be authentic, creative, and morally upright. Through the use of AI strengths and understanding of its weaknesses, brands have the opportunity to tell a story in a way that draws attention and at the same time establishes a relationship with the different consumer groups based on trust (Folorunso et al., 2023).

Measuring Brand Engagement and Equity

The last several decades were quite challenging to the marketer and researchers because they had to measure the impact of storytelling on brand performance. The qualitative, subjective nature of narratives made it challenging to follow a very specific path of exposure to brand narratives to measurable results in terms of engagement, loyalty, or purchase behavior. The previous methods were based on the principles of using indirect proxies such as periodic surveys, focus groups or general brand awareness research which, though useful, tended to be imprecise in the dynamic and real-time way of capturing consumer responses to narrative stimuli (Nikolic et al., 2020). With the emergence of AI based analytics, this picture has been turned on its head, and what marketers are measuring in terms of engagement and equity is being redefined. The brand has been accomplished by making use of cutting-edge NLP, computer vision and behavioral tracking, making it capable of quantifying emotional and behavioral responses to storytelling at a degree and degree previously unseen (Mustak et al., 2024). This evolution does not only fill this gap in historical measurements, but also allows marketers to operate on things fast, they keep on improving their stories as they continue getting new insights based on empirical information. Sentiment analysis is one of the most effective engagement measurement tools, and it involves the NLP models to classify and quantifies emotions conveyed in consumer-generated content like social media posts, online reviews, customer service communications, and so forth (Loureiro et al., 2019). AI enables marketers to understand immediate emotional responses to certain stories or campaigns by reading large volumes of data on the positive, negative, or neutral sentiment. To clarify, a cosmetics brand could track the response rates of consumers to a campaign that emphasizes the use of natural ingredients and trace the changes in brand attitude throughout the time and match it to the engagement rates, i.e. the number of comments, shares, or likes (Emon, 2025g).

In addition to general mood, sophisticated emotion recognition systems have become able to classify subtle affective states like joy or surprise, anger or sadness, in conversations between consumers (Wang et al., 2020). This granularity allows marketers to differentiate the stories that result in weak approval and those triggering passionate enthusiasm and allows them to focus on the content that elicits more emotion. Research has demonstrated that such emotional bonds play a major role in brand equity as they can create consumer loyalty and advocacy (Parris & Guzmán, 2023). In addition to NLP, computer vision technologies provide a possibility of gauging interest in visual narratives. Whereas gaze estimation systems relying on webcams can now be carried out remotely, previously eye-tracking was limited to specialized labs, wherein gaze estimation systems are utilized to analyze where and how long users gaze when exposed to digital materials (Khan et al., 2024; Shehu et al., 2021). The analysis of such patterns enables a brand to determine whether the main visual cues, such as the logo, a tagline, or a signature color, attract attention and lead the consumer focus, which are the critical elements of an effective storytelling. Furthermore, facial emotion recognition software can detect affective states when subjects look at an ad through an analysis of micro-expressions and provides an insight into the subconscious response that is usually elusive in a survey. Brand recall and recognition are other significant measures of narrative impact, the main elements of brand salience, a requirement of brand equity based on the customer-based brand equity model (Piriyakul et al., 2024). In the traditional method, the studies of recalls were based on structured interviews or delayed surveys claiming consumers to name the brands that they had seen. These are assessments that are now improved using AI to analyze online behaviors: how many times a consumer searches a brand after being introduced to a story, whether they mention the brand itself spontaneously on social media, or whether a customer revisits the website of a brand within a specific time frame. These digital clues give objective real-time evidence of the memorability of the narrative. Among the greatest contributions of AI in the field, the possibility to combine separate streams of data into holistic models of engagement and equity should be listed. Sentiment data can be used along with behavioral metrics such as click-through rates, time on content, the frequency of social sharing, conversion data, with the help of AI, to offer both individual consumer dynamic engagement profiles and can integrate insights on the segment or campaign levels (Gkikas & Theodoridis, 2022). Such combined research would allow the marketer to understand what stories not only would be able to invoke positive feelings but also would trigger actual action, such as purchase or referral, in closing the divide between telling stories and business. These combined frameworks are the foundation of algorithmic brand equity scoring, where AI allocates real-time quantitative approximations of a brand worth, according to how consumers interact on the channels. In comparison to the traditional brand audit, which is performed annually or quarterly, scoring with AI is constantly updated, and it provides a dynamic measure of brand health (Mayouf et al., 2024). This dynamic tracking enables marketers to detect potential problems in time (before engagement decreases, or negative sentiment increases) and take corrective measures as quickly as possible.

The AI-based measurement tools are also capable of more accurate consumer response segmentation, as they can determine the differences in the interactions between different demographic or psychographic groups with brand narratives. As an example, a financial services company may find, using AI analysis, that younger consumers are more receptive to less serious, meme-driven stories, whereas older generations are more receptive to more trust and stability-focused stories. Such insights can be used to develop focused storytelling strategies that maximize the engagement of every audience to increase brand equity. Notably, AI is also useful in measuring brand-consumer relationships with time. Longitudinal analyses based on AI can be used to monitor engagement trends and attitude of individual consumers towards a particular brand as they are exposed to narratives, and when and how relationships build or break. The time-oriented approaches prove to be priceless in terms of the customer lifetime value, retention optimization, and long-term brand commitment (Harris et al., 2024). Despite all these developments, AI-driven measurement does not come without its challenges. The algorithms of sentiment and emotion detection, such as them, may not be able to perform well with context, sarcasm, or cultural specifics, which means that they can fail to achieve the desired results unless tuned and controlled by humans. On the same note, facial emotion recognition software is an ethical issue when it comes to privacy and consent, especially when the consumers are not aware of being studied. Open communication and compliance with data protection rules are therefore very crucial to keep consumer trust. Furthermore, AI does not measure all the dimensions of consumer experience, as it can only quantify a wide range of factors of engagement. Cultural meaning, appreciation of humor, the subtext of visual metaphors in storytelling, and other elements are usually elements that humans must interpret to gain their full meaning. That is why it is necessary to use the hybrid model of measurement that will help to combine the accuracy of AI analytics with qualitative data that are obtained in the course of ethnographic research, focus groups, or in-depth interviews (Petersson et al., 2022).

Figure 2. AI-driven measurement of brand engagement and brand equity

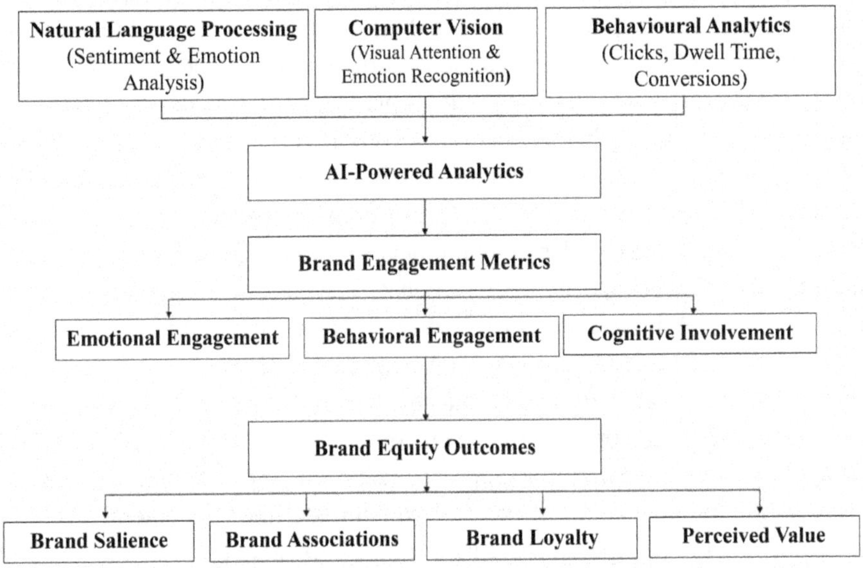

CASE STUDIES AND APPLICATIONS

The potential of AI-based narratives, which is both hypothetical and technical, is enthralling and in the context of practice-based uses, where AI-based changes come into focus most distinctly. The analysis of the ways in which the leading brands have used AI in their content strategies gives vital information on both the opportunities and challenges that come along with the deployment of narrative intelligence on scale. Among the most memorable ones is the Coca-Cola campaign "Create Real Magic" that was introduced in 2023. This program invited consumers worldwide to make original AI-generated images with the visual assets of Coca-Cola, through a partnership with the AI-based visual generative systems of DALL·E and GPT-4. Allowing people to take control of brand image creation by relying on generative AI to remix and reinterpret it gave Coca-Cola passive consumers a chance to become active contributors to its narrative (Emon & Khan, 2024). This interactive approach to narrative generation served not only to enhance engagement but it also created an enormous library of original user generated content that organically expanded the brand through social sites. Research on user-created content in related campaigns has shown that the engagement of the consumers adds emotional value and enhances the possibility of advocacy of the brand (Sykora et al., 2022). The other strong argument is the way Balenciaga has explored the issue of AI in social media marketing. The luxury fashion house applied AI-generated visuals to create stylized images in line with its avant-garde-style, which guaranteed there is a consistent visual language across Instagram, Tik Tok, and new digital platforms. In his approach, Balenciaga points to the way a luxury brand can use AI to continue to sustain a consistent brand identity and explore new forms that attract digitally native audiences. Notably, the case also illustrates a way in which AI can empower brands to react quickly to changing cultural trends, which is a vital benefit in the fashion industry, where the tastes of consumers change at a very fast pace. The case of AI-Generated Roadtrip campaign by BMW in the automotive industry is an example of how AI can enable the creation of a localized narrative on a large scale. BMW used NLP along with geospatial data to create individual road trip plans and stories based on the location, preferences, and model of a car of the customer (Sauberschwarz & Weiss, 2022). This hyper personalized narrative approach achieved 30 points higher engagement rates than generic campaigns of the past which underlines the potential AI has in contextualizing brand experiences. Elsewhere, the Mastercard Priceless Cities platform in the financial services industry included the elements of AI that personalized travel and entertainment stories of cardholders. Using the data about the transaction patterns and social media activity, the AI system suggested experiences and provided the personal storytelling content about the restaurants, concerts, and other cultural events depending on the lifestyle of each customer (Alimamy & Gnoth, 2022). The studies suggest that contextual personalization enhances the perceived value, creates more brand trust, and loyalty (Dwivedi et al., 2023). Lessons are very crucial as seen through a comparative lens. The comparative research of AI-generated and human-generated content continuously shows that the creatives of human origin will usually succeed in creating subtle, culturally relevant stories that will resonate with the subconscious or social values. An example is the Dove Real Beauty, the pioneer of emotion-oriented advertising, which was not successful due to its precision in AI but rather based on deep human understanding of social conventions of beauty. AI cannot easily reproduce this richness since it lacks first-hand experience of cultural situations and cannot feel the human plight (Galante et al., 2023).

AI-based content has obvious benefits of scale, speed, and customization. Spotify, as an example, applies AI to design personalized listening reports to millions of users annually to generate insanely large amounts of social shares and brand hype. It allows creating an emotional perception of uniqueness towards each user and provides consistency in brand across millions of individualized stories through this AI-powered personalization. The academic literature on such massive campaigns indicates that personalization may substantially increase engagement rates, at times by over half that of non-personalized campaigning, using self-relevance as a force behind share and interaction (Bonini & Magaudda, 2024). One of the most interesting studies is that by Emon & Ahmed (2025) who demonstrated a comparison of campaigns in the hospitality industry, in which hotels applied AI to create travel guides tailored to the profiles of guests. The customer satisfaction scores and repeat booking rates were higher in properties that introduced AI-driven guides as opposed to the control group that only used the traditional, manual guides and their scores grew more slowly. The study highlights the importance of scalability of AI as complemented with human strategic and cultural consideration of content to be on brand. Among the most effective ones, the hybrid solution hints at human brainstorming and AI implementation. The synergy enables creative teams to concentrate on strategic stories and general brand themes, whereas AI does the heavy lifting of making stories relevant to various audience formats and various digital platforms. An example is that the recent Nike campaigns incorporate both human-created hero videos and AI-created social media versions that are more demographic-specific to foster better engagement without compromising the brand. This strategy complies with the recent literature that urges the implementation of AI into so-called augmented creativity where artificial intelligence complements but does not suppress human creativity (Fordham et al., 2020). Such applications are also an indication of the best practices that are emerging in the minds of brands that might consider utilizing AI in the storytelling process. To begin with, transparency is paramount: the brands must communicate clearly that AI has been used to create their content to prevent the feeling of manipulation or inauthenticity, which can destroy trust (Raut et al., 2024). Second, the brands should invest in various training data and ethical control to reduce the risks of algorithmic biases, especially when creating more content based on social or cultural themes with the help of AI (Henriksen et al., 2022). Third, trial and error and manual inspection are critical; although most sophisticated AI-based systems can make use of human contextual knowledge to make stories appeal both culturally and emotionally. There are also restrictions that are pointed out in the same cases though. Although AI can produce powerful micro-narratives, it does not have the long- term strategy and understanding needed to provide a long-term campaign with a genuinely meaningful brand purpose (Balasubramaniam et al., 2023). Moreover, the risks of the AI-generated content propagating stereotypes or generating content that does not resonate with the brand values without any supervision may occur, according to the critique of AI-generated advertisements promoting negative gender stereotypes at the time of the first rollouts (Díaz-Rodríguez et al., 2023). Overall, case studies of various industries: consumer goods, high-end fashion, automotive, finance, hospitality, and entertainment alike, testify to enormous prospects of AI in narrative intelligence under careful consideration with human imagination. Such applications reveal that AI can engage a brand storytelling to provide personalization, scale, and velocity that would otherwise be unattainable by humans alone. However, it is the most effective campaigns that acknowledge the incomparable value of human cognition in the formulation of natural, culturally relevant stories that create long term emotional bonds with customers (Borau, 2025).

ETHICAL AND CREATIVE IMPLICATIONS

Although AI-driven storytelling opens promising new possibilities to engage with the brand, it also reveals ethical and creative issues of significant concern that must be considered by marketers, researchers, and policymakers. The core of these issues lies in the fact that there is a conflict between the technological ability and human aspects of the stories, namely authenticity, empathy, and cultural sensitivity, which have always been at the core of an effective brand communication. One such problem is authenticity, which has become an important concern in the age of AI-based narratives. Brands also generate trust by having authentic and transparent communication; having consumers believe that the messages a brand is sending are part of an algorithm, they can view the brand as manipulative or unauthentic (Kozinets, 2022). According to the recent research, consumer trust in AI participation in content production mechanisms could evoke skepticism triggered by the inability of brands to explicitly inform about the application of AI (Aljarah et al., 2025). This distrust is not in vain: machine-generated narratives do not have lived experience, cultural or emotional intuition, which means that they may produce a soulless narrative or fail to connect to the history and values of a brand. One of the most notorious instances of such risk became the viral spread of an AI-crafted social media post made by a fast-food chain in an awkward tone, causing scorn and a lack of brand credibility instead of making the post go viral (Park et al., 2024). The other significant ethical issue is algorithmic bias. In order to learn, AI systems rely on data; when the training data consists of historical biases, social stereotypes, unrepresentative viewpoints, the AI probably will repeat these biases in the narratives created (O'Connor & Liu, 2024).

AI systems that ascribe to Western data sets may miss out on culturally rich symbols, linguistic characteristics, or cultural values that a non-Western consumer would consider valuable and thus harm a large segment of consumers. In extreme cases, these prejudices can lead to offensive or exclusionary content, which is negative publicity on the brand and unethical towards inclusivity and respect. The studies on algorithmic fairness emphasize the need of brands to invest in diverse and representative datasets and sound bias-detection systems to avoid such a scenario (Kordzadeh & Ghasemaghaei, 2022). The other aspect of AI-driven personalization that is of paramount importance is privacy and data ethics. Personalization requires gathering and processing of behavioral, demographic, and in some cases biometric information about an individual. However, with the introduction of more stringent data collection and processing rules by global regulations such as the General Data Protection Regulation (GDPR) and the Consumer Privacy Act (CCPA) in certain states, such as the EU and California, brands are forced to enter a complex legal and ethical environment (Farhad, 2024). Crossing these limits may lead not only to fines but also to the loss of consumer confidence to a considerable extent. Besides, even in the legal framework, ethical marketing requires transparency: brands must be transparent about what kind of data they gather, how it is applied, and how consumers can gain control over the information (Manda et al., 2024). It has been a consistent finding that transparency will make consumers more willing to give information to the company and, in contrast, a perceived secrecy may cause a backlash and withdrawal (Rizzoni et al., 2022). In addition to compliance with regulations, privacy of AI-based storytelling collides with more profound ethical issues of autonomy and manipulation. Personalized narratives with the assistance of AI have the potential to form an echo chamber that causes consumers to strengthen their current preferences, potentially reducing their exposure to a variety of ideas or products (Dutta & Mishra, 2024). Other researchers claim that over-personalization has the risk of going beyond persuasion and manipulating the consumer by taking advantage of cognitive bias without the consumer noticing (Hagendorff, 2021). This tension explains why brands need to strike a balance between personalization and ethical concerns so that storytelling does not ignore the agency of consumers and its impact on making informed choices.

Creatively, although AI promises efficiency and scalability like no other tool has, it also introduces questions of homogenization of content. The algorithmic models will tend to pick patterns that are most efficient according to the engagement metrics and this may lead to formula-driven stories with no cultural sensitivity (Emon & Khan, 2024). This is especially risky when it comes to the brands which are based on different voices to make themselves stand out in congested markets. As an instance, when multiple brands in an industry work with the same AI tools trained on similar data, their communication could begin to become more and more blurred, losing distinct brand images and decreasing the overall content diversity within the marketing ecosystem (Emon & Ahmed, 2025; Haleem et al., 2022). Furthermore, AI does not possess the ability to be truly creative in the sense of making hasty decisions, challenging conventions or appealing to emotional or cultural subcontexts, which are the qualities that have created some of the most recognizable ad campaigns in the history of advertising. Ads such as the Apple Insight ad, the message of which is Think Different, or the Nike Just Do It were not based on data optimization, but on in-depth human understanding and cultural background. In this respect, scholars and practitioners increasingly propose an intermediate strategy, namely the use of AI to make human creativity stronger, but not to replace it (Emon, 2025f; Peeters et al., 2021). This paradigm shifts repetitive/data-intensive tasks, such as versioning, personalization, or performance analysis, to the AI to make creative human imaginers focus on strategic, high-level storytelling, which defies conventions and draws an emotional response. Artificial intelligence also requires strong cultural sensitivity when telling ethical stories. International brands that work within a variety of markets need to understand that a story that seems to work well within a particular culture would not be suitable in a different market. Without local human control, AI systems face the possibility of making significant mistakes that may provoke a crisis in public relations or even estrange the communities. An example of this is the use of AI to translate marketing content, which has in certain instances resulted in culturally insensitive or offensive information due to direct word-to-word translation lack of contextual meaning. Thus, local knowledge and human verification of AI-driven campaigns must be included to prevent unwanted damage and cultural respect. Moreover, creative authenticity becomes more dependent on co-creation with the consumers, who demand the possibility to form and influence brand stories. Although AI may be used to enable co-creation, which is the case with Coca-Cola in the campaign of creation of Real Magic, it must be done inclusively and openly. The brands must make sure that AI-powered co-creation platforms do not prefer one demographic or type of creativity over the others. These tools must be created with reasonable design approaches, including accessibility functionality, and representation diversity to promote actual involvement by different kinds of consumers (Zallio & Clarkson, 2021). Lastly, accountability is one of the main ethical requirements. In cases when AI-generated stories are offensive, misinformative, or lead to consumer injuries, brands cannot afford to just point the finger at the algorithm; they still stand at the final responsibility of the outputs of tools that they use (Bennett, 2023; Emon & Chowdhury, 2025). Clear lines of accountability and protocols towards a quick response and mitigation in case AI-driven content is not up to standard should therefore be defined according to ethical frameworks and governance structure. To sum up, the implementation of AI in brand narration promises game-changing opportunities, yet strict ethical thinking and artistic guardianship are needed accordingly. Brands can leverage the power of AI by foregrounding authenticity, proactively addressing bias, protecting consumer privacy, and enhancing human control to maintain the capacity of storytelling to have an emotional impact, cultural sensitivity, and trust as an essential element in establishing long-term relationships. The responsible use of AI will create the difference between empowerment and connection and alienation and mis ethical actions, as AI evolves and its responsible use in practice is determined.

Figure 3. Ethical and creative dimensions of AI-driven brand storytelling

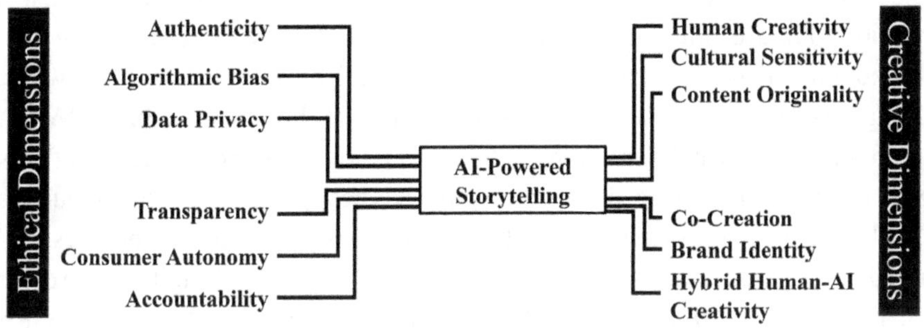

FUTURE DIRECTIONS AND RESEARCH OPPORTUNITIES

The future of narrative intelligence brings new paradigms that will transform the experience of consumers and the theoretical base of marketing communication, as the implementation of AI in brand narrative becomes even faster. The most striking result of this development is the emergence of multimodal storytelling: Artificial intelligence solutions that can combine text, graphics, video, audio, and other elements with interactive interfaces into coherent and emotionally engaging stories. The new technology, such as generative multimodal transformers, such as GPT-4o by OpenAI and CM3leon by Meta, are already showing the ability to create stories that can appeal to all senses at once, creating more immersive brand experiences (Yu & Meng, 2025). These are multimodal narratives that extend beyond the traditional post, which is the static ad or text post, allowing a brand to create experiences in which a consumer could read a personalized story, watch concurrently generated AI-made visuals, listen to synthetic but brand consistent voiceover, and choose to follow a narrative branch all in one platform. These abilities provide a rich field of practice and study because marketers seek the answers to the way sensory integration influences memory and emotional reaction and, eventually, brand equity (Bae et al., 2020; Emon, 2025e). The questions that may be explored by scholars include: Are multimodal AI-generated stories better at promoting story transportation and brand recall than single-modality content? What are the trade-offs that the consumers must face when bargaining on the complex multimodal brand stories? The other opportunity is the concept of co-creative branding, whereby the AI allows customers to turn into creators of brand narratives as opposed to mere consumers. As a follow-up of prior studies such as the role of the participatory storytelling in consumer empowerment, perceived authenticity, and brand attachment, future studies must examine the impact of the participatory storytelling on these aspects in relation to future campaigns such as Coca-Cola's "Create Real Magic" or Nike's AI-personalized sneaker designs (Huang & Guo, 2021). Are consumers who are building AI-driven narratives more likely to feel that they own the brand? What is the difference between co-creation mediated by algorithms and traditional efforts to engage the community in terms of loyalty and advocacy? The study of the questions will enhance our comprehension of the social and psychological processes of AI-enabled co-creation. Intimately connected is the necessity of longitudinal research of the long-term emotional effects of AI-generated narratives. Although the current literature is mostly based on short-term engagement metrics, the sustainability of the emotional connections established with AI-created stories has not been thoroughly studied yet. These questions will be crucial in determining the sustainability of trust, attachment, and brand equity through months and years of contentment with the use of AI in creating sustainable brand strategies, particularly over human-constructed campaigns. These studies may also demystify the question of whether being subject to repeatedly personalized algorithms leads to connection or fatigue, an aspect of increasing concern as more people become aware of the use of AI in marketing (Stray, 2020).

AI-powered storytelling also requires strong scholarly interest in terms of ethics and governance. Although this debate on algorithmic bias and data privacy is becoming more common, theories that acknowledge accountability in creative AI systems should be considered, especially regarding unintended harms in the cultural or social environment (Díaz-Rodríguez et al., 2023). Science might explore the way in which brands can execute ethical principles when creating AI-generated content and quantify the effects of AI transparency disclosure on consumer trust. Besides, comparative analysis in industries and cultural regions may show the difference in ethical perceptions, and best practices may be identified to help global brands to find their way in different markets. The other important domain is how AI and cultural adjustment interact within brand stories. Consistency and relevance: Localizing content in an expeditious and exact manner, AI offers an opportunity to global brands to reach this goal. Nevertheless, empirical studies are required to determine whether AI-based localization can be as culturally sensitive as human-translated or locally modified stories. What do consumers think about AI-localized content about its authenticity and adherence to local norms? Answering these questions could aid in brands using AI to operate in international markets in a responsible way and still manage to offer cultural sensitivity (Du & Xie, 2021; Emon, 2025c). Another potential area of research that is interesting is the emergent AI capabilities of affective computing. The capability of the systems to recognize, interpret, and even simulate human feelings also possibilities of real-time adjustment of the narratives on the affective conditions of the consumers (Puntoni et al., 2021). This may facilitate active narration in which the message of a brand changes by the minute, depending on the facial expression or voice tone of the users. However, these technologies pose deep ethical concerns of emotional control, privacy and psychological security. The studies that consider the effectiveness of affect-aware storytelling as well as the limitations would help direct brands and regulators to establish the norms of responsible use. In the methodological sense, researchers can combine AI-based analytics with conventional qualitative approaches, including in-depth interviews or ethnography, to come up with a deeper understanding of how customers feel and perceive AI-created stories. An example of mixed-method study would be investigating the difference in reception of the same AI-driven campaign among demographic subgroups, comparing the differences between behavioral (e.g. clicks, shares) and self-reported (attitudes or emotions) indicators. This would fill the existing void between the quantitative assessment of AI and more subtle and interpretive aspects of storytelling which are still the bedrock of cultural and emotional branding (Emon, 2025d; Lee et al., 2020). Lastly, the future area of interest might be the place of AI in making more brand narrative more accessible. The possibility of generating more accessible narratives by people with disabilities can be provided by AI-generated captions, audio descriptions, or adaptive content formats. What can these technologies do transform the perception of brands in marginalized groups and what best practices can brands implement so that AI serves as the source of equity, instead of the perpetuation of exclusion? Research in this field of intersection of AI, accessibility, and branding has the potential to contribute to both knowledge and social responsibility in research.

CONCLUSION

The ability to create, customize, and quantify stories through the assistance of artificial intelligence has become one of the most important boundaries of branding and marketing communication: narrative intelligence. This chapter has discussed how AI is fundamentally transforming the art and science of storytelling to provide new opportunities to personalize narratives at scale, reach a broader audience, and empirically measure brand equity with a kind of precision that was impossible only a few years ago. However, it has also highlighted that as brands move fast to use AI-based technology, they will have to face some serious ethical, creative and cultural questions to use these technologies in a responsible and efficient manner. From the very beginning, we followed the history of storytelling as the evolutionary process of handcrafted campaigns prepared by creative teams towards dynamic and AI-generated stories that can be instantly adapted to segments, platforms, and languages. The transformational power of AI consists in the fact that it processes bulk volumes of consumer behavior, preferences and sentiments, which allows marketers to customize stories that resonate with the identities, lifestyles and needs of individuals in a manner never seen. This customization is not just a technological convenience, but an effective engine of brand engagement: when the stories are based on the realities and hopes of the consumers, they become more appeals to those, get them more emotional, and persuade them to stay loyal. The core of the shift consists of the introduction of AI-based measurement systems that do away with the concept of subjective evaluation or predetermined surveys and offer the real-time and data-intensive information about the effectiveness of narratives. Using natural language processing on social media dialogues or reviews helps a brand monitor the change of sentiment and level of emotion in a story. They can then measure the strength with which visual media attract, affect and help in brand recognition through computer vision. Through these technologies, marketers can now quantify brand engagement and brand equity, long-held elusive, intangible, constructs, into measurable and practical expressions that can inform strategy and investment. The bright examples of major brands such as Coca-Cola, Balenciaga, BMW, and Mastercard demonstrate that AI-controlled narrative intelligence can be applied in practice. The radical campaigns show how AI can be used to create scalable and personalized storytelling and the potential of the new which emerges when humans and algorithms meet. They also demonstrate how AI can be used to ensure that the brands stay culturally sensitive and responsive, adjusting to changing consumer preferences in near real time. However, such examples also provide warning lessons since, without proper regulation, the created AI-mediated stories might slip into the realms of generic or culturally insensitive stories, which are what the brands are supposed to claim as being built on. The point that has emerged throughout this chapter is that the best strategy is not replacement where AI replaces human ingenuity but augmentation whereby AI supplements human ingenuity by doing repetitive data-intensive jobs. Under this hybrid system, creative teams are working on the big ideas, emotional understanding, and cultural insights that make the stories memorable and meaningful, and AI makes sure that said stories are personalized, distributed efficiently and optimized out of the feedback. This combination of computational and creative symbiosis is where narrative intelligence is the strongest.

In this new age of brands, ethics should always take the centre stage. We have touched on the risk of algorithmic bias, which can spread stereotype unwillingly or leave no population behind and threaten social justice and brand image. The privacy aspect is also pressing, as when the brands are founded on the information about the consumers to drive the AI-based systems, they must be open about the information that will be collected and stored and used and offer visual alternatives to the consumer and comply with the new regulatory environment. There are also issues of authenticity: AI should never be applied to mislead and manipulate but should be implemented to make honest and engaging communication more expressive. By predicting these ethics in advance, a brand will be able to ensure that their use of AI will be their asset, rather than a liability insofar as their reputation is concerned. Cultural sensitivity is another prerequisite. The stories are in a social, historical and cultural context, and Brands must be aware of this, that is, the stories do not exist in a vacuum. Being fully unaware of the world and lacking the cultural context, AI requires the human regulation of the control to avoid the occurrence of wrongs that may either shock the audience or lead it towards alienation. Local knowledge and wide range of perspectives should be used to design the training and implementation of AI systems whereby the content must treat and worship the difference between the global consumers. The tendencies of narrative intelligence in the future result in even more interactive, multimodal, and engaging experience in tales. AI will enable more brands to incorporate text, images, video, audio, and interactives in coherent narratives, which dynamically react to emotional responses or situational elements of the consumer. The following research and practice questions can be discussed as interesting: What are the consequences of these multimodal narratives on cognitive and emotional involvement? What are the ethical theories that would be used in the practice of affective computing in telling stories? What could the brands do to make consumers co-creators, rather than passive consumers of content through AI usage? As these possibilities are already realized, scholars and professionals will be fundamental in the process of defining an accountable, innovative and inclusive future of AI in brand narratives. To measure the impact of AI-generated stories on the long-term brand equity, trust, and cultural resonance, researchers will need to develop theories and methods of such research. The practitioners should encourage the most effective practices which constitute the compromise between technological innovation and human factors and cultural sensitivity, empathy and creativity, which are not replaceable in the process of building long-term relations with the consumers. The collaboration between academia, industry and the civil society will be paramount in such a manner that the narrative intelligence can be made in a manner that can benefit not only the brands but also the different communities that are served by these brands. Overall, it is possible to state that this chapter has disclosed that AI is not bent to taking over the art of storytelling that humans possess, but rather an efficient new medium to expand its influence and reach. By being considerate, the brands can then use them to transform their one size fits all campaigns into emotionally moving, highly personalized stories that will connect the consumers on a personal level yet still retain their identity. In the meantime, AI-assisted measurement provides the brands with a chance to quantify these stories in a strict manner and transform intuition and creativity into evidence-based strategy. Nevertheless, as we have hinted out, new code of ethical practice, respectful approach to cultures and innovative authenticity need to be written hand in hand with the implementation of AI. The way AI can do it is not what will give the narrative intelligence a future, but how the brands will choose to make use of it: in the sense of making it more engaging and personalized, becoming more inclusive and creative, in the sense of creating alienation and a loss of moral integrity, when used in the wrong hands. The possibilities and the responsibilities of the AI-powered storytelling can assist marketers not only to make smarter and more responsive brands, but also to transform them into the more human-focused ones. We are on the intersection of creativity and computation, and it is our responsibility to ensure narrative intelligence proceeds in the direction that does not overlook the ability of stories to inspire, unify, and elevate and we make sure that the next phase of branding is not just produced by machines, but also in collaboration with the various voices and lived experience of the people it hopes to communicate with.

REFERENCES

Alimamy, S., & Gnoth, J. (2022). I want it my way! The effect of perceptions of personalization through augmented reality and online shopping on customer intentions to co-create value. *Computers in Human Behavior, 128*, 107105. DOI: 10.1016/j.chb.2021.107105

Aljarah, A., Ibrahim, B., & López, M. (2025). In AI, we do not trust! The nexus between awareness of falsity in AI-generated CSR ads and online brand engagement. *Internet Research, 35*(3), 1406–1426. DOI: 10.1108/INTR-12-2023-1156

Alvarado-Karste, D., & Guzmán, F. (2020). The effect of brand identity-cognitive style fit and social influence on consumer-based brand equity. *Journal of Product and Brand Management, 29*(7), 971–984. DOI: 10.1108/JPBM-06-2019-2419

Appel, G., Grewal, L., Hadi, R., & Stephen, A. T. (2020). The future of social media in marketing. *Journal of the Academy of Marketing Science, 48*(1), 79–95. DOI: 10.1007/s11747-019-00695-1

Bae, S., Jung, T. H., Moorhouse, N., Suh, M., & Kwon, O. (2020). The Influence of Mixed Reality on Satisfaction and Brand Loyalty in Cultural Heritage Attractions: A Brand Equity Perspective. *Sustainability (Basel), 12*(7), 2956. DOI: 10.3390/su12072956

Balasubramaniam, N., Kauppinen, M., Rannisto, A., Hiekkanen, K., & Kujala, S. (2023). Transparency and explainability of AI systems: From ethical guidelines to requirements. *Information and Software Technology, 159*, 107197. DOI: 10.1016/j.infsof.2023.107197

Bennett, W. L. (2023). Killing the golden goose? A framework for regulating disruptive technologies. *Information Communication and Society, 26*(1), 16–36. DOI: 10.1080/1369118X.2021.1994625

Berber Sardinha, T. (2024). AI-generated vs human-authored texts: A multidimensional comparison. *Applied Corpus Linguistics, 4*(1), 100083. DOI: 10.1016/j.acorp.2023.100083

Berger, J., Humphreys, A., Ludwig, S., Moe, W. W., Netzer, O., & Schweidel, D. A. (2020). Uniting the Tribes: Using Text for Marketing Insight. *Journal of Marketing, 84*(1), 1–25. DOI: 10.1177/0022242919873106

Bijsterveld, K. (2023). Eavesdropping by the eye: Detecting sound events and the culture of acoustic intelligence. *Sound Studies : an Interdisciplinary Journal, 9*(2), 233–252. DOI: 10.1080/20551940.2023.2247649

Bonini, T., & Magaudda, P. (2024). *Platformed! How Streaming, Algorithms and Artificial Intelligence are Shaping Music Cultures*. Springer Nature Switzerland., DOI: 10.1007/978-3-031-43965-0

Borau, S. (2025). Deception, Discrimination, and Objectification: Ethical Issues of Female AI Agents. *Journal of Business Ethics*, *198*(1), 1–19. DOI: 10.1007/s10551-024-05754-4

Bowden, J., & Mirzaei, A. (2021). Consumer engagement within retail communication channels: An examination of online brand communities and digital content marketing initiatives. *European Journal of Marketing*, *55*(5), 1411–1439. DOI: 10.1108/EJM-01-2018-0007

Campbell, C., Sands, S., Ferraro, C., Tsao, H.-Y. J., & Mavrommatis, A. (2020). From data to action: How marketers can leverage AI. *Business Horizons*, *63*(2), 227–243. DOI: 10.1016/j.bushor.2019.12.002

Christofi, M., Vrontis, D., Leonidou, E., & Thrassou, A. (2020). Customer engagement through choice in cause-related marketing. *International Marketing Review*, *37*(4), 621–650. DOI: 10.1108/IMR-04-2018-0133

Daneshfar, F., Bartani, A., & Lotfi, P. (2024). Image captioning by diffusion models: A survey. *Engineering Applications of Artificial Intelligence*, *138*, 109288. DOI: 10.1016/j.engappai.2024.109288

Díaz-Rodríguez, N., Del Ser, J., Coeckelbergh, M., López de Prado, M., Herrera-Viedma, E., & Herrera, F. (2023). Connecting the dots in trustworthy Artificial Intelligence: From AI principles, ethics, and key requirements to responsible AI systems and regulation. *Information Fusion*, *99*, 101896. DOI: 10.1016/j.inffus.2023.101896

Du, S., & Xie, C. (2021). Paradoxes of artificial intelligence in consumer markets: Ethical challenges and opportunities. *Journal of Business Research*, *129*, 961–974. DOI: 10.1016/j.jbusres.2020.08.024

Dutta, D., & Mishra, S. K. (2024). Bots for mental health: The boundaries of human and technology agencies for enabling mental well-being within organizations. *Personnel Review*, *53*(5), 1129–1156. DOI: 10.1108/PR-11-2022-0832

Emon, M. M. H. (2025a). The Mediating Role of Supply Chain Responsiveness in the Relationship Between Key Supply Chain Drivers and Performance: Evidence from the FMCG Industry. *Brazilian Journal of Operations & Production Management*, *22*(1), 2580. DOI: 10.14488/BJOPM.2580.2025

Emon, M. M. H. (2025b). Leveraging AI on Social Media & Digital Platforms to Enhance English Language Teaching and Learning. In *AI-Powered English Teaching* (pp. 211–238). IGI Global Scientific Publishing., DOI: 10.4018/979-8-3373-1952-0.ch007

Emon, M. M. H. (2025c). Circularity Meets AI: Revolutionizing Consumer Engagement Through Green Marketing. In *Transforming Business Practices With AI-Powered Green Marketing* (pp. 169–208). IGI Global Scientific Publishing. DOI: 10.4018/979-8-3373-3017-4.ch007

Emon, M. M. H. (2025d). Ethical Intelligence in Motion: Leveraging AI for Responsible Sourcing in Supply Chain and Logistics. In *Navigating Responsible Business Practices Through Ethical AI* (pp. 207–240). DOI: 10.4018/979-8-3373-3104-1.ch008

Emon, M. M. H. (2025e). Purpose-Driven Intelligence in Green Marketing: Leveraging AI for CSR-Centric and Sustainable Brand Positioning. In *Transforming Business Practices With AI-Powered Green Marketing* (pp. 89–122). IGI Global Scientific Publishing. DOI: 10.4018/979-8-3373-3017-4.ch004

Emon, M. M. H. (2025f). Navigating the Digital Labyrinth: Personal Data Privacy and Security at Individual and Organizational Levels. In *User-Centric Cybersecurity Implications for Sustainable Digital Transformation* (pp. 257–288). IGI Global Scientific Publishing. DOI: 10.4018/979-8-3373-3171-3.ch008

Emon, M. M. H. (2025g). Digital transformation in emerging markets: Adoption dynamics of AI image generation in marketing practices. *Telematics and Informatics Reports*, *20*, 100267. DOI: 10.1016/j.teler.2025.100267

Emon, M. M. H., & Ahmed, M. (2025). Digital Readiness as a Catalyst for Talent Transformation in Hospitality. In *Talent Management in Hotels and Hospitality* (pp. 461–502). IGI Global Scientific Publishing., DOI: 10.4018/979-8-3373-4485-0.ch014

Emon, M. M. H., & Chowdhury, M. S. A. (2025). Safeguarding Student Data: Privacy and Security Challenges in AI-Powered Education Tools. In *Enhancing Student Support and Learning Through Conversational AI* (pp. 191–228). IGI Global Scientific Publishing. DOI: 10.4018/979-8-3373-3316-8.ch008

Emon, M. M. H., & Khan, T. (2024). A Systematic Literature Review on Sustainability Integration and Marketing Intelligence in the Era of Artificial Intelligence. *Review of Business and Economics Studies*, *12*(4), 6–28. DOI: 10.26794/2308-944X-2024-12-4-6-28

Emon, M. M. H., & Khan, T. (2025a). The mediating role of attitude towards the technology in shaping artificial intelligence usage among professionals. *Telematics and Informatics Reports*, *17*, 100188. DOI: 10.1016/j.teler.2025.100188

Emon, M. M. H., & Khan, T. (2025b). The transformative role of Industry 4.0 in supply chains: Exploring digital integration and innovation in the manufacturing enterprises. *Journal of Open Innovation*, *11*(2), 100516. DOI: 10.1016/j.joitmc.2025.100516

Farhad, M. A. (2024). Consumer data protection laws and their impact on business models in the tech industry. *Telecommunications Policy*, *48*(9), 102836. DOI: 10.1016/j.telpol.2024.102836

Folorunso, O., Ojo, O., Busari, M., Adebayo, M., Joshua, A., Folorunso, D., Ugwunna, C. O., Olabanjo, O., & Olabanjo, O. (2023). Exploring Machine Learning Models for Soil Nutrient Properties Prediction: A Systematic Review. *Big Data and Cognitive Computing*, *7*(2), 113. DOI: 10.3390/bdcc7020113

Fordham, J., Ratan, R., Huang, K.-T., & Silva, K. (2020). Stereotype Threat in a Video Game Context and Its Influence on Perceptions of Science, Technology, Engineering, and Mathematics (STEM): Avatar-Induced Active Self-Concept as a Possible Mitigator. *The American Behavioral Scientist*, *64*(7), 900–926. DOI: 10.1177/0002764220919148

Galante, N., Cotroneo, R., Furci, D., Lodetti, G., & Casali, M. B. (2023). Applications of artificial intelligence in forensic sciences: Current potential benefits, limitations and perspectives. *International Journal of Legal Medicine*, *137*(2), 445–458. DOI: 10.1007/s00414-022-02928-5

Gilbert, M. A. (2024). *Disrupting Marketing*., DOI: 10.4018/979-8-3693-4361-6.ch002

Gkikas, D. C., & Theodoridis, P. K. (2022). AI in consumer behavior. *Advances in Artificial Intelligence-Based Technologies: Selected Papers in Honour of Professor Nikolaos G. Bourbakis*, *1*, 147–176.

Hagendorff, T. (2021). Forbidden knowledge in machine learning reflections on the limits of research and publication. *AI & Society*, *36*(3), 767–781. DOI: 10.1007/s00146-020-01045-4

Haleem, A., Javaid, M., Asim Qadri, M., Pratap Singh, R., & Suman, R. (2022). Artificial intelligence (AI) applications for marketing: A literature-based study. *International Journal of Intelligent Networks*, *3*, 119–132. DOI: 10.1016/j.ijin.2022.08.005

Harris, S., Hadi, H. J., Ahmad, N., & Alshara, M. A. (2024). Fake News Detection Revisited: An Extensive Review of Theoretical Frameworks, Dataset Assessments, Model Constraints, and Forward-Looking Research Agendas. *Technologies*, *12*(11), 222. DOI: 10.3390/technologies12110222

Heinberg, M., Liu, Y., Huang, X., & Eisingerich, A. B. (2021). A Bad Job of Doing Good: Does Corporate Transparency on a Country and Company Level Moderate Corporate Social Responsibility Effectiveness? *Journal of International Marketing*, *29*(2), 45–61. DOI: 10.1177/1069031X20981870

Henriksen, D., Creely, E., & Mehta, R. (2022). Rethinking the Politics of Creativity: Posthumanism, Indigeneity, and Creativity Beyond the Western Anthropocene. *Qualitative Inquiry*, *28*(5), 465–475. DOI: 10.1177/10778004211065813

Huang, C., & Guo, R. (2021). The effect of a green brand story on perceived brand authenticity and brand trust: The role of narrative rhetoric. *Journal of Brand Management*, *28*(1), 60–76. DOI: 10.1057/s41262-020-00213-7

Hussain, I., Mu, S., Mohiuddin, M., Danish, R. Q., & Sair, S. A. (2020). Effects of Sustainable Brand Equity and Marketing Innovation on Market Performance in Hospitality Industry: Mediating Effects of Sustainable Competitive Advantage. *Sustainability (Basel)*, *12*(7), 2939. DOI: 10.3390/su12072939

Kang, J., Hong, S., & Hubbard, G. T. (2020). The role of storytelling in advertising: Consumer emotion, narrative engagement level, and word-of-mouth intention. *Journal of Consumer Behaviour*, *19*(1), 47–56. DOI: 10.1002/cb.1793

Ke, J., Liao, P., Li, J., & Luo, X. (2023). Effect of information load and cognitive style on cognitive load of visualized dashboards for construction-related activities. *Automation in Construction*, *154*, 105029. DOI: 10.1016/j.autcon.2023.105029

Khamaj, A., & Ali, A. M. (2024). Adapting user experience with reinforcement learning: Personalizing interfaces based on user behavior analysis in real-time. *Alexandria Engineering Journal*, *95*, 164–173. DOI: 10.1016/j.aej.2024.03.045

Khan, T., Emon, M. M. H., & Nath, A. (2024). Quantifying the Effects of AI-Driven Inventory Management on Operational Efficiency in Online Retail. *2024 27th International Conference on Computer and Information Technology (ICCIT)*, 2092–2097. DOI: 10.1109/ICCIT64611.2024.11021996

Khan, T., Emon, M. M. H., Rahman, K. M., Nipa, M. N., & Fuad, M. N. (2025). The Role of AI in Driving Customer Engagement Through Technological, Organizational and Environmental Enablers in E-Commerce. *2025 International Conference on Quantum Photonics, Artificial Intelligence, and Networking (QPAIN)*, 1–6. DOI: 10.1109/QPAIN66474.2025.11171949

Khan, T., Emon, M. M. H., & Rahman, S. (2024). Marketing Strategy Innovation via AI Adoption: A Study on Bangladeshi SMEs in the Context of Industry 5.0. *2024 6th International Conference on Sustainable Technologies for Industry 5.0 (STI)*, 1–6. DOI: 10.1109/STI64222.2024.10951050

Khan, T., & Hasan Emon, M. M. (2024). Determinants of AI Image Generator Adoption Among Marketing Agencies: The Mediating Effects of Perceived Usefulness. *2024 IEEE 3rd International Conference on Robotics, Automation, Artificial-Intelligence and Internet-of-Things (RAAICON)*, 177–182. DOI: 10.1109/RAAICON64172.2024.10928548

Kordzadeh, N., & Ghasemaghaei, M. (2022). Algorithmic bias: Review, synthesis, and future research directions. *European Journal of Information Systems, 31*(3), 388–409. DOI: 10.1080/0960085X.2021.1927212

Kozinets, R. V. (2022). Algorithmic branding through platform assemblages: Core conceptions and research directions for a new era of marketing and service management. *Journal of Service Management, 33*(3), 437–452. DOI: 10.1108/JOSM-07-2021-0263

Kumar, A., Bapat, G., Kumar, A., Hota, S. L., Abishek, G. D., & Vaz, S. (2024). Unlocking Brand Excellence: Harnessing AI Tools for Enhanced Customer Engagement and Innovation. *RAiSE, 2023*, 204. DOI: 10.3390/engproc2023059204

Lee, L. W., Dabirian, A., McCarthy, I. P., & Kietzmann, J. (2020). Making sense of text: Artificial intelligence-enabled content analysis. *European Journal of Marketing, 54*(3), 615–644. DOI: 10.1108/EJM-02-2019-0219

Lemos, M., Cardoso, P. J. S., & Rodrigues, J. M. F. (2024). Harnessing AI and NLP Tools for Innovating Brand Name Generation and Evaluation: A Comprehensive Review. *Multimodal Technologies and Interaction, 8*(7), 56. DOI: 10.3390/mti8070056

Loureiro, S. M. C., Bilro, R. G., & Japutra, A. (2019). The effect of consumer-generated media stimuli on emotions and consumer brand engagement. *Journal of Product and Brand Management, 29*(3), 387–408. DOI: 10.1108/JPBM-11-2018-2120

Manda, V. K., Sagi, S., & Yadav, A. (2024). *Blockchain in Advertising and Marketing.*, DOI: 10.4018/979-8-3693-2754-8.ch005

Mayouf, M., Jones, J., Elghaish, F., Emam, H., Ekanayake, E. M. A. C., & Ashayeri, I. (2024). Revolutionising the 4D BIM Process to Support Scheduling Requirements in Modular Construction. *Sustainability (Basel), 16*(2), 476. DOI: 10.3390/su16020476

Mustak, M., Hallikainen, H., Laukkanen, T., Plé, L., Hollebeek, L. D., & Aleem, M. (2024). Using machine learning to develop customer insights from user-generated content. *Journal of Retailing and Consumer Services, 81*, 104034. DOI: 10.1016/j.jretconser.2024.104034

Nikolic, M. V., Milovanovic, V., Vasiljevic, Z. Z., & Stamenkovic, Z. (2020). Semiconductor Gas Sensors: Materials, Technology, Design, and Application. *Sensors (Basel), 20*(22), 6694. DOI: 10.3390/s20226694

O'Connor, S., & Liu, H. (2024). Gender bias perpetuation and mitigation in AI technologies: Challenges and opportunities. *AI & Society, 39*(4), 2045–2057. DOI: 10.1007/s00146-023-01675-4

Park, J., Oh, C., & Kim, H. Y. (2024). AI vs. human-generated content and accounts on Instagram: User preferences, evaluations, and ethical considerations. *Technology in Society, 79*, 102705. DOI: 10.1016/j.techsoc.2024.102705

Parris, D. L., & Guzmán, F. (2023). Evolving brand boundaries and expectations: Looking back on brand equity, brand loyalty, and brand image research to move forward. *Journal of Product and Brand Management, 32*(2), 191–234. DOI: 10.1108/JPBM-06-2021-3528

Paul, H., & Nikolaev, A. (2021). Fake review detection on online E-commerce platforms: A systematic literature review. *Data Mining and Knowledge Discovery, 35*(5), 1830–1881. DOI: 10.1007/s10618-021-00772-6

Pedersen, C. L., & Ritter, T. (2024). Digital authenticity: Towards a research agenda for the AI-driven fifth phase of digitalization in business-to-business marketing. *Industrial Marketing Management, 123*, 162–172. DOI: 10.1016/j.indmarman.2024.10.005

Peeters, M. M. M., van Diggelen, J., van den Bosch, K., Bronkhorst, A., Neerincx, M. A., Schraagen, J. M., & Raaijmakers, S. (2021). Hybrid collective intelligence in a human–AI society. *AI & Society, 36*(1), 217–238. DOI: 10.1007/s00146-020-01005-y

Petersson, L., Larsson, I., Nygren, J. M., Nilsen, P., Neher, M., Reed, J. E., Tyskbo, D., & Svedberg, P. (2022). Challenges to implementing artificial intelligence in healthcare: A qualitative interview study with healthcare leaders in Sweden. *BMC Health Services Research, 22*(1), 850. DOI: 10.1186/s12913-022-08215-8

Piriyakul, I., Kunathikornkit, S., & Piriyakul, R. (2024). Evaluating brand equity in the hospitality industry: Insights from customer journeys and text mining. *International Journal of Information Management Data Insights*, *4*(2), 100245. DOI: 10.1016/j.jjimei.2024.100245

Puntoni, S., Reczek, R. W., Giesler, M., & Botti, S. (2021). Consumers and Artificial Intelligence: An Experiential Perspective. *Journal of Marketing*, *85*(1), 131–151. DOI: 10.1177/0022242920953847

Raut, S., Chandel, A., & Mittal, S. (2024). *Enhancing Marketing and Brand Communication With AI-Driven Content Creation.*, DOI: 10.4018/979-8-3373-0219-5.ch008

Ray, P. P. (2023). ChatGPT: A comprehensive review on background, applications, key challenges, bias, ethics, limitations and future scope. *Internet of Things and Cyber-Physical Systems*, *3*, 121–154. DOI: 10.1016/j.iotcps.2023.04.003

Rizzoni, F., Magalini, S., Casaroli, A., Mari, P., Dixon, M., & Coventry, L. (2022). Phishing simulation exercise in a large hospital: A case study. *Digital Health*, *8*, 205520762210817. DOI: 10.1177/20552076221081716

Sánchez-Aguayo, M., Urquiza-Aguiar, L., & Estrada-Jiménez, J. (2022). Predictive Fraud Analysis Applying the Fraud Triangle Theory through Data Mining Techniques. *Applied Sciences (Basel, Switzerland)*, *12*(7), 3382. DOI: 10.3390/app12073382

Santos, Z. R., Cheung, C. M. K., Coelho, P. S., & Rita, P. (2022). Consumer engagement in social media brand communities: A literature review. *International Journal of Information Management*, *63*, 102457. DOI: 10.1016/j.ijinfomgt.2021.102457

Sauberschwarz, L., & Weiss, L. (2022). Efficient Innovation with the 5C Process. In *The Corporates Strike Back* (pp. 35–135). Springer International Publishing. DOI: 10.1007/978-3-030-79114-8_2

Shehu, I. S., Wang, Y., Athuman, A. M., & Fu, X. (2021). Remote Eye Gaze Tracking Research: A Comparative Evaluation on Past and Recent Progress. *Electronics (Basel)*, *10*(24), 3165. DOI: 10.3390/electronics10243165

Stray, J. (2020). Aligning AI Optimization to Community Well-Being. *International Journal of Community Well-being*, *3*(4), 443–463. DOI: 10.1007/s42413-020-00086-3

Sykora, M., Elayan, S., Hodgkinson, I. R., Jackson, T. W., & West, A. (2022). The power of emotions: Leveraging user generated content for customer experience management. *Journal of Business Research*, *144*, 997–1006. DOI: 10.1016/j.jbusres.2022.02.048

Taheri, B., Yousaf, A., Gannon, M., & Mishra, A. (2024). e-commerce website customer engagement: Delineating the role of UTAUT, vividness, and compulsion. *Journal of Retailing and Consumer Services*, *79*, 103835. DOI: 10.1016/j.jretconser.2024.103835

Thomas, V. L., & Grigsby, J. L. (2024). Narrative transportation: A systematic literature review and future research agenda. *Psychology and Marketing*, *41*(8), 1805–1819. DOI: 10.1002/mar.22011

Verganti, R., Vendraminelli, L., & Iansiti, M. (2020). Innovation and Design in the Age of Artificial Intelligence. *Journal of Product Innovation Management*, *37*(3), 212–227. DOI: 10.1111/jpim.12523

Vredenburg, J., Kapitan, S., Spry, A., & Kemper, J. A. (2020). Brands Taking a Stand: Authentic Brand Activism or Woke Washing? *Journal of Public Policy & Marketing*, *39*(4), 444–460. DOI: 10.1177/0743915620947359

Wang, Z., Ho, S.-B., & Cambria, E. (2020). A review of emotion sensing: Categorization models and algorithms. *Multimedia Tools and Applications*, *79*(47–48), 35553–35582. DOI: 10.1007/s11042-019-08328-z

Wu, L., Zheng, Z., Qiu, Z., Wang, H., Gu, H., Shen, T., Qin, C., Zhu, C., Zhu, H., Liu, Q., Xiong, H., & Chen, E. (2024). A survey on large language models for recommendation. *World Wide Web (Bussum)*, *27*(5), 60. DOI: 10.1007/s11280-024-01291-2

Yang, D., Wei, Z., Shi, H., & Zhao, J. (2020). Market orientation, strategic flexibility and business model innovation. *Journal of Business and Industrial Marketing*, *35*(4), 771–784. DOI: 10.1108/JBIM-12-2018-0372

Yu, J., & Meng, T. (2025). Image Generative AI in Tourism: Trends, Impacts, and Future Research Directions. *Journal of Hospitality & Tourism Research (Washington, D.C.)*. Advance online publication. DOI: 10.1177/10963480251324676

Zallio, M., & Clarkson, P. J. (2021). Inclusion, diversity, equity and accessibility in the built environment: A study of architectural design practice. *Building and Environment*, *206*, 108352. DOI: 10.1016/j.buildenv.2021.108352

KEY TERMS AND DEFINITIONS

Brand Engagement: The mental, emotional, and behavioral investment customers have in a brand which is usually manifested in customer interactions, brand loyalty, and brand advocacy.

Brand Equity: This refers to the value that a brand brings to any product or service given that it includes the perception of the consumer, recognition and the brand effect on the financial results.

Computer Vision: A branch of AI that allows machines to perceive and process visual data, which could be applied in branding to measure the reaction to the image or video.

Ethical Marketing: A marketing approach identified by practices that reflect, marketing activities, including AI-enhanced narrative, that venerates customer privacy, free of bias, and increases transparency and cultural awareness.

Generative AI: Artificial intelligence systems that are used to generate new content (text, image, or video) according to a pattern that has been trained by studying a huge volume of data.

Narrative Intelligence: This is the ability of AI systems to create and modify, as well as to analyze, stories, whether in text, visual, or multimodal form, to attract audiences and convey brand messages.

Personalization: Customization of content or experience to the tastes, or behavior or demographics of individual consumers and commonly through AI-powered analytics.

Sentiment Analysis: It is a natural language processing tool used to detect and measure the emotional tone of text-based data, and it assists brands in determining consumer attitudes.

Chapter 4
Enhancing Brand Engagement Through AI-Driven Storytelling and Dynamic Content Creation in Digital Marketing

P. S. Venkateswaran
https://orcid.org/0000-0001-8958-103X
PSNA College of Engineering and Technology, Dindigul, India

S. Jeyakumar
PSNA College of Engineering and Technology, Dindigul, India

S. Devi Kamatchi
https://orcid.org/0009-0009-9464-5216
PSNA College of Engineering and Technology, Dindigul, India

S. Manimaran
PSNA College of Engineering and Technology, Dindigul, India

ABSTRACT

This study examines the impact of artificial intelligence technologies in digital marketing storytelling to enhance brand engagement through personalized, dynamic content creation strategies. A descriptive research design was used along with purposive sampling to select 376 respondents from digital marketing consumers. The

DOI: 10.4018/979-8-3373-4506-2.ch004

study analysed AI-driven storytelling frameworks to understand their application in creating adaptive marketing strategies across various digital media. AI-driven storytelling improves brand engagement by delivering personalized methods that adapt to individual consumer preferences. The technology enables real-time content optimization, resulting in higher engagement rates, improved customer retention, and enhanced brand loyalty. The effectiveness of AI-driven storytelling depends heavily on data quality, algorithm sophistication, and the balance between automation and human creativity.

1. INTRODUCTION

In today's digital economy, consumers are always connected to social media; therefore, brands can no longer talk and need to really engage. Increasingly, the audience is seeking experiences that are personal, authentic, and meaningful. Traditional marketing methods no longer meet the requirements for long-term, supportive interaction between the brand and the consumer. To address these shifting trends, organizations are now using artificial intelligence (AI) to transform how they tell brand stories. At the same time, GAI and dynamic content creation tools emerging from this technological trend have opened new possibilities for brand storytelling and real-time user personalization (Vidrih & Mayahi, 2023).

For as long as there have been brands, storytelling has been an effective means of communicating a brand's human face and fostering an emotional relationship with consumers in ways that would otherwise not be possible. Advances in AI technology have sped this process. Marketers can instantly generate text, video, or other multimedia content using tools like ChatGPT, DALL · E, and Adobe Firefly. Jasper AI enables marketing copy to align with audience preferences (Joshi et al., 2025). By these means, we are now able to deliver creative content on a scale as wide as it is sophisticated, from any device, through custom-made unified messaging.

Generative AI differs from past AI systems in that it can generate context-aware content. Formerly, AI mainly focused on data analysis and automation. Utilizing large databases and deep learning models, GAI can fabricate articles. It can also create scripts for commercials, music, and dialogue records (Nalbant & Aydin, 2025). For example, this capability has ushered in a new era of narrative branding where the content, continuously adapted to interests, behaviors, and user responses, can operate within itself.

As far as a marketing subject is concerned, the emphasis has shifted little by little over time from mass-media broadcast to very specialized interaction, according to Spinney, for example, the two main drivers of GAI adoption in digital marketing, plus, extended innovation of content communication and a new impetus for this delivered in any case by interpreting its user commands on their behalf. With these factors at work, an enterprise can cut its marketing execution in half while simultaneously forming connections with the home audience that are longer-lasting.

World-famous brands are realizing AI-assisted, instant-response storytelling strategies. It can be found in practice: Netflix uses AI to recommend personalized movies based on users' viewing habits, while Coca-Cola employs AI to design flexible campaigns tailored to a range of consumer segments. These applications have led to improvements in user stickiness, brand attention, and customer satisfaction (Joshi et al. (2025). All these annotations indicate that GAI is needed to build emotionally intelligent, audience-led campaigns full of emotional resonance rather than based on convenience alone.

The variety of form products using generative AI to create content also includes visual and audio storytelling tools. StyleGAN, WaveNet, MusicLM, and others help create rich, sensory experiences that resonate with the brand. Several relevant previous studies suggest that interactive multimedia storytelling imparts significantly more emotional recall of message stimuli for consumers (Kemp et al., 2021).

By applying AI, content strategies should not be limited to simply increasing the size of the content pool; they should also aim to improve what people actually read and how valuable this information is to them. There is no doubt that AI makes it possible to analyze consumer data quickly, effectively, and in real time (Nalbant et al., 2025). It helps to understand user intent within this worldview, better target an audience, and create scaled-down but high-quality content instead. These features enhance delivery efficiency and personalization, and improve conversion results for good measure.

The article exemplifies solid industry data; companies in Indonesia adopting AI strategies could revamp their overall marketing content for better targeting accuracy through superior "rehabilitation". This had led to campaigns with higher return on ad spend and time spent on the site by visitors Companies that engaged in a marketing GAI model appeared to be making decisions in real time. Such an approach is better adapted to changing market conditions and new consumer behaviors. (Hendrayati et al., 2024).

The changing demographics, too, suggest the relevance of GAI in digital outreach. We know that Generations Y and X like to see brands tell stories that narrate their cultural background, but are tailored to their local context. That means GAI generates the brand's identity. When consumers receive customized content from the AI that reflects not just its own viewpoint but also aspects of existence that give them happiness or frustration, we believe they will be more likely to trust and stick with it. (Vidrih and Mayahi, 2023; Joshi et al., 2025).

However, despite its attractions, GAI opens a Pandora's Box of ethical and operational problems. More Issues related to algorithmic bias, content authenticity, and transparency have come to the fore. Some cases may occur, as with Facebook- and Google-driven AI platforms, where public outcry ensues due to poor net content preparation or governance practices (Vidrih & Mayahi, 2023). It is rich in potential, but the widespread use of AI also carries great responsibility. This is because, when applied to big data gathering, the artificial intelligence engines at companies can do all kinds of discrimination that no human can.

Companies also use GAI for real-time storytelling. By facilitating two-way communication in their ad messages with the consumer group rather than a one-sided approach (i.e., information from the company to interactors), they generate much more immersive and emotionally saturated experiences than before (Nalbant and Aydin, 2025).

From a theoretical point of view, Behavior Reasoning Theory (BRT) may offer one way of thinking about how to integrate AI into storytelling. BRT, as it was used by Joshi et al., (2025) seeks to understand the grounds that lead to or hinder the adoption of specific practices — for instance, the use of GAI in digital marketing. When one considers enabling factors (e.g., personalisation) and restricting factors (e.g., ethical concerns), BRT offers a valuable approach for analysing the behaviour of marketers and consumers in AI-mediated environments. Abrokwah-Larbi, M. (2023) studied that GAI-enabled customer personalisation, which may be a significant marketing strategy for influencing customer personalisation (CP).

Previous studies have fully explored how AI is used in machine learning for data analytics or to manage large volumes of content that cannot be published all at once, its function and effect on narrative branding — on engaging oneself as a consumer of appeal — have so far gone largely ignored. By integrating these various viewpoints, the present paper seeks to assist in forming an increasingly comprehensive picture of AI-driven marketing practice.

The objectives of the study are:

- Examine generative AI within the context of digital storytelling.
- Explore ways in which AI-driven content techniques advance personalisation and emotional engagement.
- Identify the opportunities and challenges of an AI-focused story.
- Offer thoughts on the ethical, scalable, and effective ways generative AI might be used in brand communication.

1.1. Theoretical aspects of AI-based Storytelling and Brand Engagement.

The advent of AI in the online marketing sector calls for a clear-cut conceptual framework for understanding how AI-mediated processes can influence branding outcomes. This chapter features three key constructs in the analysis: storytelling with AI, fluid content generation, and brand involvement. This chapter does not treat these aspects as a collection of autonomous technological capabilities but rather as an account, in a procedural manner, of how AI capabilities are moved to appropriate consumer-brand associations.

AI-driven storytelling refers to the tactic of creating, customizing, and delivering brand narratives based on consumer information, interests, and context through artificial intelligence-driven systems. However, compared with non-interactive messages that illustrate the classic narrative, AI storytelling is concerned with how the narrative may evolve in real time based on interactions between a consumer and a robot. Brand storytelling is a branding process that allows brands to distance their words, evoke feelings, and convey figurative meaning to the consumer psyche.

The tactical ability of AI stories to be staged across alternative formats, platforms, and consumer touchpoints is known as dynamic content production. Personalization is the customization of text, pictures, sound, and interactive content in real time based on consumer profiles and situational factors. Accordingly, dynamic content is not merely an artistic expression, but an occupant that guides consumers along the experience of the AI-generated narrative. The current level of AI storytelling is highly abstract and lacks engagement unless it is dynamic.

Brand engagement is a multidimensional construct that reflects the consumer's cognitive, emotional, and behavioural investment in the brand. Engagement involves more than exposure or interaction, as it encompasses attachment, brand recall, sharing behavior, and loyalty intentions. The existing literature on branding shows that engagement can be improved when consumers find brand communication salient, heartfelt, and authentic, which can be achieved through AI-directed storytelling.

The theoretical justification for this chapter lies in the Behavioral Reasoning Theory (BRT), which posits that individuals construct reasons for and against adopting and resisting most forms of behavior by identifying the advantages and disadvantages they perceive. This can help explain how consumers weigh subjective personalization, interaction, and convenience against the perceived risks of authenticity, morality, and data security when assessing AI-infected storytelling practices (BRT to AI-inflicted branding). The sphere of AI-based storytelling influences brand interaction primarily through dynamic content creation that aligns with brand stories, the demands and needs of the situation, and the expectations of the consumer.

In this study, brand engagement cannot be directly influenced by an automatic effect of storytelling with the help of AI. Instead, it is mediated and operationalized through dynamic content creation to personalize interactive brand experiences and render them emotionally salient by focusing on, for example, social or functional aspects of the experience. The idea behind such process-based framing is a break with the concept of technological determinism. It provides a theoretical foundation for the role of AI in brand engagement in the current digital marketing environment.

2. REVIEW OF LITERATURE

2 AI The Digital Brand Storytelling.

Storytelling is central to branding research because it enables the exchange of values and meanings that go far beyond functional product qualities. Some of the earlier literature has already indicated that narrative-based brand communication would result in greater emotional appeal and brand recall than non-storytelling-based informational communication (Kemp et al., 2021; Lee, 2024). Relative to this, however, the fixed message that defines traditional storytelling would fail miserably in an online setting, since it cannot accommodate changing audience attributes.

Figure 1. AI in digital brand storytelling: Dynamic content and visual narratives

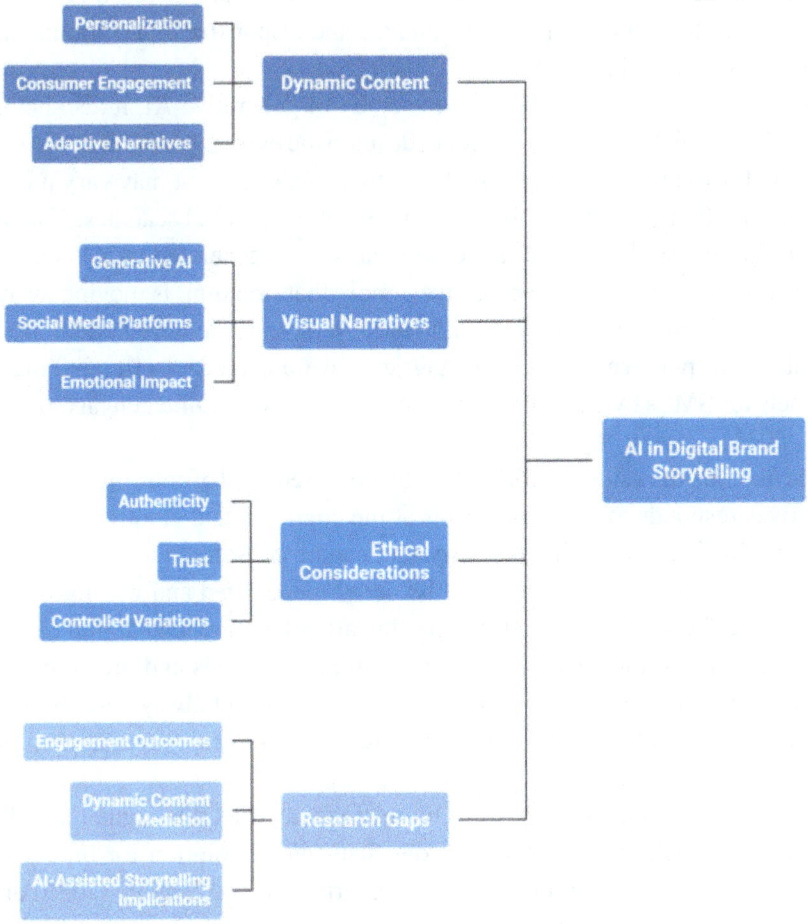

The rising adoption of artificial intelligence, however, has alleviated this limitation and provided greater flexibility in brand storytelling, which is increasingly content-driven. AI-assisted storytelling refers to the application of artificial intelligence systems to shape and tailor brand stories based on consumer data, behavioral indicators, and contextual information. Recent empirical evidence indicates that such adaptive narratives tend to generate relevance and engagement with messages, particularly in the digital environment, where consumers have developed expectations of high levels of personalization (Vidrih & Mayahi, 2023; Joshi et al., 2025).

Aarzoo & Lal (2024) suggested that advertising professionals use AI to enhance emotional storytelling and captivate audiences more effectively. AI-driven stories are not like conventional campaigns (or, actually, any media product at that), as they can adapt as the consumer interacts with them (or not). Research on AI-enabled marketing suggests that engagement outcomes are increasingly shaped by intelligent systems that support personalized and responsive brand communication (Venkateswaran et al., 2023).

Since this suggestion falls under the study of generative AI, it also helps with storytelling, which is one of the ways to develop the experiential aspect of branding. Joshi et al. Brands have to be consistent across platforms but may vary under controlled conditions, as (2025) observes. In one of the parallel searches, Nalbant and Aydin (2025) also discovered that emotional stories generated by AI can be more captivating to users. These perspectives imply that branding is moving away from a story as a fixed creative object and towards a more responsive system of stories. Social media platforms such as Instagram have emerged as effective marketing channels for SMEs by enabling visual storytelling and customer engagement (Putri et al., 2023).

On the consumer side, the differentially processed level of consumer personalized narratives responds to brand messages at the cognitive and emotive levels. Vidirh and Mayahi (2023) note that the story that can be considered as the most suitable one, in terms of personal tastes, will be better memorized and will have a greater emotional effect on the shorter the story, in particular, on young digital consumers. AI Systems make this possible through sentiment analysis and predictive models as part of the narrative design process. Such a story is not always successful. If the personalization feels too much or out of context, consumers may start doubting the message's authenticity.

Such concern is also reflected in more recent articles that argue that AI-based storytelling should not be seen as a one-size-fits-all solution for branding. The latter is also due to the prior works of Kamarunisha and Suguna (2025) and Ota et al. Narratives created by AI are no more valuable than the content formats and delivery mechanisms that support their execution (2024). Effective execution of this will make a kinescope view of AI storytelling feel like a robot rather than an engaging format. In practical terms, storytelling alone is highly unlikely to result in an effective brand engagement.

Overall, the main point of the previous research is that AI storytelling is a relatively new phenomenon in modern digital branding. It is, however, also a diffuse literature that lacks well-refined accounts of how such narratives result in actual engagement outcomes. Namely, the dynamic content generation feature, as a process that triggers touchpoint-based narratives in an AI-mediated environment, has not been studied empirically much (Hendrayati et al., 2024). In actual digital marketing scenarios, a gap in the literature exists regarding the significant implications of AI-assisted storytelling for brand engagement; therefore, this gap needs to be bridged.

2.2 Unstable Content Creation and Interactive Consumer Interactions.

Dynamic content creation has emerged as a fundamental tool in contemporary digital marketing, in a world characterized by divided attention and rapidly shifting consumer demands. Dynamic content is marketing text that is constantly modified in relation to its medium, timing, and/or form based on user information and circumstances, as well as the quality of the corresponding platform, as opposed to more stable content. In fact, past research has shown that such flexibility is essential to retaining and engaging consumers of digital brands.

Figure 2. Unveiling the multifaceted impact of dynamic content

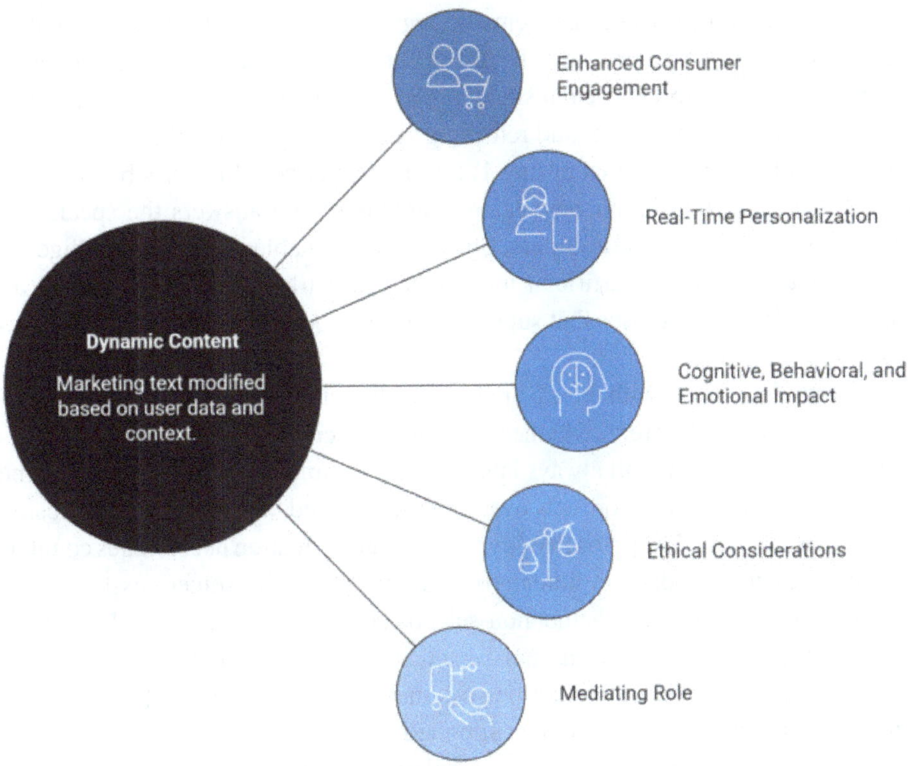

Research evidence demonstrates that content stasis is a significant element in the relationship between dynamic content and consumer engagement, through greater perceived relevance and immediacy of brand communication. Browsing behaviour or prior experience increases the likelihood that the consumer will process the message cognitively and react to it affectively. Evidence in the field of digital branding suggests that adaptive content, including customized images, videos, and interactive messages, tends to be followed by increases in engagement and dwell time (Yella, 2024; Purwanto et al., 2022).

The creation of dynamic content allows for more dynamic content, but with the development of artificial intelligence, the personalization of content at scale can now be achieved in real time. What content to convey to whom, but also the AURL (accuracy, urgency, relevance, latency) answer to why and when to convey content by streams of consumer data analysis by AI systems. Hendrayati et al., (2024) stated that firms that adopt dynamic content, such as advanced AI to customize are more responsive. Such adaptiveness is particularly relevant in a digital post-pandemic world, where consumer needs and expectations are constantly evolving.

From a consumer engagement perspective, dynamic content has a variety of impacts on several forms of engagement: cognitive, behavioral, and emotional. It is also found that the process of galvanizing information that should be frequently present and relevant to a particular situation prompts brand recall and active actions, such as sharing, commenting, and returning visits (Kemp et al., 2021; Lee, 2024). Moreover, the interaction that ensues is not only an effect of novelty but also due to the perception that brand messaging hearkens to and answers the special requirements of individual consumers. Studies on AI-enabled business intelligence suggest that the value of artificial intelligence in marketing lies in its ability to improve analytical processes that support customer-focused engagement strategies (Venkateswaran et al., 2024).

Nevertheless, along with the advantages, the literature also identifies severe limitations. This is no different; whether the content is created dynamically or not, as long as it is effective, it will always land on the consumer side. However, when the consumer becomes scared or feels overwhelmed/abused, a perception of intrusion arises. This is where the approach of dynamic content creation necessitates counterbalancing it with introductory human psychology and the consumer's expectations. However, personalization, whether non-selective or unobtrusive, can erode trust and reduce lifetime interaction. Kamarunisha and Suguna (2025) caution that long-term dynamic content strategies cannot be sustainable without proper attention to the ethics and authenticity of the content supplied.

Like the views of the above-discussed articles, recent studies assert that dynamic content creation is viewed as a mediating mechanism, independent of, rather than a driving force of, engagement. The insights generated by AI are the cornerstone of personalization, whereas dynamic content execution converts those insights into consumer experiences. Ota et al. (2024) argue that without adaptive content delivery, the strategic value of AI in marketing is mostly lost. In this perspective, the dynamic content generation serves as the connective tissue between AI-enabled capabilities and the resultant behavioral outcomes.

Overall, past studies have predominantly investigated dynamic content as a direct predictor of engagement, and limited empirical evidence has been provided to explain its mediating role in AI manipulation branding processes. These gaps stress the need for an empirical investigation of the mediating role of creating dynamic content in the association between AI-based storytelling and brand engagement, which is the objective of the present study.

2.3 Brand Visual Story Telling and AI Image Processing.

Ferraro et al. (2016) found that visual cues are critical to communicating brand meaning, as consumers tend to use visual images and videos as the most relevant information to create brand impressions in cyberspace. Branding literature over the years has shown that visual stimuli are more likely to elicit attention, emotional responses, and memory than text. In this case specifically, the recent developments in image processing with artificial intelligence open up even more possibilities for elevating the visual brand narrative to a new level of fluent management and enhancement.

Figure 3. Enhancing brand storytelling with AI image processing

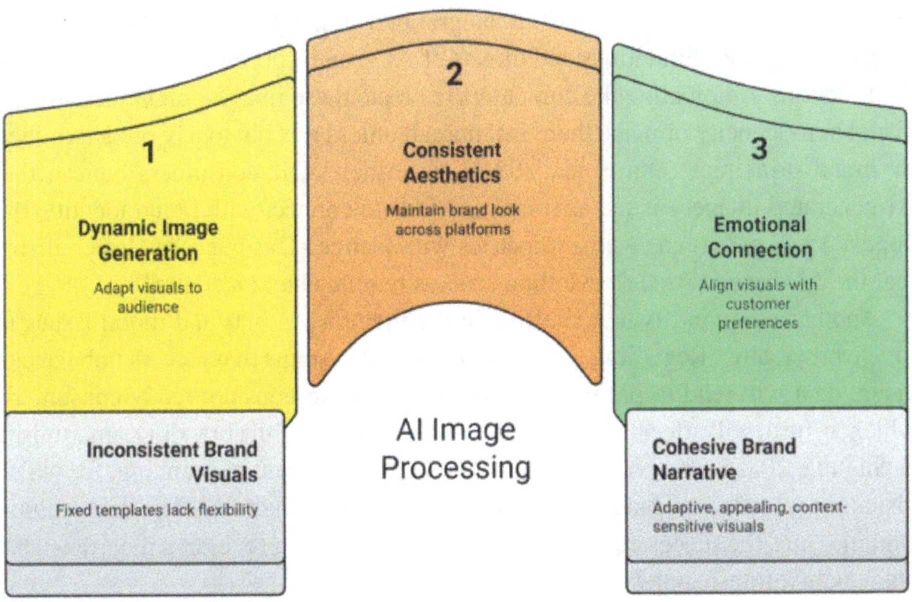

Image processing, also called AI-based image processing, is the interpretation and formulation of image content with the assistance of machine learning algorithms, providing information at a significantly larger scale. These digital branding techniques are used to manage visual consistency, enhance aesthetics, and customize images across platforms. Research has shown that when used with visual content, specifically the best visual elements portrayed, AI can improve brand recall, affective attachment by aligning the visuals presented with a brand's customer preferences (Yella, 2024), and context expectations at a higher level (Lee, 2024).

Image processing technologies enable the creation of cohesive image stories that transform in real time and vary depending on consumer touchpoints, storytelling aside. Rather than relying on fixed visual templates, AI systems can dynamically process images based on color, overlays, and subject matter to better cater to specific audience segments. This dynamic visual narrative is a potent form of experience branding because it is both consistent and flexible (Nalbant & Aydin, 2025). The balance is critical in digital channels, where consumers expect a brand to be contextually appropriate to their specific circumstances, yet visually similar to any brand recognition it may have.

Research also supports the potential to improve emotional responses to brand stimuli through AI-generated images. Visual storytelling with AI assistance has been observed to improve perceptions of creativity and immersion in the story when the images and the text or interaction unit are in correspondence and contextually relevant (Vidrih & Mayahi, 2023). The findings show that image processing is not only a technical upgrade but also an integral part of the digital branding story.

However, other limitations and threats of AI visual storytelling are described in the literature. Automating the computers to create these images might increase the visual homogeneity or make them feel unreal, unless it is obviously predetermined by brand principles (Ota et al., 2024). Nevertheless, if consumers believe that AI-generated imagery is too artificial and fails to connect with brand identity, the opposite will occur: engagement metrics will decline. This concern also confirms that the AI-driven visual storytelling process requires human control.

Another emerging issue identified in the literature is bias and moral issues in image processing. Regarding the implications, AI systems that receive unbalanced visual data will tend to promote stereotypes or fail to consider many consumers, which, in turn, will affect the reliability and dependence of the brands (Kamarunisha & Suguna, 2025). These problems are particularly relevant to branding, for which visual representations have been credited with substantial symbolic and cultural capital. Thus, the successful implementation of AI image processing requires stable data quality, transparency, and ethical controls.

Despite the increased attention to research, much of the past research has seen AI image processing and visual content generation as distinct areas of technology.

However, minimal attention has been given to visual storytelling as a component of a broader branding process using AI technologies. In particular, there are no empirical research studies that investigate the interplay between AI-generated storytelling, content generation, and visual image processing (Hendrayati et al., 2024).

The AI image processing creates a digital narrative for a brand whose venues are visually adaptive, emotionally appealing, and context-sensitive. The strength of it, lies in the visual content being combined with more central storytelling and content-delivery processes. The integration of AI-supported visual storytelling and brand engagement outcomes would enable researchers and marketers to provide a more substantial justification for AI's role in storytelling, a direct concern addressed by the current study.

Visual storytelling is growing and becoming more vibrant as AI-based image processing advances. Brand image processing helps brands deliver visual content with consistent aesthetics across different platforms to various audience segments. By automatically recognizing visual, color, and contextual patterns, AI systems facilitate the generation of imagery that aligns with brand recognition and adapts to consumer demands.

In terms of engagement, AI-powered image processing further supports the brand narrative by aligning visual imagery and emotional connection across digital channels. Visual components created or optimized using AI supplement narrative content and promote recall, attention, and affective responses. This makes image processing an essential enabler of dynamic content creation, facilitating the mediation pathway through which AI-powered storytelling impacts brand bridges. This is why it is necessary to research visual storytelling as a component of the general brand engagement strategies corporations employ to leverage AI, rather than treating it as a distinct design role.

2.4 AI Marketing Privacy, Trust, and Regulatory Issues.

Psychological, behavioral, ethical, trust, and regulatory issues surrounding the growing use of artificial intelligence in digital marketing directly affect consumer reactions to AI-based brand communications. The ability to create stories using AI, generate dynamic content, and process images offers considerable personalisation and engagement opportunities, but, as the literature claims, these opportunities can be squandered if ethics are not upheld and integrity is lost.

This raises a question of trust between the brand and consumers, particularly in AI-mediated interactions. It has been known that consumers evaluate AI-generated content not only based on its relevance and creativity but also on perceived authenticity and transparency. According to previous studies, when consumers do not know or feel uneasy about the extent of AI application in content creation, they may cast doubt on the validity of branded messages, thereby negatively affecting engagement outcomes (Vidrih & Mayahi, 2023). This is an issue primarily to be raised within the context of emotionally motivated storytelling, in which emotional involvement can be detracted by apparent manipulation or artificiality.

Recent empirical research findings indicate that AI ethics is an important predictor of brand trust. According to Kamarunisha and Suguna (2025), to make the use of AI responsible from a human rights perspective, it is necessary to prioritise data governance, minimise bias, and ensure transparency in decision-making. In the context of branding, failing to consider these problems could lead to reputational consequences, including unintentionally supporting stereotypes or misrepresenting consumer identities, in visual or narrative terms. Studies on AI-driven predictive analytics suggest that the value of artificial intelligence in digital marketing lies in its ability to support predictive decision-making processes that guide personalized and responsive content delivery (Venkateswaran & Ngo, 2025).

Figure 4. AI marketing: Unveiling the hidden depths of consumer trust

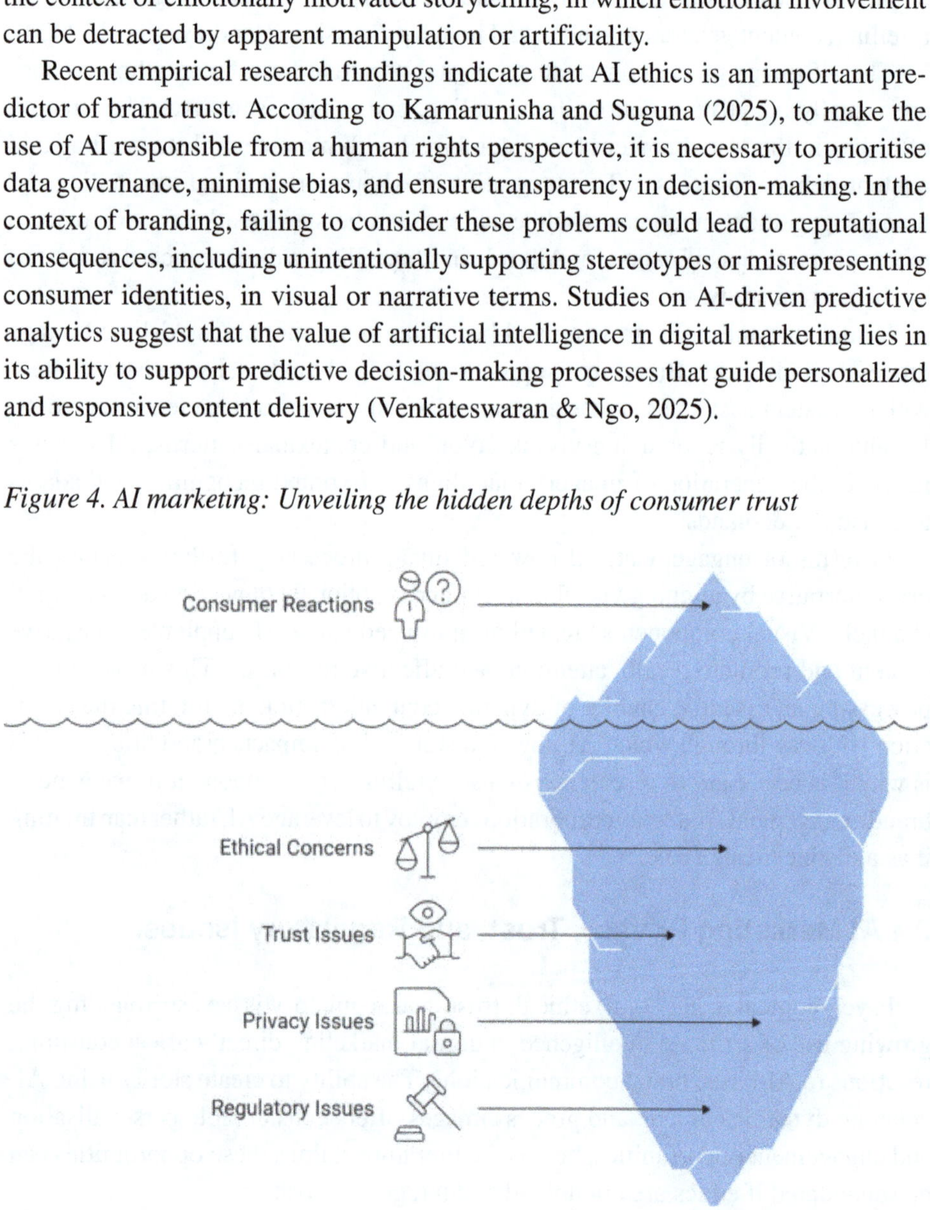

The second relevant theme identified in the literature is consumer privacy and the use of data. Nevertheless, AI-based personalization is not a noncontroversial phenomenon, as it is mainly based on the gathering and processing of consumer information, raising the questions of consent and information privacy. Hendrayati et al. (2024) state that though there is empirical evidence of the positive impact of personalization on consumers, consumers need more attention on brands to handle and process data, and the appropriate communication of how to use consumer data (Hendrayati et al., 2024). Although there is a high degree of personalization, these violations result in a weak level of engagement and trust.

Regulatory issues also complicate the use of commercial-grade AI marketing. Although to date, the literature does not focus on a unified set of international standards, researchers have already begun documenting how AI marketing practices are expected to align with evolving legal frameworks governing data protection, algorithmic accountability, and consumer rights (Ota et al., 2024). Self-sensitizing mechanisms, grounded in ethics and responsible innovation, will provide direction to firms in the absence of definitive regulations.

Real ethical and regulatory issues regarding branding should not be viewed as limitations but as defining relationships with consumers in the long term. A study in the field of digital branding finds that ethical transparency can be a competitive advantage by increasing consumer confidence and brand reputation (Lee, 2024). Consumers become less intrusive and see brand AI use as more supportive when brands clearly state they are using AI to tell a story or create content.

Though these issues are now more familiar, in ongoing research, ethical, trust, and regulatory issues have continued to be addressed as contextual rather than core processes in AI-driven branding. The number of empirical studies on issues involving the interaction between storytelling and the dynamic generation of content with the aid of AI is low, and none have explored the implications of brand engagement. Purwanto et al. (2022) highlight this gap, particularly in studies that focus solely on technological efficiency and the need to build trust mechanisms with consumers.

Overall, the literature outlines the significance of ethics, trust, and regulatory awareness in maintaining interactions with AI-enabled digital marketing. The promise of AI-driven storytelling and visual branding will only be realized when people are listened to and respond responsibly to their feelings. The insights above support the view that empirical models of AI-enabled brand engagement should incorporate ethical and trust-based dimensions, as the current study does.

2.4.1 Regulations and Data Protection in Marketing based on AI

The increased application of artificial intelligence (AI) in digital marketing has intensified scrutiny of consumer data protection, algorithmic accountability, and the ethical governance of AI. Marketers must consider their use of AI and the adoption of personalization and storytelling powered by these systems while closely adhering to data protection regulations, as they hinge on the collection and processing of personal data. Principles of informed consent, data minimization, transparency in automated decision-making, and consumer data privacy protection take centre stage in regulatory frameworks.

In terms of brand communication powered by AI, compliance now encompasses not just technical data security but also adherence to algorithmic explainability and equitable content delivery. Consumers nowadays are aware of how their data is being used to curate content that suits their interests, and this directly impacts their trust in AI-generated content messages from brands. Therefore, compliance with regulatory and ethical standards is vital, as non-compliance can harm brand credibility and engagement. Tarabieh et al., (2024) revealed that social media influencers have a significant positive direct impact on brand trust, customer brand engagement, and online repurchase intentions.

In our compliance-oriented mindset, we now often treat regulatory alignment as a burdensome minimum requirement for ethical AI marketing. Organizations that anticipate and incorporate due diligence into their marketing systems, grounded in data protection and transparent AI governance, are better positioned to maintain consumer trust and long-term relationships in digitally mediated environments.

Table 1. Key empirical studies on AI-driven storytelling, dynamic content, and brand engagement

Author(s) & Year	Study Context	Methodology	Key Findings	Relevance to the study
Kemp et al. (2021)	Digital branding	Survey-based analysis	Narrative-based brand communication enhances emotional engagement and recall	Supports role of storytelling in engagement
Lee (2024)	Brand communication	Empirical modeling	Emotional and authentic brand messages strengthen brand trust	Reinforces engagement dimensions
Vidrih & Mayahi (2023)	AI marketing	Conceptual and empirical review	AI-driven personalization improves emotional resonance and relevance	Supports AI-driven storytelling construct
Joshi et al. (2025)	Generative AI in marketing	Survey and structural modeling	AI storytelling enhances adaptive branding and engagement	Supports GAIBST role
Nalbant & Aydin (2025)	Digital storytelling	Experimental study	Emotionally responsive AI narratives sustain attention	Supports emotional mediation logic
Hendrayati et al. (2024)	AI adoption in marketing	Empirical field study	AI enables adaptive content strategies and flexibility	Supports dynamic content creation

continued on following page

Table 1. Continued

Author(s) & Year	Study Context	Methodology	Key Findings	Relevance to the study
Ota et al. (2024)	AI-generated content	Mixed-method analysis	AI content effectiveness depends on execution quality	Justifies mediating role of DYCC
Kamarunisha & Suguna (2025)	AI ethics in marketing	Review study	Ethical AI use influences trust and credibility	Supports ethics and trust dimension
Purwanto et al. (2022)	Digital content marketing	Survey analysis	Relevant content enhances engagement in post-pandemic context	Supports engagement outcomes

2.5 Research Gap

The available literature has suggested greater adoption of artificial intelligence across the digital marketing spectrum to enhance content personalization and to increase the use of AI-driven narrative strategies. The individualized content selections lead to favorable consumer experiences and brand performance. Recent work explores the potential of AI for image processing to enhance the brand's visual communication.

However, the literature has several limitations. Most research focuses on the immediate effects of AI-based storytelling on engagement, without providing much information about the intermediary processes by which AI-generated narratives lead to actual brand engagement. Second, the ability to create dynamic content is frequently cited as a key power of AI-driven marketing. Yet, studies have not tested it as an intermediary variable between AI-enhanced storytelling and brand interaction. Third, past research has typically viewed the concepts of storytelling, content execution, and visual branding individually, resulting in a piecemeal understanding. Lastly, ethical and trust factors are often treated as add-ons rather than integral to the discussion, despite their strong influence on consumers' actual reactions to AI-based brand communication.

Addressing these gaps, the research suggests and tests a process-oriented model that explores the effects of AI-powered storytelling on brand engagement by leveraging dynamic content generation and accounting for its ethical and operational consequences.

3. RESEARCH METHODOLOGY

3.1 Research Design

The research design used in this paper is to describe the effects of AI-based storytelling and personalized content creation on brand engagement. Since the study requires a systematic analysis of consumers' perceptions, attitudes, and experiences regarding AI-generated brand communication, a descriptive design is more appropriate than an experimental one, as it does not involve manipulating the study environment.

Descriptive research is more conducive to the study of technology-enabled marketing, where it is necessary to understand how consumers perceive and respond to novel practices (e.g., AI-assisted storytelling). The identified design will enable the determination of the main dimensions of online AI-based marketing and their relationship with brand engagement outcomes, within the framework of the real-life consumer experience in natural digital environments (Figure 2).

3.2 Target Population and Sample Design.

The target audience consisted of digital consumers who had previously engaged with online marketing content and had purchased a product/service online. Purposive sampling was also controlled because it is appropriate for selecting respondents with the necessary experience to evaluate AI functional and dynamic content in the digital marketing environment. The first sample comprised 565 respondents contacted via online platforms.

A total of 301 completed questionnaires were sent to this population, yielding an estimated response rate of 48.5 percent. Data screening processes led to the exclusion of 36 responses (incomplete or otherwise clinically uninformative forms, e.g., inconsistent answers to highly repeated questions or not passing the authentication test). The last sample comprised 376 usable responses, which were retained for further statistical analysis. The ultimate sample size was adequate to conduct multivariate analyses, including factor analysis, regression, and mediation tests. The results of the empirical study were evaluated using SPSS 27.

3.3 Development of Measurement Instruments and Scales.

To collect data, a questionnaire was used to measure consumers' perceptions of dynamic content generation, AI-based storytelling, and brand engagement in digital marketing settings. The questionnaire was formulated based on a literature review of the above AI-enabled marketing, digital storytelling, and consumer engagement. Prior research indicates that social media influencers significantly affect consumer brand engagement and influence managerial decision-making in digital marketing environments (Galdón et al., 2024).

The questionnaire was split into multiple sections, each addressing the various constructs examined in this study. The key constructs measured are Generative AI-Based Storytelling (GAIBST), Dynamic Content Creation (DYCC), Personalization of Marketing (PERM), Integration of Influencer Marketing and User-Generated Content (IMUGCI), Ethical and Operational Challenges (EAOC), and Brand Engagement (BRENG). Each construct was operationalized using several items to provide greater coverage of the underlying dimensions.

Measurements were based on a five-point Likert scale (1 = Strongly Disagree to 5 = Strongly Agree) to acquire all items. Because it is appropriate in a study that seeks perception, we used a five-point Likert scale since it gives the respondents the chance to indicate their level of agreement, while being responsive enough to be statistically suitable in multivariate statistics.

Pre-testing of the questionnaire was conducted to assess relevance, content validity, and clarity, in preparation for the primary survey. Slight modifications were made to improve the phrasing and make the items understandable to respondents. This was done to ensure the instrument captured important consumer perceptions of AI-enabled storytelling and dynamic content practices in digital marketing environments.

The survey was administered online, enabling rapid data collection from respondents regardless of their geographical location. The responses obtained from the questionnaire were then used in the following factor analysis, regression analysis, and mediation analyses in the research.

3.4 Construct Operationalization

Operationalisation of the key constructs in this study was based on the digital marketing literature to ensure conceptual clarity and valid measurement. The operationalization of our constructs involved two to nine items that were based on the available measures' scales based on the past conceptualization of AI-enabled brand communication from the consumer-based perspective. The operational definitions of each construct below are how the constructs were conceptualized and operationalized in the study.

Table 2. Operational definitions of study constructs

Construct	Operational Definition	Measurement Focus
Generative AI-Based Storytelling (GAIBST)	The extent to which consumers perceive brand narratives as adaptive, creative, and emotionally engaging due to the use of generative AI technologies	Narrative personalization, creativity, authenticity, emotional appeal
Dynamic Content Creation (DYCC)	The degree to which brand content is perceived as adaptable, multi-format, and responsive across digital platforms and consumer contexts	Content variability, platform responsiveness, sustained attention
Personalization of Marketing (PERM)	The extent to which marketing messages are perceived as tailored to individual preferences, needs, and behavioral patterns	Message relevance, customized interaction, perceived value
Influencer Marketing and User-Generated Content Integration (IMUGCI)	The perceived effectiveness of integrating AI-supported influencer content and user-generated brand narratives	Credibility, authenticity, community involvement
Ethical and Operational Challenges (EAOC)	Consumer perceptions regarding ethical concerns, transparency, bias, and operational risks associated with AI-driven marketing practices	Trust, transparency, data responsibility, fairness
Brand Engagement (BRENG)	The level of consumers' cognitive, emotional, and behavioral involvement with a brand in response to AI-driven content	Loyalty, emotional attachment, recall, interaction and sharing behavior

The constructs were measured using multiple items to address the concepts underlying the items adequately and to enhance their internal consistency. The constructs were operationalized based on the extant literature, which provided a solid basis for the factor analysis and subsequent regression and mediation analyses. This made it easy to determine that the extracted factors were theoretically significant dimensions of AI-Driven Marketing and brand engagement.

In the present study, consumer trust in AI-driven brand communication is conceptualized as a multidimensional perception embedded within the Ethical and Operational Challenges (EAOC) construct. Trust-related evaluations are reflected in respondents' perceptions of transparency, responsible data use, the fairness of algorithmic decisions, and the authenticity of AI-generated brand messages. Rather than treating trust as a standalone construct, this study captures trust as an outcome of ethical AI practices, consistent with prior research that positions trust as a function of perceived accountability and transparency in AI-mediated interactions.

3.5 Factor Analysis Procedure

The data were analyzed with PCA to conduct the exploratory factor analysis to find the possible underlying factors of AI-driven marketing constructs and simplify the dataset. PCA should be used in studies of perception where the researcher can be interested in reducing the number of correlated variables to give clear elements. In order to have a better interpretability of the resulting factor structure, varimax rotation using Kaiser normalization was conducted. To verify the suitability of data, Kaiser-Meyer-Olkin (KMO) measure and Bartlett Test of Sphericity were conducted. Those items that had a factor loading beyond permissible limits were reserved to an analysis follow-up.

3.6 Mediation Analysis

The mediation analysis was conducted to clarify the indirect impact of the story-telling by way of AI brand engagement and Dynamic Content Creation was used as the mediator. Mediation was analyzed through regression-based methods which give bias corrected confidence intervals (through bootstrapping) as in reference to Preacher and Hayes (2008). This method provides the mediating role of the dynamic content creation to be evaluated with confidence as a component of the proposed model.

4. ANALYSIS

Table 3. Preliminary tests for factor analysis appropriateness

KMO and Bartlett's Test		
Kaiser-Meyer-Olkin Measure of Sampling Adequacy.		**.771**
Bartlett's Test of Sphericity	Approx. Chi-Square	11692.434
	df	435
	Sig.	.000

Source: Author's computation based on survey data.

The Kaiser–Meyer–Olkin (KMO) value indicates adequate sampling adequacy, and Bartlett's Test of Sphericity is statistically significant ($p < 0.001$), confirming that the data are appropriate for conducting factor analysis.

Table 4. Component Eigenvalues and explained variance distribution

Total Variance Explained									
	Initial Eigenvalues			Extraction Sums of Squared Loadings			Rotation Sums of Squared Loadings		
Component	Total	% of Variance	Cumulative %	Total	% of Variance	Cumulative %	Total	% of Variance	Cumulative %
GAIBST	12.433	41.443	41.443	12.433	41.443	41.443	8.633	28.777	28.777
DYCC	4.146	13.819	55.262	4.146	13.819	55.262	4.141	13.804	42.581
PERM	2.207	7.356	62.618	2.207	7.356	62.618	3.646	12.152	54.733
IMUGCI	2.045	6.818	69.437	2.045	6.818	69.437	3.560	11.865	66.598
EAOC	1.693	5.644	75.081	1.693	5.644	75.081	1.946	6.486	73.085
BRENG	1.204	4.012	79.093	1.204	4.012	79.093	1.802	6.008	79.093

Extraction Method: Principal Component Analysis.
Source: Author's computation based on survey data.

The results of the principal component analysis indicate the extraction of six components with eigenvalues greater than one, collectively explaining 79.09 percent of the total variance. This level of explained variance exceeds commonly accepted thresholds in social science research, indicating a well-defined and stable factor structure. After rotation, variance is more evenly distributed across the six components, suggesting that the constructs represent distinct yet meaningful dimensions of AI-driven marketing and brand engagement.

Table 5. Rotated factor loadings and component structure matrix

	Component					
	1	2	3	4	5	6
Generative AI-Based Storytelling (GAIBST)						
AI-driven stories are distinctive and memorable.	.913					
Generative content appears more creative than traditional media.	.869					
AI makes brand storytelling feel authentic and human.	.864					
AI storytelling enhances emotional brand messaging.	.850					
I connect more with brands using AI-driven narratives.	.820					
Dynamic Content Creation (DYCC)						
Dynamic formats sustain my interest across platforms.		.912				
Diverse AI content deepens my brand connection.		.926				
I notice brands using varied content formats.		.901				
Personalized messages make me feel valued.		.880				
I prefer multimedia messaging from brands.		.830				
Personalization of Marketing (PERM)						

continued on following page

Table 5. Continued

	Component					
	1	2	3	4	5	6
AI personalization improves my digital brand experience.			.937			
AI enhances the relevance of brand interactions.			.886			
I engage more with tailored brand content.			.878			
AI-powered visuals and videos shape my brand perception.			.853			
Personalized content increases my purchase intent.			.828			
Content Integration and Influence (CIAI)						
AI-generated customer stories raise my engagement.				.887		
AI-tailored influencer content feels impactful.				.874		
I trust influencer-shared brand messages more.				.868		
I stay loyal to brands involving users in content.				.863		
UGC boosts brand authenticity.				.855		
Ethical and Operational Challenges (EAOC)						
Brands should disclose AI content usage.					.936	
Ethical AI use shapes brand trust.					.870	
I worry about AI affecting content authenticity.					.864	
I prefer brands using transparent, ethical AI.					.831	
Biased AI content reduces brand credibility.					.749	
Brand Engagement (BRENG)						
I'm loyal to brands offering tailored AI experiences.						.915
I better recall brands using dynamic AI content.						.873
AI storytelling fosters emotional brand ties.						.859
I interact more with AI-driven brands.						.839
AI content increases my likelihood to share.						.807

Extraction Method: Principal Component Analysis.
Rotation Method: Varimax with Kaiser Normalization.
a. Rotation converged in 6 iterations.
Source: Author's computation based on survey data.

The rotated factor solution yielded six distinct components corresponding to the proposed constructs, collectively explaining 79.093 percent of the total variance. All items loaded strongly on their respective factors, with factor loadings exceeding recommended thresholds, indicating good convergent validity and construct clarity.

Generative AI-Based Storytelling emerged as the dominant factor, highlighting the central role of AI-generated narratives in shaping consumer perceptions. Dynamic Content Creation and Personalization of Marketing also demonstrated strong factor structures, underscoring the importance of adaptive, tailored content in sustaining consumer engagement. The factors related to influencer and user-generated content integration, ethical and operational challenges, and brand engagement further indicate that both execution quality and ethical considerations are integral to AI-driven branding outcomes. Overall, the factor structure supports the multidimensional nature of AI-driven marketing and provides a robust foundation for subsequent regression and mediation analyses.

Hypothesis testing:

H1: Generative AI-Based Storytelling (GAIBST) has a positive significant effect on Brand Engagement (BRENG)

The multiple regression methodology was used to analyze the correlation between the Generative AI-Based Storytelling (GAIBST) and Brand Engagement (BRENG) and, at the same time, to control the other predictor variables such as Dynamic Customer Content (DYCC), Premium positioning (PREM), Image-Generated Content Impact (IMUGCI), and Emotional Appeal of Content (EAOC).

Table 6. Model summary and ANOVA results

Model	R	R^2	Adjusted R^2	Std. Error of Estimate
1	0.492	0.243	0.229	0.725

Model	Sum of Squares	df	Mean Square	F	Sig.
Regression	45.451	5	9.090	17.291	<0.001
Residual	141.942	270	0.526	-	-
Total	187.392	275	-	-	-

Source: Author's computation based on survey data.
Note: Predictors: (Constant), EAOC, GAIBST, DYCC, IMUGCI, PREM
Note: Dependent Variable: BRENG; Predictors: (Constant), EAOC, GAIBST, DYCC, IMUGCI, PREM

The regression model is statistically significant, indicating that the set of predictor variables collectively explains a meaningful proportion of variance in brand engagement. The model accounts for approximately 24 percent of the variance in brand engagement, suggesting a moderate explanatory power for consumer engagement outcomes in AI-driven marketing contexts.

Table 7. Regression coefficients

Variables	B	Std. Error	β	t	Sig.
(Constant)	1.645	0.271	-	6.070	<0.001
GAIBST	1.018	0.064	1.017	4.286	<0.001
DYCC	1.059	0.079	1.064	4.753	<0.001
PREM	0.926	0.093	0.911	2.280	0.048
IMUGCI	-0.834	0.086	-0.821	-1.393	0.095
EAOC	1.466	0.103	1.444	7.536	<0.001

Source: Author's computation based on survey data. Note: Dependent Variable: BRENG

The results provide strong support for H1, demonstrating that Generative AI-Based Storytelling has a positive and significant effect on brand engagement. This finding suggests that AI-generated narratives play an important role in shaping consumers' cognitive and emotional involvement with brands. Dynamic Content Creation also exerts a significant positive influence, underscoring the importance of adaptive, responsive content delivery in sustaining engagement.

Premium positioning positively contributes to brand engagement, though its effect is comparatively weaker. In contrast, the impact of integrating image-generated content is not statistically significant, suggesting that visual content alone may not be sufficient to drive engagement without complementary narrative or emotional elements. Among all predictors, emotional appeal emerges as the strongest determinant of brand engagement, underscoring the central role of affective content in AI-enabled brand communication.

H2: Dynamic Content Creation (DYCC) has a positive significant effect on Brand Engagement (BRENG)

Simple linear regressions were used in only taking a look at the direct connection between Dynamic Content Creation (DYCC) and Brand Engagement (BRENG), but not with the control of any other variables.

Table 8. Model summary and ANOVA results

Model	R	R^2	Adjusted R^2	Std. Error of Estimate	F Change	df1	df2	Sig. F Change
1	0.376	0.141	0.138	0.766	45.118	1	274	<0.001
Model		**Sum of Squares**		**df**	**Mean Square**		**F**	**Sig.**
Regression		26.494		1	26.494		45.118	<0.001

continued on following page

Table 8. Continued

Model	R	R^2	Adjusted R^2	Std. Error of Estimate	F Change	df1	df2	Sig. F Change
Residual		160.898		274	0.587		-	-
Total		187.392		275	-		-	-

Source: Author's computation based on survey data. Note: Predictors: (Constant), DYCC
Note: Dependent Variable: BRENG; Predictors: (Constant), DYCC

Table 9. Regression coefficients

Variables	B	Std. Error	β	t	Sig.	95% CI
(Constant)	2.373	0.199	-	11.908	<0.001	[1.981, 2.765]
DYCC	0.350	0.052	0.376	6.717	<0.001	[0.247, 0.452]

Source: Author's computation based on survey data. Note: Dependent Variable: BRENG;
CI = Confidence Interval

The simple regression results indicate a statistically significant and positive relationship between Dynamic Content Creation and Brand Engagement. The model explains a meaningful proportion of variance in brand engagement, suggesting that adaptive and responsive content plays a vital role in shaping consumer engagement outcomes.

The findings provide empirical support for H2, demonstrating that dynamic content creation directly enhances brand engagement. This result highlights the importance of continuously updated, multi-format, and interactive content in sustaining consumer interest and encouraging ongoing brand interaction in digital environments. H2 is supported.

H3: Dynamic Content Creation (DYCC) has a positive significant effect on Brand Engagement (BRENG)

The regression analysis that looks at the connection between the Generative AI-Based Storytelling (GAIBST) and Dynamic Content Creation (DYCC) has sufficient explanatory power with an R-value of 0.290 and R2 of 0.084. This means that the variance between the variable GAIBST and DYCC is 8.4 percent and the effect size is a small to medium effect as per the conventions of Cohen (1988).

Table 10. Model summary and path coefficient

Model Summary	R	R^2	MSE	F	df1	df2	p
Values	0.290	0.084	0.725	25.161	1	274	<0.001
Path	**Coefficient**	**SE**	**t**	**p**	**95% CI**		
Constant	2.018	0.273	7.396	<0.001	[1.481, 2.555]		
DYCC → BRENG (b)	0.320	0.054	5.908	<0.001	[0.213, 0.426]		
GAIBST→ BRENG (c')	0.121	0.064	1.899	0.059	[-0.005, 0.247]		

Source: Author's computation based on survey data.

The model can also be seen that the model passes the statistic barrier ($F(1,274) = 25.161$, $p < 0.001$) and the linear relationship between these two constructs is significant, and is not the result of chance.

Table 11. Path a: Effect of GAIBST on DYCC (X → M)

Path	Coefficient	SE	t	p	95% CI
Constant	2.409	0.268	9.004	<0.001	[1.882, 2.935]
GAIBST → DYCC	0.342	0.068	5.016	<0.001	[0.208, 0.476]

Source: Author's computation based on survey data.

The mediation analysis indicates that Generative AI-Based Storytelling has a significant positive effect on Dynamic Content Creation, supporting the proposed causal pathway between narrative capability and content execution. Dynamic Content Creation, in turn, demonstrates a considerable positive impact on Brand Engagement, confirming its central role in shaping consumer engagement outcomes.

When Dynamic Content Creation is included in the model, the direct effect of Generative AI-Based Storytelling on Brand Engagement becomes non-significant. This finding indicates that AI-driven storytelling's influence on brand engagement primarily operates through dynamic content creation rather than a direct pathway. The results, therefore, provide evidence of a full mediation effect, highlighting Dynamic Content Creation as the key mechanism through which AI-generated narratives translate into meaningful brand engagement. These findings support the proposed mediation hypothesis, confirming that Dynamic Content Creation mediates the relationship between AI-driven storytelling and brand engagement.

H4: Dynamic Content Creation (DYCC) has a positive significant mediating effect between GAIBST and BRENG

Table 12. Regression results for Paths b and c' (DYCC → BRENG and GAIBST BRENG)

Model Summary	R	R^2	MSE	F	df1	df2	p
Values	0.391	0.153	0.582	24.576	2	273	<0.001

Source: Author's computation based on survey data.

Path b and c': Effects on Brand Engagement (M → Y and X → Y)

The combined inclusion of Generative AI-Based Storytelling and Dynamic Content Creation significantly improves the prediction of brand engagement, indicating that the proposed mediation framework is statistically meaningful. The model explains a higher proportion of variance in brand engagement compared to the single-predictor specification, confirming the joint relevance of narrative capability and content execution.

Consistent with the mediation logic, Dynamic Content Creation demonstrates a significant effect on brand engagement, while the direct effect of Generative AI-Based Storytelling is reduced when the mediator is included. This pattern supports the view that AI-driven storytelling influences brand engagement primarily through its ability to enable dynamic and adaptive content execution. H4 is supported.

Table 13. Direct and indirect effects analysis: Mediation of GAIBST-BRENG relationship through DYCC

Effect Type	Path	Effect	SE	t/z	p	95% CI	Interpretation
Direct	c'	0.121	0.064	1.899	0.059	[-0.005, 0.247]	Not significant
Indirect	a×b	0.109	0.033	-	-	[0.054, 0.182]	Significant

Source: Author's computation based on survey data.
Note: Indirect effect confidence interval based on 5,000 bootstrap samples

Table 14. Bootstrap validation results for mediation analysis (5,000 samples)

Parameter	Original Coefficient	Bootstrap Mean	Bootstrap SE	Bootstrap 95% CI
Path a (GAIBST → DYCC)				
Constant	2.409	2.398	0.319	[1.765, 3.013]
GAIBST	0.342	0.345	0.080	[0.189, 0.504]
Paths b & c' (→ BRENG)				
Constant	2.018	2.016	0.328	[1.366, 2.656]
GAIBST (c')	0.121	0.121	0.071	[-0.012, 0.264]
DYCC (b)	0.320	0.320	0.063	[0.201, 0.446]

Source: Author's computation based on survey data.

The direct and indirect effects analysis confirms that Dynamic Content Creation mediates the relationship between Generative AI-Based Storytelling and Brand Engagement. While the indirect effect of AI-driven storytelling on brand engagement through dynamic content creation is statistically significant, the direct effect becomes non-significant when the mediator is included.

Bootstrap validation using 5,000 samples further supports the robustness of the mediation model, indicating stable and reliable parameter estimates. The findings demonstrate that AI-driven storytelling influences brand engagement primarily by enabling dynamic and adaptive content execution rather than through a direct pathway. These results provide strong evidence of full mediation, confirming that Dynamic Content Creation is the key mechanism linking AI-driven storytelling to brand engagement.

The correlation matrix indicated a high degree of positive correlations is observed across all the dimensions of AI-marketing and brand engagement using moderate and strong values of correlation coefficients. All the correlations are statistically significant and most of them are at the $p < 0.01$ level and this implies that firm bonds exist between the constructs used in the investigation.

Table 15. Relationships among AI-marketing dimensions and brand engagement

	GAIBST	DYCC	PERM	IMUGCI	EAOC	BRENG
Generative AI-Based Storytelling (GAIBST)	1					
Dynamic Content Creation (DYCC)	.282**	1				
Personalization of Marketing (PERM)	.201**	.420**	1			
Influencer Marketing and User-Generated Content Integration (IMUGCI)	.197**	.410**	.780**	1		

continued on following page

Table 15. Continued

	GAIBST	DYCC	PERM	IMUGCI	EAOC	BRENG
Ethical and Operational Challenges (EAOC)	.621**	.240**	.134*	.138*	1	
Brand Engagement (BRENG)	.322**	.439**	.300**	.261**	.335**	1

Source: Author's computation based on survey data. **. Correlation is significant at the 0.01 level (2-tailed). *. Correlation is significant at the 0.05 level (2-tailed).

The correlation analysis indicates positive and statistically significant associations among the AI-marketing dimensions and brand engagement. The pattern of correlations suggests that the constructs are related in theoretically expected directions while remaining sufficiently distinct, supporting their inclusion in subsequent regression and mediation analyses.

All AI-marketing dimensions exhibit moderate positive correlations with brand engagement, indicating that storytelling, dynamic content, personalization, influencer integration, and ethical considerations are collectively associated with consumer engagement outcomes. The absence of excessively high correlations among most constructs suggests that multicollinearity is unlikely to be a concern in the multivariate analysis.

5. FINDINGS

This study provides new empirical insights into the interrelationships among the three key dimensions of a broader AI-based marketing program and brand engagement in digital contexts. AI marketing practices affect brand engagement through a web of interconnected mechanisms rather than as simple technological effects, as the analysis establishes.

The findings confirm a positive relationship between Generative AI-Based Storytelling and brand engagement. This discovery indicates that algorithm-driven narrative abilities enhance consumers' cognitive and affective affinity with brands. But the impact of storytelling with AI is not direct. When other AI-marketing dimensions are accounted for, the strength of this relationship fluctuates, which highlights that storytelling is part of a wider process of engagement rather than a standalone driver.

Dynamic Content Creation has the most significant impact on driving brand engagement among the dimensions studied. Results showed that consumers are more responsive to adaptive, diversified, and context-sensitive content formats. This arranges the vital idea of content execution around AI-driven advertising, where the engagement results of AI-prompted insights must be streamlined to appropriately deliver brand messages across digital channels, according to timing and relevance.

Mediation analysis reveals a process-oriented relationship between AI-driven storytelling and brand engagement. In particular, the effect of Generative AI-Based Storytelling on brand engagement is mediated by Dynamic Content Creation. The results show a full mediation effect of dynamic content generation, as the direct link between AI-based storytelling and brand engagement is no longer significant when dynamic content creation is included in the model. This finding implies that AI-based narratives increase engagement through adaptive, responsive content delivery rather than directly influencing consumers.

The results also reveal that Personalization of Marketing, Influencer Marketing, and User-Generated Content Integration are positively associated with the other AI-marketing dimensions, indicating a synergistic relationship and the combined use of AI-oriented marketing activities. These linkages indicate that marketing through Artificial Intelligence is like a system of capabilities working together to provide that instant connectedness.

Furthermore, the paper reveals a strong correlation between Generative AI-Based Storytelling and Ethical and Operational Challenges. This insight is consistent with the increasing complexity of AI adoption in marketing contexts as sophisticated storytelling capabilities come alongside increasing demands for transparency, data use, and responsible implementation. The relationship itself adds another layer to the fact that ethics in AI-driven marketing environments is a critical issue rather than a fringe issue.

The overall results show that consumer processing of AI-based brand communication is multidimensional and process-oriented. Brand Engagement → Technology and creativity alone >> Excellence in execution + Ethical Consideration. These dimensions combine to represent the complexity of AI-based marketing practices and provide a structured empirical basis for the following discussion and managerial implications.

6. MANAGERIAL IMPLICATIONS AND STRATEGIC RECOMMENDATIONS

The results provide several actionable insights for managers who wish to utilise artificial intelligence in digital marketing whilst maintaining engagement with their brands. These implications underscore the need for a process-oriented, integrated, and ethically grounded approach to implementing AI-powered marketing.

6.1 Process Driven AI Marketing Approach

The results reveal that, storytelling through AI does not result in direct brand engagement; rather, it stems from dynamic content creation. As a result, managers should invest in AI technologies that deliver effective solutions to optimize internal content development processes, enabling adaptive, contextual & platform-responsive brand communication to continue to be produced indefinitely. Forget about individual storytelling capabilities and start making investment decisions based on how AI systems can enhance content workflows and execution quality.

6.2 Building AI-Driven Marketing Capabilities

This further reinforces that AI marketing dimensions are interrelated and that, to execute an effective AI marketing strategy, they must be integrated. Combine AI-driven storytelling with personalization mechanisms, influencer and user-generated content, and content management systems within a single layered marketing framework. This requires cross-functional coordination between marketing, technology, and data teams to deliver consistent AI insights that translate into coherent engagement strategies through digital touchpoints.

6.3 Ethical Transparency Turns into a Competitive Flip Side

The link between AI storytelling and ethical and operational dilemmas underscores the critical need for accountable AI governance. So instead of regarding ethical transparency as obligatory, managers should consider it a more strategic element of communication or branding. Transparency in AI use, ethical data practices, and accountability for algorithms can bolster consumer trust and ensure that consumers continue to engage with AI-driven marketing environments.

6.4 Capability Building & Performance Measurement

Since the effectiveness of AI marketing is driven more by processes than by systems, organizations should focus on organizational learning and capability development. It also involves preparing marketing teams to use AI-first tools effectively and setting up mechanisms to measure performance, not only in terms of engagement but also efficiency. No Content Strategy Is Perfect: Firms need to continuously assess the effectiveness of AI-powered content strategies to refine them further, particularly to keep up with changing consumer expectations and technologies.

7. CONCLUSION

This study investigates the impact of artificial intelligence (AI)–enabled storytelling and adaptive content design on brand engagement in digital marketing settings. The results reveal that the effectiveness of AI-enabled marketing is more of a process phenomenon than one that can be fully understood through point or direct effects, in which engagement outcomes are determined by the technological capabilities at hand through the operation of adaptive, trial-and-error content expression rather than through direct effects.

These findings show that, although generative AI can assist by enabling the creation of scalable, data-informed brand narratives, these narratives enhance brand engagement only when converted into dynamic, user-personalised, and context-responsive content. Dynamic content creation then becomes the core means by which the process of AI-driven storytelling is operationalized into tangible consumer engagement, while also highlighting the need to reassess widely held assumptions about whether simply adopting technology leads to better outcomes.

Research provides additional insights into the multifaceted coexistence of AI-initiated marketing, where engagement depends on a combination of storytelling, content personalization, user-generated content, and influencer content, integrated with technology, alongside its ethical ramifications. This link between AI-infused storytelling and ethical and operational complexities underscores the imperative of responsively governing our innovation through technology itself. In conclusion, this research offers detailed insights into AI-enabled brand communication by highlighting the emerging AI systems and consumer demands, as well as ethical frameworks that will further guide digital branding behavior.

REFERENCES

Aarzoo, & Lal, R. (2024). Artificial Intelligence-Driven Emotional Storytelling for Brand Narrative Strategies and Consumer Perception. SSRN. https://ssrn.com/abstract=4954803

Abrokwah-Larbi, M. (2023). Dynamic capabilities and generative AI in customer personalization. *Journal of Interactive Marketing*, *57*(3), 112–127.

Galdón-Salvador, J., Gil-Pechuán, I., AlFraihat, S., & Tarabieh, S. (2024). Effect of social media influencers on consumer brand engagement and its implications for business decision-making. *El Profesional de la Información*, *33*(2). Advance online publication. DOI: 10.3145/epi.2024.0210

Hendrayati, H., Achyarsyah, M., Marimon, F., Hartono, U., & Putit, L. (2024). The impact of artificial intelligence on digital marketing: Leveraging potential in a competitive business landscape. *Emerging Science Journal*, *8*(6), 2343–2348. DOI: 10.28991/ESJ-2024-08-06-012

Joshi, S., Bhattacharya, S., Pathak, P., Natraj, N. A., Saini, J., & Goswami, S. (2025). Harnessing the potential of generative AI in digital marketing using the Behavioral Reasoning Theory approach. *International Journal of Information Management Data Insights*, *5*(1), 100317. DOI: 10.1016/j.jjimei.2024.100317

Kamarunisha, M., & Suguna, M. (2025). A study on AI-powered content creation in digital marketing. [JETIR]. *Journal of Emerging Technologies and Innovative Research*, *12*(5), 541–550. http://www.jetir.org

Kemp, E., Porter, M.III, Anaza, N., & Min, D. (2021). The impact of storytelling in creating firm and customer connections in online environments. *Journal of Research in Interactive Marketing*, *15*(1), 104–124. DOI: 10.1108/JRIM-06-2020-0136

Lee, S. (2024). What triggers customer curiosity? Exploring the role of branded content experience design on customer response. *Journal of Hospitality & Tourism Research (Washington, D.C.)*, *49*(3), 403–416. DOI: 10.1177/10963480231220274

Nalbant, K. G., & Aydin, S. (2025). AI-powered digital marketing: Transforming personalized experiences. *American Research Journal of Humanities and Social Science*, *8*(1), 19–27.

Ota, R., Ray, S. S., & Alli, S. S. (2024). Exploring the impact of artificial intelligence on content creation: A comprehensive study. *International Journal of Research Publication and Reviews*, *5*(7), 597–604. DOI: 10.55248/gengpi.5.0724.1620

Purwanto, N., Pancaningrum, E., & Juwita, K. (2022). *Analysis of consumer behaviour in making decisions after the COVID-19 pandemic: perspectives on the theory of stimulus organism response (SOR)*. Kne Social Sciences., DOI: 10.18502/kss.v7i19.12425

Putri, A. A., Kywe, ChK., Temiralieva, M., Jabrayilzade, T., & Tick, A. (2023). The Utilization of Instagram as a Marketing Strategy for SME in Indonesia. *Austin J Bus Adm Manage.*, *7*(2), 1060.

Tarabieh, S., Gil-Pechuán, I., Salvador, J., & AlFraihat, S. (2024). The new game of online marketing: How social media influencers drive online repurchase intention through brand trust and customer brand engagement. *Intangible Capital, 20*(1), 103. DOI: 10.3926/ic.2515

Venkateswaran, P. S., Dominic, M. L., Agarwal, S., Oberai, H., Anand, I., & Rajest, S. S. (2023). *The role of artificial intelligence (AI) in enhancing marketing and customer loyalty. Data-driven intelligent business sustainability*. IGI Global Scientific Publishing., DOI: 10.4018/979-8-3693-0049-7.ch003

Venkateswaran, P. S., Manimaran, S., Sriramkumar, M., Reddi, L. T., Rangineni, S., & Marupaka, D. (2024). *Application of artificial intelligence to enhance business intelligence for increasing customer involvement in the FMCG industry. Cross-industry AI applications*. IGI Global Scientific Publishing., DOI: 10.4018/979-8-3693-5951-8.ch003

Venkateswaran, P. S., & Ngo, N. Q. N. (2025). *Quantitative analysis of AI-driven predictive analytics in digital marketing. Strategic blueprints for AI-driven marketing in the digital era*. IGI Global Scientific Publishing.

Vidrih, M., & Mayahi, S. (2023). Generative AI-driven storytelling: A new era for marketing. arXiv preprint. https://doi.org//arXiv.2309.09048DOI: 10.48550

Yella, S. (2024). AI-driven content creation and personalization: Revolutionizing digital marketing strategies. International Research Journal of Engineering and Technology (IRJET), 11(5), 1889–1893. https://www.irjet.net

Chapter 5
AI Innovations and Future Enterprises:
Exploring Trends, Opportunities, and Challenges Shaping Future Businesses Through Case Studies

Aliza
https://orcid.org/0000-0003-1087-7239
Banaras Hindu University, India

Abdullah
https://orcid.org/0000-0001-9487-2595
Indian Institute of Technology, Jodhpur, India

Muhammad Usman
https://orcid.org/0000-0003-1626-8477
University of Central Lancashire, UK

ABSTRACT

With the development of advanced technologies that are reshaping our future, businesses around the globe are encompassing technologies within their business frameworks. One of the technologies that is reframing business practices is artificial intelligence (AI). Presently, AI has become an integral part of enterprise operations by driving innovation and competitiveness. It has also revolutionised businesses by improving their decision-making and operations, which has a positive impact on their performance and customer experiences. The present study aims to examine AI's future in enterprises by outlining the various dimensions of AI adoption in modern enterprises. Alongside, case studies of successful AI models of three tech giants (Google, Amazon, and Meta) are provided to further facilitate a practical

DOI: 10.4018/979-8-3373-4506-2.ch005

understanding of the concepts that are underlying AI-driven enterprises. The study has managerial and practical implications, as it provides significant insights for the development and adoption of AI strategies for enterprises.

INTRODUCTION:

The advent of AI has ushered in a new era of business innovation. As AI evolves from a technological possibility to a practical tool, business enterprises are increasingly adopting AI-driven solutions for enhancing efficiency, driving growth, and maintaining competitiveness. Such transformation reflects agile business models that are not merely technological. As businesses embrace this future, there is a need to navigate a complex landscape of trends, opportunities, and challenges that accompany AI adoption in business enterprises. The ability of business organisations regarding the effective integration of AI into their core operations will ultimately determine their relevance and success in future generations of global commerce.

AI technologies are developing at a breakneck pace, which is drastically changing how businesses operate in various sectors. Global economies are undergoing a significant shift due to artificial intelligence (Lu, 2021). Artificial intelligence planning and application has steadily emerged as several businesses' primary differentiator in the development process (Li et al., 2021). Enterprises use AI for multiple reasons, such as increasing operational efficiency, generating more revenue, improving customer experiences, gaining a competitive edge, etc. In recent years, artificial intelligence (AI) has become incredibly popular as more businesses have recognised its potential to transform business practices through innovation (Jia & Wang, 2024). With the introduction of AI-powered solutions like machine learning algorithms, automation systems, natural language processing, etc., the decision-making process and business strategies are evolving. However, while adjusting to these changes, businesses need to deal with certain challenges along with the opportunities that AI brings to the enterprise. Further, since artificial intelligence (AI) technology is excellent at controlling and managing processes, its application in networking has improved performance and security (Dhingra et al., 2016). Algorithmic decision support, driven by AI fuelled by machine learning, is increasingly becoming an essential element in diverse processes across sectors (Raju et al., 2024).

Understanding the underlying potential of AI, Kulkarni et al. (2023) highlighted that future businesses will have to function in a dynamic, uncertain environment as a complex ecosystem (or system of systems) of socio-cyber-physical players, due to which they will have to keep meeting their objectives while adjusting to unanticipated changes in several areas, including customer demands, competition activity, legal requirements, regulatory frameworks, and technological advancements and obsolescence. However, there is a common concern about the performance and measurement of AI applications in the enterprise domain, despite variations in areas of interest and AI applications (Bourrasset et al., 2018). Recently, Lannon et al. (2024) studied the emergence of artificial intelligence (AI) as a significant opportunity for growth among family businesses, highlighting the need for future research to attain a clear picture of the next generation of family business successors.

AI is facilitating enterprise management through the advancement of decision-making, streamlining of operations, and driving of innovation. Enterprise management has experienced numerous changes in the digital era, and the emergence and quick growth of artificial intelligence technologies has increased its impact (Duan et al., 2019). The authors revealed the new trends and challenges of enterprise management in the context of this era and offered ideas for businesses to deal with this change by examining the effects of big data and artificial intelligence on enterprise decision-making, strategic planning, marketing, production processes, and human resource management. Kayyali (2024) aims to examine how enterprise management paradigms interact with the continuing management modernisation process in the context of artificial intelligence and suggests that to increase an organisation's competitiveness and adjust to shifting market needs, managers should aggressively investigate and implement artificial intelligence technologies and continuously update management models and practices. Artificial intelligence (AI) brings with it new organisational structures, methods of operation, optimisation niches, services, and alternative perspectives on customer interactions, which in turn create new business practices (Lahlali et al., 2021).

AI has a key role to play in service marketing. It is transforming service marketing by making consumer interaction more data-driven, individualised, and efficient. AI Innovation in Services Marketing stands out as a source of insight, unravelling the complexity surrounding the integration of AI in services marketing (Correia & Venciute, 2024). Artificial intelligence (AI) is revolutionising service marketing by enabling businesses to enhance customer engagement, personalise experiences, and optimise operations and allows marketers to tailor their strategies and offerings with precision; thus, this level of personalisation fosters stronger customer relationships and enhances loyalty (Vetrivel et al., 2024). Recently, Mari et al. (2024) explored how AI-enabled voice assistants (VAs) like Alexa can influence consumer shopping responses. It finds that AI empathy moderates the original structural model, bridging functional, relational, and social-emotional dimensions.

However, despite differences in areas of interest and AI applications, everyone has the same worry regarding the performance and measurement of AI applications in the enterprise domain (Enholm et al., 2022). AI accelerates innovation cycles by enabling faster prototyping, testing, and iteration. AI can simulate real-world scenarios, test hypotheses quickly, and analyse results in real time, accelerating product development and market entry. AI helps in attaining competitive differentiation based on user experiences. Additionally, AI opens entirely new avenues for revenue generation through subscription-based models and AI services like Microsoft Azure and Amazon Web Services. Organisations can foster a culture of innovation and reap first-mover advantages by early adoption of AI.

Despite the excessive literature acknowledging the transforming potential of AI across various enterprise functions, there is still a clear lack of empirical and integrative frameworks that can explain the systematic adoption and governance of AI across different phases that support organisational transformation. While the application and benefits of AI are highlighted in several studies, there is no consensus on holistic models or standardised metrics for measuring AI's value creation, its performance and its long-term impact on organisations. Further, there is limited empirical research to study the full lifecycle of AI adaptation, ranging from its early experimentation to its enterprise-wide integration. Moreover, there is insufficient theoretical integration that explains how user acceptance, innovation diffusion, and dynamic capabilities jointly influence the success of AI implementation. There is a lack of longitudinal research that is multi-industry case-based that examines how AI capabilities evolve over time and its influence on the sustained competitiveness of enterprises.

Figure 1. Conceptual framework for AI adoption

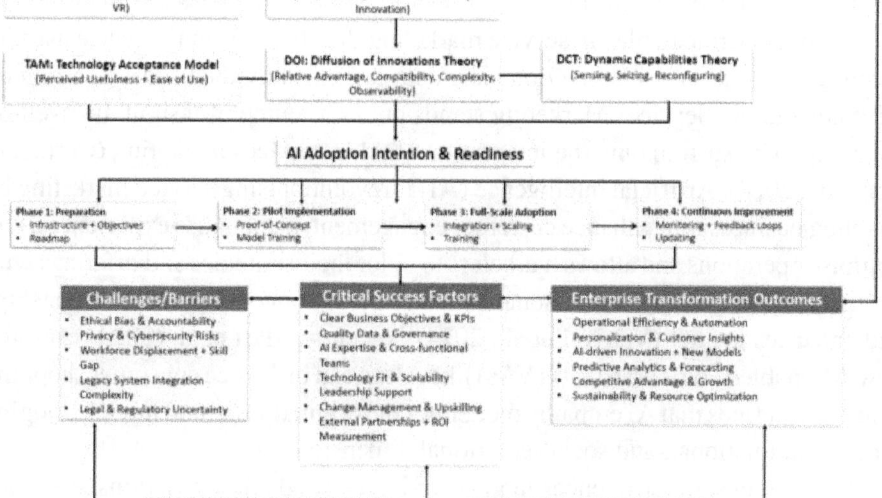

Figure 1 illustrates a conceptual framework that explains the process of enterprise AI adoption by integrating technology innovation, organisational readiness, and strategic implementation. AI innovations operate within an enterprise adoption context that emphasises competitiveness, efficiency, and innovation, supported by TAM, DOI, and DCT. These theoretical foundations shape AI adoption intention and readiness, which guide organisations through four phases: preparation, pilot implementation, full-scale adoption, and continuous improvement. Throughout this process, organisations face challenges related to ethics, privacy, skills, legacy systems, and regulation, which are addressed through critical success factors such as clear objectives, quality data, leadership support, and effective change management. Contextual factors, including language, infrastructure, regulations, and organisational culture, further influence adoption outcomes. When aligned effectively, these elements lead to enterprise transformation outcomes such as operational efficiency, AI-driven innovation, predictive analytics, and sustained competitive advantage. Empirical validation is supported through case study evidence from leading AI adopters such as Google's Gemini, Amazon's Alexa, and Meta AI.

The present study explores AI trends, possibilities, and challenges in future enterprises. In addition, the phases of AI adoption and implementation in AI-driven enterprises are also explored. Further, an analysis is made to determine the critical factors for successful AI implementation in enterprises. By examining real-world case studies, we can learn how successful businesses are becoming torchbearers in AI adoption and are mitigating the challenges that AI poses.

LITERATURE REVIEW:

The future of AI is poised to play a transformative role in the enterprise landscape. AI can revolutionise the process of business operations and value delivery. By automating tasks, AI frees up human resources for strategic and creative work, enhancing overall productivity. AI helps businesses stay agile in rapidly changing markets. AI is reshaping business scenarios in multiple ways, which are studied in previous literature. The use of AI in networking has enhanced performance and security because AI technology excels at regulating and managing tasks where humans fall short of preserving an organisation's important assets, including its financial, software, hardware, and intangible and tangible assets, which is the main goal of information security (Mishra, 2023).

With the introduction of intelligent and adaptive systems that enhance business agility and scalability, AI innovations are redefining enterprise architecture. With the advancement of AI technologies in enterprises, the field of enterprise architecture has also emerged, which is a well-known method of managing information systems following corporate objectives (Zdravković et al., 2021). Enterprise architecture is becoming more crucial in the current business environment for organisations to accomplish their objectives, and its future trends and subjects assist businesses in achieving their strategic objectives and facilitate rapid technological and business adaptation (Lankhorst, 2009). A related concept, i.e., scenario planning, has also gained popularity. It is a technique used by businesses to create their long-term plans. In their study, Sohrabi et al. (2018) demonstrate that using AI planning techniques to generate potential scenarios offers a distinct advantage for scenario planning. Recently, Bashir (2024) provided the Strategic Enterprise Artificial Intelligence (SEAI) conceptual hierarchical architecture, which has four levels: Disconnected Enterprise AI, Linked Enterprise AI, Strategist Enterprise AI, and Integrative Enterprise AI. From the early phases of adoption to the complete integration of AI across all organisational functions, the framework emphasises the significance of strategic alignment between AI projects and business objectives. The synergy between AI and enterprise architecture ensures that organisations can continuously innovate and maintain structural efficiency while aligning with their strategic goals.

Innovation in AI is radically altering the functioning of business. By utilising machine learning, natural language processing, and data-driven analytics, businesses may automate difficult tasks and obtain deeper insights for making more intelligent decisions. Sinha and Al Huraimel (2021), in their research, firmly believe that creating new AI businesses is the best way to realise AI's full potential; however, its real promise lies in facilitating the development of whole new business models that would be impossible without artificial intelligence. In a study, Abrokwah-Larbi and Awuku-Larbi (2023) found that the use of artificial intelligence in enterprise marketing can optimise the system and enhance the enterprise marketing effect. This is a crucial area for businesses in the modern era to thoroughly investigate. Guo and Wang (2021) examine the current state of big data management in businesses and examine how big data influences enterprise management decisions from five perspectives: environment, data, participants, organisation, and technology, and they suggest that to better adapt to the big data era, businesses must continuously work to enhance themselves. AI is becoming a crucial factor for strategic advantage and business transformation as it develops further.

AI innovation is revolutionising the manufacturing sector by introducing intelligent solutions that improve accuracy and productivity. Makridakis (2017) examines how Artificial Intelligence (AI) is revolutionising productivity and concluded that although AI has a lot of promise to increase productivity through automation, predictive analytics, and customised consumer experiences, there are drawbacks as well, including issues with workforce training, organisational adaptation, data privacy, and ethical application. Ethical AI concerns extend beyond fairness and transparency to include accountability, explainability, and the responsible allocation of decision authority between humans and algorithms. Akter (2024) argues how ethical AI can be integrated with corporate systems and the Internet of Things (IoT). The authors indicated that ongoing advancements in AI systems are necessary to ensure their scientific advancement while also taking societal and environmental concerns into account. Further, big data, AI, and the Internet of Things come together to offer a unique opportunity to address pressing sustainability issues. The manufacturing industry's technology options are extensive and complex as it considers growing levels of digitisation and automation in preparation for the modern competitive age (Hughes et al., 2022). With a focus on manufacturing companies, Zdarković et al. (2021) examined how symbolic and sub-symbolic AI contribute to various Enterprise Information Systems (EIS) functions, including supply chain management, inventory and logistics, customer relationship management and sales, finance and accounting, product lifecycle management, human resources, and production planning and scheduling. Further, Hansen and Bøgh (2021) provide a thorough survey and research on the prevalence of AI and the Internet of Things (IoT) among small and medium-sized manufacturing enterprises (SMEs) and suggest that SMEs should embrace knowledge-sharing strategies like open innovation and have an open mind about new business models.

Lahlali et al. (2021) conducted a study to implement an AI adoption model within the enterprise, known as the 2PS Model (Pilot, Project, and Scale), which offers the chance to capitalise on the adoption of AI by employing a comprehensive strategy. In addition, the authors discovered that disruptive technologies, machine learning (ML), robotic process automation (RPA), and artificial intelligence (AI) are crucial to corporate transformation and continue to hold enormous potential for developing new revenue streams and business models. An essential tool for improving organisational competitiveness, operational effectiveness, and decision-making is business analytics, which combines AI and ML to enable organisations to extract insightful information from data and support well-informed plans across enterprise systems (Jubi, 2023). Data-driven and AI-aided applications are crucial for intelligent transactions in finance, banking, and business, and these applications utilise powerful solutions, IoT technologies, AI-aided techniques, data analytics, and visualisation tools. However, implementing these solutions requires frameworks to support human control (Khang et al., 2024). As it develops further, AI is becoming a major force behind the development of Industry 4.0 and smart manufacturing.

AI innovation is accelerating enterprise automation by improving the intelligence, speed, and adaptability of business operations. In contrast to conventional automation, the AI-powered systems are able to make quicker and better decisions. Tschang and Almirall (2021) stated that enterprise automation is changing dramatically across several industrial sectors because of the integration of Artificial Intelligence (AI) technology. The authors emphasise the significance of an integrated approach to the implementation of AI in company management and manufacturing processes. Intelligent manufacturing, a concept within Industry 4.0, integrates smart sensors and controllers to increase competitiveness. Traditional firms are exploring AI approaches like machine learning and artificial intelligence to optimise scheduling, resource allocation, and production procedures. AI algorithms can analyse massive data volumes to identify bottlenecks and recommend fixes (Samblani & Bhatt, 2025). Additionally, AI is transforming the Web 3.0 Industrial Revolution by blending physical, digital, and biological boundaries. The digital technology interface, including AI, IoT, AR/VR, 3D printing, CPS, CC, and robotics, significantly impacts industrial performance. This transformative revolution aims to be a collaborative platform for academia and industry researchers, fostering knowledge exchange and redistributing wealth towards innovation and technology (Srivastav et al., 2024).

AI innovation supports business sustainability by enabling smarter resource management, reducing waste, and improving energy efficiency. Goralski (2020) examines the use of AI for businesses to achieve their sustainable development goals and boost economic efficiency and environmental sustainability. The findings of the study show that integrating technology into a company's operation enhances the production process, increases resource utilisation, and reduces environmental impact. Liu (2024) pointed out that businesses must implement optimisation techniques like intelligent decision-making systems and fortify the integration of external and internal data to enhance their core competitiveness and raise the calibre of managers. Antwi and Avickson (2024) examine the optimisation and automation of key business processes by using AI and ML algorithms on applications and processes in data processing systems. The study claimed that businesses must integrate AI and Systems, Applications, and Products (SAP) in Data Processing to attain operational excellence and attain a competitive edge in a changing landscape. Automation with AI results in more efficient procedures, lower costs for manual labour, higher-quality products, and increased competitiveness (Iakovlev et al., 2023). AI aids in developing eco-friendly products and processes that align with business goals and fulfil environmental and social responsibilities.

The integration of AI-driven technologies and Enterprise Resource Planning (ERP) systems is reshaping enterprise operations, making their processes more efficient and adaptive. When merged with AI, such systems become more powerful tools that can provide deeper insights, optimise workflows, and predict trends. The evolution of ERP persists, driven by advancements in AI and cloud computing (Katuu, 2020). Likewise, Varela et al. (2022) evaluate the upcoming advancements in ERP systems, including AI, cloud computing, and other customisation options. The study found that although such advancements have various uses for businesses, their successful deployment relies on careful planning and management. Yathiraju (2022) highlights that there are a lot of benefits for companies by combining AI with

ERP, including effective decision-making, enhanced competitiveness, and improved efficiency. However, such integration of AI and ERP requires meticulous preparation and teamwork so the firms can choose the best systems that guarantee accuracy and a higher quality of data to train and support staff while assessing and tracking the outcomes. Similarly, Kumar (2023) concluded that AI is useful for resource planning and has a great impact on the ERP system. Recently, Pokala (2024) conducted a system review to investigate AI's revolutionary relevance in modern ERP systems by synthesising recent results and breakthroughs from various domains. The findings show that businesses strategically integrate AI into ERP systems, focusing on commercial value creation and technological capabilities to stay competitive in a digital business environment. In contrast, Abd Elmonem et al. (2016) highlight the drawbacks of ERP, including integration issues, higher subscription fees, and loss of control, while mentioning some of its benefits, such as reduced operational costs, greater accessibility, and enhanced scalability. Kunduru (2023) concluded that with the development of automation, big data analytics, and customised user experiences, the contribution of AI in ERP systems will continue to expand in the future.

AI innovation has direct linkage with important theoretical frameworks like Diffusion of Innovation (DOI), Dynamic Capabilities Theory (DCT), and Technology Acceptance Model (TAM) as it provides the framework for understanding the role of AI in enhancing business operations. For instance, the TAM theory outlines that two key factors influencing user adoption of a particular information system and technology (IS/IT) are perceived utility and perceived ease of use, both of which have empirical backing (Chau, 1996). Frederick Davis proposed TAM in the 1980s, and Lee et al. (2003) highlighted that it was one of the most extensively used theoretical models in information systems. Also, the TAM perceives utility and ease of use functions as mediators in the relationship between system attributes (external variables) and the likelihood of system use (a measure of system success) (Legris et al., 2003). Later, King and He (2006) conducted a meta-analysis study of TAM across various sectors and concluded that it has been applied extensively and may have broader relevance. However, Wallace and Sheetz (2014) concluded that TAM can be used to assess and forecast technology acceptability, as it is not a descriptive model, indicating it cannot diagnose specific technological defects. Furthermore, Holden and Karsh (2010) examine the use of TAM in the healthcare industry and find that TAM predicts a significant amount of IT adoption or use in the industry; however, the theory needs further improvement. Chen et al. (2011) point out that TAM helps academics create user interfaces that are tailored to the needs of various online clients, leading to high user usage across various application domains. TAM has its roots in the psychological theories of reasoned action and planned behaviour and has developed into a crucial paradigm for comprehending what factors influence people's decisions to adopt or reject technology (Marangunić & Granić, 2015). In an attempt to clarify possible advancements in the technology acceptance model, Surendran (2012) recently came to the conclusion that TAM is a widely used paradigm for comprehending and elucidating user behaviour in information systems. Using the extended TAM, Aburbeian et al. (2022) examine several factors, namely self-efficiency, social norm, perceived curiosity, perceived pleasure, and price, that influence users' acceptance of metaverse technology and discovered that perceived ease of use is favourably influenced by self-efficiency, perceived interest, and perceived enjoyment.

Dynamic capabilities theory (DCT) offers a strategic perspective, emphasising the need for businesses to constantly reorganise internal capabilities in order to incorporate and capitalise on AI advancements in quickly changing markets. Teece et al. (1997) describe "dynamic capabilities" as "the firm's ability to integrate, build, and reconfigure internal and external competencies to address rapidly changing environments." Further, Eisenhardt and Martin (2000) investigated the resource-based view of the firm in general and dynamic capabilities in particular and found that the well-known organisational and strategic processes like product development and alliances are examples of dynamic capabilities, as their strategic worth comes from their capacity to direct resources into tactics that provide value. Therefore, dynamic capability is the mechanism that converts the resources and capabilities of the various levels into a competitive advantage rather than acting as an intermediate. Cavusgil et al. (2007) advocated that the dynamic capabilities (DC) perspective provides a modern understanding of how competitive advantage is maintained in changing marketplaces and that the resource-based view is the parent of the DC view. Later, Kuuluvainen (2012) presented a theoretical framework based on dynamic capabilities before conducting empirical testing of the concept. Based on the framework, it was suggested that the dynamic capabilities research programme should be refocused on the core strategic issue that businesses face (Shuen et al., 2014). Likewise, Teece (2014) developed a theoretical framework based on DC for multinational businesses to describe how dynamic capabilities and strategy work together to determine a firm's sustainable competitive advantage in global settings. Later, the author highlighted that a stronger basis for economic models of production and innovation might result from an awareness of dynamic capacities in general and the function of entrepreneurial managers in particular (Teece, 2016). Further, it was found that both the capabilities and systems frameworks embrace a comprehensive approach that demands that every component of an organisation be in harmony and acknowledge the significance of learning in some capacity for adaptation (Teece, 2018).

AI innovation closely aligns with the Theory of Diffusion of Innovations, which explains how new technologies spread within a society or organisation. As AI technologies emerge, their adoption follows the diffusion process, moving from early innovators and adopters to the majority and eventually laggards. DOI highlights variables that affect adoption rates, such as relative advantages, complexities, and observability. The theory of diffusion of innovations offers a framework for comprehending the social effects of concepts and technology resulting from these endeavours. For past years, the theory of diffusion of innovations has been used to describe how new concepts and methods spread in a wide range of contexts. Minishi-Majanja and Kiplang'at (2005) examine the suitability of the Diffusion of Innovations (DOI) Theory as a framework for elucidating elements of the adoption process of Information and Communication Technologies (ICT) innovations. Gouws and van Oudtshoorn (2011) aimed to connect the diffusion of innovations theory to contemporary ideas of product and service branding. Al-Jabri and Sohail (2012) looked at several factors influencing the uptake of mobile banking by using the Diffusion of Innovation as a baseline hypothesis and found that adoption is found to be positively impacted by observability, compatibility, and relative advantage. However, adoption is negatively impacted by perceived risk. Sundstrom (2016) lays the groundwork for applying diffusion of innovations theory to qualitative research. Dearing and Cox (2018) define dimensions of diffusion processes in the context of healthcare settings. Understanding this theory helps businesses and policymakers in designing strategies to accelerate AI adoption, overcome resistance, and maximise the transformative impact of AI across industries.

METHODOLOGY

The nature of this study is descriptive and qualitative. The secondary data employed in this study is derived from document analysis (research papers and websites). The analysis is further supported by three case studies of successful AI models of tech giants. A "case study" is a specific type of research design that focuses on performing a thorough analysis of one or a small number of cases (Tight, 2017). According to Cavaye (1996), a case study is a very flexible method that may be applied in a variety of ways. The author recommended its usage in circumstances when there is a lack of theoretical understanding of the phenomenon. Similarly, Baxter and Jack (2008) argued in earlier research that qualitative case studies are a useful method for studying complicated phenomena and that they are also an effective research methodology for formulating theories, assessing initiatives, and creating interventions. According to some studies, numerous case studies should be included in a single research study (Yin, 2012). Furthermore, Yin (2012) contends that replication, not logical reasoning, should be used in multiple-case research.

Trends and Possibilities of AI in Future Enterprises

With the rapid advancement in AI, its role in enterprise is evolving rapidly, which is discussed below:

1. **Automation and Efficiency:** AI is used for performing automated routine tasks related to customer service, data entry, supply chain management, etc. Robotic Process Automation (RPA), predictive maintenance in manufacturing, and AI-powered bots are used for handling repetitive tasks, making it possible for human resources to focus on strategic areas. Further, actionable insights in real-time for decision-making are provided by using AI to analyse vast datasets. AI helps businesses to optimise supply chains, detect bottlenecks, adjust logistics, etc., for greater cost savings and efficiency.
2. **Personalisation at Scale and Advanced Customer Insights:** AI is used by companies to analyse customer data and recommend tailored products and services based on individual preferences. Thus, companies leverage AI to create hyper-personalised experiences. Further, by helping the business to understand customers in a better way, AI provides insights for better target marketing strategies, product development, and customer satisfaction. AI algorithms are used for customer data analysis, marketing automation, and product recommendations based on sentiment analysis and behavioural analytics.
3. **AI-Driven Innovation:** AI acts as a catalyst for innovative products, services, and business models. For example, it is used to optimise energy consumption in manufacturing industries, power autonomous vehicles, help in the determination of precision medicine in the healthcare sector, etc.
4. **Human and AI Collaboration:** It is advocated that AI will augment human workers rather than replace them by improving decision-making and enhancing productivity. An AI-powered assistant helps higher-level task professionals with scheduling, data analysis, report generation, etc. Thus, AI helps in task augmentation and augmented decision-making.
5. **Predictive Analysis and Forecasting:** AI tools are used in fields like finance, retail, healthcare, etc., for analysing historical data and predicting future trends. With the improvement in AI, it is believed that its predictive accuracy will transform industries with better business forecasting and risk management.
6. **AI in Human Resources and Talent Management:** AI could play a significant role in recruitment by helping HR teams screen resumes, identifying talent gaps, and predicting future workforce needs based on business trends. Further, AI can assist in designing and tailoring programmes for the training and development of employees.

7. **Ethical AI and Governance:** Presently, businesses can seize the opportunity to lead the charge in developing an ethical AI framework that is transparent, unbiased, and accountable. With the growth in AI adoption, the ability to govern and ensure fairness in AI is becoming a key differentiator for businesses all over the world.
8. **AI in Creative Industries:** AI-generated art is becoming increasingly popular, and this trend will likely grow in various forms. Creative fields like designing and audio-based and video-based industries will increasingly rely on AI for generating content and providing recommendations. Further, AI is widely used in auto-generating graphics in the entertainment and gaming industries.

CHALLENGES OF USING AI IN FUTURE ENTERPRISES

The use of AI in enterprises poses certain challenges, which are discussed below:

1. **Ethical and Bias Concerns:** It is argued that AI systems can inadvertently perpetuate biases in the decision-making process. There is also an ethical question of using AI for decision-making that can directly affect people's lives (e.g., hiring, lending, or legal judgement), as using AI for such decisions lacks accountability.
2. **Data Privacy and Security Concerns:** Since AI systems rely on vast amounts of business and personal data, data breaches and misuse can cause serious financial and reputational damage to the enterprise. Thus, ensuring privacy and security will be paramount, and there is a need for stricter data regulations and norms. AI-driven enterprises must avoid heavy penalties by ensuring that their systems comply with privacy regulations.
3. **Workforce Displacement due to Skill Gap:** With growing automation in the workplace, there is concern regarding the displacement of workers. To cope with such challenges, businesses need to introduce new training programmes that focus on AI literacy for upskilling employees to handle new roles in the workplace.
4. **Integration with Legacy Systems:** For large organisations, integration of new AI systems with existing infrastructure and legacy systems can be quite complex and costly. Change management is required to ensure the smooth adoption and integration of new integrated systems.
5. **Legal and Regulatory Frameworks:** With the widespread use of AI, there is likely to be an increase in scrutiny and regulations. Also, the legal ramifications of AI decision-making (e.g., in healthcare, legal judgement, etc.) are still uncertain. Misalignment between AI system design and regional regulatory requirements

can create significant compliance risks, underscoring the need for adaptive governance structures and ongoing legal and ethical oversight. Governments and businesses are supposed to find ways to regulate AI and avoid its misuse without tempering the innovativeness of AI systems. Also, there is a need for a global standard for AI usage in enterprises.

AI's future in enterprise consists of a mix of challenges and opportunities. As AI becomes more embedded in enterprises, businesses will need to stay adaptable and should focus on ethical AI deployment. The key to successful AI implementation in enterprises lies in flexibility, cross-functional collaboration, and focus on ethical AI strategies.

CRITICAL FACTORS FOR SUCCESSFUL AI IMPLEMENTATION IN ENTERPRISES

Successful and smooth AI implementation in AI-driven enterprises relies on a variety of key factors to ensure that technology delivers value and addresses specific business challenges. Such key factors are discussed below:

1. **Clear Business Objectives:** AI should be seen as a tool to drive specific business outcomes. Thus, businesses need to have well-defined objectives or problem statements that AI can solve (e.g., optimising supply chain management, reducing production defectiveness, improving customer service response times, etc.). AI implementation should be aligned with strategic business goals, such as increasing efficiency, reducing costs, or enhancing customer experiences. Further, clear metrics such as KPIs (Key Performance Indicators) for coming up with measurable targets to guide AI implementation.
2. **Availability of Quality Data:** The functioning of the AI system relies on the accessibility, quality, and relevance of data. AI algorithms need a higher quality of data that is neither inconsistent nor biased for accurate decision-making. Additionally, it is necessary to integrate data from various departments or systems to provide a comprehensive view of business problems. Also, it is essential to ensure effective data governance for safeguarding sensitive data and complying with privacy regulations.
3. **AI Expertise:** The successful implementation of AI requires expertise in various disciplines due to it being a highly specialised area. To develop efficient AI models, data scientists must possess domain-specific knowledge, machine learning information, and the skill of statistical analysis. Usually, it is the re-

sponsibility of AI engineers and cross-functional teams to integrate AI solutions into an organisation's infrastructure.

4. **Appropriate AI Technology:** It is crucial to select appropriate AI technologies to ensure their successful implementation. The AI tools should be able to scale with the growing business and support real-time processing. The AI platforms should integrate easily with existing business systems (e.g., ERP or other enterprise software) to reduce the friction of incorporating AI into the workforce. Further, a choice should be made between cloud vs. on-premises AI models.
5. **Organisational Readiness and Change Management:** AI adoption requires significant shifts in the organisation's workforce and culture, which demands effective change management plans to educate the workforce and encourage collaborations to facilitate employee engagement and buy-ins. Businesses must invest in reskilling and upskilling their workforces.
6. **Strong Leadership and Vision:** AI should be part of a long-term business strategy and be driven by strong leadership support. Clear communication should be followed, and leaders must commit to AI adoption over the long term and allocate sufficient resources for its continuous improvement.
7. **Responsible Ethical AI:** Enterprises must regularly audit AI systems to ensure that AI algorithms are free from biases (e.g., race, gender, socio-economic, etc.) during decision-making. Furthermore, AI models need to be transparent so stakeholders can clearly understand the rationale behind decisions generated by AI. It must be responsible for safeguarding the data by implementing strict security measures to avoid breaches.
8. **Pilot Test and Iterative Improvements:** The successful implementation of AI involves iterating and piloting the technologies. The implementation of AI in a controlled setup allows enterprises to identify the challenges and measure its effectiveness. The AI models require continuous adoption and learning. Additionally, AI models could be refined by collecting feedback from stakeholders using feedback loops.
9. **Collaboration with External Partners:** It is beneficial for enterprises to collaborate with AI-specialised external collaborators or vendors during the implementation of AI. It will help the in-house expertise to overcome challenges by partnering with AI technology providers and consultants.
10. **ROI Measurement:** To determine the success, enterprises need to track the return on investment (ROI) of AI initiatives. Businesses require defined KPIs, including increased sales, reduced costs, improved conversion rates, and more to quantify the success of AI implementation and investigate the viability of their investment.

PHASES OF AI ADOPTION AND IMPLEMENTATION IN AI-DRIVEN ENTERPRISES

AI adoption and implementation is a multi-faceted process that requires enterprises to plan and execute. There are several steps involved in the AI adoption process:

1. **Preparation Phase:** The first phase involved in the AI adoption process is the preparation. During this phase, the enterprise assesses the readiness for AI adoption and lays the groundwork by establishing the necessary infrastructure. There are multiple dimensions to assess its readiness, including technology infrastructure, requisite skill sets, etc. Afterwards, enterprises set clear and measurable objectives for AI adoption to achieve the expected outcomes. Moreover, it includes the design of the roadmaps for AI adoption that usually involves defining the timeline and identifying necessary resources and investments.
2. **Pilot Implementation:** To test the application of AI, enterprises run a pilot project before they commit to full-scale adoption. The objective of pilot projects is to evaluate the efficiency of the AI technology, assess its impact, and identify challenges. The pilot AI project usually includes predictive maintenance, sales forecasting tools, and chatbots. During this phase, AI specialists develop and train machine learning models and evaluate their performance for accuracy, precision, and recall.
3. **Full-Scale AI Adoption:** After the successful completion of the pilot project, the enterprise proceeds to scale AI solutions for which enterprises ensure their processes, systems, and infrastructure could meet increased demand. The AI model needs to be integrated into core business processes, and feedback loops should be monitored for making necessary adjustments. Cross-functional collaboration becomes crucial at this phase to ensure AI is deployed effectively and AI models are aligned with organisational goals and user needs. Moreover, employees should be trained to use AI tools effectively within their roles.
4. **Continuous Improvement:** AI implementation is not a one-time event; rather, it is a continuous process that requires ongoing maintenance, updates, and improvements. To overcome the degradation of the machine learning model, ongoing training and A/B testing are required to ensure that models' or algorithms' efficiency and accuracy remain intact. Further, it is suggested that organisations should revisit their AI strategies regularly.

For AI adoption and implementation, it is essential to develop a comprehensive framework that can integrate AI technologies into business operations for maximising impact. The framework begins with defining AI strategy and linking it with business goals. Alongside, a clear AI roadmap is developed that can guide resource allocation for AI projects. Next, it is important to establish governance policies for data quality control. This step should be followed by identifying skill gaps and developing AI talent and skills. The AI-driven enterprise should ensure that it has the appropriate technological infrastructure to support AI models. With the right composition of AI culture and governance system, AI can be a transformative force in driving innovation, efficiency, and competitiveness.

CASE STUDIES OF SUCCESSFUL AI IMPLEMENTATION

An examination was made of the AI initiatives of three tech giants, i.e., Google, Amazon, and Meta, to showcase how these companies have leveraged AI for driving innovation and staying competitive by improving customer experiences.

Case Study 1: Google's Gemini

Overview: Introduced in 2023 by Google DeepMind, Gemini is a cutting-edge AI initiative of Google Inc. It is a next-generation AI model that focuses on integrating large language models (LLMs) into Google Search, Google Workspace, and other Google services.

Key Goals: Gemini uses state-of-the-art capabilities to help developers and enterprise customers scale with AI. Its key goals are to enhance the productivity tools with AI-powered assistance, such as writing, summarisation, translation, and scheduling recommendations. Further, it improves search results by making them more contextual and personalised.

Success Factors: Various factors contribute to the successful implementation of Gemini. Gemini is embedded into widely used Google tools like Gmail, Docs, Google Search, etc., which improves its visibility (in comparison to a standalone product) and enhances user experiences. Further, it uses sophisticated AI capabilities like natural language processing, content generation, real-time analysis, etc., to improve productivity and efficiency. For training the Gemini model, Google has access to a vast amount of data that improves its accuracy. Further, continuous improvement in its model is ensured by Google's AI research and development unit, DeepMind.

Performance & Outcomes: Google's Gemini assists in drafting and summarising in Google Workspace, which leads to productivity improvement of approximately 20-30% in knowledge-based tasks through reducing content creation and review time. It has also led to shorter query resolution cycles and enhanced user engagement that is possible via Gemini-driven contextual responses. By using Gemini, more contextual and personalised answers are provided for search results. Further, as a part of

AI-powered features in Google Workspace, it enhances productivity for businesses and individuals and makes content creation easier by automating repetitive tasks.

Cross-Cultural and Regional Adoption: In emerging economies, Gemini's adoption is shaped by internet infrastructure quality, language coverage and regulatory maturity. However, multilingual capabilities support broader accessibility. When compared to developed economy, its adoption speed is influenced by data localization norms and disparities in digital literacy.

Future Outlook: Google Gemini's future is set to accelerate as it is on the way to becoming a key intellect for Google's massive ecosystem. With the integration of deep multimodal capabilities and contextual awareness, Gemini is poised to lead the next wave of productivity AI. The company intends to develop Gemini into a real AI agent that is capable of completing commanded tasks and interacting with apps on behalf of its user. Further, Gemini 2 models are expected to dramatically enhance logic, memory, and language comprehension. In order to build user trust and meet regulatory requirements, Google is expected to make significant investments in AI safety and transparency. Gemini has successfully established a more proactive presence on Android; however, safeguarding user privacy, mitigating disinformation concerns, and staying ahead of OpenAI's rapidly growing capabilities will be a detrimental factor for its long-term success.

Case Study 2: Amazon's Alexa

Overview: Launched in 2014, Alexa is one of the most widely used AI-powered voice assistant services of Amazon Inc. It is a virtual assistant technology that is capable of natural language processing that is used to execute numerous voice-based instructions. Such tasks/instructions are performed by using automatic speech recognition, natural language processing, and other AI models.

Key Goals: Its primary goal is to improve the customer experience by making interactions more intuitive and seamless. Further, it creates a unified voice-controlled ecosystem that connects home devices, entertainment, and Amazon shopping. Via its voice interface, it enables third-party integrations with smart home systems.

Success Factors: Various factors contribute to the successful implementation of Alexa. It utilises cutting-edge natural language processing techniques that make its interaction natural. It continuously improves its speech recognition accuracy through deep learning algorithms. It is integrated with a wide range of Amazon products that makes it more valuable for customers. Third-party developers are allowed to create "skills" for enhancing Alexa's functionalities.

Performance & Outcomes: Enterprises that use Alexa for Business have noticed estimated time savings of 10-25% in their routine administrative functions that help in automating customer service and internal workflows. It has become the central hub for smart home automation. It has led to an increase in Amazon's overall ecosystem engagement in terms of repeated shopping and content consumption. It has helped businesses automate customer service and internal tasks through Alexa for Business.

Cross-Cultural and Regional Adoption: Significant variation is seen in Alexa's adoption that is caused by differences in language support, cultural attitudes towards voice interactions, and privacy norms. While its usage is high in developed economies like North America and Europe, its usability is limited in emerging economies due to considerations like device affordability, connectivity, and privacy and trust concerns in voice-based data collection.

Future Outlook: Alexa's future lies in its transition from a voice assistant to a cornerstone of ambient computing. With the advancement in generative AI, Alexa is predicted to become more context-aware, conversational, and capable of addressing complicated requests with more integration of large language models (LLMs) that can lead to shifts from scripted responses towards a more personalised engagement. Further, Amazon is working on enhancing Alexa functioning in enterprise settings with 'Alexa for Business', which acts as a productivity tool in offices and smart workspaces. Alex's reach will also expand through the company's agreement with third-party developers, automakers, and appliance manufacturers so that the assistant is being integrated into a variety of things ranging from cars to kitchen appliances. Further, rather than focusing exclusively on device sales, monetisation methods are projected to shift towards premium services, subscriptions, and smart home bundles. However, for sustaining user trust, Amazon is needed to address persistent concerns regarding privacy, data security, and voice commerce adoption.

Case Study 3: Meta AI

Overview: Launched in 2023, Meta AI is an initiative of Meta (formerly Facebook) that is aimed at improving its social media platforms (Facebook, Instagram, and WhatsApp) by enhancing advertising on these platforms and contributing to the development of the metaverse. Further, it provides voice assistance service to its user.

Key Goals: Its primary aim is to enhance user experience through AI-driven content recommendations and personalised social media experiences. Further, it drives innovation in the metaverse by integrating Augmented Reality (AR)/Virtual Reality (VR) experiences and virtual environments.

Success Factors: Various factors contribute to the successful implementation of Meta AI. It is an outcome of deep learning research that pushes Meta's AI innovation. The AI model used by Meta is used for content moderation (e.g., hate speech, misinformation, graphic violence, etc.) across its platforms.

Performance & Outcomes: Usage of Meta AI has led to an increase in user engagement and advertising efficiency by improving click-through rates. Further, automated content moderation has reduced review cycle times and operational costs. It improves the engagement of social media platforms since it offers personalised advertisement, content, and product recommendations. Also, it has been updating constantly to provide a safer social environment. Lastly, it adapts content moderation techniques and recommendations in real time.

Cross-Cultural and Regional Adoption: Deployment of Meta AI differs across the globe due to variation in cultural norms, privacy and trust concerns, regulatory frameworks, and content moderation standards. In emerging economies, challenges still remain in local language coverage and contextual accuracy.

Future Outlook: Meta AI revolves around the deep integration of AI into everyday digital and physical interactions. Meta is emerging as a prominent force in democratising powerful language models with the widespread use of its open-source Llama models. The Meta AI assistant is projected to mature into a proactive and multimodal agent that is capable of context-aware actions, visual comprehension, and seamless integration across apps, wearables, and spatial computing environments. With the expansion in smart glasses and metaverse platforms, it is expected that Meta AI will provide enhanced personalised and interactive experiences that blur the distinction between digital and physical reality. Meta AI has the potential to transform social engagement and productivity on both 2D screens and immersive 3D environments. However, its long-term success is dependent on balancing AI advancement with user privacy, ethical content creation, and meaningful monetisation techniques.

Table 1. Summary of comparative case studies

Aspects	Google Gemini	Amazon Alexa	Meta AI
Description	Revolutionizing search and AI-assisted workflows	AI-powered voice assistant revolution	Innovating with vision, NPL, and AR technologies
Primary Use Case	Enhanced search and productivity tools	Powers voice-driven interactions in smart homes and shopping	Enhances social media, AR/VR and content moderation
AI Focus	Natural language processing	Speech recognition, voice interaction	Personalization, content moderation, AR/VR
Technology Integration	Integrated with Google Services	Embedded into Echo and other Amazon devices	Integrated into Facebook, Instagram and WhatsApp
User Interaction	Text-based	Voice-Based	Text and Visual
Consumer Focus	Primarily enterprise and search-driven user	Primarily consumer-focused (smart home, shopping)	Primarily consumer-focused (social media, AR, VR)
Ecosystem	Google Products (Docs, Gmail, search)	Amazon's smart home ecosystem (Alexa, Echo)	Meta platforms (Facebook, Instagram, WhatsApp)

continued on following page

Table 1. Continued

Aspects	Google Gemini	Amazon Alexa	Meta AI
Qualitative Impact	Productivity gain in knowledge work	Time saving in routine tasks	Improved ad efficiency and reduced moderation costs
Governance Focus	Explainable AI (XAI), model safety, human-in-the-loop	Privacy-by-design, consent management	Algorithm auditing, human oversight
Adoption Variation Cause	Digital infrastructure and regulation	Language and Privacy norms	Regulatory and cultural moderation standards

These case studies demonstrated how, despite adopting different approaches towards AI adoption, Google, Amazon, and Meta are successful in shaping their business models based on customer needs and technology focuses. These tech giants have successfully embedded AI within their products and ecosystems, enabling significant user engagement, personalisation, and improvement in efficiency.

DISCUSSIONS:

AI holds immense potential in the future for enterprises, but there is a need to carefully evaluate its challenges, opportunities, and trends. Generative AI adoption is in its early stages, with organisations exploring its benefits through function-based research and innovation (Dencik et al., 2023). The successful adoption of AI requires strategic planning, expertise development, and ethical considerations. A successful AI-orientated system is one that uses the least amount of energy and provides a given accuracy in the shortest amount of time (Bourrasset et al., 2018). Recently, Sharma et al. (2021) highlighted that an efficient AI-orientated system uses the least amount of energy and improves accuracy in the shortest amount of time. To improve the decision-making process and increase efficiency, AI can spur innovation that helps companies to shift market conditions quickly (Li, 2024). Regarding AI, Kumar et al. (2023) pointed out that it is important to understand the concept of AI and its usage in commercial applications since it is so vast and complex. AI planning and application have emerged steadily as various enterprises' primary differentiator in the development process (Lu, 2019). Hence, there is a need to take AI integration techniques like deep learning and reinforcement learning, as they may spur more effectiveness and creativity (Bauskar, 2022). Automation with AI results in more efficient procedures, lower costs for manual labour, higher-quality products, and increased competitiveness (Dash et al., 2019). The continuous improvements in AI systems are required to guarantee their scientific progress while also taking societal and environmental issues into consideration. Additionally, the convergence of big data, artificial intelligence, and the Internet of Things presents a potential scope to tackle urgent sustainability concerns (Abdulqader et al., 2024). The successful implementation of AI in management and production processes will not only allow an increase in the productivity of enterprises but also contribute to the achievement of the goals of sustainable development, which, in turn, will strengthen the domestic market and the global competitiveness of the economy (Kinkel et al., 2022). Recently, Puri (2024) looks at how AI is transforming productivity and comes to the conclusion that while AI has a lot of potential to boost productivity through automation, predictive analytics, and personalised customer experiences, there are also disadvantages, such as problems with employee training, organisational adaptation, data privacy, and ethical use. In addition to ethical and regulatory concerns, AI implementation carries material failure risks that are often underestimated in opportunity-centric narratives. Technical risks such as model drift, biased training data, and hallucinations in generative AI systems can degrade performance over time and lead to erroneous or misleading outputs.

The complex and ever-changing needs of modern enterprises are becoming too much for traditional corporate management techniques to handle due to enterprise management models that incorporate AI having become a strong substitute for traditional techniques (Wang, 2023). However, to incorporate AI in a modern enterprise system, businesses must concentrate on creating an innovative and collaborative outlook. Businesses must have the necessary resources and capabilities to implement artificial intelligence systems to stay agile (Li, 2024). It is important to remember that businesses should improve the education and training of pertinent employees when implementing AI technologies (Du & Xie, 2021). Furthermore, ethical issues about data privacy, security, and fairness will become increasingly important as AI and business analytics are used more frequently. Future research should concentrate on creating ethical frameworks for responsible AI use (Tripathi & Kumar, 2025). Governments and society should simultaneously encourage the healthy growth of AI and the use of its social value, as well as tighten regulations and guidelines for its advancement (Wang, 2023).

The present study advances understanding of the AI success factors for enterprises. It has practical implications for businesses for enhancing their AI adoption strategies and their implementation. Further, the study shall help policymakers in developing supportive regulations that facilitate AI-driven enterprises. The study holds theoretical implications for researchers and academia, as it helps in advancing the area of Enterprise AI. Future studies should focus on developing a more sophisticated model of AI and exploring how AI continues to shape enterprise strategies in a dynamic business environment.

CONCLUSION:

AI acts as an enabler and transformative force for revolutionising business models, optimising operations, and uncovering new opportunities for value creation. Enterprises can leverage AI to drive innovation, efficiency, and growth. AI fuels innovations that cater to changing customer needs and market trends. It helps in personalised offerings that offer enhanced functionality. AI helps in industry transformation by enabling disruptive business models that reshape existing markets. AI-powered automation systems can help in cost reduction and less reliance on human labour. AI enables companies to model different business scenarios and access potential outcomes before final decision-making. Further, AI helps manufacturing enterprises to continuously optimise their internal operations via predictive maintenance and energy optimisation. With the use of AI-powered marketing campaigns, AI helps in scaling operations and facilitates market expansion and target marketing. However, before full implementation of AI strategies in enterprises, it is feasible to run proof-of-concept trials to test AI's viability before rolling it out on a larger scale.

REFERENCES

Abd Elmonem, M. A., Nasr, E. S., & Geith, M. H. (2016). Benefits and challenges of cloud ERP systems–A systematic literature review. *Future Computing and Informatics Journal, 1*(1–2), 1–9. DOI: 10.1016/j.fcij.2017.03.003

Abdulqader, Z., Abdulqader, D. M., Ahmed, O. M., Ismael, H. R., Ahmed, S. H., & Haji, L. (2024). A responsible AI development for sustainable enterprises: A review of integrating ethical AI with IoT and enterprise systems. *Journal of Information Technology and Informatics, 3*(2), 129–156.

Abrokwah-Larbi, K., & Awuku-Larbi, Y. (2023). The impact of artificial intelligence in marketing on the performance of business organizations: Evidence from SMEs in an emerging economy. *Journal of Entrepreneurship in Emerging Economies, 16*(4), 1090–1117. DOI: 10.1108/JEEE-07-2022-0207

Aburbeian, A. H. M., Owda, A. Y., & Owda, M. (2022). A Technology Acceptance Model Survey of the Metaverse Prospects. *AI, 3*(2), 285–302. DOI: 10.3390/ai3020018

Akter, S. (2024). Ethical AI development for sustainable enterprises: A review of integrating responsible AI with IoT and enterprise systems. *Journal of Artificial Intelligence General science (JAIGS), 6*(1), 94–125.

Al-Jabri, I., & Sohail, M. S. (2012). Mobile banking adoption: Application of diffusion of innovation theory. *Journal of Electronic Commerce Research, 13*(4), 379–391.

Antwi, B. O., & Avickson, E. K. (2024). Integrating SAP, AI, and Data Analytics for Advanced Enterprise Management. *International Journal of Research Publication and Reviews, 5*(10), 621–636. DOI: 10.55248/gengpi.5.1024.2722

Bashir, J. (2024). Strategic Enterprise Artificial Intelligence (The Conceptual Hierarchical Framework). *International Journal of Business & Management Studies, 05*(05), 131–138. DOI: 10.56734/ijbms.v5n5a13

Bauskar, S. (2022). Business analytics in enterprise system based on application of artificial intelligence. *International Research Journal of Modernization in Engineering Technology and Science, 4*(1), 1861–1870.

Baxter, P., & Jack, S. (2008). Qualitative case study methodology: Study design and implementation for novice researchers. *The Qualitative Report, 13*(4), 544–559.

Bourrasset, C., Boillod-Cerneux, F., Sauge, L., Deldossi, M., Wellenreiter, F., Bordawekar, R., & Belgodere, B. (2018, August). Requirements for an enterprise AI benchmark. In *Technology Conference on Performance Evaluation and Benchmarking* (pp. 71–81). Cham: Springer International Publishing. https://doi.org/DOI: 10.1007/978-3-030-11404-6_6

Cavaye, A. L. (1996). Case study research: A multi-faceted research approach for IS. *Information Systems Journal*, *6*(3), 227–242. DOI: 10.1111/j.1365-2575.1996.tb00015.x

Cavusgil, E., Seggie, S. H., & Talay, M. B. (2007). Dynamic capabilities view: Foundations and research agenda. *Journal of Marketing Theory and Practice*, *15*(2), 159–166. DOI: 10.2753/MTP1069-6679150205

Chau, P. Y. K. (1996). An empirical assessment of a modified technology acceptance model. *Journal of Management Information Systems*, *13*(2), 185–204. DOI: 10.1080/07421222.1996.11518128

Chen, S. C., Shing-Han, L., & Chien-Yi, L. (2011). Recent related research in technology acceptance model: A literature review. *Australian Journal of Business and Management Research*, *1*(9), 124–127. DOI: 10.52283/NSWRCA.AJBMR.20110109A14

Correia, R., & Venciute, D. (Eds.). (2024). *AI innovation in services marketing*. IGI Global. DOI: 10.4018/979-8-3693-2153-9

Dash, R., McMurtrey, M., Rebman, C., & Kar, U. K. (2019). Application of artificial intelligence in automation of supply chain management. *Journal of Strategic Innovation and Sustainability*, *14*(3), 43–53.

Dearing, J. W., & Cox, J. G. (2018). Diffusion of innovations theory, principles, and practice. *Health Affairs (Project Hope)*, *37*(2), 183–190. DOI: 10.1377/hlthaff.2017.1104

Dencik, J., Goehring, B., & Marshall, A. (2023). Managing the emerging role of generative AI in next-generation business. *Strategy and Leadership*, *51*(6), 30–36. DOI: 10.1108/SL-08-2023-0079

Dhingra, M., Jain, M., & Jadon, R. S. (2016, December). Role of artificial intelligence in enterprise information security: a review. In *2016 fourth international conference on parallel, distributed and grid computing (PDGC)* (pp. 188–191). IEEE. DOI: 10.1109/PDGC.2016.7913142

Du, S., & Xie, C. (2021). Paradoxes of artificial intelligence in consumer markets: Ethical challenges and opportunities. *Journal of Business Research*, *129*, 961–974. DOI: 10.1016/j.jbusres.2020.08.024

Duan, Y., Edwards, J. S., & Dwivedi, Y. K. (2019). Artificial intelligence for decision making in the era of Big Data–evolution, challenges and research agenda. *International Journal of Information Management*, *48*, 63–71. DOI: 10.1016/j.ijinfomgt.2019.01.021

Eisenhardt, K. M., & Martin, J. A. (2000). Dynamic capabilities: What are they? *Strategic Management Journal*, *21*(10-11), 1105–1121. DOI: 10.1002/1097-0266(200010/11)21:10/11<1105::AID-SMJ133>3.0.CO;2-E

Enholm, I. M., Papagiannidis, E., Mikalef, P., & Krogstie, J. (2022). Artificial intelligence and business value: A literature review. *Information Systems Frontiers*, *24*(5), 1709–1734. DOI: 10.1007/s10796-021-10186-w

Goralski, M. A., & Tan, T. K. (2020). Artificial intelligence and sustainable development. *International Journal of Management Education*, *18*(1), 100330. DOI: 10.1016/j.ijme.2019.100330

Gouws, T., & van Rheede van Oudtshoorn, G. P. (2011). Correlation between brand longevity and the diffusion of innovations theory. *Journal of Public Affairs*, *11*(4), 236–242. DOI: 10.1002/pa.416

Guo, J., & Wang, D. (2021). An empirical study on artificial intelligence technology based on big data to assist enterprise management decision. *International Journal of Electrical Engineering Education*, 0020720920983547. Advance online publication. DOI: 10.1177/0020720920983547

Hansen, E. B., & Bøgh, S. (2021). Artificial intelligence and internet of things in small and medium-sized enterprises: A survey. *Journal of Manufacturing Systems*, *58*, 362–372. DOI: 10.1016/j.jmsy.2020.08.009

Holden, R. J., & Karsh, B. T. (2010). The technology acceptance model: Its past and its future in health care. *Journal of Biomedical Informatics*, *43*(1), 159–172. DOI: 10.1016/j.jbi.2009.07.002

Hughes, L., Dwivedi, Y. K., Rana, N. P., Williams, M. D., & Raghavan, V. (2022). Perspectives on the future of manufacturing within the Industry 4.0 era. *Production Planning and Control*, *33*(2–3), 138–158. DOI: 10.1080/09537287.2020.1810762

Iakovlev, I., Kremleva, E., & Guzanov, R. (2023). Enterprise automation using artificial intelligence: Methods, technologies and prospects. In *E3S Web of Conferences* (Vol. 460, p. 04007). EDP Sciences., DOI: 10.1051/e3sconf/202346004007

Jia, Y., & Wang, Z. (2024). Application of artificial intelligence based on the fuzzy control algorithm in enterprise innovation. *Heliyon*, *10*(6), e28116. Advance online publication. DOI: 10.1016/j.heliyon.2024.e28116

Jubi, R. (2023). *Business Analytics-Unleashing Data Driven Decision Making.* NEHAS PUBLICATIONS.

Katuu, S. (2020). Enterprise resource planning: Past, present, and future. *New Review of Information Networking, 25*(1), 37–46. DOI: 10.1080/13614576.2020.1742770

Kayyali, M. (2024). *Building Organizational Capacity and Strategic Management in Academia.* IGI Global. DOI: 10.4018/979-8-3693-6967-8

Khang, A., Gujrati, R., Uygun, H., Tailor, R. K., & Gaur, S. (Eds.). (2024). *Data-driven modelling and predictive analytics in business and finance: concepts, designs, technologies, and applications.* CRC Press. DOI: 10.1201/9781032618845

King, W. R., & He, J. (2006). A meta-analysis of the technology acceptance model. *Information & Management, 43*(6), 740–755. DOI: 10.1016/j.im.2006.05.003

Kinkel, S., Baumgartner, M., & Cherubini, E. (2022). Prerequisites for the adoption of AI technologies in manufacturing–Evidence from a worldwide sample of manufacturing companies. *Technovation, 110*, 102375. DOI: 10.1016/j.technovation.2021.102375

Kulkarni, V., Reddy, S., Clark, T., & Proper, H. (2023). The AI-enabled enterprise. In *The AI-Enabled Enterprise* (pp. 1–12). Springer International Publishing. DOI: 10.1007/978-3-031-29053-4_1

Kumar, G. (2023). Evolution of enterprise applications through emerging technologies. *Universal Journal of Computer Sciences and Communications*, *2*(1), 1–8. DOI: 10.31586/ujcsc.2023.828

Kumar, P., Dwivedi, Y. K., & Anand, A. (2023). Responsible artificial intelligence (AI) for value formation and market performance in healthcare: The mediating role of patient's cognitive engagement. *Information Systems Frontiers, 25*(6), 2197–2220. DOI: 10.1007/s10796-021-10136-6

Kunduru, A. R. (2023). Effective usage of artificial intelligence in enterprise resource planning applications. *International Journal of Computer Trends and Technology, 71*(4), 73–80. DOI: 10.14445/22312803/IJCTT-V71I4P109

Kuuluvainen, A. (2012). How to concretize dynamic capabilities? Theory and examples. *Journal of Strategy and Management, 5*(4), 381–392. DOI: 10.1108/17554251211276353

Lahlali, M., Berbiche, N., & El Alami, J. (2021). How Enterprise must be Prepared to be "AI First"? *International Journal of Advanced Computer Science and Applications, 12*(5). Advance online publication. DOI: 10.14569/IJACSA.2021.0120542

Lankhorst, M. (2009). *Enterprise architecture at work* (Vol. 352). Springer. DOI: 10.1007/978-3-642-01310-2

Lannon, F., Lyons, R., & O'Connor, C. (2024). Generation AI and family business: A perspective article. *Journal of Family Business Management, 14*(3), 470–474. DOI: 10.1108/JFBM-07-2023-0116

Lee, Y., Kozar, K. A., & Larsen, K. R. T. (2003). The Technology acceptance model: Past, present, and future. *Communications of the Association for Information Systems, 12*. Advance online publication. DOI: 10.17705/1CAIS.01250

Legris, P., Ingham, J., & Collerette, P. (2003). Why do people use information technology? A critical review of the technology acceptance model. *Information & Management, 40*(3), 191–204. DOI: 10.1016/S0378-7206(01)00143-4

Li, J. (2024). The past, present and future of enterprise resource planning. *Journal of Enterprise and Business Intelligence*, 32–41. https://doi.org/DOI: 10.53759/5181/JEBI202404004

Li, R., Cao, Z., Ye, H., & Yue, X. (2021, April). Application and development trend of artificial intelligence in enterprise marketing. In *Journal of Physics: Conference Series* (Vol. 1881, No. 2, p. 022032). IOP Publishing. https://doi.org/DOI: 10.1088/1742-6596/1881/2/022032

Liu, C. (2024). Research on the influence of artificial intelligence on enterprise management decision-making. *Academic Journal of Business & Management, 6*(1), 108–112.

Lu, C. H. (2021). The impact of artificial intelligence on economic growth and welfare. *Journal of Macroeconomics, 69*, 103342. DOI: 10.1016/j.jmacro.2021.103342

Lu, Y. (2019). Artificial intelligence: A survey on evolution, models, applications and future trends. *Journal of Management Analytics, 6*(1), 1–29. DOI: 10.1080/23270012.2019.1570365

Makridakis, S. (2017). The forthcoming Artificial Intelligence (AI) revolution: Its impact on society and firms. *Futures, 90*, 46–60. DOI: 10.1016/j.futures.2017.03.006

Marangunić, N., & Granić, A. (2015). Technology acceptance model: A literature review from 1986 to 2013. *Universal Access in the Information Society, 14*(1), 81–95. DOI: 10.1007/s10209-014-0348-1

Mari, A., Mandelli, A., & Algesheimer, R. (2024). Empathic voice assistants: Enhancing consumer responses in voice commerce. *Journal of Business Research, 175*, 114566. DOI: 10.1016/j.jbusres.2024.114566

Minishi-Majanja, M. K., & Kiplang'at, J. (2005). The diffusion of innovations theory as a theoretical framework in library and information science research. *South African Journal of Library and Information Science, 71*(3), 211–224.

Mishra, S. (2023). Exploring the impact of AI-based cyber security financial sector management. *Applied Sciences (Basel, Switzerland), 13*(10), 5875. DOI: 10.3390/app13105875

Pokala, P. (2024). Artificial intelligence in enterprise resource planning: A systematic review of innovations, applications, and future directions. [IJRCAIT]. *International Journal of Research in Computer Applications and Information Technology, 7*(2), 1276–1289. DOI: 10.5281/zenodo.14170247

Puri, V. (2024). The future of productivity in the era of artificial intelligence: An enterprise engineering perspective. *International Journal of Innovative Research in Science, Engineering and Technology, 13*(7), 12685–12692. DOI: 10.15680/IJIRSET.2024.1307011

Raju, P., Arun, R., Turlapati, V. R., Veeran, L., & Rajesh, S. (2024). Next-Generation Management on Exploring AI-Driven Decision Support in Business. In *Optimizing Intelligent Systems for Cross-Industry Application* (pp. 61–78). IGI Global. DOI: 10.4018/979-8-3693-8659-0.ch004

Samblani, G., & Bhatt, D. P. (2025). Case Studies of Next Generation AI for Intelligent Manufacturing. In *Intelligent Manufacturing and Industry 4.0* (pp. 217–236). CRC Press.

Sharma, A., Podoplelova, E., Shapovalov, G., Tselykh, A., & Tselykh, A. (2021). Sustainable smart cities: Convergence of artificial intelligence and blockchain. *Sustainability (Basel), 13*(23), 13076. DOI: 10.3390/su132313076

Shuen, A., Feiler, P. F., & Teece, D. J. (2014). Dynamic capabilities in the upstream oil and gas sector: Managing next generation competition. *Energy Strategy Reviews, 3*, 5–13. DOI: 10.1016/j.esr.2014.05.002

Sinha, S., & Al Huraimel, K. (2021). *Reimagining businesses with AI.* John Wiley & Sons.

Sohrabi, S., Riabov, A., Katz, M., & Udrea, O. (2018). An AI planning solution to scenario generation for enterprise risk management. *Proceedings of the AAAI Conference on Artificial Intelligence, 32*(1). Advance online publication. DOI: 10.1609/aaai.v32i1.11304

Srivastav, P. K., Singhal, P., Roohani, B. S., & Sharma, N. (Eds.). (2024). *Web 3.0: The Next Generation's Internet and Understanding the Concept of the Metaverse*. CRC Press. DOI: 10.1201/9781003461418

Sundstrom, B. (2016). Mothers "Google It Up:" Extending communication channel behavior in diffusion of innovations theory. *Health Communication*, *31*(1), 91–101. DOI: 10.1080/10410236.2014.936339

Surendran, P. (2012). Technology acceptance model: A survey of literature. *International Journal of Business and Social Research*, *2*(4), 175–178.

Teece, D. J. (2014). A dynamic capabilities-based entrepreneurial theory of the multinational enterprise. *Journal of International Business Studies*, *45*(1), 8–37. DOI: 10.1057/jibs.2013.54

Teece, D. J. (2016). Dynamic capabilities and entrepreneurial management in large organizations: Toward a theory of the (entrepreneurial) firm. *European Economic Review*, *86*, 202–216. DOI: 10.1016/j.euroecorev.2015.11.006

Teece, D. J. (2018). Dynamic capabilities as (workable) management systems theory. *Journal of Management & Organization*, *24*(3), 359–368. DOI: 10.1017/jmo.2017.75

Teece, D. J., Pisano, G., & Shuen, A. (1997). Dynamic capabilities and strategic management. *Strategic Management Journal*, *18*(7), 509–533. DOI: 10.1002/(SICI)1097-0266(199708)18:7<509::AID-SMJ882>3.0.CO;2-Z

Tight, M. (2017). Understanding case study research: Small-scale research with meaning. *Sage (Atlanta, Ga.)*. Advance online publication. DOI: 10.4135/9781473920118

Tripathi, A., & Kumar, V. (2025). Ethical practices of artificial intelligence: A management framework for responsible AI deployment in businesses. *AI and Ethics*, *5*(4), 1–12. DOI: 10.1007/s43681-025-00670-3

Tschang, F. T., & Almirall, E. (2021). Artificial intelligence as augmenting automation: Implications for employment. *The Academy of Management Perspectives*, *35*(4), 642–659. DOI: 10.5465/amp.2019.0062

Varela, L., Putnik, G., & Romero, F. (2022). The concept of collaborative engineering: A systematic literature review. *Production & Manufacturing Research*, *10*(1), 784–839. DOI: 10.1080/21693277.2022.2133856

Vetrivel, S. C., Arun, V. P., Saravanan, T. P., & Maheswari, R. (2024). Harnessing AI for Next-Generation Service Marketing. In *Integrating AI-Driven Technologies into Service Marketing* (pp. 265–298). IGI Global. DOI: 10.4018/979-8-3693-7122-0.ch015

Wallace, L. G., & Sheetz, S. D. (2014). The adoption of software measures: A technology acceptance model (TAM) perspective. *Information & Management*, *51*(2), 249–259. DOI: 10.1016/j.im.2013.12.003

Wang, Y. (2023). Research on the relationship between enterprise management mode and enterprise management modernization under the background of artificial intelligence. *Academic Journal of Business & Management*, *5*(15), 53–57.

Yathiraju, N. (2022). Investigating the use of an artificial intelligence model in an ERP cloud-based system. *International Journal of Electrical. Electronics and Computers*, *7*(2), 1–26.

Yin, R. K. (2012). *Applications of Case Study Research* (3rd ed.).

Zdravković, M., Panetto, H., & Weichhart, G. (2022). AI-enabled enterprise information systems for manufacturing. *Enterprise Information Systems*, *16*(4), 668–720. DOI: 10.1080/17517575.2021.1941275

Chapter 6
Pixels and Perceptions:
Leveraging Generative AI for Real-Time Brand Equity Measurement

Rohit Yadav
https://orcid.org/0000-0002-7573-8005
IILM University, Greater Noida, India

ABSTRACT

Brand equity ceases to exist as a fixed entity but as a dynamic and perceptual process which is influenced by visual interactions in real time. This chapter will discuss how generative AI, with the help of such devices as GANs, diffusion models, and computer vision, can be used to analyze brand sentiment in real-time via user-made images. This method combines emotion recognition, social media monitoring, and latent space modeling in order to capture brand perception by geography, culture, and time. In contrast to the traditional survey-based approach, the proposed AI-powered model will provide an in-depth understanding of how visuals influence brand associations, and emotional resonance. The chapter also covers ethical issues of automation and provides a framework of a hybrid human-AI solution to transparent and culturally aware brand analytics. Such an interdisciplinary synthesis will act as a strategic framework in which marketers, artificial intelligence coders, and scientists can gauge and manipulate brand equity in the visual digital age ethically.

DOI: 10.4018/979-8-3373-4506-2.ch006

1. INTRODUCTION: VISUAL CULTURE AND THE EVOLUTION OF BRAND EQUITY

1.1 The Rise of the Visual Brandscape

→ In the contemporary digital economy, brand equity is increasingly shaped not through text or traditional media, but through images, memes, videos, and visual cues embedded in the everyday media consumption of users. The visual turn in consumer culture, amplified by the rise of platforms like Instagram, TikTok, and Pinterest, has made visual storytelling central to brand identity and value creation. Brands are no longer static assets but dynamic signifiers in continuous interaction with consumer communities through imagery, aesthetics, and symbolism (Schroeder, 2002).

While visual culture has always played a role in branding from logos and packaging to print advertisements the acceleration of visual dominance in the digital era stems from the platform design itself. Algorithms on TikTok, Instagram Reels, and YouTube Shorts prioritize visual novelty and emotional resonance, making image-based storytelling a prerequisite for virality. Even textual platforms like X (formerly Twitter) now prioritize visual cards and infographics in engagement ranking. A 2023 Nielsen study reported that visual content drives 70% more recall than text-only posts, underscoring the shift in consumer cognition. In such an environment, visual grammar composition, lighting, symbolism has become the new language of brand trust and identity. Marketers are now hiring "visual linguists" and semioticians alongside designers to interpret how images communicate meaning within cultural contexts.

1.2 Limits of Traditional Equity Metrics

→ Historically, brand equity, defined as the differential effect of brand knowledge on consumer response (Keller, 1993), was measured through consumer surveys, recall tests, and sales data. However, these approaches are increasingly inadequate in capturing the ephemeral, symbolic, and often subconscious associations that brands cultivate in a hyper-visual landscape. The modern brand lives in a stream of user-generated content, algorithmically curated feeds, and viral visual phenomena. Real-time measurement of brand sentiment now requires tools that can parse not just text, but images and videos as communicative forms. This reflects a broader shift in marketing toward integrating real-time transactional and symbolic exchanges, as seen in the use of virtual currencies to recalibrate sustainable service value (Yadav et al., 2026).

1.3 Generative AI as a Paradigm Shift

→ Generative AI, especially the developments in generative adversarial networks (GANs) and diffusion-based models, provides a revolutionary solution to this problem. Not only do these models analyze but are also able to synthesize visual data enabling brands to predict, simulate and adapt to visual trends and consumer responses. Placing brand logos, colors, or other symbolic elements within the synthetic media will allow the researchers and marketers to determine the emotional appeal of the branding strategies prior to their large-scale implementation. More to the point, generative AI allows one to transition to real-time brand equity measurement, mining sentiment, relevance, and visual prominence out of the flood of digital imagery as it appears. A newer study highlights the significance of combining AI and marketing cognition to learn more about the changing dynamics of consumers and brands. Real-time image analytics do not only deliver observational data but also actionable data to optimize campaigns and detect brand crises, as well as map emotional resonance. What is more, generative AI offers counterfactual simulation, how would brand perception appear in case of a different logo, design, or narrative? These applications are priceless in the most visual and emotionally engaging fields such as fashion, lifestyle, politics, and communication in the sphere of public health. Nonetheless, along with such a technological breakthrough comes a number of major concerns: explainability of AI generated insights, bias in training data, and the ethics of visual surveillance. Brand equity is not a calculative issue, it is highly humanistic, cultural and emotional. Therefore, this chapter offers a hybrid brand equity analytics model that merges the generative AI capabilities with interpretative oversight and ethical guidelines by human beings. This chapter begins by outlining the foundational technologies of generative AI in image analytics before moving into its specific applications in real-time brand equity measurement. It will also explore the ethical, strategic, and cultural implications of this shift, advocating for a balanced approach that enhances marketing insight without undermining user trust or interpretive nuance.

The integration of AI into marketing has evolved from rule-based personalization engines to sophisticated neural networks capable of visual synthesis. In the early 2000s, customer segmentation was driven by decision trees and regression models. The 2010s saw the rise of recommender systems (e.g., Netflix, Amazon) using collaborative filtering. Today, generative models mark a shift not just in recommendation but in the creation of visual brand assets. This shift from prediction to generation is transformative. For example, dynamic banner ads that previously required A/B testing for layout now use AI to auto-generate optimal visuals based on real-time emotional feedback. Moreover, AI can now simulate brand visuals tailored to local festivities or subcultural symbolism. Such transitions signal a broader convergence of machine creativity and human emotion, where generative AI bridges what a brand says with how it's visually perceived.

2. GENERATIVE AI IN IMAGE ANALYTICS: FROM GANS TO DIFFUSION MODELS

Generative AI will be a paradigm shift in visual computing, where machines are no longer able to analyze realistic images, simulate scenarios, and abstract representations of complex visual data. This change is particularly relevant in the context of brand analytics: as brands become more and more active in visual-first spaces, the ability to create, decode, and simulate image-based interactions in real time presents a tremendous opportunity to measure and improve brand equity. The essence of this revolution is two architectural advances, Generative Adversarial Networks (GANs) and Diffusion Models.

2.1 GANs and the Simulation of Branding Aesthetics

→ GANs were introduced by Goodfellow et al. (2014) and are a combination of the generator that creates synthetic images and the discriminator that decides whether an image is generated or real. It is an adversarial training process that generates high-fidelity visuals that can replicate real-world aesthetics. When branding, GANs can be applied to a simulation of new logos, appearances of products or advertisement mock-ups, and A/B testing can be performed without going into large scale deployment. What is more important, GANs can be reverse-engineered in order to guess the latent visual features that consumers are related to a certain brand, i.e. color palette, motifs, or emotional tone.

2.2 Diffusion Models for Controlled Visual Generation

→ The more recent diffusion models operate in a similar way, but by adding more noise to images and learning to undo this step, they produce even better images and can be controlled with even more parameters (Ho et al., 2020). These models present better image variety and are less likely to suffer mode collapse, the deficiency of GANs. The diffusion models are also used in the context of branding in the controlled production of brand-compatible imagery that can be used to meet emotional or contextual objectives. As an example, a fashion brand may replicate the seasonal aesthetics in different markets across the world based on the latent visual signals of social media in particular regions. Give image below i.e. Figure 1, This image contrasts the core workflows of GANs and diffusion models. GANs generate images through a generator-discriminator loop, while diffusion models iteratively refine noisy data into high-fidelity images.

Luxury and fashion brands have been early adopters of diffusion models for tailoring region-specific campaigns. For instance, a brand like Gucci could simulate how a culturally nuanced campaign, such as integrating traditional Korean hanbok silhouettes into contemporary fashion would resonate across Asian markets. Similarly, food and beverage companies use diffusion models to blend local iconography (e.g., lanterns for East Asian festivals) into their packaging designs. This level of control over image generation enables cultural mirroring, ensuring campaigns don't just appeal aesthetically but feel locally embedded. Unlike GANs, diffusion models offer finer control over aesthetic direction, letting brand managers specify not only the object and style but also emotional tone, lighting, or symbolism.

Figure 1. Core workflows of GANs and diffusion models

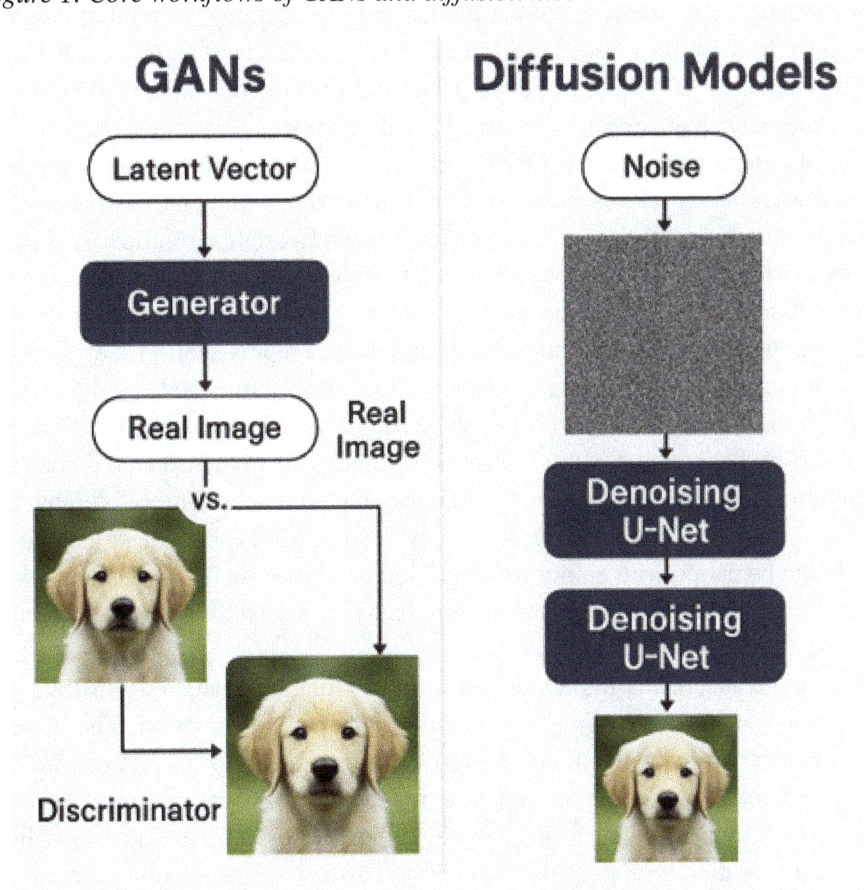

2.3 Latent Spaces and Visual Feature Extraction

→ More than generation, the latent space modeling in such AI architectures is essential to image analytics. Latent spaces are a form of abstract features of images, e.g. symmetry, color intensity, or emotional tone, which may be correlated with consumer sentiment or engagement measures. When combined with real-time social listening tools, generative AI can chart the way brand imagery is landing in different consumer groups and how slight changes in equity are affecting them through cultural events, influencer interactions, or brand scandals.

2.4 Text-to-Image Interfaces in Strategic Branding

→ The next technique on the rise is text-to-image synthesis where AI systems such as DALL·E and Imagen produce images based on verbal descriptions. It is what connects image analytics to natural language processing, where one can test a scenario: how would viewers react to an image-based advert called eco-friendly luxury? Marketers will be able to experiment with the affective bandwidth of brand stories and only create expensive campaigns after iteration through generation.

Yet, the deployment of such powerful models comes with caveats. Synthetic image generation must be responsibly managed to avoid manipulative or deceptive practices. Moreover, bias in training datasets, where AI learns from culturally skewed images, can lead to discriminatory representations or exclusionary aesthetics. As per Kim and Kim (2021)underscores, the socio-technical configuration of AI systems in marketing must embed ethical auditability and diverse representation at every layer of development. Furthermore, the black-box nature of these models complicates interpretability. Even when AI accurately predicts consumer reaction to an image, the reasoning behind such outputs may be opaque. This underscores the need for hybrid interpretive frameworks that combine computational inference with human qualitative analysis (Yadav, 2024). As the next section will explore, these generative models can be paired with emotion recognition systems, visual sentiment analysis, and multimodal integration tools to capture real-time visual impressions of brands from consumer-generated media.

Recent advancements like OpenAI's Sora or Google's Imagen 2 illustrate the convergence of natural language processing and image generation. These tools allow marketers to visualize brand narratives at the ideation stage, an eco-luxury hotel brand, for example, can prompt AI to render visualizations of "sunlit bamboo interiors with tranquil blue textures" to align with its storytelling. The result? Iterative visual ideation with no production cost. This not only streamlines creativity but democratizes design, smaller brands with limited budgets can now ideate like large creative agencies. Beyond ideation, these platforms can generate synthetic ethnographic scenes, what does sustainability look like in a Kenyan vs. Scandinavian household? empowering culturally rooted marketing.

However, the risk lies in using such tools blindly. Image generators are only as inclusive as the datasets they're trained on. A prompt like "young entrepreneur" might default to white-collar, urban male imagery. Therefore, prompt engineering and image vetting are critical in brand contexts to avoid implicit bias.

3. MAPPING BRAND SENTIMENT THROUGH VISUAL SIGNALS

Traditional sentiment analysis has long relied on textual data, social media posts, reviews, and survey responses, to gauge public perception. However, in the current media ecology dominated by images, emojis, short videos, and visual memes, a significant portion of sentiment now resides in visual expressions. For branding professionals, this shift calls for new methodologies to capture, quantify, and interpret the emotional and cognitive valences encoded in images. Generative AI-driven image analytics offers a powerful toolkit for this task, enabling real-time sentiment mapping rooted in the emotional life of visual culture.

Visual brand sentiment analysis entails examining how users interact with, represent, and co-create brand images. For example, when consumers tag products in selfies or create memes using branded content, they contribute to an evolving ecosystem of brand meaning. AI models can detect visual sentiment cues such as facial expressions, body language, object co-occurrence (e.g., branded coffee cups in work-from-home setups), and aesthetic style (e.g., minimalist, nostalgic, vibrant). When aggregated at scale, these elements function as indicators of implicit brand emotion, the subconscious attitudes and moods associated with a brand.

3.1 Facial Emotion Recognition and Brand Perception

→ Advancements in emotion recognition algorithms trained on large-scale facial expression databases (e.g., AffectNet, FER+) enable detection of nuanced emotional reactions in user-generated content. When integrated with brand logo detection, these tools can assess how different demographics emotionally respond to brand touchpoints, whether a product evokes joy, trust, anger, or indifference. Crucially, this moves brand equity measurement from explicit recall metrics to embodied affective responses captured at the point of visual engagement.

New techniques like micro-expression analysis and multi-angle facial landmark detection now allow emotion AI systems to pick up on subtle cues such as lip tension, blink rate, or furrowed brows often missed in casual human observation. Such signals are particularly useful in industries like telemedicine, edtech, or luxury fashion, where consumer trust is tied to emotional resonance. In one case, a cosmetics brand used AI-enhanced facial analytics to segment consumers not by age or gender but by their dominant facial emotional style contentment, curiosity, or assertiveness, allowing for hyper-targeted visual messaging. These tools offer non-intrusive emotional measurement, but their deployment requires guardrails to prevent over-personalization or emotional manipulation.

3.2 Aesthetic Valence and Brand Symbolism

→ Besides facial and contextual analysis, aesthetic sentiment models also break down the aesthetic tone of content related to a brand. As an example, warm color schemes and soft edges of pictures are likely to evoke a feeling of comfort or intimacy, but high contrast and the angular shapes can refer to boldness or disruption. Through training on millions of tagged pictures, AI systems can associate visual aesthetics with psychological valence and brand archetypes thus creating an emotional map of the visual ecosystem of a brand that is dynamic.

3.3 Cultural Context and Visual Sentiment

→ Another creative use case is the live surveillance of image feeds on websites such as Instagram or Pinterest to monitor changes in visual sentiment towards brand campaigns or crisis. As an example, after a controversial advertisement, a brand can find an increase in negative emotion-rich imagery, even in user-generated content that has no connection to the ad itself. This is called visual sentiment spillover and provides advance warning of brand management and public relations.

3.4 Geographic and Demographic Insights

→ Additionally, the geotagging data integration helps the brands to perform spatial sentiment analysis to determine how brand imagery is emotionally perceived across cultures or regions. A campaign that is seen to be empowering in one market may be seen as being aggressive in another. Generative AI has the potential to recreate this type of cultural differences in visual interpretation, enabling international companies to personalize and localize their visuals with care and accuracy. Particularly with Generation Alpha, whose environmental and visual expectations are digitally formed, cultural resonance must be technologically grounded (Yadav, 2025).

Nevertheless, these analytical powers have to be used in an ethical way. Another danger is that emotion mining will turn into a kind of affective surveillance when AI systems are able to read sentiment in images without their user being aware or having given consent. Kaplan and Haenlein (2019) cautions the excessive instrumentalization of consumer emotion, proposing the reflexive branding framework that supports the balance of insight with empathy and respect of user agency. Overall, generative AI will allow advancing a step further and measuring the affective dimension of brand equity, not just what consumers claim to feel, but how they visualize their feelings. This real-time, image based sentiment mapping gives the brands a strong reflection of their cultural and emotional presence in the life of the consumers.

3.5 Multimodal Sentiment Coherence

Multimodal sentiment coherence refers to the alignment between different data modalities: image, text, and audio in conveying a consistent emotional tone. When a social media post features a smiling selfie (visual) with an upbeat caption (text) and energetic music (audio), high coherence reinforces authenticity and brand connection. Conversely, dissonance e.g., sad expressions paired with promotional hashtags can create affective confusion or even mistrust.

In brand analytics, measuring this coherence is crucial. Generative AI can detect mismatches and alert managers when visual sentiment and textual engagement diverge. For instance, a promotional post may garner likes but also include sarcastic emojis or distressed facial reactions in reposted videos indicating hidden negativity. Analyzing such multimodal sentiment patterns ensures deeper emotional diagnostics.

Moreover, this approach helps brands identify influencers with aligned emotional tone, ensuring their storytelling is congruent across media types. In hybrid campaigns where imagery must match messaging, coherence analysis provides guardrails for emotional brand consistency.

4. REAL-TIME MEASURES: TEMPORAL FLUCTUATIONS AND CONSUMER SENTIMENT

The importance of real-time measurement of brand equity reaches beyond simple understanding of consumer sentiment to include the timeline of such sentiments. Brand sentiment is a dynamic variable, dependent on many factors such as cultural events, media trends, influencer commentary, and geopolitical events. Quarterly measurement of brand performance is not sufficient in a world where viral trends change consumer sentiment in a matter of hours. The presence of generative AI-based image analytics offers the capability to monitor and respond to the dynamic evolution of brand sentiment in real time across visual media.

4.1 Continuous Sentiment Streams and Alert Systems

→ Real-time metrics powered by AI rely on continuous data streams and processing pipelines. These pipelines tap the public image streams of social sites so that the AI can visually identify brand mentions, including in the case of no hashtags or text-based cues. Brands can use logo detection, product feature detection, and visual co-occurrence detection (e.g., identifying a brand's soda in users' restaurant photos) to monitor where and how they show up, in real-time. Real-time, in this case, turns brand equity into a leading indicator, not a lagging indicator, one that resonates with emergent sentiment, not with hindsight.

4.2 Emotion Trajectories and Visual Drift

→ More significantly, these systems measure the rate of emotional transition, i.e., the rate at which emotional reactions towards a brand are changing and the visual forces driving this change. Through the combination of sentiment analysis and time-series modeling, brands can forecast emotional trajectories: which images can be used as inflection points, which consumer audiences exhibit high emotional volatility, and when to apply corrective messaging or boost content visibility. Cowls and Floridi (2018) argues that real-time emotional detection, especially in visually intensive environments, is crucial to adaptive brand strategy that respects consumer emotional dynamics without lapsing into exploitation.

One of the most innovative metrics is emotion path tracking, where generative AI models observe the sequence of unfolding brand-related imagery in user feeds. As an example, a fashion brand's visual identity may change from clean, monochromatic design to rich, emotive imagery when a seasonal product launch happens, which would signal that the campaign has successfully resonated with consumers' aspirational mood. Likewise, a healthcare brand may discover that imagery transitions from empathy-based (e.g., caregiving scenes) to resistance-based (e.g., protest scenes) during moments of policy controversy, thereby signaling a potential reputational threat.

Adding to visual attention metrics enhances real-time understanding. Eye-tracking data, often created through controlled experiments or simulated approximations, train AI to learn which visual features attract attention and generate emotional interest. Used in real time, the findings inform creative optimization, determining which thumbnails, images, or brand aesthetics are most attention-grabbing within audience segments.

Consider the backlash from Pepsi's 2017 Kendall Jenner ad, an ad initially meant to represent unity was visually interpreted as trivializing social justice protests. If real-time visual sentiment tracking had been in place, the company might have detected the emotional drift within minutes of the ad's release. An increase in sarcastic memes, visual juxtapositions with real protest imagery, and anger-rich emoji overlays were immediate visual cues. Such emotion trajectories offer a post-mortem lens, but more importantly, enable crisis pre-emption.

Brands like Balenciaga faced similar backlash when imagery from campaigns was perceived as insensitive or disturbing. Generative AI can now simulate consumer reactions before launch, predicting emotional peaks or troughs through historical visual sentiment patterns. Image training based on similar cultural flashpoints enables brands to map likely drift paths.

Hence, emotional drift is not random it's culturally conditioned and often repeatable. Real-time AI mapping, when layered with historical sentiment patterns, becomes a forecasting tool, not just an analytic mirror.

4.3 Predictive Simulation for Campaign Optimization

→ Generative artificial intelligence is also applied in predictive simulation development. As an illustration, a company can use a generative model to simulate the way an image, like an advertisement that contains a particular visual theme, would be felt emotionally in different cultural contexts. This allows conducting pre-emptive campaign tests, which improves emotional resonance before release and allows it to avoid possible backlash. Kim & Kim (2021) states that such pre-emptive uses of AI are essential in creating sturdy branding systems that appeal to target markets at an emotional level.

4.4 Multimodal Integration of Data

→ Ultimately, the integration of multimodal channels, the blending of the text, image, and video signals, produces an aggregate sentiment index that is refined in real time. A brand could be tracking hashtags on Twitter, tracking facial expressions on Instagram, and tracking video engagement on TikTok all at once, and ultimately, have a synthesized emotional dashboard. This synthesis allows brand managers to respond to sentiment at the speed of cultural forces, both utilizing automated systems and human judgment. In general, the integration of generative AI to real-time image analytics streamlines brand equity from a static quantity to a flowing, dynamic emotional compact between the brand and the audience. The next section will explore the ethical implications of this real-time emotional monitoring and how brands can work through these challenges responsibly.

5. ETHICAL ISSUES REGARDING VISUAL MONITORING AND BRAND PROFILING

The generative AI function to value and generate images in real time is of serious ethical concern, especially when such technologies converge with branding, surveillance, and consumer autonomy. Real-time valuation of brand worth based on visual information requires hitherto unprecedented access to user-generated content, facial expressions, and web activity. Although this benefits marketing, it does so at the potential cost of crossing the canons of consent, privacy, and psychological intactness.

5.1 Context and Consent in Visual Data →

The biggest problem is the absence of transparency of consent in visual data mining. Unlike text-based information, which is likely to contain overt user posting or tagging behavior, image-based information is likely to be gathered from public spaces without users' open knowledge. Artificial intelligence systems can scrutinize images where brand logos incidentally feature on clothing, packaging, or background presentations—making inferences about brand sentiment based on contexts users never intended to be used as marketing commentary. This context reduces consumers' control over their digital stories. As Cowls and Floridi (2018) emphasizes, it is imperative that ethical AI systems in marketing respect the principle of contextual integrity, where the use of data is aligned with the original context of its creation.

5.2 Algorithmic Bias in Emotion AI

→ Algorithmic bias and cultural misrepresentation is also a main concern. AI systems trained on the majority on Western-oriented data are bound to misinterpret non-Western emotional, beauty, or branding expressions. For instance, an image sentiment model may classify bright colors as happiness according to Western standards and ignore their application in mourning or protest in other cultures. This may result in misreading emotional cues and culturally insensitive branding choices. Affective AI has to be diversified in training data and audited thoroughly for representational equity (Crawford, 2021).

In addition, facial recognition technology and emotion AI usage in branding analytics work enters morally delicate terrain. Since such technologies yield rich emotional data, one risks pathologizing the emotions of consumers or entering affective manipulation. When brands analyze micro-expressions or gazing behavior to maximize interaction, they are commodifying the subconscious, an act some ethicists liken to emotional extraction. Kaplan and Haenlein (2019) condemns this practice as when there is no ethical control, emotion AI can erode consumer trust and emotional dignity, especially in delicate contexts such as mental health campaigns or social justice campaigns.

Studies such as Buolamwini and Gebru's Gender Shades (2018) revealed significant racial and gender disparities in facial analysis algorithms. Models often misclassify or fail to detect emotional nuance in non-white faces. In branding, this translates to cultural erasure or misreading, which can derail inclusivity efforts. A cheerful celebration may be misread as anger due to unfamiliar facial structures or traditional attire.

Brands that rely on these flawed models may launch campaigns on misread emotions, eroding trust in marginalized communities. To mitigate this, firms must adopt diverse training datasets, audit emotion AI outputs across demographics, and apply fairness metrics before deployment. Cross-validation with human evaluators from different cultural backgrounds remains a critical safeguard.

5.3 Authenticity and Synthetic Media Ethics

→ Generative AI also poses authenticity and manipulation challenges. When synthetic images are employed to simulate brand scenarios or experiment with aesthetic directions, they confuse the creative inquiry with the deceptive representation. Brands that employ AI-generated influencer-style images, staged reviews, or synthetic product images without notice risk misleading consumers and violating advertising regulations. Regulatory guidelines are still in development to cover such uses, but ethical branding must affirmatively disclose synthetic content and keep open AI boundaries. Additionally, the real-time nature of visual surveillance obliges brands to always react to emotional change, potentially inducing reactionary branding. Without reflective judgment, real-time sentiment dashboards can lead brands to prefer short-term emotional pacification over values and integrity in the long run. This can result in algorithmic populism, where brands pursue emotional virality instead of crafting deep engagement. Human oversight, ethical review boards, and brand governance processes are necessary to balance real-time insight with strategic foresight.

In 2023, a virtual influencer with AI-generated facial features was promoted by a wellness brand without disclosure, sparking online backlash. The public perceived the brand as deceptive, undermining its credibility. These incidents highlight the blurry line between synthetic creativity and deception. Without clear labeling, consumers may feel manipulated by AI-enhanced perfection that distorts reality.

Regulators such as the FTC (USA) and the ASA (UK) have begun exploring disclosure guidelines for AI-generated content. Brands, however, must go beyond compliance to embed AI transparency as a value proposition. This could include

"AI-created" watermarks, behind-the-scenes reels, or opt-in prompts that educate users about how their data shapes branding. Ethical AI is not just technical, it's experiential.

5.4 Reflexive Branding and Participatory Ethics

→ Finally, there is an increasingly loud voice of ethical co-design, inviting consumers to participate in decision-making on how they use, interpret, and apply their data. Transparency dashboards, opt-in sentiment tracking and participatory brand feedback systems are emerging as tools that are being used to democratize brand analytics. Not only do such architectures increase ethical legitimacy but also create the consumer-brand trusts as the users no longer are treated as a remote to the analytics process. It is also important to build an external ethical AI culture that can foster transparency outside of the company as well as within internal governance systems of branding (Yadav, 2025). In short, although generative AI can help in carrying out powerful real-time image analysis, it is also causing ethical concerns that demand accountability, transparency, and inclusivity. The measurement of ethical brand equity should be held in balance between the understanding and agreement, novelty and explicability, automation and humanity. The next section will discuss how human-AI hybrid models can successfully traverse these contradictions by means of collaborative understanding and ethical vision.

6. HYBRID HUMAN-AI MODELS FOR INTERPRETABILITY AND STRATEGY

As generative artificial intelligence starts playing a more central role in brand equity analysis, the question becomes increasingly urgent: how can ethical principles and human judgment be maintained amidst a flood of algorithmic information? While AI systems excel in scalability, pattern recognition, and rapid data analysis, they lag behind in contextual understanding, moral judgment, and cultural competency that are required for subtle branding judgments. This chapter lays out the significance of hybrid human-AI models that marry computational power with human interpretive capacity to form accurate and ethically suitable insights.

6.1 Collaborative Interpretation Frameworks

→ At the heart of this hybrid methodology is the collaborative interpretation principle. Rather than relying on artificial intelligence as an independent decision-maker, brand strategists and analysts function as curators of AI output, adding context, validating, and interpreting machine-generated visual insight into meaning that resonates with culturally contented brand stories. This is in line with Yadav's epistemological approach (Yadav, 2024), which challenges AI to be a heuristic collaborator in marketing and not a strategic decision-making replacement. For example, if a generative AI model identifies a spike in negative visual sentiment around a newly launched product, it will be unable to determine if the response is due to aesthetic distaste, cultural insensitivity, or other news events that are not related. A human analyst, however, with knowledge of socio-political drivers and brand history, is able to contextualize the visual data to determine if the negative response is due to a clash with people's values or image sampling algorithmic bias.

To supplement this collaborative approach, explainable AI (XAI) models are being added to brand analytics in ever-growing numbers. XAI models give insight into how individual images are classified as positive or negative, the features that triggered emotional responses, and the variables that most impacted AI decision-making. These explanations allow human analysts to critically assess the reasoning behind the AI and modify their interpretations accordingly. Further, they provide accountability by mapping out the process of decision-making, something that is particularly vital where insights drive major strategic adjustments. Figure 6.1 illustrates the Human-AI Collaborative Analysis Loop, where AI-generated insights are continually refined through expert human feedback and ethical review to ensure cultural and contextual accuracy.

Figure 2. The human-AI collaborative analysis loop

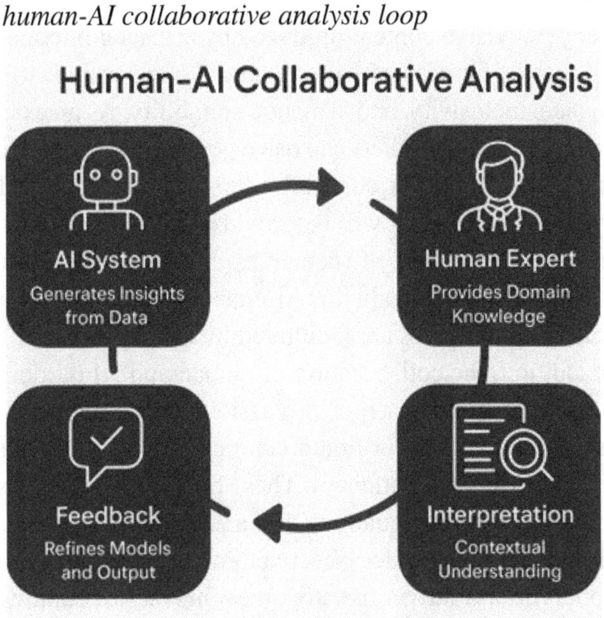

6.2 Strategic Overrides and Brand Governance

→ An important part of hybrid models is also the process of strategic overrides. In other cases, AI might propose a visual campaign based on predictive performance, but the proposal might be against the long-term ethical stance or narrative coherence of the brand. Strategic teams use override procedures to override AI-optimized but ethically flawed content. This human-in-the-loop governance protects against algorithmic myopia when short-term engagement is optimized at the cost of brand trust and authenticity.

In 2022, a consumer electronics brand's AI model suggested visuals highlighting "minimalism" with grayscale tones. While algorithmically promising, the visual conflicted with the brand's legacy of vibrant, user-centered design. The marketing team rejected the AI suggestion, instead selecting a campaign with color-coded narratives resonant with regional cultures.

Such override decisions require formal procedures: ethics committees, override dashboards, and value-alignment rubrics. Codifying when to reject AI output ensures brand integrity outpaces short-term gains. A governance model based on "ethical gates" rather than ROI metrics promotes long-term brand equity rooted in cultural consonance.

6.3 Culturally Situated Evaluation Practices

→ Hybrid systems provide a lot of promise in the context of cross-cultural branding, whereby the visual content produced by artificial intelligence is subject to critique by groups of humans of varied cultural backgrounds to determine the aspects of resonance, inclusivity, and semantic suitability. As an example, a luxury brand wishing to enter Asian markets can use a generative model to create a visual of the advertising campaign, yet culturally appropriate, emotionally appealing, and visually symbolically aligned will be provided by local analysts. Kim & Kim (2021) underlines the importance of such co-evaluative frameworks because they are essential to achieve global equality in AI-enabled marketing campaigns. Moreover, scenario planning activities are facilitated by collaboration of human and AI participants. In addition, the collaboration of human and AI participants supports scenario planning activities. Strategic professionals can integrate AI-generated visuals into narrative workshops or brand laboratories, using them as speculative tools to explore potential brand pathways. These hybrid processes foster creativity, empathy, and ethical reflection, qualities that are difficult to encode directly into machine models but are essential for effective brand stewardship.

Visual metaphors often hold contradictory meanings across cultures. For instance, while white symbolizes purity in Western wedding ads, it may signify mourning in

East Asian cultures. A fragrance brand's AI-generated campaign featuring white lilies was celebrated in Paris but criticized in Beijing. Had a hybrid evaluation system been in place with regional reviewers vetting AI outputs, this misstep could have been avoided.

Hybrid review panels, comprising semiotic experts, cultural consultants, and local creative directors, help evaluate emotional resonance at the micro-cultural level. Additionally, platforms like Canva and Adobe Firefly now integrate real-time "cultural filters" where certain visual combinations are flagged for misinterpretation risk. These are not perfect but form the first layer of cultural debugging.

Scenario planning also benefits. Brand teams use AI visuals as provocations in workshops to debate future branding paths. Such co-creative environments nurture empathy and prevent cultural faux pas in hyper-diverse markets.

6.4 Interdisciplinary Team

Structures → In an organization, this translates into interdisciplinary team structures that integrate data scientists, marketing professionals, designers, ethicists, and social scientists to co-create brand models that are not only intelligent but also compassionate. Training programs in AI literacy for marketers and branding literacy for technologists are required to bridge gaps between these disciplines. In total, hybrid human-AI systems are an excellent example of a sociotechnical solution to brand equity analytics, leveraging the strength of machine learning while grounding findings in human wisdom, cultural sensitivities, and ethics. The rest of this chapter will address the emergent applications, systemic constraints, and future possibilities of generative image analytics in branding.

Building effective human-AI branding systems requires cross-functional literacy. AI developers often lack cultural nuance, while marketers may be unaware of algorithmic limitations. A promising development is the rise of "AI Brand Stewards" professionals trained in both machine learning and brand strategy. Universities like MIT, Stanford, and INSEAD now offer joint certifications in AI ethics and digital marketing to bridge this divide. Within organizations, best practices include regular AI fluency workshops for creative teams and visual culture training for data scientists. Additionally, ethics boards are being formed with rotating consumer representatives, mirroring participatory design principles. These interdisciplinary team structures not only prevent misalignment but foster creative friction, where challenging assumptions leads to more inclusive and compelling brand narratives.

7. APPLICATIONS, LIMITATIONS, AND FUTURE DIRECTIONS

The use of generative artificial intelligence in image analysis and brand equity measurement has moved on the spectrum of speculation to practical implementation in all industries. Brands in the top fashion industry to financial technology are now adopting the use of AI technology in order to track visual sentiment, virtualize consumer reaction and enhance aesthetic appeal in real time. Nonetheless, similar to any emerging technology, generative image analytics also possesses certain in-built restrictions. The last part underlines actual applications, analyzes the limitations, and suggests possible future trends that could shape the next decade of brand intelligence.

Applications

7.1 Real-Time Brand Use Cases →

The biggest application of generative AI in the brand is that of brand monitoring visually in real-time. Using logo detection, face emotion detection and reading of scene context, the brands will be in a position to trace how their imagery is passing and how it is being experienced emotionally on the world platform. This proves useful in industries that are fast paced such as fashion, entertainment, and politics whereby the visual relevance shifts at a speed that is quicker than lightning. Another useful application involves creative testing and simulation of campaigns. Demographics test the brand stories or visual identities using imagery created by AI and then release it to the rest of the population. Such synthetic tests are risk saving and cost saving and hence agile marketing is possible. To give an example, companies such as L Or and Nike are already testing AI-generated product images, so that products fit in culturally diverse markets. Generative AI can also find application in the field of influencer analytics, where AI identifies and analyses the aesthetic of the visual branding of online influencers to match partnerships. It includes the assessment of color schemes, facial expressions and audience response to posts by the influencers and correlating it with brand tone and emotional goals. Last but not least, real-time image analysis aids crisis mitigation and detection. Where there is consumer protest, or consumer scandals, generative models can locate a visual shift in sentiment, such as peaks of anger or derisive imagery, long before a formal PR crisis has materialized.

Beyond traditional sectors, financial services and healthcare brands are turning to generative AI for trust visualization. For example, a fintech startup used AI to generate images of “financial peace” scenes like families cooking at home or elders enjoying retirement, which tested better in sentiment scores than stock photos of piggy banks or charts. Similarly, during the COVID-19 pandemic, hospitals in

Singapore used AI to track emotional response to public health imagery, adjusting campaigns based on fatigue, fear, or relief visual cues. This reflects a broader move toward emotionally intelligent branding, where visuals are not just aesthetic assets but emotional touchpoints in trust-building.

7.2 Structural and Technical Limitations →

Nevertheless, despite these applications, the generative AI in the background of brand analytics has a number of severe drawbacks. This feature, which is a western aesthetic bias in training data, creates international branding situations in which there is a misinterpretation. Representation of cross-cultural emotional expressions is the barrier to cross-cultural accuracy of AI. Deep learning models are prone to be black boxes in which the outcome cannot be easily explained. This makes strategy validation difficult, especially when it comes to matters of high stakes decision-making. AI used to optimize images is by definition a way to optimize engagement in the short term, which might lead to aesthetic homogenization with subsequent loss of brand differentiation in the long term. The gathering and analysis of user-generated imagery, especially faces and personal spaces, prompt important data protection and consent issues. With the rising synthetics media, consumers generally lack trust towards visual media, which destroys brand authenticity. The longevity of the impact of synthetic saturation on the consumer trust is an unknown variable.

7.3 Ethical and Regulatory Futures

→ This industry has lots of developments ahead. New steps of explainable emotion recognition will allow responsible visual sentiment analysis, particularly in the context of sensitive domains, such as healthcare and education. Combining image, text and audio sentiment with integrated brand equity systems is likely to allow greater, more situational comprehension. Governments and platforms are likely to develop ethical rules of marketing application of the synthetic media, such as disclosure norms and AI authorship clues. One of the aspects that policy researchers have already described regarding proactive frameworks to regulate such use in AI-driven workplaces and marketing systems is the need to pay attention to ethical use as a precondition to innovation (Yadav et al., 2025).

The European Union's AI Act proposes classifying emotion recognition systems in advertising as high-risk applications. This means brands using such systems would be subject to transparency mandates, explainability requirements, and periodic audits. Similarly, the FTC is exploring guidelines for AI-generated endorsements and manipulated visuals, mandating disclosures when synthetic media influence consumer choice.

These frameworks will alter brand strategy significantly. A brand using AI to create influencer avatars may need to label posts as "synthetic co-creation." Likewise, emotional dashboards driving campaign tweaks might be required to record interpretive rationale behind decisions.

Brands that proactively embed AI transparency into operations, such as digital footprints of synthetic elements or opt-in emotion tracking can turn compliance into a trust-building feature. Strategic use of AI Ethics Impact Statements, modeled after ESG reports, is likely to become a future norm.

7.4 Participatory and Co-Creative Trajectories

→ Brands can invite customers to leverage generative tools, facilitating collaborative visual content generation and participatory storytelling for brands, thereby developing engagement and trust. Interdisciplinary collaborations, such as researchers like Cowls and Floridi (2018), are facilitating the formation of public–private consortia that seek to co-produce inclusive, culturally responsive, and socially accountable frameworks of AI branding. In short, generative AI-integrated image analytics is a revolution in the perception, measurement, and construction of brands. The future of this method depends not only on the progress of technology but also on an unyielding ethical and strategic commitment to put human values at the forefront of visual intelligence.

As generative AI continues to evolve, its potential lies not just in image production but in building shared visual imaginaries between brands and audiences. Visual storytelling will increasingly be collaborative, predictive, and emotionally co-authored. In the coming years, we can expect custom AI models fine-tuned to brand values, community-driven visual campaigns powered by consumer-generated prompts, and dynamic dashboards that visualize not just current brand sentiment but potential futures. The challenge for scholars and practitioners alike is to build frameworks that combine algorithmic intelligence with humanistic imagination. In doing so, the field of brand analytics will move from surveillance to symbiosis from measuring perception to co-creating identity.

REFERENCES

Cowls, J., & Floridi, L. (2018). Prolegomena to a white paper on an ethical framework for a good AI society. *Minds and Machines*, *28*(4), 689–707. DOI: 10.1007/s11023-018-9482-5 PMID: 30930541

Crawford, K. (2021). *Atlas of AI: Power, politics, and the planetary costs of artificial intelligence*. Yale University Press.

Goodfellow, I., Pouget-Abadie, J., Mirza, M., Xu, B., Warde-Farley, D., Ozair, S., & Bengio, Y. (2014). Generative adversarial nets. *Advances in Neural Information Processing Systems*, *27*, 2672–2680.

Ho, J., Jain, A., & Abbeel, P. (2020). Denoising diffusion probabilistic models. *arXiv preprint arXiv:2006.11239*.

Keller, K. L. (1993). Conceptualizing, measuring, and managing customer-based brand equity. *Journal of Marketing*, *57*(1), 1–22. DOI: 10.1177/002224299305700101

Kim, D. Y., & Kim, H. Y. (2021). Trust me, trust me not: A nuanced view of influencer marketing on social media. *Journal of Business Research*, *134*, 223–232. DOI: 10.1016/j.jbusres.2021.05.024

Schroeder, J. E. (2002). *Visual consumption*. Routledge. DOI: 10.4324/9780203471630

Yadav, R. (2025). Building an ethical AI culture within organizations. In Transforming Corporate Social Responsibility and Business Ethics With AI (pp. 1–30). DOI: 10.4018/979-8-3693-9894-4.ch001

Yadav, R., Huzooree, G., Yadav, M., & Dewasiri, N. J. (2026). The influence of virtual currencies on sustainable service marketing in emerging economies. In Sustainable Service Marketing with Virtual Currencies (pp. 235–256).

Yadav, R., Singh, S. K., & Gunathilaka, D. H. P. M. (2025). Policy and regulatory frameworks for AI and global work: Navigating the challenges. In Global Work Arrangements and Outsourcing in the Age of AI (pp. 269–282).

Chapter 7
Ethical Implications of Artificial Intelligence in Market Research and the Pursuit of Trustworthy Branding Analytics

Salam Al E'mari
https://orcid.org/0000-0002-2134-4158
University of Petra, Jordan

Yousef Sanjalawe
https://orcid.org/0000-0002-4442-1865
University of Jordan, Jordan

Fuad Fataftah
https://orcid.org/0009-0009-3203-5869
Universiti Sains Malaysia, Malaysia

ABSTRACT

The rise of Artificial Intelligence (AI) in market research and branding analytics is reshaping how organizations understand and engage consumers, offering advantages such as hyper-personalized campaigns, predictive brand positioning, and real-time sentiment analysis. Yet this transformation also raises major ethical concerns, including data privacy risks, algorithmic bias, opaque decision-making, and the erosion of consumer autonomy. This chapter examines these issues through a multidisciplinary lens, proposing a framework grounded in fairness, accountability, interpretability, and informed consent. Drawing on case studies and auditing failures, it shows how

DOI: 10.4018/979-8-3373-4506-2.ch007

poorly designed or unregulated systems can damage brand integrity, foster mistrust, and produce discriminatory outcomes. The discussion highlights Explainable AI, bias detection, responsible governance, and user-centered design as essential for aligning innovation with ethics. Ultimately, it offers guidelines for building transparent, fair, and trustworthy brand–consumer relationships in the digital economy

INTRODUCTION

Artificial Intelligence (AI) has rapidly evolved from a specialized domain within computer science into a pervasive technology shaping industries, economies, and societies. Among its most profound areas of impact is marketing, particularly in market research and branding analytics. Once reliant on surveys, focus groups, and statistical models, market research has undergone a radical transformation as machine learning, natural language processing, and predictive analytics have become mainstream tools. These technologies enable businesses to extract insights from massive datasets encompassing consumer preferences, online interactions, purchasing histories, and even biometric responses (Thakur & Kushwaha, 2024). The shift has fundamentally altered the speed, scope, and precision of decision-making in consumer targeting, sentiment analysis, and brand positioning, making AI not merely an auxiliary instrument but a central driver of marketing strategy (Davenport et al., 2020).

This unprecedented transformation, however, presents a paradox. On one hand, AI allows organizations to engage in hyper-personalized communication, predict market trends with increasing accuracy, and deploy branding campaigns that resonate with targeted consumer segments. On the other hand, it introduces profound ethical challenges that risk undermining the very trust upon which effective branding depends. Concerns surrounding data privacy, algorithmic bias, opaque decision-making processes, and manipulative targeting are no longer peripheral debates; they are central to the legitimacy of AI in marketing contexts (Mittelstadt, 2019). An algorithm that promises efficiency may inadvertently perpetuate systemic discrimination if trained on biased data, while tools that analyze consumer sentiment in real time may violate personal autonomy by nudging behavior in ethically questionable ways. These dilemmas reveal that technological sophistication alone is insufficient—without ethical grounding, AI can erode consumer trust and damage brand equity (Choudhary, 2025).

The importance of addressing ethical implications in AI-driven branding extends beyond compliance with emerging legal frameworks such as the General Data Protection Regulation (GDPR, 2016), the California Consumer Privacy Act (Naqvi & Batool, 2023), or the proposed European Union Artificial Intelligence

Act (European Commission, 2021). Ethical lapses carry significant reputational, financial, and societal consequences, ranging from consumer backlash and regulatory penalties to the long-term erosion of brand credibility (Jobin et al., 2019). More importantly, the absence of ethical responsibility risks deepening inequalities by amplifying the voices of dominant groups while marginalizing others in digital marketplaces (Floridi & Cowls, 2022). In this sense, ethics in AI is not simply an abstract philosophical concern; it is a strategic imperative for sustainable marketing practices and for maintaining authentic brand–consumer relationships.

This chapter critically examines the ethical dimensions of AI in market research and branding analytics, situating the discussion at the intersection of technological innovation, consumer trust, and responsible governance. By analyzing real-world cases and highlighting instances of AI auditing failures, it illustrates how opaque models can produce unintended consequences such as discriminatory messaging, privacy breaches, or widespread consumer mistrust. It also proposes a comprehensive ethical framework that emphasizes fairness, accountability, interpretability, and informed consent, offering marketers practical tools to embed these values into their AI systems (Sun & Medaglia, 2019). The discussion extends to implementation strategies such as bias detection, explainable AI techniques, responsible data governance, and co-development of systems with user-centric design principles. These strategies are not framed as obstacles to innovation but as enablers of more trustworthy and equitable branding practices.

Finally, the chapter argues that the future of branding lies in bridging marketing innovation with ethical AI practices. Organizations that prioritize transparency, fairness, and consumer empowerment will be better positioned to cultivate loyalty and long-term trust in an era of digital skepticism. By advancing an integrated approach that combines technological possibilities with ethical accountability, this work contributes to the broader discourse on how AI can support not only more efficient but also more just and sustainable brand–consumer relationships in the digital economy.

1. THE AI-DRIVEN TRANSFORMATION OF MARKET RESEARCH

AI has emerged as a foundation of modern market research, transforming the discipline from merely looking back and describing trends to actively predicting future outcomes and prescribing strategic actions. Traditional methods—focus groups, surveys, and panel studies—were once sufficient to understand consumer behavior, but they often suffered from time lags, limited scalability, and potential biases introduced by human interpretation. In contrast, AI systems can process vast and diverse streams of data in real time, allowing firms to develop a richer, multi-dimensional picture of consumer preferences, motivations, and sentiments. These capabilities go beyond boosting operational efficiency; they are fundamentally transforming the epistemology of market research by redefining what it means to 'know' the consumer in today's digital era (Onifade et al., 2025).

The expansion of big data and the growth of digital platforms have accelerated the use of machine learning, Natural Language Processing (NLP), computer vision, and predictive modeling in marketing analytics. These technologies enable businesses to uncover subtle behavioral patterns, segment consumers with unprecedented precision, and forecast emerging market trends with remarkable accuracy. Crucially, AI not only enhances what marketers can observe but also transforms how they act on those insights—powering automated decisions in advertising, content delivery, and product innovation. Consequently, AI-driven research and branding analytics have evolved into both a competitive necessity and a defining differentiator across industries (Davenport et al., 2020).

1.1 Applications of AI in Market Research and Branding Analytics

One of the most transformative applications of AI lies in *consumer segmentation and targeting*. Traditional segmentation often relied on demographic or psychographic categories, which, while useful, lacked precision. AI enables the construction of micro-segments by analyzing behavioral, transactional, and contextual data simultaneously. For example, unsupervised clustering algorithms can reveal latent consumer groups based on purchasing sequences or browsing histories, allowing marketers to craft highly personalized campaigns (Wedel & Kannan, 2016).

Sentiment analysis and emotional AI represent another critical frontier. By applying NLP techniques to social media posts, online reviews, and customer feedback, firms can capture not just what consumers say but how they feel. Advanced models even incorporate affective computing, analyzing tone of voice, facial expressions, or biometric signals to assess emotional reactions in real time (García-Hernández et al., 2024). These insights inform dynamic brand positioning strategies and allow for adaptive marketing communication tailored to consumer mood and sentiment.

Predictive analytics and brand perception modeling further illustrate the transformative potential of AI. By training algorithms on historical and real-time data, companies can forecast market trends, anticipate shifts in consumer loyalty, and estimate the impact of potential branding campaigns before they are launched. This predictive capability reduces risk while enabling agile strategy adjustments in competitive environments (Davenport et al., 2020).

Another emerging application involves cross-channel behavioral analytics, where AI integrates data from multiple touchpoints—websites, mobile apps, in-store interactions, and IoT devices—to build holistic consumer profiles. These unified perspectives empower firms to deliver seamless brand experiences across channels, ensuring consistency and relevance in consumer engagement. Finally, AI is reshaping *creative processes* in branding. Generative AI tools such as Large Language Models (LLMs) and Generative Adversarial Networks (GANs) are being used to design advertisements, create personalized brand narratives, and even simulate consumer responses to proposed campaigns (Dwivedi et al., 2023). While still evolving, such technologies highlight the extent to which AI is not only analyzing consumer data but also actively co-creating branding strategies.

1.2 Opportunities and Strategic Advantages of AI in Market Research

The transformative applications of AI generate several strategic advantages that redefine how organizations compete in the digital economy. First, AI delivers speed and scalability. Traditional research cycles, which could take weeks or months, are now compressed into real-time dashboards, enabling marketers to make timely decisions based on the most recent consumer insights (Jabbar, Akhtar & Dani, 2020). Second, AI enhances precision and personalization. Hyper-personalized recommendations and targeted advertising are no longer aspirational; they have become baseline expectations in many industries. Algorithms can customize not only what products are recommended but also the timing, channel, and even emotional framing of marketing messages (Rust, 2020). This degree of personalization, when executed ethically, strengthens brand–consumer relationships by increasing perceived relevance and value.

Third, AI improves predictive power and risk management. By simulating consumer behavior under different conditions, organizations can test hypothetical branding strategies before implementation, reducing uncertainty and preventing costly missteps. This foresight is especially critical in volatile markets where consumer sentiment can shift rapidly due to social, political, or environmental factors (Iriani et al., 2024). Fourth, AI facilitates integrated decision-making across the enterprise. Marketing no longer operates in isolation but intersects with supply chain management, customer service, and product development. AI-powered analytics provide a common data foundation that aligns decisions across departments, fostering organizational agility and consistency in brand identity (Molakaseema, 2024).

Finally, AI offers innovation opportunities. Beyond enhancing existing methods, it opens possibilities for entirely new forms of research, such as predictive ethnography, automated focus groups powered by conversational AI, and digital twins of consumer segments that simulate evolving behaviors (Grewal et al., 2020). These innovations push market research from reactive observation to proactive experimentation, creating competitive advantages for early adopters. Despite these benefits, however, the opportunities are not without risks. As will be explored in subsequent sections, the same technologies that enable personalization and efficiency also introduce vulnerabilities around privacy, bias, transparency, and consumer autonomy. Hence, while AI-driven transformation is undeniable, its long-term success depends on embedding ethical principles within these advancements.

2. ETHICAL CHALLENGES IN AI-POWERED BRANDING ANALYTICS

AI has enabled unprecedented advances in market research and branding analytics, offering organizations the ability to predict consumer behavior, personalize campaigns, and optimize brand strategies at scale. Yet alongside these capabilities, AI also introduces a constellation of ethical challenges that threaten the foundation of consumer trust. Unlike traditional marketing practices, where human judgment and responsibility were clearly traceable, AI-driven systems often operate in opaque ways, relying on vast datasets and complex algorithms that are not easily interpretable by consumers, regulators, or even developers themselves. These issues have given rise to a set of pressing ethical concerns that are central to both academic debate and industry practice. Among the most critical are data privacy and consumer autonomy, algorithmic bias and discrimination, transparency and explainability, and accountability and responsibility.

2.1 Data Privacy and Consumer Autonomy

One of the most prominent ethical challenges of AI in market research is the question of data privacy. AI systems rely on massive datasets to generate accurate predictions and personalized recommendations, often requiring the collection and processing of highly sensitive consumer information. These datasets may include browsing histories, purchasing behavior, geolocation data, biometric indicators, and even inferred attributes such as political orientation or emotional state (Vallabhaneni et al., 2024). While the ability to integrate such diverse information enables fine-grained consumer insights, it also blurs the line between legitimate research and surveillance marketing.

From an ethical standpoint, the erosion of consumer autonomy is particularly concerning. Targeted advertising, for example, does not merely reflect consumer preferences but actively shapes them by nudging individuals toward specific products or behaviors. Such practices raise the risk of manipulation, where consumer choices are less the result of free will and more the product of algorithmic persuasion (Susser et al., 2019). The Cambridge Analytica scandal, where personal data from millions of Facebook users were harvested without consent to influence political preferences, stands as a cautionary tale of how privacy violations in AI-powered analytics can undermine democratic processes and public trust (Cadwalladr & Graham-Harrison, 2018).

Consent mechanisms further complicate privacy ethics. Although frameworks like the General Data Protection Regulation (GDPR, 2016) and the California Consumer Privacy Act (CCPA, 2018) mandate informed consent, research shows that most users do not fully understand or engage with lengthy privacy policies (Solove, 2021). As a result, consent is often more symbolic than substantive, leaving consumers vulnerable to hidden data practices. AI exacerbates this issue because data can be inferred indirectly—for example, predicting mental health states from social media activity—even when consumers have not explicitly provided such information (Kosinski et al., 2013). Thus, ethical AI in branding requires moving beyond legal compliance to embrace privacy by design, where data minimization, anonymization, and dynamic consent mechanisms are embedded directly into system architecture. Without such safeguards, firms risk undermining consumer trust, facing reputational backlash, and creating long-term damage to brand credibility.

2.2 Algorithmic Bias and Discrimination

The second major challenge is in regards to algorithm bias. Due to learning patterns from historic information, AI model is at risk of reproducing and amplifying social inequities bias, in this case focusing on social inequities in marketing and branding, it comes in the form of exclusionary targeting, discriminatory pricing, and warped representation of consumers' attitudes and behaviors (Mehrabi et al., 2021). For example, an AI sentiment analysis tool which is trained on a dataset lacking in representation of minority consumers, would consistently and systematically misinterpret the language of the speaker, providing wrong conclusions and employing ineffective (or worse, offensive) brand strategies.

Discriminatory outcomes are not limited to underrepresentation. Amazon's now-abandoned recruitment algorithm famously penalized female candidates because it was trained on historical hiring data dominated by men (Dastin, 2022). In marketing, similar dynamics could cause AI to favor high-income or majority demographics when allocating advertising budgets, inadvertently excluding marginalized groups from brand engagement. This type of bias not only undermines fairness but also contradicts the broader social responsibility that brands increasingly seek to uphold.

The ethical implications extend beyond fairness to brand reputation. Consumers are increasingly attuned to issues of social justice and inclusivity, and brands associated with discriminatory practices may suffer lasting reputational damage. Research has shown that consumers prefer companies perceived as socially responsible and are more likely to boycott brands linked to discrimination (Bhattacharya & Elsbach, 2002).

Mitigating algorithmic bias requires a proactive approach that includes diversifying training datasets, implementing fairness constraints, and conducting continuous bias audits throughout the model lifecycle (Fazelpour & Lipton, 2020). Ethical branding in the AI era thus depends not only on technical accuracy but also on ensuring equitable treatment across consumer groups.

2.3 Transparency and Explainability

Transparency is another cornerstone of ethical AI. Modern AI systems, particularly those built on deep learning architectures, often function as "black boxes," making predictions or classifications without offering human-interpretable explanations. In market research, this opacity creates significant risks. Consumers may be subjected to recommendations or targeted advertisements without understanding why they are receiving them, while marketers themselves may lack clarity about the underlying decision-making processes (Mittelstadt, 2019).

Lack of explainability undermines trust in multiple ways. For consumers, it raises questions of fairness: Why am I being shown this advertisement? Why am I excluded from this promotion? For regulators, it complicates accountability, as it becomes difficult to assess whether decisions are compliant with anti-discrimination or privacy laws. Even within organizations, opacity can lead to internal misalignment, where marketing teams deploy models they do not fully understand, potentially exposing the company to ethical and legal risks.

Explainable AI (XAI) has emerged as a promising solution, aiming to make algorithmic decisions more interpretable without sacrificing predictive performance. Techniques such as feature importance scoring, counterfactual explanations, and model-agnostic interpretability tools like LIME and SHAP are increasingly applied in marketing contexts to provide clarity about how consumer attributes influence predictions. However, the trade-off between complexity and interpretability remains a persistent challenge: the most accurate models are often the least explainable, raising difficult ethical questions about whether accuracy should ever come at the expense of transparency (Arrieta et al., 2020). Thus, in branding analytics, explainability is not just a technical requirement but an ethical imperative, directly tied to consumer trust and regulatory legitimacy.

2.4 Accountability and Responsibility

Perhaps the most complex ethical challenge is accountability. When AI systems produce harmful outcomes, responsibility is often diffused across multiple actors: data providers, algorithm developers, marketing teams, and organizational leadership. This diffusion creates what some scholars call a responsibility gap (Matthias, 2004). In branding contexts, such gaps can be particularly damaging because harm may be subtle, such as exclusionary messaging or manipulative targeting, rather than overt.

For instance, if an AI system unintentionally reinforces gender stereotypes in advertising, should accountability lie with the data scientists who built the model, the managers who approved its use, or the executives who defined the business objectives? Without clear accountability structures, organizations risk both ethical failure and public backlash.

The challenge is further compounded by the complexity of AI supply chains. Many firms rely on third-party vendors for data collection, algorithm development, or cloud infrastructure, making it difficult to trace accountability when something goes wrong (Floridi & Cowls, 2022). Moreover, current legal frameworks often lag behind technological innovation, creating regulatory vacuums where unethical practices can flourish without consequence.

Addressing accountability requires the establishment of ethical governance frameworks within organizations. This includes creating internal ethics boards, implementing auditing protocols, and ensuring cross-functional collaboration between marketers, technologists, and compliance officers. Ultimately, accountability in AI-driven branding is not only about preventing harm but also about signaling to consumers that the brand is committed to responsible practices (Jobin et al., 2019).

Taken together, these four challenges—privacy, bias, transparency, and accountability—form an interconnected web of ethical dilemmas that organizations cannot afford to ignore. Data privacy violations undermine autonomy, bias perpetuates discrimination, opacity erodes trust, and lack of accountability diffuses responsibility. Left unaddressed, these challenges threaten not only consumer welfare but also the sustainability of branding strategies in a digital economy increasingly defined by skepticism toward corporate motives. Ethical AI in market research is therefore not a matter of choosing between innovation and responsibility. Rather, it is about embedding responsibility into the innovation process itself, ensuring that technological progress aligns with societal values and consumer expectations. The following section will illustrate how these challenges manifest in practice by examining real-world case studies and auditing failures that highlight the consequences of neglecting ethical principles in AI-powered branding.

3. REAL-WORLD CASE STUDIES AND AI AUDITING FAILURES

While the ethical challenges of AI in market research and branding analytics can be discussed in theoretical terms, their gravity becomes most apparent when examined through real-world failures. Across industries, organizations have faced significant consequences—ranging from reputational backlash to regulatory penalties—because of opaque models, insufficient auditing, or neglect of ethical safeguards. These cases highlight the risks of prioritizing efficiency or profit over fairness, transparency, and accountability. They also demonstrate that ethical lapses are not merely technical shortcomings but systemic governance failures. The following case studies illustrate how AI auditing gaps and ethical oversights manifest in practice, and what lessons can be drawn for more responsible branding analytics.

3.1 Case Study 1: Cambridge Analytica and the Crisis of Consumer Trust

The Cambridge Analytica scandal remains the most emblematic case of AI-driven analytics misused at scale. By harvesting the personal data of over 50 million Facebook users without explicit consent, the firm leveraged psychographic profiling to influence voter behavior in the 2016 U.S. presidential election and the Brexit referendum (Cadwalladr & Graham-Harrison, 2018). Although this case was primarily political, its implications for market research and branding are profound.

First, it underscored the vulnerability of data privacy in digital ecosystems. The algorithms employed could infer sensitive psychological traits, such as openness or neuroticism, based on seemingly innocuous "likes" and online behaviors (Kosinski et al., 2013). Such profiling not only breached privacy but also challenged consumer autonomy by manipulating decision-making processes. Second, it revealed the failure of auditing mechanisms. At the time, Facebook had limited oversight over third-party data usage and lacked robust auditing frameworks to ensure compliance with ethical and legal standards. This governance gap allowed Cambridge Analytica to exploit systemic weaknesses for manipulative targeting.

Finally, the scandal catalyzed consumer skepticism toward digital platforms and brands associated with unethical data practices. Surveys conducted after the revelations showed declining trust in social media as a credible source of information and in brands that advertised heavily on such platforms (Isaak & Hanna, 2018). For marketers, the lesson is clear: even when tools are technically legal, their misuse can undermine long-term brand trust and legitimacy.

3.2 Case Study 2: Amazon's AI Recruitment Tool and Algorithmic Discrimination

Although not directly a branding case, Amazon's AI recruitment system provides a cautionary tale of algorithmic bias with implications for marketing and brand reputation. In 2018, reports revealed that Amazon had abandoned its AI-based hiring tool after discovering that it consistently downgraded applications containing the word "women's" (e.g., "women's chess club captain"), reflecting bias from historical data dominated by male candidates (Dastin, 2018).

In branding contexts, similar biases in AI models can skew consumer segmentation and targeting. For example, advertising platforms have been found to disproportionately exclude women from job-related ads in tech or leadership positions, reinforcing harmful stereotypes (Lambrecht & Tucker, 2019). Such discriminatory targeting undermines fairness and damages a brand's reputation as inclusive or socially responsible.

This case also highlights an auditing failure. Despite internal testing, Amazon's system was not sufficiently stress-tested for fairness across demographic groups. Effective AI auditing requires continuous monitoring, not just at deployment but throughout the model's lifecycle. The lack of transparency in training datasets and the absence of robust fairness metrics contributed to the failure. The key lesson is that bias is not an abstract risk but a measurable and preventable phenomenon. Brands that neglect bias auditing risk reputational crises, consumer boycotts, or regulatory intervention. Conversely, those that proactively audit and report on fairness can differentiate themselves as leaders in ethical innovation.

3.3 Case Study 3: Apple Card and Gender Bias in Credit Scoring

In 2019, Apple and Goldman Sachs faced a public backlash when their joint product, the Apple Card, was accused of gender discrimination. Multiple high-profile consumers reported that women were granted significantly lower credit limits than men with similar financial profiles, sparking an official investigation by the New York State Department of Financial Services (NYDFS) (Valentino-Devries, 2019).

At the heart of the controversy was the opacity of AI-driven credit scoring algorithms. Neither Apple nor Goldman Sachs could adequately explain why the algorithm allocated different limits, citing the complexity of proprietary models. This lack of transparency not only violated ethical principles of explainability but also highlighted accountability gaps: both firms initially deflected responsibility to the other, undermining public confidence. From a branding perspective, the fallout was severe. Apple, a company whose brand equity relies heavily on consumer trust and a reputation for innovation, faced criticism for neglecting ethical oversight in its partnership. The controversy illustrates that trustworthy branding is inseparable from trustworthy analytics. Even if technical responsibility lies with a partner, brands are held accountable by consumers for the ethical performance of the technologies they endorse.

The Apple Card case underscores the need for XAI and robust third-party auditing. Black-box models, when left unchecked, can produce discriminatory outcomes that not only harm individuals but also tarnish brand credibility on a global scale.

3.4 Case Study: Facebook Ad Targeting and Discriminatory Practices

Another important case that illustrates the ethical pitfalls of AI in market research is Facebook's repeated controversies over discriminatory ad targeting. In 2016, investigative reports revealed that Facebook's advertising platform allowed marketers to exclude users from seeing housing, employment, and credit-related ads based on sensitive attributes such as race, gender, or age (Angwin & Parris, 2016). Although these exclusions were framed as "audience filters," they effectively enabled digital redlining—a practice that mirrors historical patterns of discrimination in housing and finance.

The issue resurfaced in 2019, when the U.S. Department of Housing and Urban Development (HUD) filed charges against Facebook, accusing the company of violating the Fair Housing Act by enabling advertisers to discriminate against protected groups (HUD, 2019). Algorithms designed to optimize ad delivery were also implicated: even when advertisers did not specify exclusions, the system's machine learning processes disproportionately showed ads to certain groups, effectively creating biased outcomes.

This case is significant for branding analytics for several reasons. First, it highlights how algorithmic bias can emerge not only from training data but also from optimization goals. By prioritizing click-through rates or engagement, algorithms may inadvertently reinforce societal inequalities, privileging majority groups and sidelining minorities. Second, it underscores the importance of external oversight and regulatory enforcement. Facebook introduced changes to its ad targeting system only after lawsuits, regulatory pressure, and reputational harm. Third, it demonstrates that ethical lapses in AI do not remain confined to technical domains—they directly shape brand perception. Facebook's reputation as a platform was damaged, and advertisers associated with discriminatory practices risked secondary reputational fallout. The lesson for market research is that responsible AI requires auditing not just inputs but outcomes. Continuous monitoring of how algorithms distribute content across demographic groups is essential for preventing discrimination and maintaining fairness. Brands must demand transparency from platforms they partner with and ensure that ethical principles are upheld across the entire advertising ecosystem.

3.5 Lessons Learned from AI Auditing Failures

These case studies reveal several recurring themes. First, auditing failures often stem from reactive rather than proactive oversight. In each case, problems were identified only after public backlash, highlighting the insufficiency of voluntary or internal auditing mechanisms. Second, accountability is often diffused across multiple actors, leading to finger-pointing rather than responsibility. Third, consumers are increasingly unwilling to tolerate opacity: brands that fail to provide transparency in AI practices face rapid reputational erosion.

The implications for market research and branding analytics are clear. Ethical AI is not a secondary concern but a core business requirement. Robust auditing frameworks, continuous bias detection, and transparent communication with consumers must be integral components of AI governance. Organizations that adopt these practices will be better positioned to foster trust and sustain long-term brand equity. Conversely, those that neglect them risk reputational crises, regulatory sanctions, and consumer disengagement.

4. ETHICAL FRAMEWORK FOR AI IN MARKET RESEARCH

AI is now central to how organizations conduct market research and branding analytics, but its rapid rise also brings serious ethical risks—ranging from privacy violations to biased algorithms—that can erode consumer trust and damage corporate legitimacy. Addressing these challenges calls for more than just compliance with regulations; it requires a deliberate ethical framework that embeds responsibility into every stage of the AI lifecycle. As shown in *Figure 1*, this framework is built on four essential pillars: fairness, accountability, interpretability, and informed consent. Together, these principles provide the foundation for creating trustworthy branding practices and building sustainable, transparent relationships between businesses and consumers in the digital economy.

Figure 1. Ethical framework for AI in market research

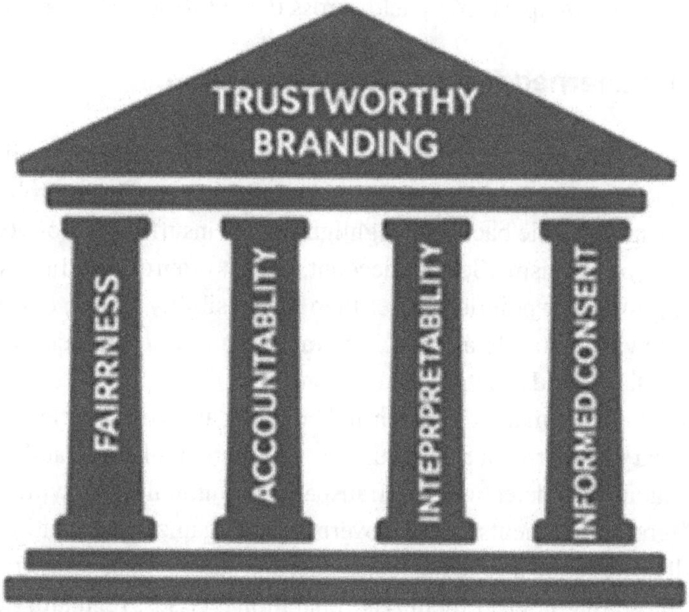

4.1 Fairness

Fairness in AI refers to ensuring equitable treatment of individuals and groups in market research processes. In branding contexts, fairness means that algorithms should not systematically exclude, misrepresent, or disadvantage marginalized populations. Yet as studies have shown, biased training data or flawed design assumptions can easily lead to discriminatory targeting or exclusionary campaigns (Mehrabi et al., 2021).

To achieve fairness, firms must adopt bias detection and mitigation practices throughout the model lifecycle. This involves diversifying datasets, applying fairness-aware machine learning techniques, and stress-testing models across demographic subgroups. For example, when deploying sentiment analysis tools, organizations should ensure linguistic inclusivity by testing performance across dialects and cultural contexts (Das & Singh., 2023). Fairness audits should also be institutionalized, with third-party reviews providing independent oversight.

Moreover, fairness is not only a technical matter but also a *societal expectation*. Brands associated with inclusivity are more likely to foster long-term loyalty, while those linked to discriminatory practices face consumer backlash (Bhattacharya &

Elsbach, 2002). Thus, fairness should be treated not as a compliance box but as a strategic value proposition.

4.2 Accountability

Accountability ensures that when AI systems in market research cause harm—whether through discriminatory targeting, privacy violations, or manipulative messaging—responsibility can be clearly assigned and addressed. This principle directly addresses the "responsibility gap" created by opaque algorithms and distributed decision-making processes (Matthias, 2004).

Organizations must establish governance structures that embed accountability at multiple levels. First, senior leadership should assume ultimate responsibility for ethical AI deployment, signaling commitment from the top. Second, cross-functional teams should be empowered to oversee the ethical performance of AI systems, including marketers, technologists, and legal experts (Jobin et al., 2019). Third, accountability must extend to external partners and vendors: firms should require transparency in third-party data and algorithms to avoid outsourcing responsibility.

Practical mechanisms include AI ethics boards, algorithmic auditing protocols, and impact assessments modeled on environmental or financial audits. Transparent reporting—such as algorithmic "nutrition labels" or impact statements—can further communicate accountability to regulators and consumers. By institutionalizing accountability, brands can preempt crises and demonstrate ethical leadership.

4.3 Interpretability and Explainability

Interpretability, often operationalized through XAI, is critical for building trust in AI-driven market research. In branding analytics, interpretability enables both organizations and consumers to understand why specific decisions were made—for example, why an individual was targeted with a particular advertisement or why a consumer segment was classified as high risk (Arrieta et al., 2020).

The absence of interpretability has already produced reputational crises, as seen in the Apple Card case where opaque credit-scoring models led to accusations of gender bias (Valentino-Devries, 2019). For market research, explainability can mitigate such risks by offering transparent rationales behind predictions and classifications. Techniques such as SHAP (Shapley Additive Explanations) or LIME (Local Interpretable Model-agnostic Explanations) can provide model-agnostic insights, while counterfactual explanations can clarify how outcomes might change under different conditions.

Interpretability also supports internal alignment within organizations. Marketing teams, executives, and compliance officers can make informed decisions only when they understand the logics driving AI systems. Beyond technical transparency, however, interpretability requires communicative clarity: explanations should be tailored for diverse audiences, from technical staff to regulators to consumers.

4.4 Informed Consent

Informed consent represents a cornerstone of ethical AI, yet in practice it remains one of the most contested principles. Market research often depends on consumer data collected directly or inferred indirectly. While regulations such as the GDPR (2016) and CCPA (2018) require informed consent, the complexity of digital ecosystems means that consumers rarely understand the scope of data collection, let alone how AI systems process that data (Solove, 2021).

An ethical framework must therefore embrace dynamic, user-centric consent mechanisms. This includes simplifying privacy policies, offering granular control over data-sharing preferences, and enabling real-time revocation of consent. For instance, consumers should be able to adjust whether their data can be used for behavioral targeting, third-party sharing, or sentiment analysis.

Beyond legal compliance, informed consent must be understood as a relational practice: by respecting consumer agency, brands signal respect and transparency, thereby fostering trust. Without meaningful consent, even technically sophisticated AI systems risk being perceived as manipulative or exploitative.

4.5 Integrating the Four Principles into Practice

AI governance can be augmented in practice and policy by adding the facets of fairness, accountability, and the rest, provided they are included in a broader and integrated governance architecture. Considered in isolation, each can create shortfalls. For example, if the focus is solely on eliminating biases, the fairness and interpretability framework may suffice, but the end result may be a confused customer. Then again, accountability that 'silences' consent may protect a corporation in the short term, but erodes societal trust in the long term. The erosion of that trust is the price for which the vigilance over application paradigm must pay, which must extend over the entire lifecycle of AI:

1. **Data Collection**: Build fairness and consent into the earliest stage through inclusive sampling methods and privacy-by-design principles.
2. **Model Development**: Introduce fairness constraints, interpretability mechanisms, and accountability checks during training to prevent issues before deployment.
3. **Deployment**: Offer clear explanations of how decisions are made, provide user-friendly consent dashboards, and ensure robust auditing protocols are in place.

4. **Monitoring and Feedback**: Carry out continuous audits, actively gather consumer feedback, and adapt systems as conditions and expectations evolve.

By integrating these four principles into every stage, organizations shift ethics from being a box-ticking exercise to becoming an everyday practice—something that guides design, builds trust, and sustains responsible innovation.

4.6 Strategic Value of Ethical AI in Branding

Embedding ethics in AI is not only a defensive practice but also a source of competitive advantage. Research indicates that consumers increasingly value brands perceived as trustworthy and transparent, and they reward ethical practices with loyalty and advocacy (Celestin et al., 2024). Ethical AI frameworks can thus enhance brand equity, reduce reputational risk, and position organizations as leaders in responsible innovation.

Moreover, regulatory trends suggest that ethical AI will soon be a legal necessity. The European Union's AI Act, for instance, explicitly emphasizes transparency, fairness, and accountability as regulatory requirements (European Commission, 2021). Early adoption of ethical frameworks therefore prepares firms for compliance while cultivating trust.

The deployment of AI in market research and branding analytics offers unparalleled opportunities for personalization, efficiency, and predictive insight. Yet without robust ethical grounding, these opportunities risk devolving into crises of trust, fairness, and accountability. The proposed framework—anchored in fairness, accountability, interpretability, and informed consent—provides a structured pathway for organizations to align innovation with responsibility. By embedding these principles across the AI lifecycle, firms can not only mitigate risks but also strengthen brand equity in an era where ethical credibility has become a defining competitive asset.

5. IMPLEMENTATION GUIDELINES FOR ETHICAL AI PRACTICES

While the preceding sections have emphasized ethical principles and illustrated failures, organizations require concrete guidance on how to operationalize ethical AI in market research and branding analytics. Implementing such practices is not a one-time exercise but an ongoing process spanning data collection, algorithm design, deployment, and post-deployment monitoring. The following guidelines outline actionable steps that firms can adopt to ensure AI systems are trustworthy, transparent, and aligned with consumer expectations.

5.1 Bias Detection and Mitigation Techniques

Bias is one of the most pervasive risks in AI-driven branding analytics, often arising from imbalanced training datasets or optimization goals that reinforce inequality. To address this challenge, firms must embed bias detection and mitigation strategies throughout the AI lifecycle.

1. **Dataset Diversification**: Training data should represent diverse demographic groups, dialects, and contexts. For example, sentiment analysis systems should be stress-tested across languages and cultural expressions to avoid misclassification (Das & Singh., 2023).
2. **Fairness-Aware Algorithms**: Implement machine learning techniques that incorporate fairness constraints, such as demographic parity, equal opportunity, or disparate impact reduction (Mehrabi et al., 2021).
3. **Pre-processing and Post-processing Techniques**: Methods like reweighting datasets before training or calibrating model outputs afterward can reduce disparities without severely compromising accuracy.
4. **Continuous Bias Audits**: Organizations should institutionalize third-party or independent audits that test AI systems for bias on an ongoing basis. Audits must extend beyond inputs to examine outcomes—who benefits, who is excluded, and who might be harmed.

Embedding bias detection at every stage ensures that fairness is not treated as an afterthought but as a core design principle.

5.2 Responsible Data Governance

Data is the raw material of AI, and responsible governance is crucial for maintaining trust. In market research, where personal and behavioral data are routinely collected, organizations must prioritize privacy, security, and transparency.

1. **Privacy by Design**: Systems should minimize data collection to what is strictly necessary, employ anonymization or pseudonymization techniques, and store data securely in compliance with regulations like GDPR (2016) and CCPA (2018).

2. **Dynamic Consent Mechanisms**: Instead of relying on static, lengthy privacy policies, firms should implement user-friendly dashboards where consumers can adjust consent preferences in real time (Solove, 2021).
3. **Data Provenance Tracking**: Organizations must document how data is collected, processed, and shared. Blockchain-based data provenance tools are emerging as powerful means to guarantee traceability and accountability in data use (Zyskind et al., 2015).
4. **Third-Party Data Oversight**: Because many firms rely on purchased datasets, strict vetting of external data providers is necessary. Contracts should mandate transparency and adherence to ethical data standards.

Strong governance practices ensure that consumer data is not only legally protected but also ethically respected.

5.3 Co-Development with Ethical Design Principles

AI systems are most effective when designed collaboratively, incorporating multiple perspectives from the outset. Co-development with ethical design principles ensures that marketing innovation is aligned with consumer values and societal norms.

1. **Human-Centered Design**: Involve end-users in system design, particularly marginalized groups who may be disproportionately affected by algorithmic decisions. Participatory workshops, consumer panels, and iterative testing can reveal blind spots.
2. **Stakeholder Engagement**: Ethical AI requires input not only from technologists and marketers but also from ethicists, legal experts, and social scientists (Jobin et al., 2019). Cross-disciplinary teams can balance technical feasibility with ethical obligations.
3. **Ethics by Design**: Incorporate ethical requirements (fairness, explainability, accountability) directly into technical specifications. For example, interpretability metrics should be treated as performance benchmarks alongside accuracy.
4. **Corporate Culture Alignment**: Ethical AI practices cannot thrive in isolation; they must be embedded into organizational culture through training, leadership commitment, and incentive structures. Firms like Microsoft and Google have institutionalized internal AI ethics committees, demonstrating the importance of governance culture (Whittaker et al., 2018).

By co-developing with ethics as a design principle, firms can move from reactive fixes to proactive prevention of ethical failures.

5.4 Integration of Guidelines Across the AI Lifecycle

The effectiveness of ethical AI practices depends not on isolated implementation but on their integration across the entire AI lifecycle. Each stage of development and deployment presents unique ethical risks, which must be addressed through targeted safeguards. As illustrated in Figure 2, the lifecycle of ethical AI in market research begins with data collection, proceeds through model training and deployment, and continues with ongoing monitoring and auditing.

Figure 2. Implementation of ethical AI practices across the AI lifecycle in market research

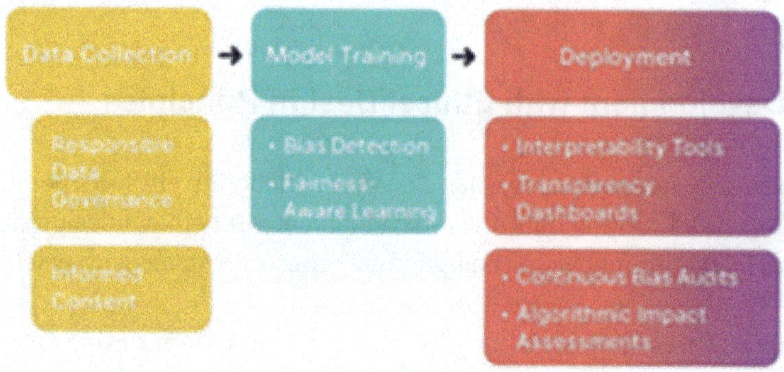

In the data collection stage, responsible governance and informed consent form the foundation of ethical practice. By ensuring transparency in data provenance and empowering consumers with granular consent mechanisms, organizations establish the basis of trust before analytics even begin. During model training, bias detection and fairness-aware learning ensure that predictive systems do not perpetuate historical inequities or marginalize underrepresented groups. At this stage, technical interventions such as reweighting datasets, auditing for fairness metrics, and employing fairness-constrained optimization are essential to align outcomes with principles of justice and inclusion.

Once models are deployed, organizations must prioritize interpretability and transparency. Tools such as explainable AI frameworks, consumer-facing transparency dashboards, and clear communication of targeting criteria help maintain trust while allowing both internal teams and external stakeholders to scrutinize decision processes. Finally, in the monitoring and auditing stage, continuous bias audits and algorithmic impact assessments provide safeguards against drift, unintended harms, or discriminatory outcomes. By institutionalizing these practices, firms ensure that ethical oversight is not a one-time effort but a sustained responsibility.

The implementation of ethical AI in market research requires deliberate and systematic action. By embedding bias detection, responsible data governance, co-development with ethical design, and regulatory compliance strategies, organizations can align technological innovation with consumer trust. These guidelines demonstrate that ethical AI is not an obstacle to innovation but an enabler of sustainable branding. Brands that adopt them will not only avoid reputational crises but also strengthen their competitive advantage in an increasingly skeptical digital marketplace.

6. BRIDGING MARKETING INNOVATION AND ETHICAL AI

AI has redefined market research and branding analytics, yet its sustainability depends on integrating ethical principles into innovation. Far from being a constraint, ethics can act as a catalyst for creative marketing strategies, consumer trust, and long-term competitiveness. This section organizes the discussion into three interrelated dimensions: balancing commercial goals with consumer trust, positioning ethics as competitive advantage, and fostering collaborative ecosystems for responsible innovation.

6.1 Balancing Commercial Goals with Consumer Trust

AI-driven marketing often focuses on short-term performance metrics—such as click-through rates, engagement, and conversions—that can conflict with consumer expectations for fairness, privacy, and autonomy. While hyper-personalization can increase relevance, it may also feel intrusive if consumers believe their privacy is being compromised (Susser et al., 2019). The challenge, therefore, is to balance traditional KPIs with measures that reflect consumer trust. As shown in Table 1, integrating ethical AI metrics—such as transparency, fairness, explainability, and informed consent—alongside conventional indicators helps organizations design campaigns that are not only effective but also ethically resilient, ultimately strengthening long-term brand reputation and loyalty.

Table 1. Balancing commercial metrics with ethical trust indicators.

Traditional Marketing KPIs	Ethical AI Metrics for Trust	Strategic Impact on Branding
Click-through rate (CTR)	Transparency in targeting	Higher consumer confidence in messaging
Conversion rate	Data minimization & informed consent	Reduced perception of manipulation
Return on Investment (ROI)	Fairness in audience segmentation	Stronger inclusivity and brand reputation
Engagement rate	Explainability of recommendations	Improved consumer loyalty and satisfaction

Each pairing in Table 1 highlights how ethical considerations reshape conventional marketing performance indicators into trust-building mechanisms. Transparency in targeting not only maintains strong click-through rates but also reassures consumers that recommendations are based on clear and legitimate criteria, increasing their confidence in brand messaging. Data minimization and informed consent, when linked to conversion rates, reduce the perception of manipulation by ensuring that customers feel their choices are respected and not coerced by hidden profiling. Fairness in audience segmentation strengthens inclusivity by broadening market reach and improving brand reputation, which in turn enhances the long-term impact of Return on Investment (ROI). Finally, explainability of recommendations turns engagement into genuine loyalty, as consumers are more likely to remain satisfied when they understand why they are being shown certain content or offers. Taken together, these integrations demonstrate that ethical AI metrics do not compete with commercial goals but instead reinforce them, creating a sustainable foundation for both brand growth and consumer trust.

6.2 Ethical Branding as a Competitive Advantage

In increasingly competitive markets, where products and services are often commoditized, consumers differentiate brands less by functional attributes and more by their values, commitments, and ethical conduct. Ethical AI practices, when embedded in branding and market research, can therefore become a powerful source of competitive advantage. Rather than being perceived as a regulatory burden, ethical AI provides opportunities for organizations to strengthen brand equity, build trust-based loyalty, and align with the values of socially conscious consumers.

Research shows that younger generations, particularly millennials and Gen Z, are especially attentive to ethical considerations. A global McKinsey study, for example, found that Gen Z consumers actively seek brands that demonstrate inclusivity, sustainability, and transparency, with nearly 70% indicating they are more likely to purchase from companies they perceive as socially responsible (Francis & Hoefel, 2018). By contrast, brands associated with unethical data use, algorithmic bias, or lack of transparency face reputational damage and consumer disengagement.

Ethical AI practices can also translate into market expansion opportunities. For instance, training sentiment analysis models on diverse linguistic and cultural datasets allows brands to reach broader audiences without alienating underrepresented groups. Similarly, fairness audits in advertising systems not only reduce legal risk but also unlock new segments by ensuring inclusive targeting strategies. In this sense, ethics is not simply about avoiding harm, it actively broadens market reach and enhances competitiveness.

The relationship between ethics, trust, and innovation is best understood as a cycle, where each element reinforces the others. As shown in Figure 3, ethical AI practices enhance consumer trust, which in turn generates competitive advantage. Competitive advantage, once achieved, incentivizes further ethical investment, thereby perpetuating the cycle of innovation and trust-building. This dynamic underscores the strategic role of ethics not as a constraint but as a flywheel for brand growth.

Figure 3. The ethics–innovation–trust cycle in branding.

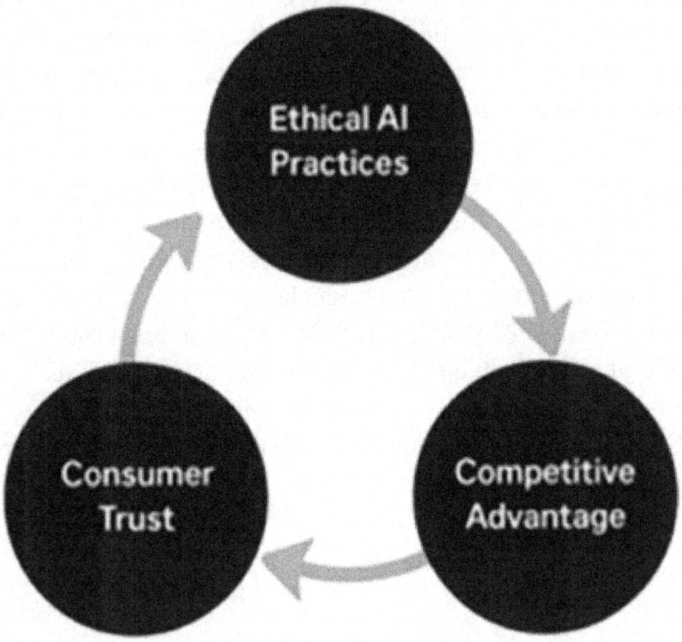

6.3 Collaborative Ecosystems for Responsible Innovation

While individual organizations can integrate ethical AI practices into their branding strategies, the complexity of modern data ecosystems requires broader collaboration across stakeholders. AI supply chains involve multiple actors including businesses, regulators, data providers, technology vendors, and consumers, making it impossible for any single entity to address ethical challenges comprehensively. Collaboration ensures that innovation remains socially legitimate, legally compliant, and responsive to evolving consumer expectations.

Industry consortia and partnerships are central to these ecosystems. For example, initiatives such as the Partnership on AI bring together companies, academics, and civil society organizations to develop guidelines, benchmarks, and research that shape responsible AI practices across industries. Participation in such alliances not only mitigates reputational risk but also provides access to shared innovations that can enhance both ethical alignment and market performance.

Regulatory collaboration is equally critical. Anticipating evolving frameworks such as the EU Artificial Intelligence Act (European Commission, 2021) or sector-specific privacy laws allows organizations to build compliance into their systems from the outset. Proactive alignment with regulators also strengthens legitimacy, positioning brands as leaders rather than laggards in ethical innovation.

Consumers must also be included as active participants rather than passive data subjects. Co-creation initiatives, such as participatory design workshops for consent interfaces or consumer-led fairness testing, ensure that ethical AI reflects real-world needs and expectations. By giving consumers agency, organizations not only enhance inclusivity but also signal respect, deepening brand authenticity.

The roles of different stakeholders in such ecosystems can be visualized through Table 2, which maps how businesses, regulators, consumers, and civil society contribute to responsible AI practices and the corresponding benefits for branding innovation. For instance, while businesses drive the technical development of AI, regulators provide accountability, consumers reinforce authenticity, and NGOs ensure public oversight. This division of responsibilities highlights that responsible innovation is inherently collective.

Table 2. Collaborative ecosystem roles in ethical AI marketing

Stakeholder Group	Role in Ethical AI Implementation	Benefit for Branding Innovation
Businesses	Develop and deploy responsible AI systems	Enhance reputation and reduce risk
Regulators	Define standards and enforce accountability	Provide legal legitimacy and consumer trust
Consumers	Participate in co-design and consent processes	Strengthen agency and brand authenticity
Civil society/ NGOs	Provide oversight and ethical guidance	Increase transparency and public credibility

Collaboration thus enables brands to move beyond compliance-driven ethics toward systemic responsibility, where the interplay of diverse actors ensures that AI systems serve both commercial goals and societal interests. For organizations, participating in such ecosystems is not optional but a strategic necessity in building credibility, resilience, and long-term competitive advantage.

Bridging marketing innovation and ethical AI requires moving beyond a compliance-driven approach to one that treats ethics as a strategic driver. By balancing commercial objectives with trust, positioning ethics as a differentiator, and engaging in collaborative ecosystems, organizations can turn responsibility into resilience. The integration of ethics and innovation does not slow progress; rather, it builds the foundation for *trustworthy, future-proof branding*.

7. CONCLUSION

AI has rapidly transformed market research and branding analytics, offering unprecedented opportunities for personalization, predictive insight, and strategic decision-making, yet this progress has also exposed organizations to profound ethical challenges that strike at the core of consumer trust. As the chapter has shown, concerns around data privacy, algorithmic bias, opacity, and accountability are not hypothetical but recurring issues that have materialized in real-world controversies such as Cambridge Analytica's data misuse, Amazon's biased recruitment tool, the Apple Card's gender discrimination, and Facebook's exclusionary ad targeting practices. These failures demonstrate that without responsible oversight, AI can undermine brand credibility, invite regulatory penalties, and erode the long-term trust upon which effective branding depends. To address these risks, the chapter proposed a comprehensive ethical framework built on the principles of fairness, accountability, interpretability, and informed consent, which together provide the foundation for aligning technological innovation with societal expectations. Crucially, these principles must be operationalized across the AI lifecycle, from responsible data governance and dynamic consent in data collection, to fairness-aware learning in model training, explainability tools in deployment, and continuous audits in monitoring. Implementation guidelines emphasized that ethics must be embedded as an ongoing process rather than treated as a one-off compliance exercise, ensuring that systems remain transparent, equitable, and responsive to consumer concerns.

The discussion also highlighted that ethics should not be viewed merely as a constraint on innovation but as a catalyst for competitive advantage: by balancing commercial goals with consumer trust, integrating ethical branding into corporate identity, and participating in collaborative ecosystems with regulators, consumers, and civil society, organizations can transform responsibility into resilience and differentiation. Ethical AI thus emerges as both a moral imperative and a strategic resource, enabling brands to cultivate loyalty, broaden market inclusivity, and future-proof themselves against tightening regulations and rising consumer expectations. Ultimately, the chapter argued that bridging marketing innovation with ethical AI is the pathway to building transparent, equitable, and trustworthy brand–consumer relationships in the digital economy, where consumers increasingly evaluate brands not only on what they sell but on how they act. In this context, ethics is not a barrier to progress but a foundation for sustainable innovation, ensuring that AI serves as a driver of both commercial value and societal good.

REFERENCES

Angwin, J., & Parris, T. (2016). Facebook lets advertisers exclude users by race. *ProPublica.* https://www.propublica.org/article/facebook-lets-advertisers-exclude-users-by-race

Arrieta, A. B., Díaz-Rodríguez, N., Del Ser, J., Bennetot, A., Tabik, S., Barbado, A., & Herrera, F. (2020). Explainable Artificial Intelligence (XAI): Concepts, taxonomies, opportunities and challenges toward responsible AI. *Information Fusion, 58*, 82–115. DOI: 10.1016/j.inffus.2019.12.012

Bhattacharya, C. B., & Elsbach, K. D. (2002). Us versus them: The roles of organizational identification and disidentification in social marketing initiatives. *Journal of Public Policy & Marketing, 21*(1), 26–36. DOI: 10.1509/jppm.21.1.26.17608

Cadwalladr, C., & Graham-Harrison, E. (2018). Revealed: 50 million Facebook profiles harvested for Cambridge Analytica in major data breach. *The guardian, 17*(1), 22.

California Consumer Privacy Act (CCPA). (2018). State of California Department of Justice. https://oag.ca.gov/privacy/ccpa

Celestin, M., Sujatha, S., & Kumar, A. D. (2024). Analyzing the role of ethical business practices in building consumer trust and long-term brand loyalty: Leveraging corporate ethics as a competitive advantage. *WORLD (Oakland, Calif.), 1*. Advance online publication. DOI: 10.5281/zenodo.14010882

Choudhary, M. (2025). The Algorithmic Persuader: Ethical Challenges in AI-Powered Behavioral Manipulation in Digital Marketing. https://doi.org/DOI: 10.5281/zenodo.15474169

Das, R., & Singh, T. D. (2023). Multimodal sentiment analysis: A survey of methods, trends, and challenges. *ACM Computing Surveys, 55*(13s), 1–38. DOI: 10.1145/3586075

Dastin, J. (2018). *Amazon scraps secret AI recruiting tool that showed bias against women. Reuters (2018).*

Dastin, J. (2022). Amazon scraps secret AI recruiting tool that showed bias against women. In *Ethics of data and analytics* (pp. 296–299). Auerbach Publications. DOI: 10.1201/9781003278290-44

Davenport, T., Guha, A., Grewal, D., & Bressgott, T. (2020). How artificial intelligence will change the future of marketing. *Journal of the Academy of Marketing Science, 48*(1), 24–42. DOI: 10.1007/s11747-019-00696-0

Dwivedi, Y. K., Hughes, L., Wang, Y., Alalwan, A. A., Ahn, S. J., Balakrishnan, J., Barta, S., Belk, R., Buhalis, D., Dutot, V., Felix, R., Filieri, R., Flavián, C., Gustafsson, A., Hinsch, C., Hollensen, S., Jain, V., Kim, J., Krishen, A. S., & Wirtz, J. (2023). Metaverse marketing: How the metaverse will shape the future of consumer research and practice. *Psychology and Marketing, 40*(4), 750–776. DOI: 10.1002/mar.21767

European Commission. (2021). "Proposal for a Regulation laying down harmonised rules on artificial intelligence (Artificial Intelligence Act)." https://eur-lex.europa.eu/legal-content/EN/TXT/?uri=CELEX%3A52021PC0206

Fazelpour, S., & Lipton, Z. C. (2020, February). Algorithmic fairness from a non-ideal perspective. In *Proceedings of the AAAI/ACM Conference on AI, Ethics, and Society* (pp. 57-63). https://doi.org/DOI: 10.1145/3375627.3375828

Floridi, L., & Cowls, J. (2022). A unified framework of five principles for AI in society. *Machine learning and the city: Applications in architecture and urban design*, 535-545. https://doi.org/DOI: 10.1002/9781119815075.ch45

Francis, T., & Hoefel, F. (2018). True Gen': Generation Z and its implications for companies. *McKinsey & Company, 12*(2), 1-10.

García-Hernández, R. A., Luna-García, H., Celaya-Padilla, J. M., García-Hernández, A., Reveles-Gómez, L. C., Flores-Chaires, L. A., Delgado-Contreras, J. R., Rondon, D., & Villalba-Condori, K. O. (2024). A systematic literature review of modalities, trends, and limitations in emotion recognition, affective computing, and sentiment analysis. *Applied Sciences (Basel, Switzerland), 14*(16), 7165. DOI: 10.3390/app14167165

General Data Protection Regulation (GDPR). (2016). [EU]. *Regulation, 2016*(679). https://gdpr.eu/

Grewal, D., Hulland, J., Kopalle, P. K., & Karahanna, E. (2020). The future of technology and marketing: A multidisciplinary perspective. *Journal of the Academy of Marketing Science, 48*(1), 1–8. DOI: 10.1007/s11747-019-00711-4

Iriani, N., Agustianti, A., Sucianti, R., Rahman, A., & Putera, W. (2024). Understanding risk and uncertainty management: A qualitative inquiry into developing business strategies amidst global economic shifts, government policies, and market volatility. *Golden Ratio of Finance Management, 4*(2), 62–77. DOI: 10.52970/grfm.v4i2.444

Isaak, J., & Hanna, M. J. (2018). User data privacy: Facebook, Cambridge Analytica, and privacy protection. *Computer*, *51*(8), 56–59. DOI: 10.1109/MC.2018.3191268

Jabbar, A., Akhtar, P., & Dani, S. (2020). Real-time big data processing for instantaneous marketing decisions: A problematization approach. *Industrial Marketing Management*, *90*, 558–569. DOI: 10.1016/j.indmarman.2019.09.001

Jobin, A., Ienca, M., & Vayena, E. (2019). The global landscape of AI ethics guidelines. *Nature Machine Intelligence*, *1*(9), 389–399. DOI: 10.1038/s42256-019-0088-2

Kosinski, M., Stillwell, D., & Graepel, T. (2013). Private traits and attributes are predictable from digital records of human behavior. *Proceedings of the National Academy of Sciences of the United States of America*, *110*(15), 5802–5805. DOI: 10.1073/pnas.1218772110

Lambrecht, A., & Tucker, C. (2019). Algorithmic bias? An empirical study of apparent gender-based discrimination in the display of STEM career ads. *Management Science*, *65*(7), 2966–2981. DOI: 10.1287/mnsc.2018.3093

Matthias, A. (2004). The responsibility gap: Ascribing responsibility for the actions of learning automata. *Ethics and Information Technology*, *6*(3), 175–183. DOI: 10.1007/s10676-004-3422-1

Mehrabi, N., Morstatter, F., Saxena, N., Lerman, K., & Galstyan, A. (2021). A survey on bias and fairness in machine learning. *ACM Computing Surveys*, *54*(6), 1–35. DOI: 10.1145/3457607

Mittelstadt, B. (2019). Principles alone cannot guarantee ethical AI. *Nature Machine Intelligence*, *1*(11), 501–507. DOI: 10.1038/s42256-019-0114-4

Molakaseema, S. K. R. (2024). Leadership and Organizational Transformation in the Era of Digitalization Powered by Artificial Intelligence–An Analysis of Challenges and Opportunities. DOI: 10.34726/hss.2024.127206

Naqvi, S. K. H., & Batool, K. (2023). A comparative analysis between general data protection regulations and California consumer privacy act. *Journal of Computer Science. Information Technology and Telecommunication Engineering*, *4*(1), 326–332.

Onifade, A. Y., Ogeawuchi, J. C., & Abayomi, A. A. (2025). Scaling AI-Driven Sales Analytics for Predicting Consumer Behavior and Enhancing Data-Driven Business Decisions. *International Journal of Advanced Multidisciplinary Research and Studies*, *4*(6), 2181–2201. DOI: 10.62225/2583049X.2024.4.6.4269

Rust, R. T. (2020). The future of marketing. *International Journal of Research in Marketing*, *37*(1), 15–26. DOI: 10.1016/j.ijresmar.2019.08.002

Solove, D. J. (2021). The Myth of the Privacy Paradox. 89 George Washington Law Review 1. *GWU Legal Studies Research Paper*, (2020-10).

Sun, T. Q., & Medaglia, R. (2019). Mapping the challenges of Artificial Intelligence in the public sector: Evidence from public healthcare. *Government Information Quarterly*, *36*(2), 368–383. DOI: 10.1016/j.giq.2018.09.008

Susser, D., Roessler, B., & Nissenbaum, H. (2019). Online manipulation: Hidden influences in a digital world. *Geo. L. Tech. Rev.*, *4*, 1.

Thakur, J., & Kushwaha, B. P. (2024). Artificial intelligence in marketing research and future research directions: Science mapping and research clustering using bibliometric analysis. *Global Business and Organizational Excellence*, *43*(3), 139–155. DOI: 10.1002/joe.22233

U.S. Department of Housing and Urban Development (HUD). (2019). HUD charges Facebook with housing discrimination. *HUD Press Release.* https://archives.hud.gov/news/2019/pr19-035.cfm

Valentino-Devries, J. (2019). How E-Commerce Sites Manipulate You Into Buying Things You May Not Want. *International New York Times*, NA-NA.

Vallabhaneni, A. S., Perla, A., Regalla, R. R., & Kumari, N. (2024). The power of personalization: AI-driven recommendations. In *Minds Unveiled* (pp. 111–127). Productivity Press., DOI: 10.4324/9781032711089-9

Wedel, M., & Kannan, P. K. (2016). Marketing analytics for data-rich environments. *Journal of Marketing*, *80*(6), 97–121. DOI: 10.1509/jm.15.0413

Whittaker, M., Crawford, K., Dobbe, R., Fried, G., Kaziunas, E., Mathur, V., West, S. M., Richardson, R., Schultz, J., & Schwartz, O. (2018). *AI now report 2018*. AI Now Institute at New York University.

Zyskind, G., & Nathan, O. (2015, May). *Decentralizing privacy: Using blockchain to protect personal data. In 2015 IEEE security and privacy workshops*. IEEE., DOI: 10.1109/SPW.2015.27

Chapter 8
Ethical Aspects and Considerations of Machine Learning, Artificial Intelligence, and Image Processing in Marketing Research and Branding

Achakkagari Shashidhar
https://orcid.org/0009-0003-1467-8250
University of Hyderabad, India

Parvez Ahmad
https://orcid.org/0009-0008-3144-4006
SRM University, India

ABSTRACT

The integration of Artificial Intelligence (AI), Machine Learning (ML), and image processing in marketing research and branding enables predictive analytics, hyper-personalisation, and real-time consumer engagement. However, these technologies raise ethical concerns over privacy, surveillance, consent, and behavioural manipulation. Personal and biometric data are often collected without user awareness, undermining autonomy. Risks include targeting based on inferred emotions, loss of agency, and algorithmic biases that may cause discrimination in segmentation and representation. The chapter also evaluates synthetic media, such as AI-generated

DOI: 10.4018/979-8-3373-4506-2.ch008

influencers, for their impact on authenticity, trust, and perception. While legal frameworks like GDPR and CCPA exist, their limitations are noted. To address these challenges, the chapter proposes ethical frameworks stressing transparency, accountability, and interdisciplinary governance to foster fairness, trust, and societal benefit in AI-driven marketing.

1. INTRODUCTION: THE RISE OF INTELLIGENT MARKETING AND THE ETHICAL IMPERATIVE

The rapid proliferation of Artificial Intelligence (AI), Machine Learning (ML), and image processing technologies is reshaping the landscape of modern marketing and branding. These tools are no longer limited to back-end analytics or operational enhancements; they now lie at the heart of customer engagement strategies. AI is an emerging technology that is commonly defined as the "capability of a computer program to perform tasks or reasoning processes that we usually associate to intelligence in a human being" (Rossi, 2016). AI acts as an umbrella term for various technologies such as machine learning or deep learning (Jordan & Mitchell, 2015), involves the development of computer programs and systems that can perform tasks that normally require human intelligence, such as understanding natural language, recognizing patterns in data, and making decisions based on data analysis. From AI-powered recommendation engines to real-time sentiment analysis, and from facial recognition tools in retail stores to AI-generated promotional content, the digital marketing ecosystem has become increasingly intelligent, automated, and visually immersive. Predictive analytics, on the other hand, is the use of statistical algorithms and ML techniques to analyze data and make predictions about future events or trends (Letourneau-Guillon et al., 2020). Brands today are able to anticipate consumer needs, personalize interactions at scale, and adapt their messaging in real time. While these developments bring unprecedented strategic advantages, they also give rise to deep and pressing ethical concerns that cannot be relegated to afterthoughts.

Understanding the role of predictive analytics in anticipating customer needs and improving service delivery provides businesses with actionable insights that can strengthen customer loyalty. The ability to leverage data effectively allows organizations to not only meet but exceed customer expectations, thereby driving long-term success in an increasingly competitive marketplace (Rane et al., 2023; Alatyat et al., 2023). The strategic implementation of predictive analytics is essential for organizations aiming to enhance customer experience and retention. By harnessing the power of data, businesses can anticipate customer needs, tailor their offerings, and foster loyalty, ultimately driving sustainable growth in a competitive landscape (Oyegbade et al., 2021).

In marketing research and branding, the use of AI and ML often involves the collection and analysis of vast amounts of personal data. This includes not only explicit user input likebrowsing behavior and purchasing history, but also implicit signals like facial expressions, voice tone, emotional states, and biometric identifiers. Image processing, in particular, has enabled the use of facial recognition and emotion detection in both physical and digital environments, making it possible to infer consumer reactions and tailor experiences in real time. However, the accelerated adoption of AI in the marketing industry raises significant ethical and legal concerns. Concerns regarding data privacy, user consent, prejudice, discrimination and the possibility of algorithmic bias are merely a subset of the larger problems at hand (Borenstein & Howard, 2020; Hagendorff, 2020; Jobin et al., 2019; Kumar & Suthar, 2024). As these tools evolve, the ethical stakes increase, forcing marketers, technologists, and regulators to confront a fundamental question: how can we leverage technological innovation without compromising ethical responsibility?

At its core, this chapter argues that the ethical considerations surrounding AI, ML, and image processing are not peripheral; they are central to the sustainable and trustworthy use of these technologies in marketing. Ethical missteps in this domain can lead to not only reputational harm and legal consequences but also long-term damage to consumer trust and societal well-being. Marketers seeks to influence behavior; when combined with algorithmic systems capable of predicting, personalizing, and even manipulating human preferences, the power imbalance between brands and consumers grows significantly. This new paradigm demands a rethinking of ethical obligations, accountability mechanisms, and governance structures. The integration of these technologies has also blurred the line between persuasion and manipulation. AI systems can be designed to nudge users toward specific outcomes, whether that's purchasing a product, clicking an ad, or engaging with content. When powered by emotion detection and real-time data analysis, such systems can subtly shape user behavior without their conscious awareness. While this capability holds marketing appeal, it raises serious questions about informed consent, cognitive autonomy, and the psychological integrity of consumer decision-making.

Furthermore, the ethical risks extend beyond individual harm to systemic issues like algorithmic bias and discrimination. ML systems are trained on historical data, which often reflects existing social inequalities. As a result, AI systems used in branding and targeting may replicate and even amplify these biases, excluding certain groups from marketing campaigns, misclassifying facial features based on race or gender, or reinforcing stereotypes through content recommendations. The consequences of such missteps are particularly profound in an era where brand identity is closely linked to social values and inclusivity.

A major issue is the lack of consumer awareness regarding how their data is being used. The lack of transparency can lead to unauthorised data sharing or misuse (Wirtz et al., 2022). Transparency, fairness, and accountability become not just ideals but operational imperatives. Yet many AI-driven systems remain "black boxes"; their inner workings are not understandable even to the developers who build them, let alone the consumers they affect. This lack of explainability undermines consumer trust and complicates regulatory oversight. It also challenges the traditional marketing principles of clarity, honesty, and relationship-building. When consumers don't know how or why they are being targeted, trust in the brand erodes.

Although there has been substantial research on the ethical and legal dimensions of AI across various sectors like health care and finance (Gerke et al., 2020; Jobin et al., 2019), there is a noticeable gap within the marketing domain (Kumar & Suthar, 2024). This chapter seeks to provide a comprehensive ethical framework for understanding and evaluating the use of AI, ML, and image processing in marketing and branding. It begins by establishing the technological landscape and the key ways these tools are transforming marketing practices, which delves into critical ethical domains: data privacy, surveillance, manipulation, algorithmic bias, transparency, consent, and the use of synthetic media. Exploring the emerging legal and regulatory contexts and offers practical strategies for ethical governance, including ethical audits, responsible AI design, and interdisciplinary collaboration.

Ultimately, ethical marketing in the age of AI is not about resisting innovation; it is about guiding it. It requires a commitment to embedding ethical reflection into every stage of system design, deployment, and communication. This chapter is written for researchers, practitioners, and policymakers, who recognize that the future of marketing is not only intelligent but also accountable, transparent, and humane. By critically examining the intersection of technology and ethics, we can chart a path forward where innovation serves not just business interests, but societal good.

2. APPLICATIONS AND TRANSFORMATIONS IN BRANDING AND MARKETING

The integration of ML, AI, and image processing into marketing research and branding has fundamentally altered how brands interact with consumers. These technologies have enabled hyper-personalization, real-time engagement, predictive modeling, and data-driven decision-making that surpass the capabilities of traditional marketing. While these developments offer operational and strategic advantages, they introduce ethical complexities at every stage of the marketing pipeline, from data collection to consumer targeting and content generation. AI tools can automate the management of marketing campaigns by analyzing consumer data and predicting the best times to engage with customers. Techniques like decision trees and random forests help in determining the optimal timing and content of marketing messages, ensuring that consumers receive relevant communications (Blake et al., 2015).

AI and ML models analyze large volumes of structured and unstructured data to uncover patterns and predict consumer behavior. In branding, this translates into deeply personalized experiences where every touchpoint, from advertisements to product recommendations, is dynamically tailored to individual preferences. Retailers use ML to forecast demand and optimize pricing; media companies use it to curate content; and e-commerce platforms apply predictive analytics to influence purchasing decisions. These applications enable brands to stay competitive, but they also create ethical tensions related to autonomy, consent, and manipulation, which this chapter will address in depth.

Another critical application of predictive analytics in customer retention is churn prediction and prevention. By analyzing historical data, businesses can identify customers who are at risk of leaving based on behavioral patterns, transaction history, engagement levels, and sentiment analysis (Chukwuemeka et al., 2021). By applying advanced statistical models, machine learning algorithms, and artificial intelligence, organizations can identify patterns in customer behavior, predict potential churn, optimize loyalty programs, and refine pricing strategies to maintain a competitive edge (Nnagha et al., 2023).

Personalization is another key application, like predictive model-powered recommendation engines used by companies like Amazon or Netflix, which suggest products or content based on browsing habits and previous interactions. Personalization is a key factor in optimizing loyalty programs, and predictive analytics enables businesses to tailor incentives to individual customer preferences. Rather than offering generic rewards, companies can use predictive insights to determine what incentives will be most effective for each customer segment. For example, a travel company can offer frequent flyers exclusive discounts on destinations they have previously searched for, while a retail business can provide customized product discounts based on past purchases (Awoyemi et al., 2023).

Image processing adds another dimension to these capabilities. Brands now use computer vision techniques to assess consumer reactions through facial expression analysis, track in-store movement patterns, and evaluate visual engagement with advertisements. Facial recognition systems deployed in retail environments can identify returning customers and trigger personalized offers, while emotion detection algorithms gauge real-time sentiment from video interactions or social media images. Though these technologies aim to enhance user experience and optimize marketing strategies, their use raises serious concerns about surveillance, biometric data privacy, and the potential for non-consensual emotional profiling.

Generative AI has also emerged as a transformative force in branding. Tools that create realistic human avatars, deepfake influencers, or AI-generated ad visuals blur the line between authentic and synthetic content. These outputs can be indistinguishable from human-created materials, raising ethical concerns about deception and the erosion of authenticity in brand-customer relationships. In marketing contexts, where trust and relatability are central, the use of synthetic media without clear disclosure may undermine brand credibility and mislead consumers.

Another major transformation is in segmentation and targeting. Traditional demographic-based marketing is increasingly being replaced with behavior-based segmentation powered by ML algorithms. These systems cluster users based on predictive signals, purchase intent, browsing habits, and social media engagement, and adjust brand messaging accordingly. On the surface, this improves relevance and efficiency. However, when such systems make inferences about users' identities, preferences, or vulnerabilities, especially without transparency, the risk of discriminatory or manipulative targeting increases. Vulnerable populations such as children, the elderly, or individuals with cognitive impairments may be particularly susceptible to algorithmically optimized messaging.

Programmatic advertising further exemplifies the ethical challenges embedded in AI-powered branding. These systems automate ad placements based on real-time user behavior and contextual data. While efficient, the lack of transparency around how and why ads are shown can make consumers feel surveilled or targeted unfairly. Moreover, ad algorithms may unintentionally reinforce harmful stereotypes or exclude certain user groups if they are trained on biased data. Without ethical guardrails, AI-driven targeting can become a form of digital redlining, where certain users receive fewer opportunities or biased representations based on algorithmic assumptions.

In influencer marketing and branded content, AI is now used to identify potential collaborators by analyzing their follower metrics, sentiment, and engagement patterns. Predictive algorithms determine which influencers are most likely to drive conversions. At the same time, synthetic influencers, virtual characters generated using AI, are gaining popularity for their consistency and cost-effectiveness. While these developments offer novel marketing strategies, they prompt questions about authenticity, disclosure, and the psychological impact of presenting synthetic personas as real.

At a broader level, AI and ML systems are now involved in strategic brand decision-making. Marketers use AI to simulate campaign outcomes, assess brand perception through sentiment analysis, and adjust strategy in real time based on consumer feedback. These applications enhance agility but can also prioritize short-term metrics like engagement or clicks over long-term values such as trust and ethical integrity. As systems optimize for performance, they may recommend tactics that cross ethical boundaries, such as exploiting behavioral weaknesses or leveraging emotional states, if not deliberately designed to align with ethical principles.

This technological transformation has also shifted power dynamics in the marketer-consumer relationship. AI-driven branding gives companies unprecedented insight into consumer psychology, preferences, and routines. The asymmetry of knowledge and control creates an ethical imbalance: while brands operate with advanced tools and real-time data, consumers often lack clarity about how their information is used or how their decisions are being shaped. This imbalance underlines the urgency of embedding ethics directly into the design, deployment, and communication of marketing technologies.

3. ETHICAL ISSUES IN DATA PRIVACY AND CONSENT

One of the most pressing ethical concerns in AI marketing is data privacy. AI systems often rely on extensive data collection and processing, which raises significant privacy and security issues (Mittelstadt et al., 2016). At the core of ethical marketing lies the principle of respecting consumer privacy and obtaining meaningful consent. The capability of AI algorithms to amass and analyse extensive sets of personal data, such as browser histories and purchasing behaviours, has led to heightened concerns about data privacy (Wirtz et al., 2022). The use of AI, ML, and image processing in marketing research and branding fundamentally relies on access to large datasets, much of which includes personal and often sensitive information. These systems process browsing behavior, location data, purchase history, facial features, and emotional states frequently without the explicit knowledge or informed consent of the individual. AI can enhance predictive analytics, but it poses risks like biased data, privacy breaches, overreliance on technology, unfair decisions, and a lack of transparency. To mitigate harm, it's crucial to ensure careful data handling, privacy safeguards, and continuous evaluation of AI systems to maintain fairness, accuracy, and accountability in predictions (Radanliev et al., 2020). As marketing shifts toward greater personalization and predictive targeting, the risk of infringing on individual privacy increases significantly.

The ethical problem begins with data collection. AI and ML systems require extensive input data to function effectively, which often leads marketers to gather consumer information across a wide range of platforms: websites, mobile apps, social media, customer relationship management (CRM) systems, and physical stores equipped with cameras and sensors. Image processing tools can identify customers through facial recognition, assess sentiment through micro-expressions, or infer demographics from visual data. This ambient and continuous collection process is largely invisible to consumers, making it difficult for them to be aware of how much personal information they are sharing, let alone how it is being used.

One major concern is the absence of informed consent. While many digital platforms include privacy policies or consent checkboxes, these mechanisms are often insufficient. They are usually written in technical or vague language, do not offer meaningful choice, and fail to explain how AI and image processing technologies specifically use personal data. For consent to be ethically valid, it must be informed, freely given, specific, and revocable. In practice, most marketing systems fail to meet these standards, especially when passive data such as facial expressions or online behavior is used to infer intent or emotional states without active participation.

Data minimization, a key ethical principle, is often overlooked. Instead of collecting only what is necessary, many marketing systems operate under a logic of maximum data extraction, assuming that more data will lead to better performance. This mindset increases the risk of overreach, data breaches, and misuse. From an ethical standpoint, marketers should limit data collection to what is relevant and proportionate to their stated purpose and implement strict controls to prevent secondary or unintended uses.

Image processing technologies pose additional risks. Unlike textual data, biometric data, such as facial images, is permanent and uniquely identifiable. If compromised, it cannot be changed like a password. When used in marketing, such data is often extracted without clear disclosure, particularly in public spaces or via user-uploaded content. For example, facial recognition technology used to customize digital signage based on viewer age or mood may function without users' awareness. This practice not only undermines privacy but also violates ethical norms of autonomy and human dignity.

A related concern is function creep, where data collected for one purpose is repurposed for another without the user's knowledge. For instance, images shared on social media may initially be analyzed for engagement metrics but later be used to train emotion detection models or infer product preferences. Consumers rarely have control over these secondary uses, nor are they provided with mechanisms to opt out. This violates the ethical principle of purpose limitation and erodes trust in digital platforms.

The risks are compounded when personal data is combined across systems. Cross-platform tracking, where behavior from one site or app is matched with information from another, allows marketers to create highly detailed consumer profiles. While this improves targeting accuracy, it also increases exposure to privacy violations. Without robust safeguards and user-centric controls, consumers are left vulnerable to hyper-surveillance and manipulation.

Children and vulnerable populations face even greater ethical risks. Minors often do not fully understand consent implications, and yet their behavior is increasingly tracked and analyzed. Image recognition systems used in education or entertainment apps may identify and profile young users without adequate safeguards. Ethically, the bar for consent and data protection must be significantly higher for vulnerable users, but in practice, these groups are often more exposed to intrusive data practices.

Ethical marketing also requires transparency, not only in how data is collected but in how it is used to make decisions. Many AI-driven campaigns operate in opaque ways, with little visibility into how consumer segments are formed, how personalization works, or why certain individuals are targeted with specific content. This lack of transparency makes it nearly impossible for consumers to challenge or correct inaccuracies in their profiles or understand how they are being influenced. It also raises concerns about algorithmic determinism, where individuals are reduced to data-driven probabilities and stripped of context and nuance.

To address these concerns, ethical frameworks must promote user agency and control. Consumers should be able to access their data, understand how it is processed, and make informed decisions about its use. Opt-in models, granular consent settings, and data dashboards are tools that can empower users, but only if implemented clearly and accessibly. Ethical marketing design should avoid dark patterns, user interface tricks that push consumers toward sharing more data than they intend. Instead, interfaces should facilitate ethical choices by default.

Security is also a vital component of ethical data handling. When companies collect sensitive consumer data, they assume a duty of care to protect it from unauthorized access, theft, or misuse. Data breaches not only violate privacy but also undermine consumer confidence in brands and digital ecosystems. Encrypting personal information, limiting access based on roles, and conducting regular audits are basic ethical obligations. Yet, these practices are inconsistently followed across industries.

From a regulatory perspective, laws like the General Data Protection Regulation (GDPR) in Europe and the California Consumer Privacy Act (CCPA) in the U.S. attempt to formalize some of these ethical concerns into legal requirements. These include data subject rights, consent protocols, and limits on automated profiling. However, regulatory frameworks often lag behind technological developments, particularly in areas like real-time emotion detection or synthetic image generation. Therefore, compliance alone is insufficient; ethical marketing requires a proactive, principle-based approach.

4. SURVEILLANCE, MANIPULATION, AND CONSUMER AUTONOMY

Transparency is another critical ethical concern. The algorithms used in AI are often complex and opaque, making it difficult to understand how decisions are made and who is accountable for them (Mittelstadt et al., 2019). As Artificial Intelligence (AI), Machine Learning (ML), and image processing technologies become increasingly integrated into marketing, significant ethical concerns arise around surveillance and its implications for consumer autonomy. These tools enable marketers to monitor, analyze, and influence consumer behavior across digital and physical domains, often in ways that are opaque or imperceptible to consumers. This expanding capacity for surveillance, combined with algorithmic precision, raises profound ethical questions about behavioral manipulation and the gradual erosion of consumers' ability to make free, informed decisions. AI allows firms to anticipate and control consumers' decisions (Lippi et al., 2020).

Surveillance in marketing involves the continuous observation and data collection of individual behaviors. AI systems routinely track online browsing patterns, app usage, social media interactions, and physical location data. When coupled with image processing, marketers gain access to additional layers of information such as facial expressions, emotional states, and body language. In retail environments, cameras interpret shopper movement and reaction; online, sentiment analysis tools analyze selfies or profile images to infer mood. These inputs are used to generate adaptive, real-time responses, such as altering advertising content based on detected emotions.

While these systems promise enhanced personalization, they frequently operate without meaningful consent or consumer awareness. Unlike traditional market research methods, which involve voluntary participation, AI-based surveillance is typically passive and embedded within user environments. Consumers are often unaware of when they are being analyzed or what data is being collected, limiting their ability to contest or withdraw from these processes. This invisibility undermines informed consent and compromises the individual's right to autonomy.

Ethical concerns become more acute when surveillance evolves from observation to active manipulation. AI systems are not merely predicting behavior, they are increasingly designed to shape it. Real-time emotion detection and predictive modeling allow marketers to deploy targeted strategies at moments of emotional vulnerability. For instance, if a user exhibits signs of anxiety, algorithms might prompt the promotion of comforting products or escapist media. Although such interventions may drive engagement, they do so by exploiting psychological states that the consumer did not knowingly disclose or agree to have used for marketing purposes.

The notion of dark patterns illustrates these practices, which can be aggravated by A.I.-based algorithm implementation. Dark patterns are user interfaces whose designers knowingly confuse users, make it difficult for users to express their actual preferences, or manipulate users into taking specific actions (Luguri & Strahilevitz, 2019). They cover all the profiling methods, algorithmic proposals, or user interfaces that can restrict the ability to make a free and informed choice on the consumer's part. Dark patterns are also called dark nudges or bad sludges. Therefore, they cover strategies that increase the opacity of consumers' choices, making it more difficult for them to express their preferences freely, or that lead them to make decisions that they would not have made spontaneously (see, for instance, Gray et al., 2018; Sunstein, 2020). The dark pattern can be produced by the design of the site or the modes of presentation of the choices (Acquisti et al., 2020). It is not just a matter of using consumers' and users' vulnerabilities to induce them to make choices they could rationally try to curb, but also a matter of eliciting these preferences (Mulligan et al., 2020). Thus, "manipulative by design" devices exist (Obar & Oeldorf-Hirsch, 2018).

This manipulation challenges the foundational concept of autonomy, the right to make independent, rational decisions. Unlike transparent persuasion, which allows consumers to weigh options, AI-driven influence operates through opaque mechanisms, often below the level of conscious awareness. Consumers may believe their decisions are self-directed when, in reality, they are being subtly steered by systems optimized for engagement or conversion metrics.

Vulnerable populations are especially at risk. Children, the elderly, and individuals with cognitive impairments are less equipped to recognize or resist algorithmic influence. These groups can be easily profiled and targeted in ways that encourage overconsumption, dependence, or emotionally driven decisions, raising serious ethical concerns.

Moreover, as personalization strategies intensify, the boundary between relevance and coercion becomes increasingly blurred. When AI is used to trigger urgency, shape emotional states, or algorithmically time offers, personalization may give way to manipulation. The absence of transparency in these adjustments further compromises consumer autonomy.

There is also a growing risk that constant surveillance becomes normalized, masked as convenience. As users adapt to personalized interfaces and algorithmically tailored content, they may become desensitized to the trade-offs involved, ultimately accepting reduced privacy and diminished self-determination as the norm. This normalization extends beyond marketing, potentially weakening public resistance to surveillance in other societal domains.

To mitigate these risks, ethical marketing must draw a clear distinction between persuasion and manipulation. It must be guided by three key principles: transparency, protection of vulnerable users, and autonomy by design. Consumers should be clearly informed when AI influences their content; safeguards should be in place to prevent exploitation of psychological vulnerabilities; and systems should allow users to opt out, override automated decisions, or access neutral, non-personalized content.

5. BIAS AND DISCRIMINATION IN AI AND ML SYSTEMS

Bias in AI and ML systems presents a pressing ethical challenge, particularly when these technologies are applied in marketing and branding. These systems rely on data-driven learning to make decisions, yet the datasets they are trained on often reflect historical and societal biases. When deployed in marketing contexts, such biases can lead to discriminatory outcomes in targeting strategies, content personalization, visual representation, and customer segmentation. The consequences are not only ethically problematic, resulting in unfair treatment of individuals and groups, but also reputationally damaging for brands, as such practices deepen social inequalities and undermine public trust.

AI and ML models in marketing derive insights from historical patterns to determine audience targeting, predict conversion likelihood, or tailor visual content to specific demographics. However, historical data is rarely neutral. It encapsulates entrenched social hierarchies, consumption patterns, and cultural biases. For instance, if men predominantly purchased a particular product in the past, an ML model may unjustly prioritize male audiences for future campaigns, thereby perpetuating rather than challenging gender norms.

Bias is not limited to text-based or numerical data. Image processing systems used in branding, particularly those involving facial recognition or emotion detection, often exhibit reduced accuracy for individuals with darker skin tones, non-Western facial features, or culturally variant expressions. These discrepancies can lead to misclassification or exclusion of entire demographic groups, resulting in inconsistent, alienating, or offensive consumer experiences.

Such bias extends to targeted advertising. Predictive algorithms may undervalue users from underrepresented backgrounds, assigning them lower relevance scores and subsequently excluding them from high-value opportunities, including employment, housing, or premium products. While the aim may be optimization, the outcome often reinforces structural disadvantage and social stratification.

Content personalization systems further intensify this issue. Algorithms trained to maximize engagement frequently serve users content that mirrors their previous behavior, reinforcing existing preferences and stereotypes. A fitness enthusiast might repeatedly be shown content promoting narrow body ideals, excluding diverse representations. This creates a feedback loop in which algorithmic bias informs future predictions, narrowing the diversity of user experiences and skewing brand messaging.

Generative AI used in producing marketing copy, visuals, or avatars can also replicate implicit biases present in its training data. These may manifest as stereotypical portrayals of gender, race, culture, or age. In branding, where representation plays a central role, such outputs can alienate audiences and result in public backlash, reputational harm, and lost trust.

Crucially, bias can be introduced long before model deployment during data collection and labeling. If training datasets are geographically or culturally skewed, or if human annotators apply inconsistent labels, the model will inevitably inherit those distortions. In global marketing, this can lead to poorly localized content or culturally insensitive campaigns.

Addressing bias requires sustained ethical intervention. First, brands must recognize that bias is not simply a technical issue, but a human one. Data collection must reflect diversity across gender, race, age, and geography. Datasets should be audited and models tested for disparate outcomes across demographics. Second, algorithmic mitigation techniques such as fairness-aware modeling and de-biasing must be paired with human oversight, including ethical review involving diverse perspectives. Third, transparency is vital: consumers deserve to know when AI influences decisions and how those decisions are made. Finally, brands must be accountable for societal impacts, actively monitoring outcomes, collecting user feedback, and correcting inequities when discovered.

6. TRANSPARENCY AND EXPLAINABILITY IN AI-DRIVEN MARKETING

Transparency and explainability are essential to the ethical use of AI, machine learning, and image processing in marketing. As these technologies increasingly shape decisions about who sees what content, when, and why, the underlying processes often remain opaque. This lack of clarity creates serious ethical concerns. Consumers are left unaware of how their data is used, how their profiles are constructed, or why they are shown certain ads and not others. More importantly, they are unable to contest decisions that affect their access to information, services, or opportunities.

AI models, especially those built on deep learning, often operate in ways that are difficult to interpret. Even developers and marketers who deploy them may not fully understand why a system behaves as it does. In practical terms, this means a user may be targeted with specific content or excluded from a discount offer without knowing the basis for that decision. When systems use personal data to make inferences that affect people's experiences or options, those individuals deserve a basic explanation. Ethical systems cannot be black boxes.

The consequences of opacity are especially evident when algorithms create consumer segments, assign value scores, or personalize prices. For instance, if a user is categorized as low priority based on past behavior, they might receive fewer rewards, lower quality recommendations, or even less responsive customer service. If they are unaware that this categorization exists, they cannot challenge its accuracy or fairness. The system quietly shapes their experience while denying them both awareness and agency. The ethical cost is not only unequal treatment but the absence of any route for redress.

Explainability matters just as much in image processing systems. Technologies like facial recognition or emotion detection are often used to infer mood or intent based on visual input. These inferences are probabilistic, based on training data that may not reflect the diversity of real users. A system may misread emotion, misunderstand cultural differences, or make assumptions that are simply wrong. When these interpretations inform real-time marketing decisions, such as which product is shown or which message is delivered, they influence behavior without consent or understanding. A person may be nudged, excluded, or categorized based on data they never agreed to share and signals they never intended to communicate.

The problem is compounded by vague or inaccessible privacy policies. Consumers rarely receive clear information about what data is collected, how it is used, or what role AI plays in shaping their experience. Even when companies do provide this information, it is often buried in dense language or abstract summaries. The result is a gap between what companies know and what users are allowed to know. That imbalance erodes trust and undermines the ethical foundation of consent.

Meaningful transparency must be built into the systems themselves. That includes letting users know when AI is involved in personalizing content, showing them what kinds of data are being collected, and giving them a way to understand how they've been categorized. These aren't just user interface features they are ethical design choices. They create the conditions for consent, accountability, and informed decision-making.

Internal transparency is just as important. Marketers, product teams, and data scientists need to understand the tools they are using. If no one can explain how a model works, or why it produced a certain outcome, it becomes impossible to audit its fairness or correct its mistakes. Tools for interpreting models—such as attribution analysis or visual mapping—should be standard practice. Without them, errors go unnoticed, and bias becomes harder to detect.

Regulatory frameworks like the GDPR and CCPA require some level of algorithmic transparency, but they often fall short of what is needed. Compliance alone does not ensure ethical practice. Many systems remain legally permissible while still functioning in ways that distort choice or reproduce inequality. Ethical transparency must go beyond legal requirements and reflect a broader commitment to fairness and accountability.

There is also the trade-off between model complexity and interpretability. It is often assumed that the most accurate models must be the most complex, and therefore the least explainable. But when systems influence pricing, segmentation, or emotional targeting, accuracy alone is not enough. In such cases, it is reasonable to accept slightly less precision in exchange for greater transparency. People have a right to understand how decisions about them are made, even if that means choosing simpler or more interpretable tools.

7: RISKS OF SYNTHETIC MEDIA AND AI-GENERATED BRANDING

The use of synthetic media in marketing, such as AI-generated images, deepfake videos, and virtual influencers, introduces a new layer of ethical complexity in branding. These technologies allow marketers to create content that closely resembles human-generated material, often to the point of being indistinguishable from reality. While such tools offer creative flexibility and efficiency, they also blur the line between authenticity and fabrication. This erosion of clarity can lead to deception, manipulated trust, and confusion among consumers who may not realize they are engaging with artificial content.

Brands increasingly use AI-generated visuals to promote products, simulate scenarios, or represent idealized customers. These assets are often created through generative adversarial networks (GANs) and other deep learning models that can fabricate human-like faces, voices, or behaviors. In many cases, consumers are not informed that the people or scenes they are interacting with do not exist. When marketing relies on this type of content without explicit disclosure, it risks deceiving the audience, even if unintentionally. Consumers may make decisions or form emotional connections based on false representations, raising serious concerns about trust and transparency.

Virtual influencers exemplify this ethical dilemma. These are digital personas designed to act like real individuals, often with social media accounts, brand partnerships, and follower engagement. Though they may seem harmless, their interactions are scripted by teams or algorithms, and their presence may create unrealistic standards or false narratives. When users engage with such influencers without knowing their artificial nature, the line between marketing and manipulation becomes dangerously thin. These personas may promote products, values, or lifestyles that consumers assume are endorsed by real people, influencing behavior under false pretenses.

Another risk of synthetic media is its potential to reinforce stereotypes or biases. AI-generated content often reflects the data it is trained on, which can include skewed or problematic representations. If these models are trained on images that overrepresent certain races, genders, or body types, they may perpetuate narrow ideals of beauty, success, or identity in branding campaigns. When used without critical oversight, synthetic media can thus unintentionally amplify exclusionary messages and reduce the visibility of underrepresented groups in marketing narratives.

The rapid production and customization of synthetic content also raise concerns about the commodification of human likeness and emotion. AI tools can simulate facial expressions, tones of voice, and micro-movements to evoke empathy or relatability. Brands may use these cues to trigger specific emotional responses such as trust, nostalgia, or urgency without the involvement of real people. While such tactics may improve engagement, they risk crossing ethical boundaries by using fabricated emotion as a tool of influence. The consumer believes they are reacting to a genuine human expression, when in fact they are responding to a programmed output.

A further complication arises in user-generated content platforms and interactive environments. AI tools now enable brands to allow users to "interact" with virtual personas or co-create content that appears personalized. These experiences can feel authentic, even though they are governed entirely by automated logic. When synthetic agents participate in conversations, respond to emotional cues, or simulate social feedback, they create a sense of relationship that is not real. This can distort the user's understanding of human connection, raise concerns about emotional manipulation, and obscure the true intent of the brand.

Legal and regulatory frameworks have yet to fully catch up with the implications of synthetic media. In many jurisdictions, there is no requirement to disclose when media is AI-generated, leaving ethical discretion entirely to the organization. This lack of oversight increases the risk that brands will prioritize efficiency and novelty over responsibility and integrity. Without clear guidelines or consumer protections, synthetic content may be used in ways that erode public confidence not only in marketing, but in media and communication more broadly.

Ethical branding must acknowledge that authenticity is a foundational value in consumer relationships. When synthetic media is used, it should be clearly labeled and contextualized to prevent deception. Consumers should be able to distinguish between real and artificial content, especially when it influences purchasing decisions or emotional engagement. Transparency about the nature of the content helps preserve trust and aligns with principles of informed consent.

Furthermore, brands should avoid using synthetic media to simulate endorsements, testimonials, or lived experiences that did not occur. Creating fake reviews, customer stories, or emotional reactions undermines the credibility of the message and violates the ethical principle of honesty. If consumers learn that such content is fabricated, it can cause long-term damage to brand reputation and customer loyalty.

8: ACCOUNTABILITY AND ETHICAL RESPONSIBILITY FRAMEWORKS

The increasing complexity of AI, machine learning, and image processing systems in marketing makes accountability an urgent ethical issue. As these systems make decisions about customer segmentation, pricing, and brand messaging, responsibility becomes more difficult to trace. When a model excludes certain groups, misuses data, or causes unintended harm, it is rarely clear who is answerable. Is it the data scientist, the marketer, the executive team, or the system itself?

Ethical responsibility cannot be placed on a single actor. AI in marketing is the result of layered decisions across data collection, model training, system design, and strategic use. Each of these steps involves human judgment and ethical trade-offs. For that reason, accountability must be shared across the full lifecycle. Distributing responsibility across roles helps prevent the common excuse that an outcome was simply the product of automation or the system behaving unpredictably.

One major challenge is that AI models, particularly in marketing, make decisions not through explicit instructions but by identifying statistical patterns. This makes intent hard to prove. A model might learn to exclude certain demographics not because anyone intended harm, but because biased data led to biased outcomes. Still, the absence of intent does not remove responsibility. If a model discriminates even subtly, the organization that built and deployed it is still accountable for its effects.

Addressing this requires proactive frameworks. Algorithmic impact assessments, for example, can help identify risks before deployment. They allow teams to consider questions of fairness, privacy, and potential misuse in advance. This kind of structured review is as essential to AI as product safety testing is to physical goods.

Interdisciplinary review boards are another key mechanism. These should include not just engineers and marketers, but ethicists, legal experts, and ideally representatives from affected communities. Their role is to assess how a system is designed, what data it relies on, and what assumptions shape its outcomes. Their feedback can improve the ethical grounding of everything from targeting strategies to user interfaces.

Documentation also plays a central role in accountability. Every system should have a clear record of who developed it, what data it was trained on, what goals it was designed to achieve, and how it was evaluated. This information enables traceability and ensures that ethical responsibility is assigned, not lost in abstraction.

When documentation is done with accountability in mind, it becomes harder for organizations to distance themselves from harmful outcomes.

Training is equally essential. Developers, marketers, and managers must be educated on the ethical dimensions of AI especially how marketing goals can conflict with user autonomy or fairness. Without this understanding, even well-meaning teams may cause harm they don't recognize. Ethics training should be standard practice, not a one-time seminar or compliance checkbox.

Leadership also matters. Ethical standards must come from the top and be integrated into the organization's strategic goals. If leaders treat ethical risk as seriously as financial risk, teams will follow suit. This includes making clear that long-term trust is more important than short-term optimization.

Finally, accountability is not a one-time task. AI systems evolve as they collect new data and adapt to user behavior. Their ethical risks also shift over time. Ongoing monitoring, regular audits, and mechanisms for user feedback are essential to ensure that a system remains aligned with ethical standards long after it launches.

9: LEGAL AND REGULATORY IMPLICATIONS

As AI, ML, and image processing technologies become central to modern marketing, the need for legal and regulatory oversight grows increasingly urgent. These systems routinely process personal data, influence consumer behavior, and automate decisions that were once made by humans. The potential for misuse, whether intentional or inadvertent, has prompted legal systems worldwide to begin regulating how personal data is collected, processed, and applied in algorithmic marketing. However, current regulatory frameworks often lag behind technological capabilities, leaving critical ethical issues inadequately addressed. Moreover, the existing literature often proposes generalised solutions that may not directly apply to the marketing context. Research is needed to explore the ethical and legal challenges specific to AI in marketing and propose solutions tailored to this domain (Kumar & Suthar, 2024). Bridging this gap is essential for aligning legal compliance with ethical responsibility.

The most influential legal frameworks governing data-driven marketing today are the General Data Protection Regulation (GDPR) in the European Union and the California Consumer Privacy Act (CCPA) in the United States. Both aim to give individuals greater control over their personal data through transparency, informed consent, and the right to access, delete, or correct information. GDPR goes further by requiring that organizations provide meaningful explanations for automated decisions that significantly affect individuals. This is particularly relevant in marketing, where systems frequently assign value scores, target ads, or personalize user experiences based on automated logic.

In theory, these regulations apply directly to AI-driven marketing. Systems that recommend products, tailor content, or infer consumer preferences must operate within the boundaries of lawful data use. However, in practice, compliance is uneven. Many companies adopt vague or overly broad privacy policies, fail to obtain informed consent, or deploy opaque models that contradict the intent of transparency. Users may technically have rights, but the systems they interact with rarely make it easy to exercise them. As a result, individuals remain exposed to automated profiling, data exploitation, and behavioral manipulation with limited understanding or control.

CCPA, while narrower than GDPR, grants consumers the right to know what data is collected, request its deletion, and opt out of its sale. Businesses are required to disclose data categories and provide accessible opt-out mechanisms. Yet similar to GDPR, enforcement is limited, and the legislation struggles to keep pace with newer technologies such as facial recognition, emotion detection, and synthetic media generation. These tools often fall outside existing legal definitions, creating gaps in protection and oversight.

A central challenge is that many of the categories now relevant to marketing emotional states, inferred intentions, and biometric traits are not clearly defined as personal data under existing laws. AI systems can make inferences about a user's preferences, vulnerabilities, or psychological state without direct input. Whether those inferences deserve the same legal protection as explicit personal data is still under debate. Until this is resolved, sensitive data can be collected, processed, and monetized with little legal friction.

Another issue lies in the mismatch between the theoretical ideal of consent and the operational realities of AI. AI systems in marketing adapt constantly, responding to real-time inputs and behavior. It is impractical to seek explicit consent for every instance of data use. As a result, consent becomes a one-time event, often buried in generic interfaces. This is legally compliant but ethically insufficient. Informed consent must be ongoing, contextual, and supported by clear user interfaces, privacy-friendly defaults, and the ability to easily opt out.

Regulatory requirements for explainability also create tension. GDPR mandates that users receive meaningful insight into how automated decisions are made. Yet many AI systems, particularly deep learning models, are difficult to interpret even for developers. While this technical complexity is real, it cannot excuse the absence of explanation. If a system influences access to pricing, offers, or content, users should be able to understand the basis of those decisions. Ethically responsible marketing requires the use of interpretable models or supplementary explanation tools, even if that means sacrificing a degree of performance.

Beyond GDPR and CCPA, new legislation is emerging. The proposed EU AI Act, for example, would classify emotion recognition and biometric profiling in marketing as high-risk, subject to stricter oversight and transparency requirements. Canada, Brazil, and other countries are also developing laws that center on transparency, data minimization, and user control. However, global regulation remains fragmented, and most laws lag behind the speed of innovation. In this context, ethical marketing cannot wait for regulation to catch up.

10: FUTURE ETHICAL MARKETING – TRUST, INNOVATION, AND INTERDISCIPLINARY ACTION

As AI, ML, and image processing technologies continue to evolve and shape the future of marketing, the ethical landscape will only become more complex. The challenge ahead is not to resist innovation, but to ensure it is developed and deployed in ways that preserve human dignity, fairness, and trust. Ethical marketing must move beyond reactive compliance and embrace a proactive, principled approach that integrates transparency, accountability, and inclusion into every stage of technological advancement. The future of marketing lies not in technological dominance but in ethical leadership.

Trust will become the defining currency of digital branding. In a world where consumers are increasingly aware of how their data is collected and used, brands that demonstrate ethical integrity will stand out. This means adopting privacy-by-design principles, giving consumers control over how their data is used, and being transparent about the use of AI in decision-making. Ethical trust-building also includes clear communication; consumers should know when a recommendation is algorithmic, when content is AI-generated, and how their profiles are constructed. When people feel respected and informed, they are more likely to remain loyal and engaged.

At the same time, innovation must not be constrained by fear of ethical risk but rather guided by ethical foresight. AI offers tremendous opportunities to improve personalization, accessibility, and responsiveness in marketing. For example, it can help brands reach underserved communities with relevant content, design more inclusive campaigns, and deliver support services at scale. These benefits are only fully realized when systems are designed to avoid harm and maximize social value. Innovation that is inclusive and reflective of diverse needs contributes to a more ethical and equitable marketing ecosystem.

To achieve this balance, interdisciplinary collaboration is essential. Ethical marketing in the AI era cannot be managed by technologists alone, nor should it be left entirely to marketers or legal teams. Ethical oversight must include voices from across disciplines, ethicists, designers, legal experts, social scientists, consumer advocates, and affected communities. Together, these stakeholders can evaluate risks, challenge assumptions, and propose alternatives that balance efficiency with responsibility. Embedding ethical reflection into every stage of AI system development, from ideation to deployment, ensures that ethical considerations are not afterthoughts but are integral to system design.

Educational institutions and professional organizations also have a role to play. Curricula in business, data science, marketing, and design should include ethical training that focuses on real-world dilemmas in AI-driven environments. Practitioners must be equipped with the critical thinking skills necessary to recognize and respond to ethical trade-offs. Certification programs, ethical guidelines, and continuing education can reinforce these competencies and help foster a culture of responsibility within the industry.

Ethical marketing must also be adaptive. AI systems are dynamic; they evolve through learning and interaction. New risks and challenges will emerge over time, such as deepfakes, voice cloning, hyper-personalization, emotion prediction, and real-time influence mechanisms, which will test existing ethical standards. This means ethical frameworks must be regularly reviewed and updated. What is acceptable today may become unethical tomorrow as technology outpaces public understanding or regulatory control. Ethical marketing requires flexibility, vigilance, and continuous learning to remain effective in a rapidly changing environment.

Furthermore, organizations should view ethical practices not only as risk mitigation but as opportunities for differentiation. Brands that are transparent, inclusive, and respectful in their use of AI gain a strategic edge in consumer trust, regulatory preparedness, and societal reputation. Ethical branding is no longer optional; it is a competitive advantage. Companies that fail to adapt may face consumer backlash, legal penalties, or lasting damage to credibility. Conversely, those who lead in ethical innovation can shape industry standards and influence public expectations.

This future also requires a cultural shift within organizations. Ethical behavior must be valued at every level, not just in corporate mission statements but in day-to-day operations, performance metrics, and team incentives. Ethics must be integrated into key performance indicators (KPIs), product roadmaps, and decision-making frameworks. When ethical considerations are embedded into the core strategy, they guide innovation instead of slowing it down. This cultural embedding is what transforms ethical marketing from a set of external rules into an internal norm.

Public engagement is also critical. As marketing technologies become more sophisticated, consumers must be educated about how AI works and what their rights are. Transparent dialogue between brands and the public fosters mutual understanding and accountability. Brands should communicate clearly not only what they do, but why they do it, and they should invite feedback. Participatory design, open consultation, and ethical advisory boards with public input can strengthen legitimacy and build resilience in the face of ethical challenges.

Finally, ethical marketing must always return to its human purpose. Technology is a tool, not a goal. The goal of marketing is to connect meaningfully with people to understand needs, provide value, and build relationships. When AI is used to support these goals, rather than override them, it can enhance both business success and social good. But when AI is used to exploit, manipulate, or marginalize, it erodes the very foundation of marketing itself. Ethics reminds us of this purpose and keeps technology in service of it.

In conclusion, the future of ethical marketing lies at the intersection of trust, innovation, and interdisciplinary action. It requires a holistic approach that spans technical design, organizational culture, legal frameworks, and public engagement. AI, ML, and image processing will continue to reshape marketing, but whether this transformation benefits society depends on the values we embed into these systems now. Ethical vigilance is not a constraint on innovation; it is its most reliable guide. By aligning technological advancement with ethical principles, brands can lead with integrity and build a marketing future that is intelligent, inclusive, and just.

CONCLUSION

The evolution of marketing through AI, ML, and image processing technologies has introduced extraordinary capabilities in personalization, targeting, and engagement. These tools have fundamentally redefined how brands understand and interact with consumers, enabling real-time insights, emotion-aware messaging, and data-driven branding strategies at an unprecedented scale. Yet, with this transformation comes a parallel responsibility: to ensure that innovation does not compromise ethics, individual rights, or social equity.

Throughout this chapter, we have examined the key ethical challenges associated with the use of intelligent systems in marketing. These include violations of privacy through large-scale data extraction, lack of informed consent, behavioral surveillance, and algorithmic manipulation that threatens consumer autonomy. The deployment of systems that learn from biased data introduces real risks of discrimination and exclusion, particularly in customer segmentation, ad targeting, and content personalization. Image processing, especially emotion detection and facial recognition, raises further concerns when used without transparency or accountability.

We have also analyzed the ethical complexities surrounding synthetic media such as AI-generated influencers and deepfake content, which blur the line between authentic and fabricated brand communication. While these tools offer creative potential, they must be used responsibly to avoid deception and erosion of consumer trust.

Legal and regulatory frameworks such as the GDPR and CCPA provide foundational protections, but they are often reactive, limited in scope, and lag behind technological advancements. This reinforces the need for internal governance structures, proactive ethical frameworks, and interdisciplinary collaboration to guide the ethical development and deployment of AI in marketing.

Accountability must be shared across all stakeholders: developers, marketers, data scientists, executives, and policy-makers. Ethical responsibility must be integrated into the entire AI lifecycle, from data collection and algorithm design to implementation and consumer interaction. This includes regular audits, bias mitigation strategies, transparency protocols, and public engagement.

Importantly, the ethical use of AI in marketing is not only a matter of risk avoidance it is an opportunity for strategic leadership. Brands that adopt transparent, inclusive, and ethically sound practices are more likely to build lasting relationships with consumers, foster loyalty, and contribute positively to public discourse on technology and trust. Ethical marketing is not a limitation on innovation; it is the condition that enables its legitimacy and long-term sustainability.

As we move forward, the challenge is not simply how to innovate faster, but how to innovate more responsibly. Marketing must remain a human-centered discipline, one that respects autonomy, fairness, and truth even as it embraces the power of machines. The future of marketing depends not only on what AI can do, but on what we choose to do with it. Aligning technological advancement with ethical principles is not just a professional duty; it is a societal imperative.

This chapter has aimed to provide a foundational roadmap for understanding and navigating the ethical dimensions of AI in marketing. As these technologies evolve, so too must our ethical frameworks, ensuring that intelligent systems serve both business goals and the broader values of trust, respect, and justice.

REFERENCES

Acquisti, A., Brandimarte, L., & Loewenstein, G. (2020). Secrets and Likes: The Drive for Privacy and the Difficulty of Achieving It in the Digital Age. *Journal of Consumer Psychology, 30*(4), 736–758. Advance online publication. DOI: 10.1002/jcpy.1191

Alatyat, Z., Atiat, H. S., Al-Qatawneh, M. I., Alrahamneh, N. H. Y., Alrahamneh, H. Y., Alzyadat, M. A., & Jalil, M. M. A. (2023). The Impact of Branding in Building and Enhancing Customer Loyalty for Banking Services: An Applied Study of Commercial Bank Customers in Jordan. *International Journal of Professional Business Review, 8*(4), e01138–e01138. DOI: 10.26668/businessreview/2023.v8i4.1138

Awoyemi, N. O., Uchenna, R., Ozigi, J., None Iveren M. Leghemo, & Onwuzulike, C. (2023). Revolutionizing corporate governance: A framework for solving leadership inefficiencies in entrepreneurial and small business organizations. *International Journal of Multidisciplinary Research Updates, 6*(1), 045–052. DOI: 10.53430/ijmru.2023.6.1.0066

Blake, T., Nosko, C., & Tadelis, S. (2015). Consumer Heterogeneity and Paid Search Effectiveness: A Large-Scale Field Experiment. *Econometrica, 83*(1), 155–174. DOI: 10.3982/ECTA12423

Borenstein, J., & Howard, A. (2020). Emerging challenges in AI and the need for AI ethics education. *AI and Ethics, 1*(1), 61–65. Advance online publication. DOI: 10.1007/s43681-020-00002-7

Chukwuemeka, C., Ige, B., Adeola, S., Adeyemo, P., None Olukunle Oladipupo Amoo, & Adeoye, N. (2021). Redefining zero trust architecture in cloud networks: A conceptual shift towards granular, dynamic access control and policy enforcement. *Magna Scientia Advanced Research and Reviews, 2*(1), 074–086. DOI: 10.30574/msarr.2021.2.1.0032

Gerke, S., Minssen, T., & Cohen, G. (2020). Ethical and Legal Challenges of Artificial intelligence-driven Healthcare. *Artificial Intelligence in Health, 1*(1), 295–336. DOI: 10.1016/B978-0-12-818438-7.00012-5

Gray, C. M., Kou, Y., Battles, B., Hoggatt, J., & Toombs, A. L. (2018). The Dark (Patterns) Side of UX Design. *Proceedings of the 2018 CHI Conference on Human Factors in Computing Systems - CHI '18*, 1–14. DOI: 10.1145/3173574.3174108

Hagendorff, T. (2020). The Ethics of AI ethics: An Evaluation of Guidelines. *Minds and Machines, 30*(1), 99–120. DOI: 10.1007/s11023-020-09517-8

Jobin, A., Ienca, M., & Vayena, E. (2019). The Global Landscape of AI Ethics Guidelines. *Nature Machine Intelligence, 1*(9), 389–399. DOI: 10.1038/s42256-019-0088-2

Jordan, M. I., & Mitchell, T. M. (2015). Machine learning: Trends, perspectives, and prospects. *Science, 349*(6245), 255–260. DOI: 10.1126/science.aaa8415

Kumar, D., & Suthar, N. (2024). Ethical and Legal Challenges of AI in Marketing: An Exploration of Solutions. *Journal of Information. Communication and Ethics in Society, 22*(1), 124–144. DOI: 10.1108/JICES-05-2023-0068

Letourneau-Guillon, L., Camirand, D., Guilbert, F., & Forghani, R. (2020). Artificial Intelligence Applications for Workflow, Process Optimization and Predictive Analytics. *Neuroimaging Clinics of North America, 30*(4), e1–e15. DOI: 10.1016/j.nic.2020.08.008

Lippi, M., Contissa, G., Jablonowska, A., Lagioia, F., Micklitz, H.-W., Palka, P., Sartor, G., & Torroni, P. (2020). The Force Awakens: Artificial Intelligence for Consumer Law. *Journal of Artificial Intelligence Research, 67*, 169–190. DOI: 10.1613/jair.1.11519

Luguri, J., & Strahilevitz, L. (2019). Shining a Light on Dark Patterns. SSRN *Electronic Journal, 13*(1). DOI: 10.2139/ssrn.3431205

Mittelstadt, B., Russell, C., & Wachter, S. (2019). Explaining Explanations in AI. *Proceedings of the Conference on Fairness, Accountability, and Transparency - FAT* '19*, 279–288. DOI: 10.1145/3287560.3287574

Mittelstadt, B. D., Allo, P., Taddeo, M., Wachter, S., & Floridi, L. (2016). The Ethics of algorithms: Mapping the Debate. *Big Data & Society, 3*(2), 1–21. DOI: 10.1177/2053951716679679

Mulligan, D. K., Regan, P. M., & King, J. (2020). The Fertile Dark Matter of Privacy takes on the Dark Patterns of Surveillance. *Journal of Consumer Psychology, 30*(4), 767–773. Advance online publication. DOI: 10.1002/jcpy.1190

Nnagha, E. M., Ademola, M. K., Izevbizua, E. A., Uwishema, O., Nazir, A., & Wellington, J. (2023). Tackling sickle cell crisis in Nigeria: The need for newer therapeutic solutions in sickle cell crisis management - short communication. *Annals of Medicine and Surgery (London), 85*(5), 2282–2286. DOI: 10.1097/MS9.0000000000000696

Obar, J. A., & Oeldorf-Hirsch, A. (2018). The Clickwrap: A Political Economic Mechanism for Manufacturing Consent on Social Media. *Social Media + Society, 4*(3), 2056305118784770. Advance online publication. DOI: 10.1177/2056305118784770

Oyegbade, I. K., Igwe, A. N., Ofodile, O. C., & Azubuike, C. (2021). Innovative financial planning and governance models for emerging markets: Insights from startups and banking audits. *Open Access Research Journal of Multidisciplinary Studies, 1*(2), 108–116. DOI: 10.53022/oarjms.2021.1.2.0033

Radanliev, P., De Roure, D., Page, K., Nurse, J. R. C., Mantilla Montalvo, R., Santos, O., Maddox, L., & Burnap, P. (2020). Cyber risk at the edge: Current and future trends on cyber risk analytics and artificial intelligence in the industrial internet of things and industry 4.0 supply chains. *Cybersecurity, 3*(1), 13. Advance online publication. DOI: 10.1186/s42400-020-00052-8

Rane, N., Achari, A., & Choudhary, S. P. (2023). Enhancing customer loyalty through quality of service: Effective strategies to improve customer satisfaction, experience, relationship, and engagement. *International Research Journal of Modernization in Engineering Technology and Science, 5*(5), 427–452. ResearchGate. DOI: 10.56726/IRJMETS38104

Sunstein, C. R. (2020). Sludge Audits. *Behavioural Public Policy, 6*(4), 1–20. DOI: 10.1017/bpp.2019.32

Wirtz, J., Tarbit, J., Hartley, N., & Kunz, W. (2022). Corporate digital responsibility: Dealing with ethical, privacy and fairness challenges of AI. *Journal of AI. Robotics & Workplace Automation, 1*(4), 325. DOI: 10.69554/EJDV6502

Chapter 9
Data Privacy and Regulatory Concerns in AI-Powered Market Research

Ansuman Samal
https://orcid.org/0000-0002-4213-5988
Siksha 'O' Anusandhan University, India

P. Selvakumar
https://orcid.org/0000-0002-3650-4548
Department of Science and Humanities, Nehru Institute of Technology, Coimbatore, India

Pamarthi Satyanarayana
https://orcid.org/0009-0008-4041-3674
VEL TECH University, India

Dhananjay Kulkarni
Sri Balaji University, Pune, India

Shiney Chib
https://orcid.org/0000-0001-7648-9963
Datta Meghe Institute of Management Studies, India

S. Guru Basava Aradhya
https://orcid.org/0000-0002-3335-2681
Dr. D.Y. Patil B-School, Pune, India

ABSTRACT

AI-powered market research leverages diverse sources—transactions, surveys, browsing behavior, and more—to derive actionable insights that guide strategic decision-making. However, this data-intensive approach raises significant concerns regarding data privacy, a fundamental issue that must be rigorously addressed to maintain trust, ensure compliance with legal frameworks, and protect individual rights. Data privacy, broadly defined, refers to the handling, processing, storage, and sharing in ways safeguard prevent unauthorized access or misuse. In AI-driven market research, data privacy involves a complex interplay of ethical, technical,

DOI: 10.4018/979-8-3373-4506-2.ch009

considerations influence, anonymized, encrypted, ultimately utilized. ensuring data privacy -powered market research need for detailed, high-quality data against privacy safeguards. AI algorithms thrive on detailed, granular data to detect subtle patterns and provide nuanced insights; however, this often involves processing sensitive or personally identifiable information.

THE IMPORTANCE OF DATA PRIVACY IN AI-POWERED MARKET RESEARCH

AI-powered market research leverages diverse sources—transactions, surveys, browsing behavior, and more—to derive actionable insights that guide strategic decision-making. However, this data-intensive approach raises significant concerns regarding data privacy, a fundamental issue that must be rigorously addressed to maintain trust, ensure compliance with legal frameworks, and protect individual rights. Data privacy, broadly defined, refers to the handling, processing, storage, and sharing in ways safeguard prevent unauthorized access or misuse. In AI-driven market research, data privacy involves a complex interplay of ethical, technical, considerations influence, anonymized, encrypted, ultimately utilized. ensuring data privacy -powered market research need for detailed, high-quality data against privacy safeguards. AI algorithms thrive on detailed, granular data to detect subtle patterns and provide nuanced insights; however, this often involves processing sensitive or personally identifiable information. To mitigate risks, organizations employ various replaces identifiable information with artificial identifiers but retains a key that can re-link the data under strict controls. Encryption protects data during storage and transmission, These technical measures, when combined with robust access controls, audit trails, and secure data infrastructures, form the backbone of a privacy-conscious AI research framework. Beyond technical safeguards, ethical stewardship of data privacy is equally vital in AI-powered market research. maintaining privacy also involves rigorous scrutiny of the datasets and algorithms to ensure fairness and accountability. This ethical dimension reinforces the trust relationship between consumers and companies, fostering a market environment where data subjects feel respected and secure.

Data privacy in AI-powered market research also has profound implications for business strategy and marketplace by building consumer trust and loyalty, which is increasingly critical in an era of heightened privacy awareness. Transparent privacy practices serve as a brand asset, signaling responsibility and respect for consumer rights. Furthermore, compliance with data protection laws helps avoid costly fines and legal battles that can erode financial stability and damage corporate reputation. and even disruption of research operations due to regulatory sanctions. As a result, many organizations are investing in privacy governance frameworks, appointing data protection officers, and integrating privacy impact assessments into their AI market research processes to proactively manage risks. necessitate continuous vigilance and adaptation in data privacy practices. AI capabilities are advancing rapidly, introducing new possibilities but also novel privacy challenges, such as the use of facial recognition, location tracking, and behavioral biometrics in market research. Regulators are also tightening requirements and expanding the scope of protected data, demanding greater transparency and accountability. To navigate this complex environment, organizations must foster In conclusion, merely regulatory cornerstone of, effective, and sustainable AI-powered market research. Protecting the privacy of personal data ensures that AI technologies can be harnessed responsibly to generate valuable market insights without compromising individual rights or public trust. By embedding robust privacy measures, embracing ethical principles, and maintaining compliance with evolving legal standards, data subjects they serve. (Kumar A. et al. 2025) This balance between innovation and privacy protection is critical for fostering a trustworthy digital ecosystem where both businesses and consumers thrive.

AI-POWERED MARKET RESEARCH: OPPORTUNITIES AND CHALLENGES

The regulatory landscape governing data protection has become increasingly complex and stringent in response to the exponential growth of data collection, processing, and analysis in today's digital economy, particularly within AI-powered market research. Data protection laws. These laws vary significantly across regions, reflecting differing cultural values, political priorities, and historical approaches to privacy, (Kotte K. R. et al. 2025) yet there is a clear global trend toward more comprehensive and enforceable data protection regulations. Understanding this regulatory environment is crucial for organizations engaged in AI market research, as Beyond the EU, many countries have introduced or updated data protection laws inspired by GDPR's framework, reflecting its global influence. closely mirrors GDPR principles despite Brexit. In Asia, countries like Japan have implemented (PIPL), effective since 2021, represents a significant development in the Asia-Pacific region, introducing stringent data handling requirements, cross-border transfer restrictions, and strong individual rights. The PIPL emphasizes data localization and consent, reflecting China's unique regulatory environment and geopolitical considerations. In India, the Personal Data Protection Bill, though still under consideration, aims to establish a robust data privacy regime modeled in part after GDPR, signaling increasing global harmonization. introduce a dedicated enforcement agency. (Thirunagalingam A. et al. 2025) Other U.S. states like Virginia, Colorado, and Utah have enacted similar laws, contributing to a growing mosaic of privacy regulations. This fragmented landscape requires companies to carefully navigate compliance based on where their consumers reside, often adopting multi-jurisdictional privacy strategies.

Internationally, various multi-lateral frameworks and agreements seek to privacy protections. Asia-Pacific Economic Cooperation (APEC) Privacy Framework promotes interoperability among member economies, emphasizing accountability and data security. ongoing negotiations for new agreements. These cross-border data transfer mechanisms are critical for global AI-powered market research, which often relies on data collected and processed across multiple jurisdictions. allows for human oversight and intervention. Additionally, there is growing recognition of the need to prevent algorithmic bias and discrimination, which may violate principles of fairness embedded in data protection frameworks. (Sakthivel M. et al. 2025) Enforcement of data protection laws is carried out by dedicated and state agencies in the U.S. These bodies possess investigative and sanctioning powers and play a vital role in guiding compliance through guidelines, audits, and public awareness campaigns. High-profile enforcement actions, such as those against tech giants for data breaches or misuse of consumer data, highlight the increasing vigilance of regulators worldwide and underscore the risks of non-compliance. They also encourage companies to invest in privacy training, data governance frameworks, and technological safeguards as part of comprehensive compliance programs. (Bahangulu J. K. et al. 2025) The evolving regulatory landscape also impacts the ethical and operational aspects (Upadhyaya A. N. et al. 2025) of AI-powered market research. Researchers and organizations must remain agile, regularly updating Collaboration with legal experts, data protection officers, and ethicists is essential to interpret complex regulatory mandates and implement them effectively within AI workflows. Moreover, organizations are encouraged to foster a culture of privacy awareness, not only to ensure compliance but to build long-term consumer trust. Laws like the GDPR set high standards that are being emulated worldwide, while regional differences necessitate tailored compliance approaches. For AI-powered market research, responsibly, protecting individual rights, and maintaining competitive advantage. As technology and societal expectations evolve, so too will data protection regulations, demanding continuous (Maheswaran K. et al. 2025) vigilance, adaptability, and commitment to privacy as a core organizational value. Successfully managing this regulatory environment enables organizations to not only comply with the law but to uphold ethical standards and foster trust in the digital age.

PERSONAL DATA PROTECTION: ENSURING ANONYMITY AND CONFIDENTIALITY

AI-powered market research represents a transformative shift in the way businesses gather, analyze, and interpret consumer insights, fundamentally altering the traditional landscape of market intelligence. By harnessing advanced algorithms, enables organizations process vast and complex datasets far beyond human capacity, delivering deeper, faster, and more predictive revolution presents tremendous opportunities for market researchers to unlock new levels of precision, personalization, and (Hubballi R. B. et al. 2025) efficiency, while simultaneously introducing a range of challenges that require careful navigation to realize AI's full potential in an ethical, accurate, and privacy-conscious manner. Traditional market research methods—surveys, focus groups, and manual data analysis—are often time-consuming, expensive, and limited in scale. AI technologies can process data e-commerce platforms, customer reviews, and IoT devices in real time, providing dynamic and continuously updated insights. For example, sentiment analysis powered by natural language processing (NLP) can scan thousands of customer comments across multiple languages to detect emerging opinions and emotional trends, enabling businesses within large datasets, uncovering hidden consumer segments or predicting future buying behaviors with higher accuracy than traditional statistical methods. (Soundariya A. et al. 2025) Furthermore, AI facilitates enhanced personalization and targeting in market research. By integrating data from various touchpoints—websites, mobile apps, purchase histories, and demographic information—AI models can create detailed consumer profiles and personas that help marketers tailor their products, messaging, and campaigns to specific audiences. This level of granularity not only improves customer engagement but also optimizes marketing spend by reducing waste and increasing conversion rates. Additionally, interact with respondents market research surveys, improving response rates and data quality through adaptive questioning and immediate feedback. These interactive technologies enhance participant experience and help capture richer, more nuanced data.

AI also enables predictive and prescriptive analytics that transform market research from descriptive hindsight to forward-looking strategy. Predictive models forecast customer behaviors such as churn, product preferences, or lifetime value, allowing companies to proactively design retention strategies or develop new offerings. Prescriptive analytics go a step further by suggesting optimal actions based on predictive insights, guiding decisions around pricing, promotions, or inventory management. This shift empowers organizations to move beyond understanding what happened to influencing what will happen, driving competitive advantage in rapidly evolving markets. (Thirunagalingam A. et al. 2025) Data privacy and ethical concerns represent another critical challenge. any breach of trust can have serious reputational and legal consequences for companies. Market researchers must implement stringent data protection measures, anonymization techniques, and transparent consent processes to maintain compliance and consumer confidence. Ethical dilemmas also arise regarding the use of AI to influence consumer behavior, requiring careful consideration of fairness, transparency, and potential manipulation. Technical challenges in AI deployment also complicate market research. Developing, training, and maintaining AI models require significant expertise, infrastructure, and ongoing monitoring to ensure accuracy and relevance. This lack of transparency poses risks for regulatory compliance and ethical governance, as it may be unclear how AI systems arrive at particular conclusions or recommendations. Consequently, there is a growing demand for explainable AI (XAI) methods that offer clearer insights into algorithmic processes and enable human oversight. Moreover, AI models are vulnerable to evolving market dynamics and adversarial manipulation. As consumer behavior shifts, AI algorithms must be continually retrained and updated to maintain relevance and accuracy. Adversarial attacks—where malicious actors deliberately input misleading or manipulated data—pose security (Samal A. et al. 2025) threats that can compromise research outcomes.

DATA COLLECTION AND USAGE: TRANSPARENCY AND CONSENT: DISCUSSION OF DATA COLLECTION AND USAGE.

Anonymity and confidentiality, while related, address distinct facets of privacy: anonymity ensures that data subjects cannot be identified within datasets, while confidentiality focuses on protecting personal data from unauthorized exposure or use during its lifecycle. Effective personal data protection less apparent data points like IP addresses, browsing histories, purchase patterns, biometric data, and location information. (Upadhyaya A. N. et al. 2025) The sensitive nature of this data means that breaches or improper handling powered market research, where large volumes of personal data are analyzed to discern consumer preferences and behaviors, protecting this data is critical to prevent harm and maintain ethical integrity. Ensuring anonymity is a primary strategy to protect personal data, particularly when sharing datasets for analysis or research purposes. Anonymization involves removing or irreversibly modifying personal identifiers such that individuals cannot be re-identified, even when datasets are combined with other information. Techniques for anonymization include data masking, generalization, suppression, and noise addition. Data masking replaces sensitive information with fictional or scrambled data; suppression eliminates certain data points entirely; and noise addition introduces random data variations to obscure (Chib S. et al. 2025) individual records. The goal is to maintain the analytical value of the data while breaking any direct or indirect link to identifiable individuals. However, achieving true anonymization is challenging, as advanced re-identification attacks using auxiliary data sources or AI techniques can sometimes reconstruct identities from anonymized datasets, especially when data is rich and multi-dimensional. Therefore, organizations must continuously assess re-identification risks and apply robust anonymization methodologies.

Complementing these technical safeguards are organizational policies and procedures designed to embed data protection into daily operations. Data governance frameworks outline clear rules for data handling, retention, and destruction, Legal frameworks worldwide provide the regulatory backbone for personal data protection, with stringent requirements for both anonymity and confidentiality. (Soundariya A. et al. 2025) The sheer scale and velocity of data generation, combined with increasingly sophisticated AI analytics, amplify the potential for privacy risks. AI models often require large, diverse datasets to train effectively, which can conflict with data minimization principles that advocate limiting data collection to what is strictly necessary. Furthermore, AI algorithms may inadvertently memorize or infer sensitive information during training, raising concerns about model inversion attacks where confidential data can be extracted from AI models. To mitigate these risks, emerging techniques such as differential privacy introduce mathematical noise into datasets or model outputs to protect individual data points without significantly degrading overall accuracy. Federated learning is another promising approach, enabling AI models to be trained across decentralized devices without transferring raw personal data, thus preserving confidentiality. The importance of protecting anonymity and confidentiality extends beyond compliance to building trust between consumers and organizations. In market research, where consumer participation is voluntary, trust is a critical determinant of data quality and engagement. When individuals are confident accurate data, enhancing the validity and usefulness of research findings. Conversely, high-profile data breaches or misuse can erode public trust, leading to decreased participation, negative publicity, and financial losses. (Alhitmi H. K. et al. 2024) It requires a comprehensive approach combining advanced technical safeguards, rigorous organizational policies, legal compliance, and a strong ethical commitment to privacy. As data volumes grow and AI capabilities evolve, continuous innovation in privacy-enhancing technologies and governance practices is imperative to keep pace with emerging risks. By prioritizing anonymity and confidentiality, reinforce the social contract of trust that underpins sustainable and responsible data-driven innovation.

DATA SECURITY: PROTECTING AGAINST BREACHES AND CYBER THREATS

This means that organizations must provide data subjects with comprehensive information before collecting any data, typically through privacy notices or transfers to third parties or across borders. It requires moving away from dense, jargon-filled legalese toward clear language that ensures meaningful comprehension by diverse audiences. Enhanced transparency builds trust by reducing uncertainty and enabling individuals. (Samal A. et al. 2025) Organizations must provide data subjects with real choices and avoid coercive or manipulative practices that undermine autonomy. For instance, consent for different data processing activities, such as marketing communications, behavioral profiling, or data sharing with partners, should be granular and separable, allowing individuals to accept some uses while declining others. Despite these legal frameworks, implementing transparency and consent in practice presents multiple challenges. One major obstacle is the complexity and scale of modern data ecosystems, where data collection often involves multiple Maintaining clear communication and accountability across these entities is difficult, particularly when data flows occur behind the scenes or across international borders with varying legal standards. Users may struggle to understand which organizations hold their data and for what purposes, leading to confusion and mistrust (Nebeker C. et al. 2022) Furthermore, the prevalence of lengthy privacy policies and consent forms can overwhelm users, resulting in "consent fatigue" where individuals mechanically accept terms without genuine understanding. Technological advancements also complicate transparency and consent. For example, AI-driven data collection mechanisms, such as behavioral tracking, biometric recognition, and IoT devices, often operate invisibly or continuously, challenging traditional consent models that rely on explicit user interaction. Real-time grasp the full scope of data usage. To address these issues, innovative solutions are emerging, including dynamic consent frameworks that allow ongoing, context-aware consent management; privacy (Ara A. et al. 2025) dashboards that provide that facilitate automated compliance checks and personalized privacy settings.

Another critical dimension is the ethical responsibility of organizations to go beyond minimum legal compliance and foster genuine transparency and meaningful consent as part of their corporate culture and social responsibility. This involves embedding into product development, ensuring that data protection is considered at every stage of the data lifecycle. It also means engaging with consumers through clear communication channels, education, and dialogue to build trust and demonstrate respect for individual autonomy. (Chib S. et al. 2025) Transparency reporting, where companies disclose their data practices and compliance efforts publicly, further enhances accountability and consumer confidence. Importantly, transparency and consent are not static achievements but ongoing commitments that require continuous evaluation and adaptation as technologies, consumer expectations, and regulatory landscapes evolve. They must also invest in training employees and developing cross-functional teams that include privacy experts, legal counsel, technologists, and communication specialists to ensure comprehensive oversight. (Abolaji E. O. et al. 2024) From a consumer perspective, transparency and consent digital interactions and protect themselves from privacy risks.. Achieving effective transparency and consent requires a holistic approach combining clear communication, robust legal compliance, innovative technology solutions, ethical leadership, and ongoing vigilance. (Alhitmi H. K. et al. 2024) As data-driven technologies continue to advance and permeate every aspect of life, organizations must prioritize transparency and consent not only as regulatory obligations but as core values that underpin sustainable and respectful relationships with individuals and society at large.

GDPR AND CCPA: UNDERSTANDING KEY REGULATIONS

Data breaches, which involve unauthorized access, disclosure, alteration, or destruction of sensitive information, have surged in frequency and sophistication, exploiting vulnerabilities in technological infrastructures, human factors, and organizational processes. Cyber threats now encompass a broad and evolving spectrum of malicious activities—including hacking, Data today exists in multiple environments—on-premises servers, public and private clouds, mobile devices, and edge networks—each (Nebeker C. et al. 2022) presenting unique security considerations. Moreover, data is transmitted continuously across networks, requiring protection both at rest and in transit. Attackers leverage automated tools, social engineering techniques, To protect against these pervasive threats, organizations create overlapping protections that reduce the likelihood and impact of breaches. This strategy typically includes technical, administrative, and physical safeguards. Access control is fundamental to data security, ensuring that only authorized monitoring, providing granular visibility and control over who accesses what data and when. Additionally, privileged access management (PAM) targets high-level accounts that pose elevated risks if compromised, enforcing stricter controls and oversight. information outside the organizational perimeter, whether accidentally or maliciously. These tools classify data based on sensitivity and apply policies to control its usage, such as blocking the upload of confidential files to external websites or flagging unusual email attachments. Security information and event management investigate, and respond to threats rapidly. Complementing SIEM are advanced (Kumar D. et al. 2024) analytics and artificial intelligence that identify patterns indicative of cyberattacks, insider threats, or policy violations.

Figure 1. Role of AI in data privacy

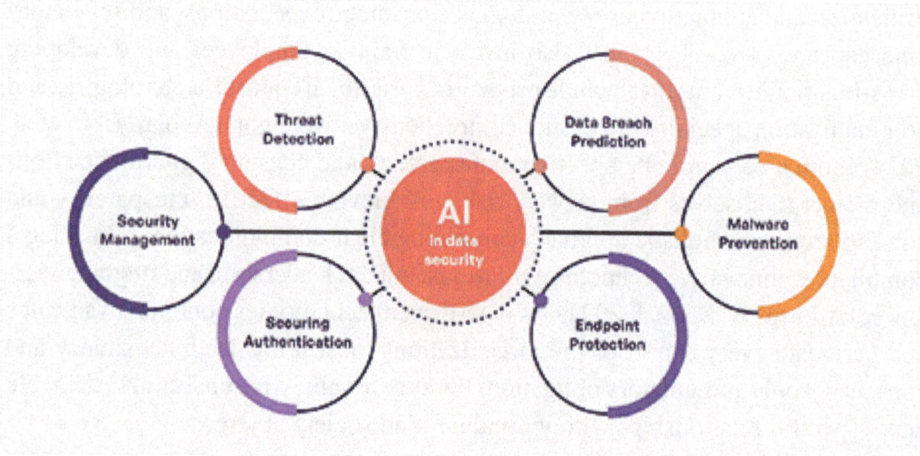

Incident response and disaster recovery capabilities are vital components of a comprehensive data security posture. Despite preventive measures, breaches may still occur, and the ability to quickly detect, contain, and remediate incidents can drastically reduce their impact. Well-defined incident response plans outline roles, communication protocols, and technical steps for managing breaches. Regular testing through simulations and tabletop exercises ensures preparedness and continuous improvement. Backup and recovery solutions (Abolaji E. O. et al. 2024) Emerging technologies offer both opportunities and risks for data security, automate routine security tasks, and predict potential attack vectors. However, these same technologies can be weaponized by cybercriminals to craft more convincing phishing campaigns, automate vulnerability discovery, and evade detection systems. Blockchain technology presents potential for securing data integrity and enhancing transparency in transactions, though it is still evolving and not a panacea for all security challenges. Human factors remain a critical element in data security. Employee awareness training is essential to reduce susceptibility to supports a proactive defense. Policies governing device usage, password hygiene, and reporting of suspicious activity reinforce these efforts. (Zangana H. M. et al. 2025) In conclusion, data security against breaches and cyber threats demands a holistic, multi-layered approach encompassing advanced technologies, rigorous policies, skilled personnel, and continuous adaptation to evolving threats. As data becomes an increasingly valuable asset and cyber adversaries grow more sophisticated, organizations must prioritize data security as a strategic imperative.

DATA LOCALIZATION: CHALLENGES AND OPPORTUNITIES

The significant and regulations globally, setting comprehensive standards Both laws emerged widespread collection and ensure transparency, accountability, and security. Despite their shared objective of enhancing data privacy rights, GDPR and CCPA differ in scope, geographic applicability, key provisions, enforcement mechanisms, and overall approach, reflecting distinct regulatory philosophies and legal traditions in landmark European Union that harmonizes data protection laws across its 27 member states. (Kumar D. et al. 2024) It replaces the 1995 One of the regulation's foundational principles is the empowerment of data subjects through explicit appropriate. evidenced by The regulation places a heavy emphasis on transparency, requiring organizations to provide clear, GDPR's accountability principle mandates that organizations proactively. alongside potential civil litigation and reputational harm. In contrast, pioneering role in data privacy legislation. While it shares GDPR's focus on consumer rights and business accountability, CCPA's scope is limited to for-profit Unlike GDPR prior in most cases focuses on transparency and consumer choice, particularly to third parties. mandates privacy at or before data collection, including "Do Not Sell My Personal Information" link. While CCPA respond consumer requests within specified timeframes it lacks GDPR's explicit data protection officer requirements or the comprehensive approach to data protection impact assessments. The CCPA authorizes enforcement by the California Attorney General, who may issue fines for violations up to (Anidjar L. et al. 2023) Despite these differences, GDPR and CCPA share common themes that underscore the global shift toward enhanced data privacy and protection. Both laws recognize the importance of individual rights over personal data and seek to increase transparency around data collection and usage. They emphasize accountability by requiring businesses promptly. Moreover, both regulations have inspired a wave of similar privacy laws worldwide, such as Brazil's LGPD and Virginia's CDPA, indicating a growing trend toward comprehensive data privacy governance.

The impact of GDPR and CCPA on businesses is profound and multifaceted. Enforcement of GDPR has been marked by a series of high-profile investigations and fines targeting multinational technology companies, telecommunications providers, and other sectors, signaling regulatory authorities' commitment to uphold data protection standards. These enforcement actions have clarified regulatory expectations and encouraged organizations to prioritize privacy risk management proactively. (Zangana H. M. et al. 2025) CCPA enforcement, while still evolving, has seen increased scrutiny and settlements related to consumer complaints and data breach disclosures, prompting businesses to enhance their compliance programs and consumer communication strategies. In conclusion, GDPR and CCPA represent pivotal frameworks in the ongoing evolution of global data privacy regulation.

They establish robust rights for individuals rigorous safeguard personal information through transparency, accountability, key provisions, (Prabha C. et al. 2024) similarities, distinctions essential seeking to navigate the complex regulatory landscape and build trust with consumers. As data privacy continues to gain prominence on the global stage, GDPR and CCPA will remain foundational models influencing future legislation and corporate data governance practices worldwide.

CROSS-BORDER DATA TRANSFERS: NAVIGATING REGULATORY COMPLEXITIES

Data localization refers to the regulatory requirement that organizations collect, process, and store data—particularly personal and sensitive information—within the borders of a specific country or region. This concept has gained prominence over recent years as governments worldwide seek to assert greater control over data generated by their citizens and within their jurisdictions. (Anidjar L. et al. 2023) Data localization is often driven by concerns related to national security, privacy protection, economic development, regulatory compliance, and sovereignty over digital assets. Beyond privacy, data localization is also viewed as a means to promote economic growth and digital sovereignty. By requiring local data storage, governments aim to foster the development of domestic data centers, cloud infrastructure, and related industries, thereby creating jobs and stimulating investment in technology sectors. This approach supports the concept of digital sovereignty, where nations seek to maintain control over their digital infrastructure, resources, and technological ecosystems to reduce dependence on foreign providers. For emerging economies, data localization can be seen as a strategy to build local digital capabilities and participate more actively in the global digital economy. Additionally, data localization can support government efforts to ensure critical infrastructure resilience by maintaining key data assets on domestic soil. However, the implementation of data localization policies poses significant challenges for multinational corporations and cloud service providers that rely on global data flows to deliver seamless services, optimize costs, and leverage economies of scale. The fragmentation of data across multiple jurisdictions increases operational complexity and costs, as organizations must build or lease data storage facilities in each country with localization mandates. (Gemiharto I. et al. 2024) This duplication of infrastructure leads to inefficiencies, hinders applications that depend on large, integrated datasets. Data localization can also impact service latency and quality, particularly for users who benefit from distributed cloud architectures that optimize data access speed and reliability across regions.

The lack of harmonization across countries complicates efforts to implement consistent data governance frameworks, forcing organizations to develop tailored compliance strategies that increase administrative overhead. (Prabha C. et al. 2024) From a technical perspective, data localization demands robust security and governance measures to ensure that localized data centers meet stringent standards for confidentiality, integrity, and availability. Organizations must implement strong encryption, access controls, monitoring, Additionally, localization may necessitate enhanced collaboration with local authorities and adherence to domestic regulations regarding data access, retention, and sharing. This raises privacy concerns related to potential government surveillance and the protection of civil liberties, particularly in jurisdictions with less transparent or authoritarian legal frameworks. Despite these challenges, data localization also presents several opportunities. It encourages investment in local technology infrastructure, which can drive innovation, create skilled jobs, and improve digital literacy within the country. Localization policies may foster the growth of local cloud service providers and data management companies, strengthening the domestic technology ecosystem. (Gemiharto I. et al. 2024) By ensuring data sovereignty, countries can assert greater control over their digital future, negotiate better terms with multinational tech giants, and promote trust among citizens who may be concerned about the handling of their data abroad. Additionally, localized data storage can enhance disaster recovery and business continuity by reducing dependence on foreign infrastructure. Global initiatives and dialogues are increasingly focusing on finding balanced approaches that reconcile data localization with (although invalidated, a new framework is under negotiation) seek to facilitate trusted data transfers while respecting privacy and security principles. Emerging technologies like edge computing and hybrid cloud architectures offer technical solutions that can support compliance with localization requirements while maintaining performance and scalability. Privacy-enhancing technologies (PETs), including data anonymization, encryption, and federated learning, also provide mechanisms to minimize risks when data moves across borders. In conclusion, data localization complex evolving modern, reflecting a confluence of privacy, security, economic, and sovereignty considerations. (Pandey A. S. et al. 2024) While it offers significant local economic development, it also introduces operational challenges, compliance complexities, and potential trade-offs impacting global data flows and innovation.

BIAS AND FAIRNESS: ENSURING AI SYSTEMS ARE UNBIASED: ANALYSIS OF BIAS AND FAIRNESS.

Navigating the intricate landscape of cross-border data transfers requires organizations to understand and comply with a patchwork of legal frameworks that govern when, how, and under what conditions data may leave a jurisdiction. (Raji M. A. et al. 2024) This challenge is compounded by varying definitions of personal data, differences in enforcement approaches, and the rapid evolution of privacy regulations in response to emerging technological and geopolitical developments. Consequently, effective management of cross-border data flows necessitates the adoption of robust compliance mechanisms that reconcile global business needs with local legal obligations. The cornerstone of cross-border data transfer regulation is the recognition that personal data processed outside its country of origin can be subject to increased privacy risks due to jurisdictional gaps, differing legal protections, and challenges in enforcement. The recent against U.S. government surveillance, thus intensifying scrutiny on transfers to the U.S. and prompting organizations to reassess their compliance strategies. This landmark ruling underscored during transfers and catalyzed efforts to negotiate a new transatlantic data transfer framework. In parallel, other regions have introduced or strengthened their own data transfer regulations. requires security assessments and government approval for certain data transfers abroad, while Brazil's LGPD mandates compliance with international data transfer standards. Apart from legal obligations, organizations must grapple with operational complexities (Gupta A. et al. 2025) associated with cross-border transfers. Identifying data flows, mapping data transfers, and understanding the jurisdictions involved are critical initial steps to ensure compliance. Many organizations lack clear visibility into their data ecosystems, especially when relying on third-party cloud providers, subprocessors, or international supply chains. This opacity increases the risk of non-compliance and inadvertent exposure to enforcement actions. (Abbas E. et al. 2024).

However, the effectiveness of SCCs depends on the ability to verify that the recipient's local environment—including government access and surveillance practices—does not undermine data protection. This assessment often requires technical safeguards such as encryption, pseudonymization, or anonymization, which add complexity and cost but enhance security and privacy. Binding Corporate enabling intra-group transfers under approved, enforceable data protection policies. However, obtaining regulatory approval for BCRs can be time-consuming and resource-intensive. (Kumar A. et al. 2025) Data transfer compliance also intersects with emerging technologies and new data paradigms. Cloud computing, for instance, enables dynamic data storage and processing across multiple global data centers, complicating the enforcement of location-specific restrictions. analytics generate massive streams of data that frequently cross borders, necessitating innovative compliance solutions. Additionally, artificial intelligence applications depend on aggregated, diverse datasets from multiple countries, challenging organizations to reconcile data localization laws with the need for data integration and sharing. vital to align privacy requirements with operational realities. Investments in privacy-enhancing technologies—such as data encryption, (Raji M. A. et al. 2024) tokenization, and federated learning—can reduce exposure by minimizing the amount of personal data transferred or by protecting data in transit. Transparency with data subjects through clear privacy notices and effective mechanisms for exercising data rights is essential to meet regulatory expectations and build trust. International cooperation and harmonization efforts continue to shape the future of cross-border data transfers. Multilateral agreements, global privacy standards, and cross-border regulatory dialogues aim to create interoperable frameworks that facilitate safe data flows while respecting national sovereignty and privacy rights. Organizations that proactively engage in these developments and adopt flexible, risk-based compliance strategies will be better positioned meeting regulatory demands. In conclusion, the digital economy but are accompanied by complex regulatory, operational, and technological challenges. (Gupta A. et al. 2025) Successfully navigating this landscape requires organizations to understand diverse legal regimes, implement robust governance and technical controls, and maintain agility in response to evolving privacy expectations and geopolitical dynamics.

EXPLAINABILITY AND TRANSPARENCY: UNDERSTANDING AI DECISION-MAKING

Algorithmic bias may also result from design choices, such as the selection of features, objective functions, or decision thresholds that inadvertently prioritize certain groups over others. Moreover, feedback loops in AI systems can reinforce existing biases, as decisions made by AI influence future data collection and model retraining, potentially entrenching disparities over time. Fairness in social dimensions, making its operationalization challenging. Various definitions of fairness exist, often reflecting different perspectives and trade-offs. Group fairness, for instance, focuses on ensuring that protected groups—such as those defined by race, gender, or age— (Ara A. et al. 2025) receive equitable outcomes or treatment from AI systems. Individual fairness, in contrast, emphasizes treating similar individuals similarly, regardless of group membership. Other fairness metrics include demographic parity, equal opportunity, and predictive parity, each capturing different aspects of fairness and sometimes conflicting with one another. The choice of fairness criteria depends on the application context, stakeholder values, and regulatory requirements, necessitating transparent and participatory decision-making processes. The consequences of bias in AI systems are far-reaching and can result in discriminatory practices, social injustice, and erosion of public trust. In hiring algorithms, biased models may systematically disadvantage minority candidates, perpetuating workforce inequalities. In criminal justice, predictive policing or sentencing tools biased against certain demographics can exacerbate systemic racism and undermine due process. Healthcare AI systems trained on skewed data health disparities. Furthermore, biased AI can contribute to digital exclusion, marginalizing vulnerable groups and exacerbating the digital divide. These harms not only affect individuals but also raise significant ethical and legal challenges for organizations deploying AI, as many jurisdictions now recognize fairness as a key principle in data protection and anti-discrimination laws. (Akter S. et al. 2023) Detecting bias Statistical analysis of model outputs across demographic groups can reveal disparities in error rates, false positives, and false negatives. Visualization techniques and fairness dashboards enable stakeholders to monitor and interpret model behavior. However, detecting bias is complicated by data limitations, ambiguous definitions of protected attributes, and challenges in capturing intersectional identities. Qualitative approaches, including stakeholder interviews, impact assessments, and ethical audits, provide contextual insights into how AI systems affect different communities. Continuous monitoring and periodic re-evaluation are necessary, as models may degrade or become biased over time due to changes in data or environment.

Mitigating bias involves interventions at multiple stages of the AI development lifecycle. Pre-processing techniques focus on curating balanced and representative datasets, addressing missing or skewed data, and augmenting underrepresented groups. (Farooqi S. A. et al. 2024) In-processing methods involve modifying the training algorithms to incorporate fairness constraints or adversarial debiasing, which aims to reduce unwanted correlations between sensitive attributes and model predictions. Post-processing approaches adjust model (Pandey A. S. et al. 2024) outputs to meet fairness criteria, such as recalibrating probabilities or applying decision thresholds to equalize outcomes. Combining these techniques can improve fairness, but trade-offs often exist between fairness, accuracy, and other performance metrics. It is also essential to integrate human oversight, domain deployment to ensure meaningful fairness beyond technical fixes. Transparency and explainability are integral to addressing bias and promoting fairness. Explainable AI (XAI) techniques and facilitate accountability. Transparency extends to documenting datasets, model development processes, and fairness evaluations through tools like datasheets for datasets and model cards. Engaging diverse stakeholders—ensures that fairness considerations reflect societal values and lived experiences. Legal and regulatory frameworks increasingly emphasize fairness as a fundamental requirement for AI systems. intersect with AI fairness concerns, prompting calls for algorithmic accountability. Organizations must therefore align AI development with these evolving legal norms to mitigate liability and uphold ethical responsibilities. In conclusion, ensuring (Abbas E. et al. 2024) AI systems are unbiased and fair is a complex, ongoing endeavor that demands multidisciplinary collaboration, robust technical solutions, ethical foresight, and inclusive governance.

ACCOUNTABILITY: ASSIGNING RESPONSIBILITY FOR AI-DRIVEN DECISIONS

Explainability refers to the ability to clearly articulate the logic, rationale, and factors behind an AI system's outputs, while transparency encompasses the openness regarding Together, these concepts empower stakeholders—including developers, regulators, users, and affected individuals—to scrutinize, challenge, and improve AI models, fostering an environment of trust and responsible innovation. This comprehensive discussion explores why explainability and transparency matter, the challenges inherent in achieving them, the technical methods employed, and their broader social, legal, (Leitner-Hanetseder S. et al. 2022) and ethical implications. The demand for explainability and transparency arises primarily from the need to mitigate parameters and nonlinear transformations, making their internal workings opaque even to their creators. This opacity can lead to uncertainty, mistrust, and difficulties in diagnosing errors or biases, potentially resulting in harmful consequences when AI-driven decisions affect individuals' lives and rights. For instance, a loan denial or medical diagnosis generated by an AI system without understandable reasoning can cause confusion and frustration for consumers and patients, undermining their ability to contest or seek redress. In regulated industries, explainability is often a legal or compliance requirement to ensure accountability and adherence to anti-discrimination and data protection laws. For regulators and auditors, explainability facilitates the assessment of compliance with fairness, (Rauf M. A. et al. 2024) norms. For end-users and affected individuals, understanding AI decisions enhances trust, empowerment, and acceptance by clarifying how decisions are made and what data is used. Explainability also supports organizational governance by providing mechanisms to oversee AI deployment, manage risks, and ensure alignment with corporate values and societal expectations.

Achieving explainability and transparency, however, is a significant technical and conceptual challenge, particularly with the proliferation of "black box" AI models. Simplistic models like decision trees or linear regressions are inherently interpretable, as their decision rules are explicit and comprehensible. (Bhamidipaty V. et al. 2025) However, such models often lack the predictive power of more complex approaches like deep learning, ensemble methods, or reinforcement learning, which excel in tasks involving unstructured data such as images, speech, and natural language. The challenge lies in balancing model accuracy with interpretability—commonly referred to as the accuracy-interpretability trade-off. To address this, researchers and practitioners employ a variety of techniques to explain complex AI models post hoc or design inherently interpretable models that offer transparency by construction. Post hoc explainability methods aim to provide human-understandable explanations after the AI system has made a decision. These include techniques such as feature importance ranking, which identifies the input variables that most influence a prediction; individual predictions based on cooperative game theory; and counterfactual explanations, which show how minimal changes to input features could alter an AI decision. Visualization tools like partial dependence plots and saliency maps further aid interpretation by highlighting model behavior and influential data regions. While powerful, these methods have limitations, including potential oversimplification, approximations that may misrepresent model behavior, (Prince N. U. et al. 2024) and challenges in communicating complex explanations to non-technical users. Technical complexities, the risk of exposing proprietary information or trade secrets, and the difficulty of translating technical explanations into accessible language pose barriers. (Almeida D. et al. 2025) To overcome these challenges, interdisciplinary collaboration among AI researchers, ethicists, legal experts, and user experience designers is vital to develop explanations that are accurate, meaningful, and actionable.

DATA MINIMIZATION: COLLECTING ONLY NECESSARY DATA: ANALYSIS OF DATA MINIMIZATION.

One of the fundamental challenges in assigning accountability for AI-driven decisions arises from the multifaceted and systems. Unlike traditional AI decisions may result from intricate interactions among data inputs, algorithms, automated learning, and system updates, which can be difficult to trace or explain. The involvement of multiple actors—data providers, algorithm developers, platform operators, end-users, and third-party vendors—complicates identifying who is responsible for specific outcomes. Moreover, (Kumar R. S. et al. 2024) the use of machine learning models that continuously evolve through self-improvement or reinforcement learning adds layers of unpredictability and dynamic behavior that challenge conventional accountability models based on human agency and intent. This diffusion of responsibility creates "accountability gaps" where it is unclear who should bear liability for errors, harms, or discriminatory effects (Madanchian M. et al. 2024) This includes designing systems that enable human intervention, review, and override, thereby preventing unchecked autonomous operation. Organizations are encouraged to establish governance structures regulatory oversight, audits, certification schemes, and mechanisms for affected individuals to seek redress and challenge AI decisions. Legal accountability characteristics of AI. Traditional liability concepts—such as product liability, negligence, and strict liability—may not neatly apply to AI systems, especially those that learn and adapt post-deployment. Some jurisdictions are exploring new legal constructs specifically tailored to AI accountability, including mandatory transparency requirements, certification of AI systems, and obligations to demonstrate due diligence in risk management. impose risk-based obligations on AI providers and users, emphasizing accountability through documentation, monitoring, and incident reporting.

Logging and monitoring tools record AI system inputs, outputs, and model changes, creating an audit trail that supports investigations and accountability claims. Robust testing and validation protocols, including stress testing and fairness audits, ensure AI behaves as intended under diverse conditions. These technical safeguards complement organizational processes and regulatory requirements, forming an integrated accountability framework. Accountability also involves ethical considerations related to fairness, justice, and respect for human rights. prevent discrimination, protect privacy, and avoid harm. (Bahangulu J. K. et al. 2025) When AI decisions negatively impact individuals or communities, accountability requires not only identifying the responsible parties but also providing mechanisms for remediation, compensation, and systemic improvements. This necessitates participatory governance models that include affected stakeholders, promote transparency about AI use, and foster ongoing dialogue between developers, regulators, and society. Building a culture of responsibility within organizations—through training, ethical guidelines, and leadership commitment—is essential for embedding accountability into everyday AI practice. In practice, achieving accountability for AI-driven decisions is an ongoing process that requires balancing innovation with risk management.

ANONYMIZATION AND PSEUDONYMIZATION: PROTECTING DATA

At its core, data minimization involves critically assessing only directly relevant and necessary to fulfill that purpose are gathered. This requires organizations to define clear objectives before collecting data and to avoid indiscriminate or excessive accumulation of information. collection to demographic details, purchase history, and relevant preferences rather than gathering extraneous sensitive information such as biometric data or unrelated personal identifiers. Adhering to data minimization reduces the volume of stored data, thereby lowering exposure to security vulnerabilities (Almeida D. et al. 2025) and the complexity of data governance. It also respects individuals' privacy by minimizing intrusive data capture, aligning with ethical principles of autonomy and informed consent. Legal frameworks worldwide enshrine data minimization as a key requirement. "adequate, relevant, and limited to what is necessary in relation to the purposes for which they are processed." organizations must conduct necessity and proportionality assessments, demonstrating that data collection is justified and cannot be achieved with less data. Similarly, the CCPA provide services or comply with legal obligations. These regulations also mandate transparency with data subjects about what data is collected and why, supporting informed consent and user control. Despite its clear benefits, implementing data minimization poses practical challenges, especially in complex data ecosystems and AI-driven environments. Modern AI and machine learning systems often require large datasets to train models effectively, leading to tensions between data minimization and the desire for extensive data to improve accuracy and innovation.

To overcome these challenges, organizations minimization. This starts with conducting thorough data mapping and inventory exercises to understand what data is collected, stored, and processed across all systems. Purpose specification should be explicit and granular, enabling focused data collection aligned with clearly defined goals. (Bhamidipaty V. et al. 2025) Data governance frameworks must incorporate data minimization policies, supported by technical controls such as automated data classification, retention limits, and access restrictions. Privacy by design principles encourage embedding data minimization early in system development, ensuring that data collection interfaces and workflows only capture essential information. For AI systems, techniques like federated learning, synthetic data generation, and differential privacy can reduce the need for raw personal data, enabling model training while preserving privacy. Transparency and communication with data subjects are vital components of data minimization. Organizations should purposes, and the retention periods, offering choices where feasible. (Madanchian M. et al. 2024) Providing clear, accessible privacy notices and mechanisms to opt-out or limit data sharing reinforces user autonomy and trust. When organizations collect less data, they also reduce the burden of data subject access requests and deletion obligations, enhancing operational efficiency. It requires deliberate, context-aware strategies that focus on collecting only what is necessary, supported by strong governance, transparency, and technological innovation. While challenges remain—especially in (Rauf M. A. et al. 2024) AI contexts—advances in privacy-enhancing technologies and regulatory guidance provide pathways for organizations to implement effective data minimization.

REGULAR AUDITS AND COMPLIANCE: ENSURING REGULATORY ADHERENCE

Anonymization and pseudonymization are critical decision-making. Although both aim to reduce the risk of exposing personal information, anonymization and pseudonymization differ significantly in approach, effectiveness, and regulatory implications. (Leitner-Hanetseder S. et al. 2022) This discussion explores the concepts, methodologies, advantages, limitations, and practical considerations surrounding anonymization and pseudonymization, highlighting their essential roles in responsible data management. True anonymization requires more than simply deleting obvious identifiers like names or social security numbers; it involves mitigating risks of re-identification through techniques such as data masking, aggregation, generalization, noise addition, and k-anonymity. For example singling out an individual. Other advanced techniques include differential privacy, which introduces controlled randomness into data queries to preserve statistical properties while preventing disclosure of individual records. (Farooqi S. A. et al. 2024) Pseudonymization, by contrast, entails replacing direct identifiers within a data set—or pseudonyms. Unlike anonymization, pseudonymization does not irreversibly sever the link between the data and the individual. The mapping between pseudonyms and real identities is maintained separately and securely, enabling the data to be re-identified if necessary under controlled circumstances. As a result, pseudonymized data remains personal data under regulations like the GDPR and requires ongoing protection and compliance measures. However, pseudonymization substantially reduces privacy risks by limiting direct exposure of personal identifiers and restricting access to the re-identification key. It facilitates lawful data processing activities such as longitudinal studies, fraud detection, or personalized services, where retaining the ability to re-link data to individuals is essential for operational or legal reasons. The benefits of anonymization and pseudonymization are multifaceted. Both techniques enhance data privacy, anonymized patient records to study (Kumar R. S. et al. 2024) disease patterns while protecting patient confidentiality. Similarly, pseudonymization allows companies to analyze customer behavior over time without directly revealing identities, balancing personalization with privacy.

Despite their advantages, implementing anonymization and pseudonymization presents technical and practical challenges. Cases of successful re-identification attacks have demonstrated that naive anonymization—such as simply removing names—may be insufficient, especially when combined with other publicly available datasets. Therefore, continuous evaluation and updating of anonymization methods are necessary to address evolving risks. Pseudonymization requires robust security controls to protect the mapping keys and ensure that only authorized personnel can re-identify individuals, as any compromise of these keys undermines privacy safeguards. Additionally, organizations must balance data utility against privacy; excessive anonymization can degrade data quality and limit its usefulness for analysis, while insufficient measures increase re-identification risks. The legal and regulatory context underscores the importance of these techniques. The GDPR explicitly promotes pseudonymization as a valuable data protection measure that can reduce risks and facilitate compliance, although it does not exempt pseudonymized data from protection obligations. Recital 28 of the (Akter S. et al. 2023) GDPR highlights pseudonymization as a means to enhance security and enable data processing under certain conditions. Government agencies anonymize census and population data before public release, ensuring transparency and research utility while protecting citizens. As data ecosystems grow (Prince N. U. et al. 2024) increasingly complex, the effective application of these techniques, combined with comprehensive governance and technological safeguards, will be vital for sustaining public trust and unlocking the transformative potential of data-driven innovation without compromising individual privacy.

THE FUTURE OF DATA PRIVACY IN AI-POWERED MARKET RESEARCH

Regular audits and compliance activities are fundamental pillars for ensuring that organizations adhere to regulatory requirements, internal policies, and ethical standards, particularly in domains involving sensitive data, such as privacy, security, and financial management. In an increasingly complex regulatory environment marked by mitigating risks, and sustaining competitive advantage. Audits serve as systematic, independent examinations of organizational processes, controls, and records, designed to (Kotte K. R. et al. 2025) verify compliance with applicable laws and standards, identify gaps or weaknesses, and recommend corrective actions. This comprehensive overview explores the role of regular audits in enforcing compliance, the methodologies involved, common challenges faced by organizations, and best practices to build resilient. Compliance audits can be internal—conducted by dedicated compliance teams or internal auditors—or external, performed by independent auditors, certification bodies, or regulatory agencies. Both types are essential: internal audits enable proactive identification and remediation of compliance issues, while external audits provide validation and assurance to stakeholders, including regulators, customers, and business partners. They collect documentation, such as privacy policies, risk assessments, training records, and technical configurations, to understand the control environment. (Sakthivel M. et al. 2025) Execution involves detailed testing of controls through interviews, process walkthroughs, data sampling, and technical reviews, such as penetration testing or system configuration audits. Auditors assess both the design adequacy of controls and their operational effectiveness over a defined period. Organizations must therefore maintain agility to adapt their compliance frameworks and audit methodologies accordingly.

To address these challenges, organizations adopt risk-based audit approaches that prioritize high-risk areas, such as processing of sensitive personal data or critical business functions. Leveraging automation and data analytics enhances audit efficiency by enabling continuous monitoring of compliance controls, real-time anomaly detection, and more comprehensive coverage than traditional manual audits. (Maheswaran K. et al. 2025) Regulatory technology (RegTech) solutions offer tools for tracking regulatory changes, managing audit workflows, and maintaining evidence trails. This cultural foundation empowers employees to recognize compliance obligations and embed privacy and security best practices into everyday operations. In highly regulated industries like finance, healthcare, and telecommunications, audit readiness is a competitive differentiator and often a contractual requirement. Additionally, audit findings provide actionable insights that enable organizations to improve processes, reduce risks of data breaches or regulatory fines, and align operational practices with ethical standards. An integral component of audit and compliance programs is the documentation and reporting framework. Comprehensive record-keeping ensures traceability of compliance activities, facilitates regulatory inquiries, and supports accountability. Documentation includes policy manuals, risk assessments, training records, incident logs, and evidence of control operation. Transparent communication with regulators during audits fosters cooperative relationships and can mitigate enforcement actions in case of identified non-compliance. (Hubballi R. B. et al. 2025) Organizations are increasingly adopting governance, risk, and compliance (GRC) platforms to centralize documentation, automate workflows, and provide dashboards for monitoring compliance status across departments and geographies.

CONCLUSION

The future of data privacy in AI-powered market research presents a complex yet dynamic interplay of emerging opportunities and formidable challenges. As artificial intelligence continues to revolutionize how market research is conducted—transforming the collection, analysis, and interpretation of consumer data—questions around privacy, transparency, and accountability become increasingly pivotal. AI technologies generative models are enabling unprecedented insights into consumer behavior, preferences, and intentions. These advancements promise richer, real-time, and more personalized market insights, allowing businesses to craft products and campaigns with surgical precision. However, they also usher in critical concerns about in an age where surveillance capitalism and data monetization have drawn widespread scrutiny. The future of this intersection hinges on how stakeholders balance innovation with the ethical and legal imperative to respect individual privacy rights. This enables organizations to gain deep consumer insights without relying solely on traditional survey-based methods. Predictive models can anticipate trends, segment audiences with precision, and optimize product-market fit. Moreover, the rise of generative AI opens new doors for simulating consumer personas, drafting marketing content, or generating synthetic data to train models when real data access is limited. Yet this immense power introduces considerable risk: when AI systems mine public or semi-private digital content, they may inadvertently collect personal or sensitive information without explicit consent. Furthermore, the increasing opacity of algorithmic models makes it harder for companies to determine whether privacy principles are being upheld internally or across third-party data partnerships. In the coming years, the central privacy challenge for AI-powered market research will be navigating an increasingly rigorous and globally fragmented regulatory landscape. As regulators gain technological literacy and enforcement capabilities, organizations will face heightened scrutiny over automated profiling, targeted advertising, and data sharing practices. Moreover, proposed legislation will bring AI-specific compliance obligations, including risk assessments, algorithmic transparency, fairness auditing, and human oversight. Future market research operations must be engineered with compliance in mind, integrating "privacy by design" and "accountability by default" into every layer value chain. However, technological innovation alone is not sufficient. The future of data privacy in AI-driven market research will also depend heavily on organizational culture, consumer trust, and cross-sector collaboration. Thus, cultivating a culture of privacy and ethical data use will be critical. This involves not only meeting regulatory standards but exceeding them—providing transparency, offering clear opt-ins and opt-outs, educating users, and demonstrating tangible respect for user preferences. Ethical AI guidelines, internal review boards, and privacy impact assessments should become standard practice, ensuring that innovations are deployed responsibly and inclusively.

Cross-industry collaboration will be essential to shape a cohesive and forward-looking privacy ecosystem. Regulators, technology providers, academic researchers, advocacy groups, and industry leaders must work together to develop harmonized standards, interoperable compliance frameworks, and shared best practices. The emergence of global certifications for data protection and AI ethics—and upcoming AI governance standards—will support this effort by providing clear benchmarks for responsible data practices. Industry-specific consortia ethical market research powered by AI. Moreover, public-private partnerships could foster innovation in privacy technology, promote data stewardship, and facilitate responsible data sharing through trusted intermediaries. Looking ahead, the future of data privacy in AI-powered market research will likely feature a shift toward decentralization, user-centric control, and greater transparency. Personal data vaults, blockchain-based own, manage, and selectively share their data on their terms. Companies may shift to consent-based data ecosystems, where users actively participate in data monetization or insight generation, incentivized by tokens or rewards. Explainable AI (XAI) will become vital, ensuring that users and regulators understand how insights are derived, particularly when they affect individuals through profiling or segmentation. Market research tools will evolve to offer built-in privacy controls,

REFERENCES

Abbas, E., & Qazi, A. A. (2024). Customized Ai-powered Security and Privacy Configurations for Social MEDIA Websites. *BULLET: Jurnal Multidisiplin Ilmu, 3*(1), 108–117.

Abolaji, E. O., & Akinwande, O. T. (2024). AI powered privacy protection: A survey of current state and future directions. *World Journal of Advanced Research and Reviews, 23*(3), 2687–2696. DOI: 10.30574/wjarr.2024.23.3.2869

Akter, S., Hossain, M. A., Sajib, S., Sultana, S., Rahman, M., Vrontis, D., & McCarthy, G. (2023). A framework for AI-powered service innovation capability: Review and agenda for future research. *Technovation, 125*, 102768. DOI: 10.1016/j.technovation.2023.102768

Alhitmi, H. K., Mardiah, A., Al-Sulaiti, K. I., & Abbas, J. (2024). Data security and privacy concerns of AI-driven marketing in the context of economics and business field: An exploration into possible solutions. *Cogent Business & Management, 11*(1), 2393743. DOI: 10.1080/23311975.2024.2393743

Almeida, D., & Barr, N. (2025). Innovations in Health Data Protection Ethical, Legal, and Technological Perspectives in a Global Context: AI-Powered Diagnosis Systems and Health Data Innovation. In *Navigating Privacy, Innovation, and Patient Empowerment Through Ethical Healthcare Technology* (pp. 171-196). IGI Global Scientific Publishing.

Anidjar, L., Packin, N. G., & Panezi, A. (2023). The matrix of privacy: Data infrastructure in the AI-Powered Metaverse. *SSRN, 18*, 59. DOI: 10.2139/ssrn.4363208

Ara, A., & Thomas, A. (2025). Exploring Consumer Perceptions and Ethical Considerations in AI-Powered E-Commerce. In *Data Visualization Tools for Business Applications* (pp. 347–368). IGI Global.

Bahangulu, J. K., & Owusu-Berko, L. (2025). Algorithmic bias, data ethics, and governance: Ensuring fairness, transparency, and compliance in AI-powered business analytics applications. *World J Adv Res Rev*, 1746-1763.

Bhamidipaty, V., Bhamidipaty, D. L., Guntoory, I., Bhamidipaty, K. D. P., Iyengar, K. P., Botchu, B., & Botchu, R. (2025). Revolutionizing Healthcare: The Impact of AI-Powered Sensors. *Generative Artificial Intelligence for Biomedical and Smart Health Informatics*, 355-373.

Chib, S., Mehta, A. K., Saravanan, A., Mishra, B. R., & Manjunath, T. C. (2025). Mental Health Challenges and Solutions in High-Pressure Work Environments. In Harriott, S. (Ed.), *Innovative Approaches to Managing Conflict and Change in Diverse Work Environments* (pp. 247–272). IGI Global Scientific Publishing. DOI: 10.4018/979-8-3693-9556-1.ch011

Farooqi, S. A., Memon, A., Zamir, S., Malik, K., Batool, W., & Zahid, H. (2024). NAVIGATING AI IN THE REAL WORLD: TRANSFORMATIONS, REGULATIONS, AND CHALLENGES. *Policy Research Journal*, *2*(4), 1083–1099.

Gemiharto, I., & Masrina, D. (2024). User privacy preservation in AI-powered digital communication systems. *Jurnal Communio: Jurnal Jurusan Ilmu Komunikasi*, *13*(2), 349–359. DOI: 10.35508/jikom.v13i2.9420

Gupta, A., Amarnani, M., Soanki, S., & Kishore, J. (2025). AI and Data Privacy in Business. In *2025 First International Conference on Advances in Computer Science, Electrical, Electronics, and Communication Technologies (CE2CT)* (pp. 109-114). IEEE.

Hubballi, R. B., Selvakumar, P., Seenivasan, R., & Basava Aradhya, S. G., Dinesh, N., & Seelam, P. K. (2025). Overview of Current AI Technologies in Education. In L. Kyei-Blankson & E. Ntuli (Eds.), *Transformative AI Practices for Personalized Learning Strategies* (pp. 1-26). IGI Global Scientific Publishing.

Kotte, K. R., Attaluri, V., & Selvakumar, P. (2025). Revolutionising Retail Banking with AI and Virtual Technologies AI-Driven Financial Training. In Nair, A. J., Manohar, S., Limbu, Y. B., & Huhmann, B. A. (Eds.), *Intersecting Natural Language Processing and FinTech Innovations in Service Marketing* (pp. 421–440). IGI Global Scientific Publishing. DOI: 10.4018/979-8-3693-9944-6.ch020

Kumar, A., Sharma, A., Dhanka, S., Bist, Y., Maini, S., & Bhatnagar, P. (2025). Data Privacy, Ethics, and the Role of AI in Customer Relationship Management. In *Demystifying Emotion AI, Robotics AI, and Sentiment Analysis in Customer Relationship Management* (pp. 283-318). IGI Global Scientific Publishing.

Kumar, D., & Suthar, N. (2024). Ethical and legal challenges of AI in marketing: An exploration of solutions. *Journal of Information. Communication and Ethics in Society*, *22*(1), 124–144. DOI: 10.1108/JICES-05-2023-0068

Kumar, R. S., Lokeshwari, J., & Shanmugam, S. K. (2024, November). AI-Powered Privacy Preservation: A Novel Framework for Adaptive Data Protection. In *2024 2nd International Conference on Computing and Data Analytics (ICCDA)* (pp. 1-6). IEEE.

Leitner-Hanetseder, S., & Lehner, O. M. (2022). AI-powered information and Big Data: Current regulations and ways forward in IFRS reporting. *Journal of Applied Accounting Research, 24*(2), 282–298. DOI: 10.1108/JAAR-01-2022-0022

Madanchian, M., & Taherdoost, H. (2024). AI-Powered Innovations in High-Tech Research and Development: From Theory to Practice. *Computers, Materials & Continua, 81*(2), 2133–2159. DOI: 10.32604/cmc.2024.057094

Maheswaran, K., Selvakumar, P., Shaikh, M., Shashank, G., Gupta, S., & Manjunath, T. C. (2025). The Evolution of Smart Urban Mobility With Emerging Technologies. In Ponnusamy, S., Assaf, M., Youssef, B., Jeon, G., & Kalyanaraman, S. (Eds.), *Leveraging VANETs and Blockchain Technology for Urban Mobility* (pp. 1–28). IGI Global Scientific Publishing. DOI: 10.4018/979-8-3373-0265-2.ch001

Nebeker, C., Parrish, E. M., & Graham, S. (2022). The AI-powered digital health sector: ethical and regulatory considerations when developing digital mental health tools for the older adult demographic. In *Artificial Intelligence in Brain and Mental Health: Philosophical, Ethical & Policy Issues* (pp. 159–176). Springer International Publishing.

Pandey, A. S., Sharma, Y., Tiwari, A., Chauhan, R., Tyagi, S., & Kumari, J. (2024). Ethical Implications of AI-Powered Communication Tool. In *2024 International Conference on Communication, Computer Sciences and Engineering (IC3SE)* (pp. 1857-1861). IEEE. DOI: 10.1109/IC3SE62002.2024.10593350

Prabha, C., & Saluja, S. (2024). Consumer Policy: The Relationship Between AI and Data Privacy. In *Ethical AI and Data Management Strategies in Marketing* (pp. 41-55). IGI Global.

Prince, N. U., Faheem, M. A., Khan, O. U., Hossain, K., Alkhayyat, A., Hamdache, A., & Elmouki, I. (2024). AI-powered data-driven cybersecurity techniques: Boosting threat identification and reaction. *Nanotechnology Perceptions, 20*, 332–353. DOI: 10.62441/nano-ntp.v20iS10.1804

Raji, M. A., Olodo, H. B., Oke, T. T., Addy, W. A., Ofodile, O. C., & Oyewole, A. T. (2024). E-commerce and consumer behavior: A review of AI-powered personalization and market trends. *GSC Advanced Research and Reviews, 18*(3), 066-077.

Rauf, M. A., Jim, M. M. I., Rahman, M. M., & Tariquzzaman, M. (2024). AI-Powered Predictive Analytics for Intellectual Property Risk Management in Supply Chain Operations: A Big Data Approach. *Global Mainstream Journal, 1*(4), 10–62304. DOI: 10.62304/ijse.v1i04.184

Sakthivel, M., Jaganathan, A., & Mohanraj, M. Mohit, & Manjunath, T. (2025). Brand Loyalty through AI and Personalisation AI-Generated Content for Financial Marketing. In A. J Nair, S. Manohar, Y. B. Limbu, & B. A. Huhmann (Eds.), *Intersecting Natural Language Processing and FinTech Innovations in Service Marketing* (pp. 77-96). IGI Global Scientific Publishing.

Samal, A., & Misra, L. I. Mohit, Pougajendy, S., Chandel, P. S., Manjunath, T. C., & (2025). Musealization and Tourism Practices. In S. Oflazoğlu & M. Dora (Eds.), *Preserving Cultural Heritage in Post-Disaster Urban Renewal* (pp. 115-142). IGI Global Scientific Publishing.

Soundariya, A., Behera, N. K., Chandel, P. S., Gupta, S., & Manjunath, T. C. (2025). AI and Environmental Ethics: The Role of AI in Addressing Climate Change Ethical Considerations in AI-Driven Environmental Solutions. In Chakraborty, S. (Ed.), *Human Values, Ethics, and Dignity in the Age of Artificial Intelligence* (pp. 321–346). IGI Global Scientific Publishing. DOI: 10.4018/979-8-3693-9035-1.ch013

Thirunagalingam, A., & Selvakumar, P. (2025). Application of Automation and Robotics in the Oil and Gas Industry. In Abdullayev, V., & Khang, A. (Eds.), *Revolutionizing AI and Robotics in the Oil and Gas Industry* (pp. 229–244). IGI Global Scientific Publishing. DOI: 10.4018/979-8-3693-8156-4.ch011

Upadhyaya, A. N., Debnath, P., Rani, P., Manjunath, T. C., & Bhattacharya, S. (2025). AI-Based Disaster Prediction and Early Warning Systems. In Mobo, F. (Ed.), *AI and Emerging Technologies for Emergency Response and Smart Cities* (pp. 55–74). IGI Global Scientific Publishing. DOI: 10.4018/979-8-3693-9770-1.ch003

Zangana, H. M., Omar, M., & Al-Karaki, J. N. (2025). Data Privacy and Security Standards in AI-Powered Scientific Research. In *Ensuring Secure and Ethical STM Research in the AI Era* (pp. 1–42). IGI Global Scientific Publishing. DOI: 10.4018/979-8-3373-4252-8.ch001

Compilation of References

Aarthi, S., Ravikumar, R. N., & Pardaev, J. (2025). Synergizing multimodal generative AI and blockchain for the future of digital media. In *Advances in Computational Intelligence and Robotics* (pp. 1–34). IGI Global Scientific Publishing. DOI: 10.4018/979-8-3373-1504-1.ch001

Aarzoo, & Lal, R. (2024). Artificial Intelligence-Driven Emotional Storytelling for Brand Narrative Strategies and Consumer Perception. SSRN. https://ssrn.com/abstract=4954803

Abbas, E., & Qazi, A. A. (2024). Customized Ai-powered Security and Privacy Configurations for Social MEDIA Websites. *BULLET: Jurnal Multidisiplin Ilmu*, *3*(1), 108–117.

Abd Elmonem, M. A., Nasr, E. S., & Geith, M. H. (2016). Benefits and challenges of cloud ERP systems–A systematic literature review. *Future Computing and Informatics Journal*, *1*(1–2), 1–9. DOI: 10.1016/j.fcij.2017.03.003

Abdulqader, Z., Abdulqader, D. M., Ahmed, O. M., Ismael, H. R., Ahmed, S. H., & Haji, L. (2024). A responsible AI development for sustainable enterprises: A review of integrating ethical AI with IoT and enterprise systems. *Journal of Information Technology and Informatics*, *3*(2), 129–156.

Abolaji, E. O., & Akinwande, O. T. (2024). AI powered privacy protection: A survey of current state and future directions. *World Journal of Advanced Research and Reviews*, *23*(3), 2687–2696. DOI: 10.30574/wjarr.2024.23.3.2869

Abrokwah-Larbi, K., & Awuku-Larbi, Y. (2023). The impact of artificial intelligence in marketing on the performance of business organizations: Evidence from SMEs in an emerging economy. *Journal of Entrepreneurship in Emerging Economies*, *16*(4), 1090–1117. DOI: 10.1108/JEEE-07-2022-0207

Abrokwah-Larbi, M. (2023). Dynamic capabilities and generative AI in customer personalization. *Journal of Interactive Marketing*, *57*(3), 112–127.

Aburbeian, A. H. M., Owda, A. Y., & Owda, M. (2022). A Technology Acceptance Model Survey of the Metaverse Prospects. *AI*, *3*(2), 285–302. DOI: 10.3390/ai3020018

Acquisti, A., Brandimarte, L., & Loewenstein, G. (2020). Secrets and Likes: The Drive for Privacy and the Difficulty of Achieving It in the Digital Age. *Journal of Consumer Psychology*, *30*(4), 736–758. Advance online publication. DOI: 10.1002/jcpy.1191

Ahlawat, R., & Swami, P. (2024). *The Right Color Attracts the Right Customer.*, DOI: 10.4018/979-8-3693-4236-7.ch017

Akter, S. (2024). Ethical AI development for sustainable enterprises: A review of integrating responsible AI with IoT and enterprise systems. *Journal of Artificial Intelligence General science (JAIGS)*, *6*(1), 94–125.

Akter, S., Hossain, M. A., Sajib, S., Sultana, S., Rahman, M., Vrontis, D., & McCarthy, G. (2023). A framework for AI-powered service innovation capability: Review and agenda for future research. *Technovation*, *125*, 102768. DOI: 10.1016/j.technovation.2023.102768

Al Balushi, M. K., Soliman, M., Al Hosni, M. S., & Al Mamari, A. (2024). Artificial Intelligence and Destination Branding. In Advances in Hospitality, Tourism, and the Services Industry (pp. 141–164). IGI Global. DOI: 10.4018/979-8-3693-6700-1.ch006

Alanadoly, A. B., Sidhu, S. K., & Richards-Carpenter, N. (2024). *AI Landscape in Fashion: Insights on Transforming Design, Supply Chains, Marketing, and Consumer Experiences* (pp. 417–439). DOI: 10.1007/978-3-031-71052-0_16

Alatyat, Z., Atiat, H. S., Al-Qatawneh, M. I., Alrahamneh, N. H. Y., Alrahamneh, H. Y., Alzyadat, M. A., & Jalil, M. M. A. (2023). The Impact of Branding in Building and Enhancing Customer Loyalty for Banking Services: An Applied Study of Commercial Bank Customers in Jordan. *International Journal of Professional Business Review*, *8*(4), e01138–e01138. DOI: 10.26668/businessreview/2023.v8i4.1138

Alhitmi, H. K., Mardiah, A., Al-Sulaiti, K. I., & Abbas, J. (2024). Data security and privacy concerns of AI-driven marketing in the context of economics and business field: An exploration into possible solutions. *Cogent Business & Management*, *11*(1), 2393743. DOI: 10.1080/23311975.2024.2393743

Alimamy, S., & Gnoth, J. (2022). I want it my way! The effect of perceptions of personalization through augmented reality and online shopping on customer intentions to co-create value. *Computers in Human Behavior*, *128*, 107105. DOI: 10.1016/j.chb.2021.107105

Al-Jabri, I., & Sohail, M. S. (2012). Mobile banking adoption: Application of diffusion of innovation theory. *Journal of Electronic Commerce Research, 13*(4), 379–391.

Aljarah, A., Ibrahim, B., & López, M. (2025). In AI, we do not trust! The nexus between awareness of falsity in AI-generated CSR ads and online brand engagement. *Internet Research, 35*(3), 1406–1426. DOI: 10.1108/INTR-12-2023-1156

Almeida, D., & Barr, N. (2025). Innovations in Health Data Protection Ethical, Legal, and Technological Perspectives in a Global Context: AI-Powered Diagnosis Systems and Health Data Innovation. In *Navigating Privacy, Innovation, and Patient Empowerment Through Ethical Healthcare Technology* (pp. 171-196). IGI Global Scientific Publishing.

Almeida, S., & Lelis, C. (2024). *Implications of New Media in Brands' Visual Identities: A Systematic Literature Review* (pp. 809–825). DOI: 10.1007/978-3-031-47281-7_66

Alvarado-Karste, D., & Guzmán, F. (2020). The effect of brand identity-cognitive style fit and social influence on consumer-based brand equity. *Journal of Product and Brand Management, 29*(7), 971–984. DOI: 10.1108/JPBM-06-2019-2419

Angwin, J., & Parris, T. (2016). Facebook lets advertisers exclude users by race. *ProPublica.* https://www.propublica.org/article/facebook-lets-advertisers-exclude-users-by-race

Anidjar, L., Packin, N. G., & Panezi, A. (2023). The matrix of privacy: Data infrastructure in the AI-Powered Metaverse. *SSRN, 18*, 59. DOI: 10.2139/ssrn.4363208

Antwi, B. O., & Avickson, E. K. (2024). Integrating SAP, AI, and Data Analytics for Advanced Enterprise Management. *International Journal of Research Publication and Reviews, 5*(10), 621–636. DOI: 10.55248/gengpi.5.1024.2722

Appel, G., Grewal, L., Hadi, R., & Stephen, A. T. (2020). The future of social media in marketing. *Journal of the Academy of Marketing Science, 48*(1), 79–95. DOI: 10.1007/s11747-019-00695-1

Ara, A., & Thomas, A. (2025). Exploring Consumer Perceptions and Ethical Considerations in AI-Powered E-Commerce. In *Data Visualization Tools for Business Applications* (pp. 347–368). IGI Global.

Arrieta, A. B., Díaz-Rodríguez, N., Del Ser, J., Bennetot, A., Tabik, S., Barbado, A., & Herrera, F. (2020). Explainable Artificial Intelligence (XAI): Concepts, taxonomies, opportunities and challenges toward responsible AI. *Information Fusion, 58*, 82–115. DOI: 10.1016/j.inffus.2019.12.012

Atienza, R. (2021). *Vision Transformer for Fast and Efficient Scene Text Recognition.*, DOI: 10.1007/978-3-030-86549-8_21

Awoyemi, N. O., Uchenna, R., Ozigi, J., None Iveren M. Leghemo, & Onwuzulike, C. (2023). Revolutionizing corporate governance: A framework for solving leadership inefficiencies in entrepreneurial and small business organizations. *International Journal of Multidisciplinary Research Updates, 6*(1), 045–052. DOI: 10.53430/ijmru.2023.6.1.0066

Babadoğan, B. (2024b). Exploring the role of AI in automating content marketing: Unlocking opportunities and navigating challenges. *Next Frontier For Life Sciences and AI, 8*(1), 67. DOI: 10.62802/gkj6f352

Baele, S. J., Brace, L., & Coan, T. G. (2023). Uncovering the Far-Right Online Ecosystem: An Analytical Framework and Research Agenda. *Studies in Conflict and Terrorism, 46*(9), 1599–1623. DOI: 10.1080/1057610X.2020.1862895

Bae, S., Jung, T. H., Moorhouse, N., Suh, M., & Kwon, O. (2020). The Influence of Mixed Reality on Satisfaction and Brand Loyalty in Cultural Heritage Attractions: A Brand Equity Perspective. *Sustainability (Basel), 12*(7), 2956. DOI: 10.3390/su12072956

Bagga, P., & Kaur, J. (2025b). Understanding artificial intelligence and its impact on branding. In Advances in Marketing, Customer Relationship Management, and E-Services (pp. 231–258). IGI Global. DOI: 10.4018/979-8-3693-9461-8.ch009

Bahangulu, J. K., & Owusu-Berko, L. (2025). Algorithmic bias, data ethics, and governance: Ensuring fairness, transparency, and compliance in AI-powered business analytics applications. *World J Adv Res Rev*, 1746-1763.

Balakrishna, S., & Mustapha, A. A. (2023). Progress in multi-object detection models: A comprehensive survey. *Multimedia Tools and Applications, 82*(15), 22405–22439. DOI: 10.1007/s11042-022-14131-0

Balasubramaniam, N., Kauppinen, M., Rannisto, A., Hiekkanen, K., & Kujala, S. (2023). Transparency and explainability of AI systems: From ethical guidelines to requirements. *Information and Software Technology, 159*, 107197. DOI: 10.1016/j.infsof.2023.107197

Balmer, J. M. T. (2023). Design, corporate brand design, and corporate heritage brand design: What are they? what of them? *Journal of Brand Management, 30*(2), 97–115. DOI: 10.1057/s41262-023-00314-z

Bashir, J. (2024). Strategic Enterprise Artificial Intelligence (The Conceptual Hierarchical Framework). *International Journal of Business & Management Studies*, *05*(05), 131–138. DOI: 10.56734/ijbms.v5n5a13

Basole, R. C., Park, H., & Seuss, C. D. (2024). Complex business ecosystem intelligence using AI-powered visual analytics. *Decision Support Systems*, *178*, 114133. DOI: 10.1016/j.dss.2023.114133

Bauskar, S. (2022). Business analytics in enterprise system based on application of artificial intelligence. *International Research Journal of Modernization in Engineering Technology and Science*, *4*(1), 1861–1870.

Baxter, P., & Jack, S. (2008). Qualitative case study methodology: Study design and implementation for novice researchers. *The Qualitative Report*, *13*(4), 544–559.

Bennett, W. L. (2023). Killing the golden goose? A framework for regulating disruptive technologies. *Information Communication and Society*, *26*(1), 16–36. DOI: 10.1080/1369118X.2021.1994625

Berber Sardinha, T. (2024). AI-generated vs human-authored texts: A multidimensional comparison. *Applied Corpus Linguistics*, *4*(1), 100083. DOI: 10.1016/j.acorp.2023.100083

Berger, J., Humphreys, A., Ludwig, S., Moe, W. W., Netzer, O., & Schweidel, D. A. (2020). Uniting the Tribes: Using Text for Marketing Insight. *Journal of Marketing*, *84*(1), 1–25. DOI: 10.1177/0022242919873106

Bertão, R. A., Yeoun, M.-H., & Joo, J. (2025). A blind spot in AI-powered logo makers: Visual design principles. *Visual Communication*, *24*(1), 222–250. DOI: 10.1177/14703572231155593

Bhamidipaty, V., Bhamidipaty, D. L., Guntoory, I., Bhamidipaty, K. D. P., Iyengar, K. P., Botchu, B., & Botchu, R. (2025). Revolutionizing Healthcare: The Impact of AI-Powered Sensors. *Generative Artificial Intelligence for Biomedical and Smart Health Informatics*, 355-373.

Bhattacharya, C. B., & Elsbach, K. D. (2002). Us versus them: The roles of organizational identification and disidentification in social marketing initiatives. *Journal of Public Policy & Marketing*, *21*(1), 26–36. DOI: 10.1509/jppm.21.1.26.17608

Bijsterveld, K. (2023). Eavesdropping by the eye: Detecting sound events and the culture of acoustic intelligence. *Sound Studies : an Interdisciplinary Journal*, *9*(2), 233–252. DOI: 10.1080/20551940.2023.2247649

Blake, T., Nosko, C., & Tadelis, S. (2015). Consumer Heterogeneity and Paid Search Effectiveness: A Large-Scale Field Experiment. *Econometrica, 83*(1), 155–174. DOI: 10.3982/ECTA12423

Bonini, T., & Magaudda, P. (2024). *Platformed! How Streaming, Algorithms and Artificial Intelligence are Shaping Music Cultures*. Springer Nature Switzerland., DOI: 10.1007/978-3-031-43965-0

Borau, S. (2025). Deception, Discrimination, and Objectification: Ethical Issues of Female AI Agents. *Journal of Business Ethics, 198*(1), 1–19. DOI: 10.1007/s10551-024-05754-4

Borenstein, J., & Howard, A. (2020). Emerging challenges in AI and the need for AI ethics education. *AI and Ethics, 1*(1), 61–65. Advance online publication. DOI: 10.1007/s43681-020-00002-7

Bourrasset, C., Boillod-Cerneux, F., Sauge, L., Deldossi, M., Wellenreiter, F., Bordawekar, R., & Belgodere, B. (2018, August). Requirements for an enterprise AI benchmark. In *Technology Conference on Performance Evaluation and Benchmarking* (pp. 71–81). Cham: Springer International Publishing. https://doi.org/DOI: 10.1007/978-3-030-11404-6_6

Bowden, J., & Mirzaei, A. (2021). Consumer engagement within retail communication channels: An examination of online brand communities and digital content marketing initiatives. *European Journal of Marketing, 55*(5), 1411–1439. DOI: 10.1108/EJM-01-2018-0007

Cadwalladr, C., & Graham-Harrison, E. (2018). Revealed: 50 million Facebook profiles harvested for Cambridge Analytica in major data breach. *The guardian, 17*(1), 22.

Caires, C. S. (2025). *From Words to Icons*. Advancements in Prompting Text-to-Image Models for Logo Design with Artificial Intelligence., DOI: 10.1007/978-3-031-76156-0_12

Cai, Y. (2025b). Innovative design and development of brand visual system under the background of Artificial Intelligence-assisted visual communication design. In *Research Square*.

California Consumer Privacy Act (CCPA). (2018). State of California Department of Justice. https://oag.ca.gov/privacy/ccpa

Campbell, C., Sands, S., Ferraro, C., Tsao, H.-Y. J., & Mavrommatis, A. (2020). From data to action: How marketers can leverage AI. *Business Horizons, 63*(2), 227–243. DOI: 10.1016/j.bushor.2019.12.002

Castañeda-García, J. A., Frías-Jamilena, D. M., Del Barrio-García, S., & Rodríguez-Molina, M. A. (2020). The Effect of Message Consistency and Destination-Positioning Brand Strategy Type on Consumer-Based Destination Brand Equity. *Journal of Travel Research*, *59*(8), 1447–1463. DOI: 10.1177/0047287519881506

Cavaye, A. L. (1996). Case study research: A multi-faceted research approach for IS. *Information Systems Journal*, *6*(3), 227–242. DOI: 10.1111/j.1365-2575.1996.tb00015.x

Cavusgil, E., Seggie, S. H., & Talay, M. B. (2007). Dynamic capabilities view: Foundations and research agenda. *Journal of Marketing Theory and Practice*, *15*(2), 159–166. DOI: 10.2753/MTP1069-6679150205

Celestin, M., Sujatha, S., & Kumar, A. D. (2024). Analyzing the role of ethical business practices in building consumer trust and long-term brand loyalty: Leveraging corporate ethics as a competitive advantage. *WORLD (Oakland, Calif.)*, *1*. Advance online publication. DOI: 10.5281/zenodo.14010882

Çelik, T., & Akagün Ergin, E. (2025). AI-driven design exploration: Utilizing brand logos as an inspiration source for architectural design. *Artificial Intelligence for Engineering Design, Analysis and Manufacturing*, *39*(e5), e5. DOI: 10.1017/S0890060425000046

César, I., Pereira, I., Rodrigues, F., Miguéis, V., Nicola, S., & Madureira, A. (2025). Exploring multimodal learning applications in marketing: A critical perspective. *International Journal of Hybrid Intelligent Systems*, *21*(1), 29–46. DOI: 10.3233/HIS-240018

Chaki, J., & Dey, N. (2021). *Introduction to Image Color Feature*., DOI: 10.1007/978-981-15-5761-3_1

Chau, P. Y. K. (1996). An empirical assessment of a modified technology acceptance model. *Journal of Management Information Systems*, *13*(2), 185–204. DOI: 10.1080/07421222.1996.11518128

Chen, S. C., Shing-Han, L., & Chien-Yi, L. (2011). Recent related research in technology acceptance model: A literature review. *Australian Journal of Business and Management Research*, *1*(9), 124–127. DOI: 10.52283/NSWRCA.AJBMR.20110109A14

Chib, S., Mehta, A. K., Saravanan, A., Mishra, B. R., & Manjunath, T. C. (2025). Mental Health Challenges and Solutions in High-Pressure Work Environments. In Harriott, S. (Ed.), *Innovative Approaches to Managing Conflict and Change in Diverse Work Environments* (pp. 247–272). IGI Global Scientific Publishing. DOI: 10.4018/979-8-3693-9556-1.ch011

Choudhary, M. (2025). The Algorithmic Persuader: Ethical Challenges in AI-Powered Behavioral Manipulation in Digital Marketing. https://doi.org/DOI: 10.5281/zenodo.15474169

Christofi, M., Vrontis, D., Leonidou, E., & Thrassou, A. (2020). Customer engagement through choice in cause-related marketing. *International Marketing Review*, *37*(4), 621–650. DOI: 10.1108/IMR-04-2018-0133

Chukwuemeka, C., Ige, B., Adeola, S., Adeyemo, P., None Olukunle Oladipupo Amoo, & Adeoye, N. (2021). Redefining zero trust architecture in cloud networks: A conceptual shift towards granular, dynamic access control and policy enforcement. *Magna Scientia Advanced Research and Reviews, 2*(1), 074–086. DOI: 10.30574/msarr.2021.2.1.0032

Correia, R., & Venciute, D. (Eds.). (2024). *AI innovation in services marketing*. IGI Global. DOI: 10.4018/979-8-3693-2153-9

Cowls, J., & Floridi, L. (2018). Prolegomena to a white paper on an ethical framework for a good AI society. *Minds and Machines*, *28*(4), 689–707. DOI: 10.1007/s11023-018-9482-5 PMID: 30930541

Crawford, K. (2021). *Atlas of AI: Power, politics, and the planetary costs of artificial intelligence.* Yale University Press.

Daneshfar, F., Bartani, A., & Lotfi, P. (2024). Image captioning by diffusion models: A survey. *Engineering Applications of Artificial Intelligence*, *138*, 109288. DOI: 10.1016/j.engappai.2024.109288

Dash, R., McMurtrey, M., Rebman, C., & Kar, U. K. (2019). Application of artificial intelligence in automation of supply chain management. *Journal of Strategic Innovation and Sustainability*, *14*(3), 43–53.

Das, R., & Singh, T. D. (2023). Multimodal sentiment analysis: A survey of methods, trends, and challenges. *ACM Computing Surveys*, *55*(13s), 1–38. DOI: 10.1145/3586075

Dastin, J. (2018). *Amazon scraps secret AI recruiting tool that showed bias against women. Reuters (2018).*

Dastin, J. (2022). Amazon scraps secret AI recruiting tool that showed bias against women. In *Ethics of data and analytics* (pp. 296–299). Auerbach Publications. DOI: 10.1201/9781003278290-44

Davenport, T., Guha, A., Grewal, D., & Bressgott, T. (2020). How artificial intelligence will change the future of marketing. *Journal of the Academy of Marketing Science*, *48*(1), 24–42. DOI: 10.1007/s11747-019-00696-0

Davtyan, N. (2024). AI in consumer behavior analysis and digital marketing: A strategic approach. The Integration of AI and Technology in Modern Business, 61–70.

Dearing, J. W., & Cox, J. G. (2018). Diffusion of innovations theory, principles, and practice. *Health Affairs (Project Hope)*, *37*(2), 183–190. DOI: 10.1377/hlthaff.2017.1104

Dencik, J., Goehring, B., & Marshall, A. (2023). Managing the emerging role of generative AI in next-generation business. *Strategy and Leadership*, *51*(6), 30–36. DOI: 10.1108/SL-08-2023-0079

Dey, A. U., Ghosh, S. K., Valveny, E., & Harit, G. (2021). Beyond visual semantics: Exploring the role of scene text in image understanding. *Pattern Recognition Letters*, *149*, 164–171. DOI: 10.1016/j.patrec.2021.06.011

Dhingra, M., Jain, M., & Jadon, R. S. (2016, December). Role of artificial intelligence in enterprise information security: a review. In *2016 fourth international conference on parallel, distributed and grid computing (PDGC)* (pp. 188–191). IEEE. DOI: 10.1109/PDGC.2016.7913142

Díaz-Rodríguez, N., Del Ser, J., Coeckelbergh, M., López de Prado, M., Herrera-Viedma, E., & Herrera, F. (2023). Connecting the dots in trustworthy Artificial Intelligence: From AI principles, ethics, and key requirements to responsible AI systems and regulation. *Information Fusion*, *99*, 101896. DOI: 10.1016/j.inffus.2023.101896

Divea, K., & Surjit, R. (2022). *Blockchain Utility by Pioneers in Fashion and Apparel Industry*., DOI: 10.1007/978-981-19-6569-2_4

Dixit, U. D., Shirdhonkar, M. S., & Sinha, G. R. (2023). Automatic logo detection from document image using HOG features. *Multimedia Tools and Applications*, *82*(1), 863–878. DOI: 10.1007/s11042-022-13300-5

Du Plessis, C. (2025). Ethical requirements for generative AI in brand content creation: A qualitative comparative analysis. *Frontiers in Communication*, *10*, 10. DOI: 10.3389/fcomm.2025.1523077

Duan, Y., Edwards, J. S., & Dwivedi, Y. K. (2019). Artificial intelligence for decision making in the era of Big Data–evolution, challenges and research agenda. *International Journal of Information Management*, *48*, 63–71. DOI: 10.1016/j.ijinfomgt.2019.01.021

Dulloo, R., & Struweg, I. (2025). The Rise of Experience Economy and Marketing 5.0. In *Leveraging AI-Powered Marketing in the Experience-Driven Economy* (pp. 1–38). IGI Global., DOI: 10.4018/979-8-3693-9561-5.ch001

Du, S., & Xie, C. (2021). Paradoxes of artificial intelligence in consumer markets: Ethical challenges and opportunities. *Journal of Business Research*, *129*, 961–974. DOI: 10.1016/j.jbusres.2020.08.024

Dutta, D., & Mishra, S. K. (2024). Bots for mental health: The boundaries of human and technology agencies for enabling mental well-being within organizations. *Personnel Review*, *53*(5), 1129–1156. DOI: 10.1108/PR-11-2022-0832

Dwivedi, Y. K., Hughes, L., Wang, Y., Alalwan, A. A., Ahn, S. J., Balakrishnan, J., Barta, S., Belk, R., Buhalis, D., Dutot, V., Felix, R., Filieri, R., Flavián, C., Gustafsson, A., Hinsch, C., Hollensen, S., Jain, V., Kim, J., Krishen, A. S., & Wirtz, J. (2023). Metaverse marketing: How the metaverse will shape the future of consumer research and practice. *Psychology and Marketing*, *40*(4), 750–776. DOI: 10.1002/mar.21767

Eisenhardt, K. M., & Martin, J. A. (2000). Dynamic capabilities: What are they? *Strategic Management Journal*, *21*(10-11), 1105–1121. DOI: 10.1002/1097-0266(200010/11)21:10/11<1105::AID-SMJ133>3.0.CO;2-E

Emon, M. M. H. (2025c). Circularity Meets AI: Revolutionizing Consumer Engagement Through Green Marketing. In *Transforming Business Practices With AI-Powered Green Marketing* (pp. 169–208). IGI Global Scientific Publishing. DOI: 10.4018/979-8-3373-3017-4.ch007

Emon, M. M. H. (2025d). Ethical Intelligence in Motion: Leveraging AI for Responsible Sourcing in Supply Chain and Logistics. In *Navigating Responsible Business Practices Through Ethical AI* (pp. 207–240). DOI: 10.4018/979-8-3373-3104-1.ch008

Emon, M. M. H. (2025e). Purpose-Driven Intelligence in Green Marketing: Leveraging AI for CSR-Centric and Sustainable Brand Positioning. In *Transforming Business Practices With AI-Powered Green Marketing* (pp. 89–122). IGI Global Scientific Publishing. DOI: 10.4018/979-8-3373-3017-4.ch004

Emon, M. M. H. (2025f). Navigating the Digital Labyrinth: Personal Data Privacy and Security at Individual and Organizational Levels. In *User-Centric Cybersecurity Implications for Sustainable Digital Transformation* (pp. 257–288). IGI Global Scientific Publishing. DOI: 10.4018/979-8-3373-3171-3.ch008

Emon, M. M. H., & Chowdhury, M. S. A. (2025). Safeguarding Student Data: Privacy and Security Challenges in AI-Powered Education Tools. In *Enhancing Student Support and Learning Through Conversational AI* (pp. 191–228). IGI Global Scientific Publishing. DOI: 10.4018/979-8-3373-3316-8.ch008

Emon, M. M. H. (2025). The Mediating Role of Supply Chain Responsiveness in the Relationship Between Key Supply Chain Drivers and Performance: Evidence from the FMCG Industry. *Brazilian Journal of Operations & Production Management, 22*(1), 2580. DOI: 10.14488/BJOPM.2580.2025

Emon, M. M. H. (2025b). Leveraging AI on Social Media & Digital Platforms to Enhance English Language Teaching and Learning. In *AI-Powered English Teaching* (pp. 211–238). IGI Global Scientific Publishing., DOI: 10.4018/979-8-3373-1952-0.ch007

Emon, M. M. H. (2025g). Digital transformation in emerging markets: Adoption dynamics of AI image generation in marketing practices. *Telematics and Informatics Reports, 20*, 100267. DOI: 10.1016/j.teler.2025.100267

Emon, M. M. H., & Ahmed, M. (2025). Digital Readiness as a Catalyst for Talent Transformation in Hospitality. In *Talent Management in Hotels and Hospitality* (pp. 461–502). IGI Global Scientific Publishing., DOI: 10.4018/979-8-3373-4485-0.ch014

Emon, M. M. H., & Khan, T. (2024). A Systematic Literature Review on Sustainability Integration and Marketing Intelligence in the Era of Artificial Intelligence. *Review of Business and Economics Studies, 12*(4), 6–28. DOI: 10.26794/2308-944X-2024-12-4-6-28

Emon, M. M. H., & Khan, T. (2025). The mediating role of attitude towards the technology in shaping artificial intelligence usage among professionals. *Telematics and Informatics Reports, 17*, 100188. DOI: 10.1016/j.teler.2025.100188

Emon, M. M. H., & Khan, T. (2025b). The transformative role of Industry 4.0 in supply chains: Exploring digital integration and innovation in the manufacturing enterprises. *Journal of Open Innovation, 11*(2), 100516. DOI: 10.1016/j.joitmc.2025.100516

Enholm, I. M., Papagiannidis, E., Mikalef, P., & Krogstie, J. (2022). Artificial intelligence and business value: A literature review. *Information Systems Frontiers, 24*(5), 1709–1734. DOI: 10.1007/s10796-021-10186-w

European Commission. (2021). "Proposal for a Regulation laying down harmonised rules on artificial intelligence (Artificial Intelligence Act)." https://eur-lex.europa.eu/legal-content/EN/TXT/?uri=CELEX%3A52021PC0206

Fang, H., Chen, D., Huang, Q., Zhang, J., Ma, Z., Zhang, W., & Yu, N. (2021). Deep Template-Based Watermarking. *IEEE Transactions on Circuits and Systems for Video Technology*, *31*(4), 1436–1451. DOI: 10.1109/TCSVT.2020.3009349

Farhad, M. A. (2024). Consumer data protection laws and their impact on business models in the tech industry. *Telecommunications Policy*, *48*(9), 102836. DOI: 10.1016/j.telpol.2024.102836

Farooqi, S. A., Memon, A., Zamir, S., Malik, K., Batool, W., & Zahid, H. (2024). NAVIGATING AI IN THE REAL WORLD: TRANSFORMATIONS, REGULATIONS, AND CHALLENGES. *Policy Research Journal*, *2*(4), 1083–1099.

Farseev, A., Lepikhin, K., Schwartz, H., Ang, E. K., & Powar, K. (2018). SoMin.ai. *Proceedings of the 26th ACM International Conference On*, 1234–1236.

Fazelpour, S., & Lipton, Z. C. (2020, February). Algorithmic fairness from a non-ideal perspective. In *Proceedings of the AAAI/ACM Conference on AI, Ethics, and Society* (pp. 57-63). https://doi.org/DOI: 10.1145/3375627.3375828

Figoli, F. A., Rampino, L., & Mattioli, F. (2022). Ai in the design process: Training the human-Ai collaboration. DS 117: Proceedings of the 24th International Conference on Engineering and Product Design Education (E&PDE 2022), London South Bank University in London, UK. 8th - 9th 2022.

Floridi, L., & Cowls, J. (2022). A unified framework of five principles for AI in society. *Machine learning and the city: Applications in architecture and urban design*, 535-545. https://doi.org/DOI: 10.1002/9781119815075.ch45

Folorunso, O., Ojo, O., Busari, M., Adebayo, M., Joshua, A., Folorunso, D., Ugwunna, C. O., Olabanjo, O., & Olabanjo, O. (2023). Exploring Machine Learning Models for Soil Nutrient Properties Prediction: A Systematic Review. *Big Data and Cognitive Computing*, *7*(2), 113. DOI: 10.3390/bdcc7020113

Fordham, J., Ratan, R., Huang, K.-T., & Silva, K. (2020). Stereotype Threat in a Video Game Context and Its Influence on Perceptions of Science, Technology, Engineering, and Mathematics (STEM): Avatar-Induced Active Self-Concept as a Possible Mitigator. *The American Behavioral Scientist*, *64*(7), 900–926. DOI: 10.1177/0002764220919148

Francis, T., & Hoefel, F. (2018). True Gen': Generation Z and its implications for companies. *McKinsey & Company, 12*(2), 1-10.

Friatin, L. Y. (2025). Revolutionizing writing: The impact of technology on enhancing students' writing skills. [Journal of Applied Linguistics and Literacy]. *JALL*, *9*(1), 87. DOI: 10.25157/jall.v9i1.17963

Galante, N., Cotroneo, R., Furci, D., Lodetti, G., & Casali, M. B. (2023). Applications of artificial intelligence in forensic sciences: Current potential benefits, limitations and perspectives. *International Journal of Legal Medicine, 137*(2), 445–458. DOI: 10.1007/s00414-022-02928-5

Galdón-Salvador, J., Gil-Pechuán, I., AlFraihat, S., & Tarabieh, S. (2024). Effect of social media influencers on consumer brand engagement and its implications for business decision-making. *El Profesional de la Información, 33*(2). Advance online publication. DOI: 10.3145/epi.2024.0210

García-Hernández, R. A., Luna-García, H., Celaya-Padilla, J. M., García-Hernández, A., Reveles-Gómez, L. C., Flores-Chaires, L. A., Delgado-Contreras, J. R., Rondon, D., & Villalba-Condori, K. O. (2024). A systematic literature review of modalities, trends, and limitations in emotion recognition, affective computing, and sentiment analysis. *Applied Sciences (Basel, Switzerland), 14*(16), 7165. DOI: 10.3390/app14167165

Gemiharto, I., & Masrina, D. (2024). User privacy preservation in AI-powered digital communication systems. *Jurnal Communio: Jurnal Jurusan Ilmu Komunikasi, 13*(2), 349–359. DOI: 10.35508/jikom.v13i2.9420

General Data Protection Regulation (GDPR). (2016). [EU]. *Regulation, 2016*(679). https://gdpr.eu/

George, R. (2025). Tourism and Hospitality Product-Offerings, Branding, and Pricing. In *Marketing Tourism and Hospitality* (pp. 225–255). Springer Nature Switzerland., DOI: 10.1007/978-3-031-65983-6_8

Gerke, S., Minssen, T., & Cohen, G. (2020). Ethical and Legal Challenges of Artificial intelligence-driven Healthcare. *Artificial Intelligence in Health, 1*(1), 295–336. DOI: 10.1016/B978-0-12-818438-7.00012-5

Gilbert, M. A. (2024). Disrupting marketing. In Advances in Marketing, Customer Relationship Management, and E-Services (pp. 21–56). IGI Global. Gual-Ort\'\i, J., Juan-Verdoy, P., Amat-Cózar, J., & Mart\'\inez-Moya, J. A. (2025). Exploring the role of Artificial Intelligence in brand image creation. In Research Square. DOI: 10.4018/979-8-3693-4361-6.ch002

Gkikas, D. C., & Theodoridis, P. K. (2022). AI in consumer behavior. *Advances in Artificial Intelligence-Based Technologies: Selected Papers in Honour of Professor Nikolaos G. Bourbakis, 1*, 147–176.

Goodfellow, I., Pouget-Abadie, J., Mirza, M., Xu, B., Warde-Farley, D., Ozair, S., & Bengio, Y. (2014). Generative adversarial nets. *Advances in Neural Information Processing Systems*, *27*, 2672–2680.

Goralski, M. A., & Tan, T. K. (2020). Artificial intelligence and sustainable development. *International Journal of Management Education*, *18*(1), 100330. DOI: 10.1016/j.ijme.2019.100330

Gouws, T., & van Rheede van Oudtshoorn, G. P. (2011). Correlation between brand longevity and the diffusion of innovations theory. *Journal of Public Affairs*, *11*(4), 236–242. DOI: 10.1002/pa.416

Gray, C. M., Kou, Y., Battles, B., Hoggatt, J., & Toombs, A. L. (2018). The Dark (Patterns) Side of UX Design. *Proceedings of the 2018 CHI Conference on Human Factors in Computing Systems - CHI '18*, 1–14. DOI: 10.1145/3173574.3174108

Grewal, D., Hulland, J., Kopalle, P. K., & Karahanna, E. (2020). The future of technology and marketing: A multidisciplinary perspective. *Journal of the Academy of Marketing Science*, *48*(1), 1–8. DOI: 10.1007/s11747-019-00711-4

Guerra-Tamez, C. R., Kraul Flores, K., Serna-Mendiburu, G. M., Chavelas Robles, D., & Ibarra Cortés, J. (2024). Decoding Gen Z: AI's influence on brand trust and purchasing behavior. *Frontiers in Artificial Intelligence*, *7*, 1323512. DOI: 10.3389/frai.2024.1323512

Guo, E. (2025). Redefining exclusivity: The role of generative AI in luxury brand strategies. Advances in Economics. *Management and Political Sciences*, *165*(1), 80–85.

Guo, J., & Wang, D. (2021). An empirical study on artificial intelligence technology based on big data to assist enterprise management decision. *International Journal of Electrical Engineering Education*, 0020720920983547. Advance online publication. DOI: 10.1177/0020720920983547

Gupta, A., Amarnani, M., Soanki, S., & Kishore, J. (2025). AI and Data Privacy in Business. In *2025 First International Conference on Advances in Computer Science, Electrical, Electronics, and Communication Technologies (CE2CT)* (pp. 109-114). IEEE.

Hagendorff, T. (2020). The Ethics of AI ethics: An Evaluation of Guidelines. *Minds and Machines*, *30*(1), 99–120. DOI: 10.1007/s11023-020-09517-8

Hagendorff, T. (2021). Forbidden knowledge in machine learning reflections on the limits of research and publication. *AI & Society*, *36*(3), 767–781. DOI: 10.1007/s00146-020-01045-4

Haleem, A., Javaid, M., Asim Qadri, M., Pratap Singh, R., & Suman, R. (2022). Artificial intelligence (AI) applications for marketing: A literature-based study. *International Journal of Intelligent Networks*, *3*, 119–132. DOI: 10.1016/j.ijin.2022.08.005

Hamatta, H. S. A., Deepika, C. L. N., Rjoub, G., Kassaymeh, S., Manikandan, R., Suman, S. K., & Bhagyalakshmi, L. (2025). Integration of Deep Learning and Image Segmentation in Computational Modeling for Improved Biospeckle Image Analysis. *SN Computer Science*, *6*(4), 350. DOI: 10.1007/s42979-025-03872-y

Hanna, S., Rowley, J., & Keegan, B. (2021). Place and Destination Branding: A Review and Conceptual Mapping of the Domain. *European Management Review*, *18*(2), 105–117. DOI: 10.1111/emre.12433

Hansen, E. B., & Bøgh, S. (2021). Artificial intelligence and internet of things in small and medium-sized enterprises: A survey. *Journal of Manufacturing Systems*, *58*, 362–372. DOI: 10.1016/j.jmsy.2020.08.009

Harris, S., Hadi, H. J., Ahmad, N., & Alshara, M. A. (2024). Fake News Detection Revisited: An Extensive Review of Theoretical Frameworks, Dataset Assessments, Model Constraints, and Forward-Looking Research Agendas. *Technologies*, *12*(11), 222. DOI: 10.3390/technologies12110222

Hauser, J. R., Li, Z., & Mao, C. (2023). *Artificial Intelligence and User-Generated Data Are Transforming How Firms Come to Understand Customer Needs*., DOI: 10.1108/S1548-643520230000020007

Havale, D. S., Raut, N., Anute, N., Ahluwalia, G. K., Kalshetti, P., & Selvakumar, P. (2025). Ethical challenges and bias in AI marketing. In *Advances in Computational Intelligence and Robotics* (pp. 27–54). IGI Global.

He, H., Zhao, S., Xi, Y., & Ho, J. C. (2023). MedDiff: Generating electronic health records using accelerated denoising diffusion model.

Heinberg, M., Liu, Y., Huang, X., & Eisingerich, A. B. (2021). A Bad Job of Doing Good: Does Corporate Transparency on a Country and Company Level Moderate Corporate Social Responsibility Effectiveness? *Journal of International Marketing*, *29*(2), 45–61. DOI: 10.1177/1069031X20981870

Hemalatha, A. (2023). *AI-driven marketing: Leveraging Artificial Intelligence for Enhanced Customer Engagement*. Jupiter Publications Consortium. DOI: 10.47715/JPC.B.978-93-91303-61-7

Hendrayati, H., Achyarsyah, M., Marimon, F., Hartono, U., & Putit, L. (2024). The impact of artificial intelligence on digital marketing: Leveraging potential in a competitive business landscape. *Emerging Science Journal*, *8*(6), 2343–2348. DOI: 10.28991/ESJ-2024-08-06-012

Henriksen, D., Creely, E., & Mehta, R. (2022). Rethinking the Politics of Creativity: Posthumanism, Indigeneity, and Creativity Beyond the Western Anthropocene. *Qualitative Inquiry*, *28*(5), 465–475. DOI: 10.1177/10778004211065813

Ho, J., Jain, A., & Abbeel, P. (2020). Denoising diffusion probabilistic models. *arXiv preprint arXiv:2006.11239.*

Holden, R. J., & Karsh, B. T. (2010). The technology acceptance model: Its past and its future in health care. *Journal of Biomedical Informatics*, *43*(1), 159–172. DOI: 10.1016/j.jbi.2009.07.002

Hoppe, D. (2018). Linking employer branding and internal branding: Establishing perceived employer brand image as an antecedent of favourable employee brand attitudes and behaviours. *Journal of Product and Brand Management*, *27*(4), 452–467. DOI: 10.1108/JPBM-12-2016-1374

Huang, C., & Guo, R. (2021). The effect of a green brand story on perceived brand authenticity and brand trust: The role of narrative rhetoric. *Journal of Brand Management*, *28*(1), 60–76. DOI: 10.1057/s41262-020-00213-7

Huang, H., Cai, Y., & Xu, L. (2021). Stability or instability: The impact of brand concepts on logo design preferences. *Journal of Brand Management*, *28*(5), 465–480. DOI: 10.1057/s41262-021-00238-6

Huang, M.-H., & Rust, R. T. (2021). A strategic framework for artificial intelligence in marketing. *Journal of the Academy of Marketing Science*, *49*(1), 30–50. DOI: 10.1007/s11747-020-00749-9

Hubballi, R. B., Selvakumar, P., Seenivasan, R., & Basava Aradhya, S. G., Dinesh, N., & Seelam, P. K. (2025). Overview of Current AI Technologies in Education. In L. Kyei-Blankson & E. Ntuli (Eds.), *Transformative AI Practices for Personalized Learning Strategies* (pp. 1-26). IGI Global Scientific Publishing.

Hughes, C., Swaminathan, V., & Brooks, G. (2019). Driving Brand Engagement Through Online Social Influencers: An Empirical Investigation of Sponsored Blogging Campaigns. *Journal of Marketing*, *83*(5), 78–96. DOI: 10.1177/0022242919854374

Hughes, L., Dwivedi, Y. K., Rana, N. P., Williams, M. D., & Raghavan, V. (2022). Perspectives on the future of manufacturing within the Industry 4.0 era. *Production Planning and Control*, *33*(2–3), 138–158. DOI: 10.1080/09537287.2020.1810762

Hussain, I., Mu, S., Mohiuddin, M., Danish, R. Q., & Sair, S. A. (2020). Effects of Sustainable Brand Equity and Marketing Innovation on Market Performance in Hospitality Industry: Mediating Effects of Sustainable Competitive Advantage. *Sustainability (Basel)*, *12*(7), 2939. DOI: 10.3390/su12072939

Huynh, T., Nguyen, H. D., Zelinka, I., Nguyen, K. V., Pham, V. T., & Hoang, S. N. (2021). ADVO: A system to manage influencer marketing campaigns on social networks. *Applied Sciences (Basel, Switzerland)*, *11*(14), 6497. DOI: 10.3390/app11146497

Iakovlev, I., Kremleva, E., & Guzanov, R. (2023). Enterprise automation using artificial intelligence: Methods, technologies and prospects. E3S Web Conf., 460, 4007.

Iakovlev, I., Kremleva, E., & Guzanov, R. (2023). Enterprise automation using artificial intelligence: Methods, technologies and prospects. In *E3S Web of Conferences* (Vol. 460, p. 04007). EDP Sciences., DOI: 10.1051/e3sconf/202346004007

Ip, K. (2023). Revolutionising content recommendation: The impact of AI in marketing. Journal of AI. *Robotics & Workplace Automation*, *2*(4), 382. DOI: 10.69554/AMHI2323

Iriani, N., Agustianti, A., Sucianti, R., Rahman, A., & Putera, W. (2024). Understanding risk and uncertainty management: A qualitative inquiry into developing business strategies amidst global economic shifts, government policies, and market volatility. *Golden Ratio of Finance Management*, *4*(2), 62–77. DOI: 10.52970/grfm.v4i2.444

Isaak, J., & Hanna, M. J. (2018). User data privacy: Facebook, Cambridge Analytica, and privacy protection. *Computer*, *51*(8), 56–59. DOI: 10.1109/MC.2018.3191268

Isohanni, J. (2024). Recognising small colour changes with unsupervised learning, comparison of methods. *Advances in Computational Intelligence*, *4*(2), 6. DOI: 10.1007/s43674-024-00073-7

Jabbar, A., Akhtar, P., & Dani, S. (2020). Real-time big data processing for instantaneous marketing decisions: A problematization approach. *Industrial Marketing Management*, *90*, 558–569. DOI: 10.1016/j.indmarman.2019.09.001

Jia, Y., & Wang, Z. (2024). Application of artificial intelligence based on the fuzzy control algorithm in enterprise innovation. *Heliyon*, *10*(6), e28116. Advance online publication. DOI: 10.1016/j.heliyon.2024.e28116

Jobin, A., Ienca, M., & Vayena, E. (2019). The global landscape of AI ethics guidelines. *Nature Machine Intelligence*, *1*(9), 389–399. DOI: 10.1038/s42256-019-0088-2

Jordan, M. I., & Mitchell, T. M. (2015). Machine learning: Trends, perspectives, and prospects. *Science, 349*(6245), 255–260. DOI: 10.1126/science.aaa8415

Joshi, S., Bhattacharya, S., Pathak, P., Natraj, N. A., Saini, J., & Goswami, S. (2025). Harnessing the potential of generative AI in digital marketing using the Behavioral Reasoning Theory approach. *International Journal of Information Management Data Insights, 5*(1), 100317. DOI: 10.1016/j.jjimei.2024.100317

Jubi, R. (2023). *Business Analytics-Unleashing Data Driven Decision Making*. NEHAS PUBLICATIONS.

Juska, J. M. (2021). *Integrated Marketing Communication*. Routledge., DOI: 10.4324/9780367443382

Kamarunisha, M., & Suguna, M. (2025). A study on AI-powered content creation in digital marketing. [JETIR]. *Journal of Emerging Technologies and Innovative Research, 12*(5), 541–550. http://www.jetir.org

Kang, J., Hong, S., & Hubbard, G. T. (2020). The role of storytelling in advertising: Consumer emotion, narrative engagement level, and word-of-mouth intention. *Journal of Consumer Behaviour, 19*(1), 47–56. DOI: 10.1002/cb.1793

Karjalainen, T.-M., & Snelders, D. (2010). Designing Visual Recognition for the Brand. *Journal of Product Innovation Management, 27*(1), 6–22. DOI: 10.1111/j.1540-5885.2009.00696.x

Katuu, S. (2020). Enterprise resource planning: Past, present, and future. *New Review of Information Networking, 25*(1), 37–46. DOI: 10.1080/13614576.2020.1742770

Kayyali, M. (2024). *Building Organizational Capacity and Strategic Management in Academia*. IGI Global. DOI: 10.4018/979-8-3693-6967-8

Kazi, K. S. L., Shinde, S. S., Nerkar, P. M., Kazi, S. S., & Kazi, V. S. (2025). *Machine Learning for Brand Protection*., DOI: 10.4018/979-8-3693-7041-4.ch007

Ke, J., Liao, P., Li, J., & Luo, X. (2023). Effect of information load and cognitive style on cognitive load of visualized dashboards for construction-related activities. *Automation in Construction, 154*, 105029. DOI: 10.1016/j.autcon.2023.105029

Keller, K. L. (1993). Conceptualizing, measuring, and managing customer-based brand equity. *Journal of Marketing, 57*(1), 1–22. DOI: 10.1177/002224299305700101

Kemp, E., Porter, M.III, Anaza, N., & Min, D. (2021). The impact of storytelling in creating firm and customer connections in online environments. *Journal of Research in Interactive Marketing, 15*(1), 104–124. DOI: 10.1108/JRIM-06-2020-0136

Kesavan, V., Polisetty, A., & Dash, G. (2024). *The Application of AI in Transitioning Business Houses Towards New Product Development Process.*, DOI: 10.4018/979-8-3693-9122-8.ch017

Khamaj, A., & Ali, A. M. (2024). Adapting user experience with reinforcement learning: Personalizing interfaces based on user behavior analysis in real-time. *Alexandria Engineering Journal, 95*, 164–173. DOI: 10.1016/j.aej.2024.03.045

Khan, T., & Hasan Emon, M. M. (2024). Determinants of AI Image Generator Adoption Among Marketing Agencies: The Mediating Effects of Perceived Usefulness. *2024 IEEE 3rd International Conference on Robotics, Automation, Artificial-Intelligence and Internet-of-Things (RAAICON)*, 177–182. DOI: 10.1109/RAAICON64172.2024.10928548

Khan, T., Emon, M. M. H., & Nath, A. (2024). Quantifying the Effects of AI-Driven Inventory Management on Operational Efficiency in Online Retail. *2024 27th International Conference on Computer and Information Technology (ICCIT)*, 2092–2097. DOI: 10.1109/ICCIT64611.2024.11021996

Khan, T., Emon, M. M. H., & Rahman, S. (2024). Marketing Strategy Innovation via AI Adoption: A Study on Bangladeshi SMEs in the Context of Industry 5.0. *2024 6th International Conference on Sustainable Technologies for Industry 5.0 (STI)*, 1–6. DOI: 10.1109/STI64222.2024.10951050

Khang, A., Gujrati, R., Uygun, H., Tailor, R. K., & Gaur, S. (Eds.). (2024). *Data-driven modelling and predictive analytics in business and finance: concepts, designs, technologies, and applications*. CRC Press. DOI: 10.1201/9781032618845

Khan, T., Emon, M. M. H., Rahman, K. M., Nipa, M. N., & Fuad, M. N. (2025). The Role of AI in Driving Customer Engagement Through Technological, Organizational and Environmental Enablers in E-Commerce. *2025 International Conference on Quantum Photonics, Artificial Intelligence, and Networking (QPAIN)*, 1–6. DOI: 10.1109/QPAIN66474.2025.11171949

Kim, D. Y., & Kim, H. Y. (2021). Trust me, trust me not: A nuanced view of influencer marketing on social media. *Journal of Business Research, 134*, 223–232. DOI: 10.1016/j.jbusres.2021.05.024

Kim, J., Kim, M., & Lee, S.-M. (2025). Unlocking Trust Dynamics: An Exploration of Playfulness, Expertise, and Consumer Behavior in Virtual Influencer Marketing. *International Journal of Human-Computer Interaction, 41*(1), 378–390. DOI: 10.1080/10447318.2023.2300018

King, W. R., & He, J. (2006). A meta-analysis of the technology acceptance model. *Information & Management*, *43*(6), 740–755. DOI: 10.1016/j.im.2006.05.003

Kinkel, S., Baumgartner, M., & Cherubini, E. (2022). Prerequisites for the adoption of AI technologies in manufacturing–Evidence from a worldwide sample of manufacturing companies. *Technovation*, *110*, 102375. DOI: 10.1016/j.technovation.2021.102375

Kirkby, A., Baumgarth, C., & Henseler, J. (2023). To disclose or not disclose, is no longer the question – effect of AI-disclosed brand voice on brand authenticity and attitude. *Journal of Product and Brand Management*, *32*(7), 1108–1122. DOI: 10.1108/JPBM-02-2022-3864

Kohrs, K. (2021). The language of luxury fashion advertising: Technology of the self and spectacle. *Journal of Fashion Marketing and Management*, *25*(2), 257–273. DOI: 10.1108/JFMM-02-2020-0029

Kordzadeh, N., & Ghasemaghaei, M. (2022). Algorithmic bias: Review, synthesis, and future research directions. *European Journal of Information Systems*, *31*(3), 388–409. DOI: 10.1080/0960085X.2021.1927212

Kosinski, M., Stillwell, D., & Graepel, T. (2013). Private traits and attributes are predictable from digital records of human behavior. *Proceedings of the National Academy of Sciences of the United States of America*, *110*(15), 5802–5805. DOI: 10.1073/pnas.1218772110

Koswara, A. (2025). The intersection of generative AI and applied linguistics in modern marketing & Advertising practices. LinguaEducare. *Journal of English and Linguistic Studies*, *2*(1), 19–28.

Kotapati, S. P. (2025). Artificial Intelligence in Scalable Content Creation for Micro-influencer Marketing Agencies. *Asian J. Res. Com. Sci.*, *18*(6), 215–222. DOI: 10.9734/ajrcos/2025/v18i6692

Kotte, K. R., Attaluri, V., & Selvakumar, P. (2025). Revolutionising Retail Banking with AI and Virtual Technologies AI-Driven Financial Training. In Nair, A. J., Manohar, S., Limbu, Y. B., & Huhmann, B. A. (Eds.), *Intersecting Natural Language Processing and FinTech Innovations in Service Marketing* (pp. 421–440). IGI Global Scientific Publishing. DOI: 10.4018/979-8-3693-9944-6.ch020

Kozinets, R. V. (2022). Algorithmic branding through platform assemblages: Core conceptions and research directions for a new era of marketing and service management. *Journal of Service Management*, *33*(3), 437–452. DOI: 10.1108/JOSM-07-2021-0263

Kubovics, M. (2024). Innovative Content Production in Marketing Communication Through AI. *Proc. Eur. Conf. Entrep. Innov.*, *19*(1), 377–383. DOI: 10.34190/ecie.19.1.2877

Kubovics, M. (2025). AI in the creation of Marketing Communication content. *INTERANTIONAL JOURNAL OF SCIENTIFIC RESEARCH IN ENGINEERING AND*, *09*(04), 1–9. DOI: 10.55041/IJSREM42613

Kulkarni, V., Reddy, S., Clark, T., & Proper, H. (2023). The AI-enabled enterprise. In *The AI-Enabled Enterprise* (pp. 1–12). Springer International Publishing. DOI: 10.1007/978-3-031-29053-4_1

Kumar, A., Sharma, A., Dhanka, S., Bist, Y., Maini, S., & Bhatnagar, P. (2025). Data Privacy, Ethics, and the Role of AI in Customer Relationship Management. In *Demystifying Emotion AI, Robotics AI, and Sentiment Analysis in Customer Relationship Management* (pp. 283-318). IGI Global Scientific Publishing.

Kumar, R. S., Lokeshwari, J., & Shanmugam, S. K. (2024, November). AI-Powered Privacy Preservation: A Novel Framework for Adaptive Data Protection. In *2024 2nd International Conference on Computing and Data Analytics (ICCDA)* (pp. 1-6). IEEE.

Kumar, A., Bapat, G., Kumar, A., Hota, S. L., Abishek, G. D., & Vaz, S. (2024). Unlocking Brand Excellence: Harnessing AI Tools for Enhanced Customer Engagement and Innovation. *RAiSE*, *2023*, 204. DOI: 10.3390/engproc2023059204

Kumar, D., & Suthar, N. (2024). Ethical and Legal Challenges of AI in Marketing: An Exploration of Solutions. *Journal of Information. Communication and Ethics in Society*, *22*(1), 124–144. DOI: 10.1108/JICES-05-2023-0068

Kumar, G. (2023). Evolution of enterprise applications through emerging technologies. *Universal Journal of Computer Sciences and Communications*, *2*(1), 1–8. DOI: 10.31586/ujcsc.2023.828

Kumar, P., Dwivedi, Y. K., & Anand, A. (2023). Responsible artificial intelligence (AI) for value formation and market performance in healthcare: The mediating role of patient's cognitive engagement. *Information Systems Frontiers*, *25*(6), 2197–2220. DOI: 10.1007/s10796-021-10136-6

Kunduru, A. R. (2023). Effective usage of artificial intelligence in enterprise resource planning applications. *International Journal of Computer Trends and Technology*, *71*(4), 73–80. DOI: 10.14445/22312803/IJCTT-V71I4P109

Kuuluvainen, A. (2012). How to concretize dynamic capabilities? Theory and examples. *Journal of Strategy and Management, 5*(4), 381–392. DOI: 10.1108/17554251211276353

Lahlali, M., Berbiche, N., & El Alami, J. (2021). How Enterprise must be Prepared to be "AI First"? *International Journal of Advanced Computer Science and Applications, 12*(5). Advance online publication. DOI: 10.14569/IJACSA.2021.0120542

Lambrecht, A., & Tucker, C. (2019). Algorithmic bias? An empirical study of apparent gender-based discrimination in the display of STEM career ads. *Management Science, 65*(7), 2966–2981. DOI: 10.1287/mnsc.2018.3093

Lankhorst, M. (2009). *Enterprise architecture at work* (Vol. 352). Springer. DOI: 10.1007/978-3-642-01310-2

Lannon, F., Lyons, R., & O'Connor, C. (2024). Generation AI and family business: A perspective article. *Journal of Family Business Management, 14*(3), 470–474. DOI: 10.1108/JFBM-07-2023-0116

Lee, L. W., Dabirian, A., McCarthy, I. P., & Kietzmann, J. (2020). Making sense of text: Artificial intelligence-enabled content analysis. *European Journal of Marketing, 54*(3), 615–644. DOI: 10.1108/EJM-02-2019-0219

Lee, S. (2024). What triggers customer curiosity? Exploring the role of branded content experience design on customer response. *Journal of Hospitality & Tourism Research (Washington, D.C.), 49*(3), 403–416. DOI: 10.1177/10963480231220274

Lee, Y., Kozar, K. A., & Larsen, K. R. T. (2003). The Technology acceptance model: Past, present, and future. *Communications of the Association for Information Systems, 12*. Advance online publication. DOI: 10.17705/1CAIS.01250

Legris, P., Ingham, J., & Collerette, P. (2003). Why do people use information technology? A critical review of the technology acceptance model. *Information & Management, 40*(3), 191–204. DOI: 10.1016/S0378-7206(01)00143-4

Leitner-Hanetseder, S., & Lehner, O. M. (2022). AI-powered information and Big Data: Current regulations and ways forward in IFRS reporting. *Journal of Applied Accounting Research, 24*(2), 282–298. DOI: 10.1108/JAAR-01-2022-0022

Lemos, M., Cardoso, P. J. S., & Rodrigues, J. M. F. (2024). Harnessing AI and NLP Tools for Innovating Brand Name Generation and Evaluation: A Comprehensive Review. *Multimodal Technologies and Interaction, 8*(7), 56. DOI: 10.3390/mti8070056

Letourneau-Guillon, L., Camirand, D., Guilbert, F., & Forghani, R. (2020). Artificial Intelligence Applications for Workflow, Process Optimization and Predictive Analytics. *Neuroimaging Clinics of North America, 30*(4), e1–e15. DOI: 10.1016/j.nic.2020.08.008

Li, J. (2024). The past, present and future of enterprise resource planning. *Journal of Enterprise and Business Intelligence*, 32–41. https://doi.org/DOI: 10.53759/5181/JEBI202404004

Li, R., Cao, Z., Ye, H., & Yue, X. (2021, April). Application and development trend of artificial intelligence in enterprise marketing. In *Journal of Physics: Conference Series* (Vol. 1881, No. 2, p. 022032). IOP Publishing. https://doi.org/DOI: 10.1088/1742-6596/1881/2/022032

Limantara, Q. R. (2024). Exploring the role of Generative Artificial Intelligence in crafting brand experiences: Insights from selected case studies. *International Journal of Creative Multimedia, 5*(2), 88–100. DOI: 10.33093/ijcm.2024.5.2.6

Lippi, M., Contissa, G., Jablonowska, A., Lagioia, F., Micklitz, H.-W., Palka, P., Sartor, G., & Torroni, P. (2020). The Force Awakens: Artificial Intelligence for Consumer Law. *Journal of Artificial Intelligence Research, 67*, 169–190. DOI: 10.1613/jair.1.11519

Liu, C. (2024). Research on the influence of artificial intelligence on enterprise management decision-making. *Academic Journal of Business & Management, 6*(1), 108–112.

Loureiro, S. M. C., Bilro, R. G., & Japutra, A. (2019). The effect of consumer-generated media stimuli on emotions and consumer brand engagement. *Journal of Product and Brand Management, 29*(3), 387–408. DOI: 10.1108/JPBM-11-2018-2120

Lu, C. H. (2021). The impact of artificial intelligence on economic growth and welfare. *Journal of Macroeconomics, 69*, 103342. DOI: 10.1016/j.jmacro.2021.103342

Luguri, J., & Strahilevitz, L. (2019). Shining a Light on Dark Patterns. SSRN *Electronic Journal, 13*(1). DOI: 10.2139/ssrn.3431205

Luo, L., Liu, L., Zheng, Y., & Chen, J. (2024). Visual information and appearance: The impact of visual attributes of user-generated photos on review helpfulness. *Telematics and Informatics, 92*, 102164. DOI: 10.1016/j.tele.2024.102164

Lu, Y. (2019). Artificial intelligence: A survey on evolution, models, applications and future trends. *Journal of Management Analytics, 6*(1), 1–29. DOI: 10.1080/23270012.2019.1570365

Madanchian, M., & Taherdoost, H. (2024). AI-Powered Innovations in High-Tech Research and Development: From Theory to Practice. *Computers, Materials & Continua*, *81*(2), 2133–2159. DOI: 10.32604/cmc.2024.057094

Maheswaran, K., Selvakumar, P., Shaikh, M., Shashank, G., Gupta, S., & Manjunath, T. C. (2025). The Evolution of Smart Urban Mobility With Emerging Technologies. In Ponnusamy, S., Assaf, M., Youssef, B., Jeon, G., & Kalyanaraman, S. (Eds.), *Leveraging VANETs and Blockchain Technology for Urban Mobility* (pp. 1–28). IGI Global Scientific Publishing. DOI: 10.4018/979-8-3373-0265-2.ch001

Makridakis, S. (2017). The forthcoming Artificial Intelligence (AI) revolution: Its impact on society and firms. *Futures*, *90*, 46–60. DOI: 10.1016/j.futures.2017.03.006

Manda, V. K., Sagi, S., & Yadav, A. (2024). *Blockchain in Advertising and Marketing.*, DOI: 10.4018/979-8-3693-2754-8.ch005

Marangunić, N., & Granić, A. (2015). Technology acceptance model: A literature review from 1986 to 2013. *Universal Access in the Information Society*, *14*(1), 81–95. DOI: 10.1007/s10209-014-0348-1

Mari, A., Mandelli, A., & Algesheimer, R. (2024). Empathic voice assistants: Enhancing consumer responses in voice commerce. *Journal of Business Research*, *175*, 114566. DOI: 10.1016/j.jbusres.2024.114566

Massoudi, A. H., Birdawod, H. Q., & Raewf, M. B. (2023). Personal Digital Marketing Influence on Successful Marketing Campaign in Today's Digital Age. *Cihan U Erbil J H SOC SCI*, *7*(1), 158–165. DOI: 10.24086/cuejhss.v7n1y2023.pp158-165

Matthias, A. (2004). The responsibility gap: Ascribing responsibility for the actions of learning automata. *Ethics and Information Technology*, *6*(3), 175–183. DOI: 10.1007/s10676-004-3422-1

Mayouf, M., Jones, J., Elghaish, F., Emam, H., Ekanayake, E. M. A. C., & Ashayeri, I. (2024). Revolutionising the 4D BIM Process to Support Scheduling Requirements in Modular Construction. *Sustainability (Basel)*, *16*(2), 476. DOI: 10.3390/su16020476

Mehrabi, N., Morstatter, F., Saxena, N., Lerman, K., & Galstyan, A. (2021). A survey on bias and fairness in machine learning. *ACM Computing Surveys*, *54*(6), 1–35. DOI: 10.1145/3457607

Minishi-Majanja, M. K., & Kiplang'at, J. (2005). The diffusion of innovations theory as a theoretical framework in library and information science research. *South African Journal of Library and Information Science*, *71*(3), 211–224.

Mishra, S. (2023). Exploring the impact of AI-based cyber security financial sector management. *Applied Sciences (Basel, Switzerland)*, *13*(10), 5875. DOI: 10.3390/app13105875

Mittelstadt, B. (2019). Principles alone cannot guarantee ethical AI. *Nature Machine Intelligence*, *1*(11), 501–507. DOI: 10.1038/s42256-019-0114-4

Mittelstadt, B. D., Allo, P., Taddeo, M., Wachter, S., & Floridi, L. (2016). The Ethics of algorithms: Mapping the Debate. *Big Data & Society*, *3*(2), 1–21. DOI: 10.1177/2053951716679679

Mittelstadt, B., Russell, C., & Wachter, S. (2019). Explaining Explanations in AI. *Proceedings of the Conference on Fairness, Accountability, and Transparency - FAT* '19*, 279–288. DOI: 10.1145/3287560.3287574

Mogaji, E. (2021). Brand Identity. In *Brand Management* (pp. 85–122). Springer International Publishing., DOI: 10.1007/978-3-030-66119-9_5

Moharam, M. M. R., & Tawalbeh, A. (2025). The role of gen AI in enhancing creativity and efficiency in content marketing creation: Scoping review and future insights. *Ijirss*, *8*(1), 2804–2814. DOI: 10.53894/ijirss.v8i1.5060

Molakaseema, S. K. R. (2024). Leadership and Organizational Transformation in the Era of Digitalization Powered by Artificial Intelligence–An Analysis of Challenges and Opportunities. DOI: 10.34726/hss.2024.127206

Mora Cortez, R., Ghosh Dastidar, A., Cortez, R. M., & Dastidar, A. G. (2022). A longitudinal study of B2B customer engagement in LinkedIn: The role of brand personality. *Journal of Business Research*, *145*, 92–105. DOI: 10.1016/j.jbusres.2022.02.086

Mulligan, D. K., Regan, P. M., & King, J. (2020). The Fertile Dark Matter of Privacy takes on the Dark Patterns of Surveillance. *Journal of Consumer Psychology*, *30*(4), 767–773. Advance online publication. DOI: 10.1002/jcpy.1190

Murár, P., Kubovics, M., & Jurišová, V. (2024). The impact of brand-voice integration and artificial Intelligence on social media marketing. *Communication Today*, 50–63. DOI: 10.34135/communicationtoday.2024.Vol.15.No.1.4

Mustak, M., Hallikainen, H., Laukkanen, T., Plé, L., Hollebeek, L. D., & Aleem, M. (2024). Using machine learning to develop customer insights from user-generated content. *Journal of Retailing and Consumer Services*, *81*, 104034. DOI: 10.1016/j.jretconser.2024.104034

Nalbant, K. G., & Aydin, S. (2025). AI-powered digital marketing: Transforming personalized experiences. *American Research Journal of Humanities and Social Science*, *8*(1), 19–27.

Nanne, A. J., Antheunis, M. L., Van Der Lee, C. G., Postma, E. O., Wubben, S., & Van Noort, G. (2020). The Use of Computer Vision to Analyze Brand-Related User Generated Image Content. *Journal of Interactive Marketing*, *50*(1), 156–167. DOI: 10.1016/j.intmar.2019.09.003

Naqvi, S. K. H., & Batool, K. (2023). A comparative analysis between general data protection regulations and California consumer privacy act. *Journal of Computer Science. Information Technology and Telecommunication Engineering*, *4*(1), 326–332.

Nebeker, C., Parrish, E. M., & Graham, S. (2022). The AI-powered digital health sector: ethical and regulatory considerations when developing digital mental health tools for the older adult demographic. In *Artificial Intelligence in Brain and Mental Health: Philosophical, Ethical & Policy Issues* (pp. 159–176). Springer International Publishing.

Nikolic, M. V., Milovanovic, V., Vasiljevic, Z. Z., & Stamenkovic, Z. (2020). Semiconductor Gas Sensors: Materials, Technology, Design, and Application. *Sensors (Basel)*, *20*(22), 6694. DOI: 10.3390/s20226694

Nnagha, E. M., Ademola, M. K., Izevbizua, E. A., Uwishema, O., Nazir, A., & Wellington, J. (2023). Tackling sickle cell crisis in Nigeria: The need for newer therapeutic solutions in sickle cell crisis management - short communication. *Annals of Medicine and Surgery (London)*, *85*(5), 2282–2286. DOI: 10.1097/MS9.0000000000000696

O'Connor, S., & Liu, H. (2024). Gender bias perpetuation and mitigation in AI technologies: Challenges and opportunities. *AI & Society*, *39*(4), 2045–2057. DOI: 10.1007/s00146-023-01675-4

Obar, J. A., & Oeldorf-Hirsch, A. (2018). The Clickwrap: A Political Economic Mechanism for Manufacturing Consent on Social Media. *Social Media + Society*, *4*(3), 2056305118784770. Advance online publication. DOI: 10.1177/2056305118784770

Onifade, A. Y., Ogeawuchi, J. C., & Abayomi, A. A. (2025). Scaling AI-Driven Sales Analytics for Predicting Consumer Behavior and Enhancing Data-Driven Business Decisions. *International Journal of Advanced Multidisciplinary Research and Studies*, *4*(6), 2181–2201. DOI: 10.62225/2583049X.2024.4.6.4269

Orth, U. R., Nickel, K., Böhm, R., & Röwe, K. (2020). Agreement by design: The effect of visual harmony on responses to surveys. *Journal of Consumer Behaviour*, *19*(2), 196–207. DOI: 10.1002/cb.1804

Ota, R., Ray, S. S., & Alli, S. S. (2024). Exploring the impact of artificial intelligence on content creation: A comprehensive study. *International Journal of Research Publication and Reviews*, *5*(7), 597–604. DOI: 10.55248/gengpi.5.0724.1620

Overgoor, G., Rand, W., van Dolen, W., & Mazloom, M. (2022). Simplicity is not key: Understanding firm-generated social media images and consumer liking. *International Journal of Research in Marketing*, *39*(3), 639–655. DOI: 10.1016/j.ijresmar.2021.12.005

Oyegbade, I. K., Igwe, A. N., Ofodile, O. C., & Azubuike, C. (2021). Innovative financial planning and governance models for emerging markets: Insights from startups and banking audits. *Open Access Research Journal of Multidisciplinary Studies*, *1*(2), 108–116. DOI: 10.53022/oarjms.2021.1.2.0033

Pandey, A. S., Sharma, Y., Tiwari, A., Chauhan, R., Tyagi, S., & Kumari, J. (2024). Ethical Implications of AI-Powered Communication Tool. In *2024 International Conference on Communication, Computer Sciences and Engineering (IC3SE)* (pp. 1857-1861). IEEE. DOI: 10.1109/IC3SE62002.2024.10593350

Park, J., Oh, C., & Kim, H. Y. (2024). AI vs. human-generated content and accounts on Instagram: User preferences, evaluations, and ethical considerations. *Technology in Society*, *79*, 102705. DOI: 10.1016/j.techsoc.2024.102705

Parris, D. L., & Guzmán, F. (2023). Evolving brand boundaries and expectations: Looking back on brand equity, brand loyalty, and brand image research to move forward. *Journal of Product and Brand Management*, *32*(2), 191–234. DOI: 10.1108/JPBM-06-2021-3528

Pascucci, F., Savelli, E., & Gistri, G. (2023). How digital technologies reshape marketing: evidence from a qualitative investigation. *Italian Journal of Marketing*. DOI: 10.1007/s43039-023-00063-6

Paul, H., & Nikolaev, A. (2021). Fake review detection on online E-commerce platforms: A systematic literature review. *Data Mining and Knowledge Discovery*, *35*(5), 1830–1881. DOI: 10.1007/s10618-021-00772-6

Pedersen, C. L., & Ritter, T. (2024). Digital authenticity: Towards a research agenda for the AI-driven fifth phase of digitalization in business-to-business marketing. *Industrial Marketing Management*, *123*, 162–172. DOI: 10.1016/j.indmarman.2024.10.005

Peeters, M. M. M., van Diggelen, J., van den Bosch, K., Bronkhorst, A., Neerincx, M. A., Schraagen, J. M., & Raaijmakers, S. (2021). Hybrid collective intelligence in a human–AI society. *AI & Society*, *36*(1), 217–238. DOI: 10.1007/s00146-020-01005-y

Peng, Y. (2024). A comparative analysis between GAN and Diffusion Models in image generation. *Transactions on Computer Science and Intelligent Systems*, *5*, 189–195. DOI: 10.62051/0f1va465

Peng, Y., Lock, I., & Ali Salah, A. (2024). Automated Visual Analysis for the Study of Social Media Effects: Opportunities, Approaches, and Challenges. *Communication Methods and Measures*, *18*(2), 163–185. DOI: 10.1080/19312458.2023.2277956

Petersson, L., Larsson, I., Nygren, J. M., Nilsen, P., Neher, M., Reed, J. E., Tyskbo, D., & Svedberg, P. (2022). Challenges to implementing artificial intelligence in healthcare: A qualitative interview study with healthcare leaders in Sweden. *BMC Health Services Research*, *22*(1), 850. DOI: 10.1186/s12913-022-08215-8

Piriyakul, I., Kunathikornkit, S., & Piriyakul, R. (2024). Evaluating brand equity in the hospitality industry: Insights from customer journeys and text mining. *International Journal of Information Management Data Insights*, *4*(2), 100245. DOI: 10.1016/j.jjimei.2024.100245

Pokala, P. (2024). Artificial intelligence in enterprise resource planning: A systematic review of innovations, applications, and future directions. [IJRCAIT]. *International Journal of Research in Computer Applications and Information Technology*, *7*(2), 1276–1289. DOI: 10.5281/zenodo.14170247

Prabha, C., & Saluja, S. (2024). Consumer Policy: The Relationship Between AI and Data Privacy. In *Ethical AI and Data Management Strategies in Marketing* (pp. 41-55). IGI Global.

Prince, N. U., Faheem, M. A., Khan, O. U., Hossain, K., Alkhayyat, A., Hamdache, A., & Elmouki, I. (2024). AI-powered data-driven cybersecurity techniques: Boosting threat identification and reaction. *Nanotechnology Perceptions*, *20*, 332–353. DOI: 10.62441/nano-ntp.v20iS10.1804

Puntoni, S., Reczek, R. W., Giesler, M., & Botti, S. (2021). Consumers and Artificial Intelligence: An Experiential Perspective. *Journal of Marketing*, *85*(1), 131–151. DOI: 10.1177/0022242920953847

Puri, V. (2024). The future of productivity in the era of artificial intelligence: An enterprise engineering perspective. *International Journal of Innovative Research in Science, Engineering and Technology*, *13*(7), 12685–12692. DOI: 10.15680/IJIRSET.2024.1307011

Purwanto, N., Pancaningrum, E., & Juwita, K. (2022). *Analysis of consumer behaviour in making decisions after the COVID-19 pandemic: perspectives on the theory of stimulus organism response (SOR)*. Kne Social Sciences., DOI: 10.18502/kss.v7i19.12425

Putri, A. A., Kywe, ChK., Temiralieva, M., Jabrayilzade, T., & Tick, A. (2023). The Utilization of Instagram as a Marketing Strategy for SME in Indonesia. *Austin J Bus Adm Manage.*, *7*(2), 1060.

Qian, S., Lu, Y., Peng, Y., Shen, C., & Xu, H. (2024). Convergence or divergence? A cross-platform analysis of climate change visual content categories, features, and social media engagement on Twitter and Instagram. *Public Relations Review*, *50*(2), 102454. DOI: 10.1016/j.pubrev.2024.102454

Radanliev, P., De Roure, D., Page, K., Nurse, J. R. C., Mantilla Montalvo, R., Santos, O., Maddox, L., & Burnap, P. (2020). Cyber risk at the edge: Current and future trends on cyber risk analytics and artificial intelligence in the industrial internet of things and industry 4.0 supply chains. *Cybersecurity*, *3*(1), 13. Advance online publication. DOI: 10.1186/s42400-020-00052-8

Raji, M. A., Olodo, H. B., Oke, T. T., Addy, W. A., Ofodile, O. C., & Oyewole, A. T. (2024). E-commerce and consumer behavior: A review of AI-powered personalization and market trends. *GSC Advanced Research and Reviews, 18*(3), 066-077.

Raju, P., Arun, R., Turlapati, V. R., Veeran, L., & Rajesh, S. (2024). Next-Generation Management on Exploring AI-Driven Decision Support in Business. In *Optimizing Intelligent Systems for Cross-Industry Application* (pp. 61–78). IGI Global. DOI: 10.4018/979-8-3693-8659-0.ch004

Ramalli, E. (2024). Data Quality, Data Diversity and Data Provenance. *Ethical Perspectives*, •••, 39–48. DOI: 10.1007/978-3-031-52962-7_4

Rane, N., Achari, A., & Choudhary, S. P. (2023). Enhancing customer loyalty through quality of service: Effective strategies to improve customer satisfaction, experience, relationship, and engagement. *International Research Journal of Modernization in Engineering Technology and Science, 5*(5), 427–452. ResearchGate. DOI: 10.56726/IRJMETS38104

Rauf, M. A., Jim, M. M. I., Rahman, M. M., & Tariquzzaman, M. (2024). AI-Powered Predictive Analytics for Intellectual Property Risk Management in Supply Chain Operations: A Big Data Approach. *Global Mainstream Journal*, *1*(4), 10–62304. DOI: 10.62304/ijse.v1i04.184

Raut, S., Chandel, A., & Mittal, S. (2024). Enhancing marketing and brand communication with AI-driven content creation. In Advances in Marketing, Customer Relationship Management, and E-Services (pp. 139–172). IGI Global.

Raut, S., Chandel, A., & Mittal, S. (2024). *Enhancing Marketing and Brand Communication With AI-Driven Content Creation.*, DOI: 10.4018/979-8-3373-0219-5.ch008

Ravikumar, R. N., & Aarthi, S. (2025). AI-driven governance. In *Advances in Computational Intelligence and Robotics* (pp. 343–372). IGI Global Scientific Publishing. DOI: 10.4018/979-8-3373-3760-9.ch012

Ray, P. P. (2023). ChatGPT: A comprehensive review on background, applications, key challenges, bias, ethics, limitations and future scope. *Internet of Things and Cyber-Physical Systems*, *3*, 121–154. DOI: 10.1016/j.iotcps.2023.04.003

Reed, C., Wynn, M., & Bown, R. (2025). Artificial intelligence in digital marketing: Towards an analytical framework for revealing and mitigating bias. *Big Data and Cognitive Computing*, *9*(2), 40. DOI: 10.3390/bdcc9020040

Rizzoni, F., Magalini, S., Casaroli, A., Mari, P., Dixon, M., & Coventry, L. (2022). Phishing simulation exercise in a large hospital: A case study. *Digital Health*, *8*, 205520762210817. DOI: 10.1177/20552076221081716

Rust, R. T. (2020). The future of marketing. *International Journal of Research in Marketing*, *37*(1), 15–26. DOI: 10.1016/j.ijresmar.2019.08.002

Sakthivel, M., Jaganathan, A., & Mohanraj, M. Mohit, & Manjunath, T. (2025). Brand Loyalty through AI and Personalisation AI-Generated Content for Financial Marketing. In A. J Nair, S. Manohar, Y. B. Limbu, & B. A. Huhmann (Eds.), *Intersecting Natural Language Processing and FinTech Innovations in Service Marketing* (pp. 77-96). IGI Global Scientific Publishing.

Samal, A., & Misra, L. I. Mohit, Pougajendy, S., Chandel, P. S., Manjunath, T. C., & (2025). Musealization and Tourism Practices. In S. Oflazoğlu & M. Dora (Eds.), *Preserving Cultural Heritage in Post-Disaster Urban Renewal* (pp. 115-142). IGI Global Scientific Publishing.

Samayamantri, L. S., Singhal, S., Krishnamurthy, O., & Regin, R. (2024). *AI-Driven Multimodal Approaches to Human Behavior Analysis.*, DOI: 10.4018/979-8-3693-3739-4.ch025

Samblani, G., & Bhatt, D. P. (2025). Case Studies of Next Generation AI for Intelligent Manufacturing. In *Intelligent Manufacturing and Industry 4.0* (pp. 217–236). CRC Press.

Sánchez-Aguayo, M., Urquiza-Aguiar, L., & Estrada-Jiménez, J. (2022). Predictive Fraud Analysis Applying the Fraud Triangle Theory through Data Mining Techniques. *Applied Sciences (Basel, Switzerland)*, *12*(7), 3382. DOI: 10.3390/app12073382

Santos, Z. R., Cheung, C. M. K., Coelho, P. S., & Rita, P. (2022). Consumer engagement in social media brand communities: A literature review. *International Journal of Information Management*, *63*, 102457. DOI: 10.1016/j.ijinfomgt.2021.102457

Sauberschwarz, L., & Weiss, L. (2022). Efficient Innovation with the 5C Process. In *The Corporates Strike Back* (pp. 35–135). Springer International Publishing. DOI: 10.1007/978-3-030-79114-8_2

Schroeder, J. E. (2002). *Visual consumption*. Routledge. DOI: 10.4324/9780203471630

Shaban, A. (2024). Digital Rights, Digital Representation, and Digital Justice—Towards Digital Democracy and Freedom of Expression. In *Digital Geographies—Theory, Space, and Communities* (pp. 765–899). Springer Nature Singapore. DOI: 10.1007/978-981-97-4734-4_7

Sharakhina, L., Ilyina, I., Kaplun, D., Teor, T., & Kulibanova, V. (2024). AI technologies in the analysis of visual advertising messages: Survey and application. *Journal of Marketing Analytics*, *12*(4), 1066–1089. DOI: 10.1057/s41270-023-00255-1

Sharma, A., Podoplelova, E., Shapovalov, G., Tselykh, A., & Tselykh, A. (2021). Sustainable smart cities: Convergence of artificial intelligence and blockchain. *Sustainability (Basel)*, *13*(23), 13076. DOI: 10.3390/su132313076

Sharma, V., Gupta, M., Kumar, A., & Mishra, D. (2021). Video Processing Using Deep Learning Techniques: A Systematic Literature Review. *IEEE Access : Practical Innovations, Open Solutions*, *9*, 139489–139507. DOI: 10.1109/ACCESS.2021.3118541

Shehu, I. S., Wang, Y., Athuman, A. M., & Fu, X. (2021). Remote Eye Gaze Tracking Research: A Comparative Evaluation on Past and Recent Progress. *Electronics (Basel)*, *10*(24), 3165. DOI: 10.3390/electronics10243165

Shuen, A., Feiler, P. F., & Teece, D. J. (2014). Dynamic capabilities in the upstream oil and gas sector: Managing next generation competition. *Energy Strategy Reviews*, *3*, 5–13. DOI: 10.1016/j.esr.2014.05.002

Shukla, A. (2024). Innovative ways of utilizing generative AI for graphical big data analysis. *J Arti Inte & Cloud Comp*, *3*(1), 1–3. DOI: 10.47363/JAICC/2024(3)222

Shukla, M., Misra, R., & Singh, D. (2023). Exploring relationship among semiotic product packaging, brand experience dimensions, brand trust and purchase intentions in an Asian emerging market. *Asia Pacific Journal of Marketing and Logistics, 35*(2), 249–265. DOI: 10.1108/APJML-10-2021-0718

Singh, D., Sharma, A., Singh, R. K., & Rana, P. S. (2025). Artificial intelligence enabled supply chain resilience: insights from FMCG industry. *Journal of Global Operations and Strategic Sourcing*. DOI: 10.1108/JGOSS-02-2024-0017

Singh, D., & Arora, D. (2024). *Cloud-Based Object Detection Model Using Amazon Rekognition.*, DOI: 10.1007/978-981-99-9811-1_13

Sinha, S., & Al Huraimel, K. (2021). *Reimagining businesses with AI*. John Wiley & Sons.

Sohrabi, S., Riabov, A., Katz, M., & Udrea, O. (2018). An AI planning solution to scenario generation for enterprise risk management. *Proceedings of the AAAI Conference on Artificial Intelligence, 32*(1). Advance online publication. DOI: 10.1609/aaai.v32i1.11304

Solove, D. J. (2021). The Myth of the Privacy Paradox. 89 George Washington Law Review 1. *GWU Legal Studies Research Paper*, (2020-10).

Soundariya, A., Behera, N. K., Chandel, P. S., Gupta, S., & Manjunath, T. C. (2025). AI and Environmental Ethics: The Role of AI in Addressing Climate Change Ethical Considerations in AI-Driven Environmental Solutions. In Chakraborty, S. (Ed.), *Human Values, Ethics, and Dignity in the Age of Artificial Intelligence* (pp. 321–346). IGI Global Scientific Publishing. DOI: 10.4018/979-8-3693-9035-1.ch013

Srivastav, P. K., Singhal, P., Roohani, B. S., & Sharma, N. (Eds.). (2024). *Web 3.0: The Next Generation's Internet and Understanding the Concept of the Metaverse*. CRC Press. DOI: 10.1201/9781003461418

Stray, J. (2020). Aligning AI Optimization to Community Well-Being. *International Journal of Community Well-being, 3*(4), 443–463. DOI: 10.1007/s42413-020-00086-3

Sundstrom, B. (2016). Mothers "Google It Up:" Extending communication channel behavior in diffusion of innovations theory. *Health Communication, 31*(1), 91–101. DOI: 10.1080/10410236.2014.936339

Sunstein, C. R. (2020). Sludge Audits. *Behavioural Public Policy, 6*(4), 1–20. DOI: 10.1017/bpp.2019.32

Sun, T. Q., & Medaglia, R. (2019). Mapping the challenges of Artificial Intelligence in the public sector: Evidence from public healthcare. *Government Information Quarterly*, *36*(2), 368–383. DOI: 10.1016/j.giq.2018.09.008

Surendran, P. (2012). Technology acceptance model: A survey of literature. *International Journal of Business and Social Research*, *2*(4), 175–178.

Susser, D., Roessler, B., & Nissenbaum, H. (2019). Online manipulation: Hidden influences in a digital world. *Geo. L. Tech. Rev.*, *4*, 1.

Sykora, M., Elayan, S., Hodgkinson, I. R., Jackson, T. W., & West, A. (2022). The power of emotions: Leveraging user generated content for customer experience management. *Journal of Business Research*, *144*, 997–1006. DOI: 10.1016/j.jbusres.2022.02.048

Taheri, B., Yousaf, A., Gannon, M., & Mishra, A. (2024). e-commerce website customer engagement: Delineating the role of UTAUT, vividness, and compulsion. *Journal of Retailing and Consumer Services*, *79*, 103835. DOI: 10.1016/j.jretconser.2024.103835

Tao, M., Li, X., Alam, F., Yan, Y., & Chau, T. (2025). Unveiling the impact of AI technological anxiety on the marketers' intention to adopt Generative AI. *Journal of Global Information Management*, *33*(1), 1–22. DOI: 10.4018/JGIM.372177

Tarabieh, S., Gil-Pechuán, I., Salvador, J., & AlFraihat, S. (2024). The new game of online marketing: How social media influencers drive online repurchase intention through brand trust and customer brand engagement. *Intangible Capital*, *20*(1), 103. DOI: 10.3926/ic.2515

Teece, D. J. (2014). A dynamic capabilities-based entrepreneurial theory of the multinational enterprise. *Journal of International Business Studies*, *45*(1), 8–37. DOI: 10.1057/jibs.2013.54

Teece, D. J. (2016). Dynamic capabilities and entrepreneurial management in large organizations: Toward a theory of the (entrepreneurial) firm. *European Economic Review*, *86*, 202–216. DOI: 10.1016/j.euroecorev.2015.11.006

Teece, D. J. (2018). Dynamic capabilities as (workable) management systems theory. *Journal of Management & Organization*, *24*(3), 359–368. DOI: 10.1017/jmo.2017.75

Teece, D. J., Pisano, G., & Shuen, A. (1997). Dynamic capabilities and strategic management. *Strategic Management Journal*, *18*(7), 509–533. DOI: 10.1002/(SICI)1097-0266(199708)18:7<509::AID-SMJ882>3.0.CO;2-Z

Thakur, J., & Kushwaha, B. P. (2024). Artificial intelligence in marketing research and future research directions: Science mapping and research clustering using bibliometric analysis. *Global Business and Organizational Excellence*, *43*(3), 139–155. DOI: 10.1002/joe.22233

Theurer, C. P., Tumasjan, A., Welpe, I. M., & Lievens, F. (2018). Employer branding: A brand equity-based literature review and research agenda. *International Journal of Management Reviews*, *20*(1), 155–179. DOI: 10.1111/ijmr.12121

Thirunagalingam, A., & Selvakumar, P. (2025). Application of Automation and Robotics in the Oil and Gas Industry. In Abdullayev, V., & Khang, A. (Eds.), *Revolutionizing AI and Robotics in the Oil and Gas Industry* (pp. 229–244). IGI Global Scientific Publishing. DOI: 10.4018/979-8-3693-8156-4.ch011

Thomas, V. L., & Grigsby, J. L. (2024). Narrative transportation: A systematic literature review and future research agenda. *Psychology and Marketing*, *41*(8), 1805–1819. DOI: 10.1002/mar.22011

Tight, M. (2017). Understanding case study research: Small-scale research with meaning. *Sage (Atlanta, Ga.)*. Advance online publication. DOI: 10.4135/9781473920118

Tripathi, A., & Kumar, V. (2025). Ethical practices of artificial intelligence: A management framework for responsible AI deployment in businesses. *AI and Ethics*, *5*(4), 1–12. DOI: 10.1007/s43681-025-00670-3

Tschang, F. T., & Almirall, E. (2021). Artificial intelligence as augmenting automation: Implications for employment. *The Academy of Management Perspectives*, *35*(4), 642–659. DOI: 10.5465/amp.2019.0062

U.S. Department of Housing and Urban Development (HUD). (2019). HUD charges Facebook with housing discrimination. *HUD Press Release.* https://archives.hud.gov/news/2019/pr19-035.cfm

Upadhyaya, A. N., Debnath, P., Rani, P., Manjunath, T. C., & Bhattacharya, S. (2025). AI-Based Disaster Prediction and Early Warning Systems. In Mobo, F. (Ed.), *AI and Emerging Technologies for Emergency Response and Smart Cities* (pp. 55–74). IGI Global Scientific Publishing. DOI: 10.4018/979-8-3693-9770-1.ch003

Valentino-Devries, J. (2019). How E-Commerce Sites Manipulate You Into Buying Things You May Not Want. *International New York Times*, NA-NA.

Vallabhaneni, A. S., Perla, A., Regalla, R. R., & Kumari, N. (2024). The power of personalization: AI-driven recommendations. In *Minds Unveiled* (pp. 111–127). Productivity Press., DOI: 10.4324/9781032711089-9

Varela, L., Putnik, G., & Romero, F. (2022). The concept of collaborative engineering: A systematic literature review. *Production & Manufacturing Research, 10*(1), 784–839. DOI: 10.1080/21693277.2022.2133856

Varsha, P. S., Akter, S., Kumar, A., Gochhait, S., & Patagundi, B. (2021). The impact of artificial intelligence on branding. *Journal of Global Information Management, 29*(4), 221–246. DOI: 10.4018/JGIM.20210701.oa10

Venkateswaran, P. S., Dominic, M. L., Agarwal, S., Oberai, H., Anand, I., & Rajest, S. S. (2023). *The role of artificial intelligence (AI) in enhancing marketing and customer loyalty. Data-driven intelligent business sustainability*. IGI Global Scientific Publishing., DOI: 10.4018/979-8-3693-0049-7.ch003

Venkateswaran, P. S., Manimaran, S., Sriramkumar, M., Reddi, L. T., Rangineni, S., & Marupaka, D. (2024). *Application of artificial intelligence to enhance business intelligence for increasing customer involvement in the FMCG industry. Cross-industry AI applications*. IGI Global Scientific Publishing., DOI: 10.4018/979-8-3693-5951-8.ch003

Venkateswaran, P. S., & Ngo, N. Q. N. (2025). *Quantitative analysis of AI-driven predictive analytics in digital marketing. Strategic blueprints for AI-driven marketing in the digital era*. IGI Global Scientific Publishing.

Verganti, R., Vendraminelli, L., & Iansiti, M. (2020). Innovation and Design in the Age of Artificial Intelligence. *Journal of Product Innovation Management, 37*(3), 212–227. DOI: 10.1111/jpim.12523

Verma, A. (2025). Social Media Marketing. In Marketing in a Digital World: Strategies, Evolution and Global Impact (pp. 179–205). BENTHAM SCIENCE PUBLISHERS. DOI: 10.2174/9789815305456125010009

Vetrivel, S. C., Arun, V. P., Saravanan, T. P., & Maheswari, R. (2024). Harnessing AI for Next-Generation Service Marketing. In *Integrating AI-Driven Technologies into Service Marketing* (pp. 265–298). IGI Global. DOI: 10.4018/979-8-3693-7122-0.ch015

Vidrih, M., & Mayahi, S. (2023). Generative AI-driven storytelling: A new era for marketing. arXiv preprint. https://doi.org//arXiv.2309.09048DOI: 10.48550

Vredenburg, J., Kapitan, S., Spry, A., & Kemper, J. A. (2020). Brands Taking a Stand: Authentic Brand Activism or Woke Washing? *Journal of Public Policy & Marketing, 39*(4), 444–460. DOI: 10.1177/0743915620947359

Wallace, L. G., & Sheetz, S. D. (2014). The adoption of software measures: A technology acceptance model (TAM) perspective. *Information & Management, 51*(2), 249–259. DOI: 10.1016/j.im.2013.12.003

Wang, H., Du, Q., Wang, Y., Xu, H., Wei, Z., & Wang, X. (2024). GPro: Generative AI-empowered toolkit for promoter design. *Bioinformatics (Oxford, England), 40*(3), btae123. DOI: 10.1093/bioinformatics/btae123

Wang, Y. (2023). Research on the relationship between enterprise management mode and enterprise management modernization under the background of artificial intelligence. *Academic Journal of Business & Management, 5*(15), 53–57.

Wang, Y. (2024). KOL strategy under the empowerment of AI: A new chapter in brand marketing. Advances in Economics. *Management and Political Sciences, 113*(1), 116–122.

Wang, Z., Ho, S.-B., & Cambria, E. (2020). A review of emotion sensing: Categorization models and algorithms. *Multimedia Tools and Applications, 79*(47–48), 35553–35582. DOI: 10.1007/s11042-019-08328-z

Waqas, M., Hamzah, Z. L., & Mohd Salleh, N. A. (2021). Customer experience with the branded content: A social media perspective. *Online Information Review, 45*(5), 964–982. DOI: 10.1108/OIR-10-2019-0333

Wedel, M., & Kannan, P. K. (2016). Marketing analytics for data-rich environments. *Journal of Marketing, 80*(6), 97–121. DOI: 10.1509/jm.15.0413

Wen, Y., & Laporte, S. (2025). Experiential Narratives in Marketing: A Comparison of Generative AI and Human Content. *Journal of Public Policy & Marketing, 44*(3), 392–410. DOI: 10.1177/07439156241297973

Whittaker, M., Crawford, K., Dobbe, R., Fried, G., Kaziunas, E., Mathur, V., West, S. M., Richardson, R., Schultz, J., & Schwartz, O. (2018). *AI now report 2018.* AI Now Institute at New York University.

Wirtz, J., Tarbit, J., Hartley, N., & Kunz, W. (2022). Corporate digital responsibility: Dealing with ethical, privacy and fairness challenges of AI. *Journal of AI. Robotics & Workplace Automation, 1*(4), 325. DOI: 10.69554/EJDV6502

Wu, L., Zheng, Z., Qiu, Z., Wang, H., Gu, H., Shen, T., Qin, C., Zhu, C., Zhu, H., Liu, Q., Xiong, H., & Chen, E. (2024). A survey on large language models for recommendation. *World Wide Web (Bussum), 27*(5), 60. DOI: 10.1007/s11280-024-01291-2

Wu, Z., Shen, C., & van den Hengel, A. (2019). Wider or Deeper: Revisiting the ResNet Model for Visual Recognition. *Pattern Recognition*, *90*, 119–133. DOI: 10.1016/j.patcog.2019.01.006

Yadav, R. (2025). Building an ethical AI culture within organizations. In Transforming Corporate Social Responsibility and Business Ethics With AI (pp. 1–30). DOI: 10.4018/979-8-3693-9894-4.ch001

Yadav, R., Huzooree, G., Yadav, M., & Dewasiri, N. J. (2026). The influence of virtual currencies on sustainable service marketing in emerging economies. In Sustainable Service Marketing with Virtual Currencies (pp. 235–256).

Yadav, R., Singh, S. K., & Gunathilaka, D. H. P. M. (2025). Policy and regulatory frameworks for AI and global work: Navigating the challenges. In Global Work Arrangements and Outsourcing in the Age of AI (pp. 269–282).

Yadav, S. P., Jindal, M., Rani, P., de Albuquerque, V. H. C., dos Santos Nascimento, C., & Kumar, M. (2023). An improved deep learning-based optimal object detection system from images. *Multimedia Tools and Applications*, *83*(10), 30045–30072. DOI: 10.1007/s11042-023-16736-5

Yang, D., Wei, Z., Shi, H., & Zhao, J. (2020). Market orientation, strategic flexibility and business model innovation. *Journal of Business and Industrial Marketing*, *35*(4), 771–784. DOI: 10.1108/JBIM-12-2018-0372

Yari, N., Lankut, E., Alon, I., & Richter, N. F. (2020). Cultural intelligence, global mindset, and cross-cultural competencies: A systematic review using bibliometric methods. *European Journal of International Management*, *14*(2), 210. DOI: 10.1504/EJIM.2020.105567

Yathiraju, N. (2022). Investigating the use of an artificial intelligence model in an ERP cloud-based system. *International Journal of Electrical. Electronics and Computers*, *7*(2), 1–26.

Yella, S. (2024). AI-driven content creation and personalization: Revolutionizing digital marketing strategies. International Research Journal of Engineering and Technology (IRJET), 11(5), 1889–1893. https://www.irjet.net

Yin, R. K. (2012). *Applications of Case Study Research* (3rd ed.).

Yuan, P. (2024). A research on the dynamization effect of brand visual identity design: Mediated by digital information smart media. *Journal of Information Systems Engineering & Management*, *9*(1), 24153. DOI: 10.55267/iadt.07.14078

Yu, J., & Meng, T. (2025). Image Generative AI in Tourism: Trends, Impacts, and Future Research Directions. *Journal of Hospitality & Tourism Research (Washington, D.C.)*. Advance online publication. DOI: 10.1177/10963480251324676

Zallio, M., & Clarkson, P. J. (2021). Inclusion, diversity, equity and accessibility in the built environment: A study of architectural design practice. *Building and Environment, 206*, 108352. DOI: 10.1016/j.buildenv.2021.108352

Zangana, H. M., Omar, M., & Al-Karaki, J. N. (2025). Data Privacy and Security Standards in AI-Powered Scientific Research. In *Ensuring Secure and Ethical STM Research in the AI Era* (pp. 1–42). IGI Global Scientific Publishing. DOI: 10.4018/979-8-3373-4252-8.ch001

Zdravković, M., Panetto, H., & Weichhart, G. (2022). AI-enabled enterprise information systems for manufacturing. *Enterprise Information Systems, 16*(4), 668–720. DOI: 10.1080/17517575.2021.1941275

Zhao, X., Wang, L., Zhang, Y., Han, X., Deveci, M., & Parmar, M. (2024). A review of convolutional neural networks in computer vision. *Artificial Intelligence Review, 57*(4), 99. DOI: 10.1007/s10462-024-10721-6

Zheng, H., & Huang, L. (2022). Owned Social Media Advertising: Cannibalization and Competition. *Journal of Interactive Marketing, 57*(3), 442–456. DOI: 10.1177/10949968221095555

Zyskind, G., & Nathan, O. (2015, May). *Decentralizing privacy: Using blockchain to protect personal data. In 2015 IEEE security and privacy workshops*. IEEE., DOI: 10.1109/SPW.2015.27

About the Contributors

Md Faiz Ahmad, an academician and researcher specializing in marketing specially consumer behaviour in emerging digital marketing trends, holds a Ph.D. in Management Studies from the University of Hyderabad, India. With over 9 years of experience in research, academia and industry, he has developed a strong foundation in marketing research and business strategies. He is currently an Assistant Professor at Department of Management, Paari School of Business, SRM University-AP, where he teaches and mentors students in contemporary marketing practices. His work has been published in renowned journals indexed in ABDC, SCOPUS, and Web of Science (WoS). In addition to research, he collaborates with industry professionals and academic peers to conduct market research and data-driven marketing analysis. Passionate about education and innovation, he strives to bridge the gap between theory and practice.

Mudassir Rafi is an accomplished academic and researcher in the field of Computer Science, currently serving as an Assistant Professor at King Khalid University, Saudi Arabia, and SRM University, AP, India. With a strong background in digital image processing, artificial intelligence, and machine learning applications, he has made significant contributions to academia through teaching, research, and innovation. Dr. Rafi earned his Ph.D. from the Indian Institute of Technology (IIT), Dhanbad, specializing in texture processing and analysis. Prior to that, he completed his Master of Computer Applications (M.C.A.) from Jamia Millia Islamia, New Delhi, and his Bachelor of Science (Honors) from Aligarh Muslim University. His academic career spans various prestigious institutions, including NIT Jamshedpur, KL University Hyderabad, and NIST Berhampur, where he has taught and mentored students across multiple disciplines. Research Contributions & Achievements Dr. Rafi's research interests revolve around image segmentation, texture analysis, object detection, and medical image processing. His work has been published in renowned journals such as Springer's Multimedia Tools and Applications and the International

Arab Journal of Information Technology. He has also presented his findings at numerous IEEE and international conferences. His achievements include receiving a Silver Certificate at the IEEE International Conference ICCSPCIT-2015 for his outstanding research contributions. Dr. Rafi holds patents in AI-driven solutions, including a Smart Water Heater System and an AI-based Recommendation System for Products and Services, reflecting his commitment to technological advancements. Beyond research, Dr. Rafi has played a key role in academic governance, serving as a Research Committee Member and Course Coordinator for AI-related courses. He has also been an active reviewer for high-impact journals such as IET Image Processing and Digital Signal Processing. An advocate for knowledge dissemination, he has delivered expert talks on AI, machine learning, and scientific writing at international faculty development programs and workshops. With a distinguished academic career and a passion for research-driven innovation, Dr. Mudassir Rafi continues to shape the future of computer science through his contributions in academia and industry collaborations.

Mohd Danish Kirmani, a dedicated educator and researcher in marketing, holds a Ph.D. in Management and has over 8 years of teaching experience. He is currently an Assistant Professor at the School of Management, IILM University, Greater Noida where he teaches courses on Consumer Behavior, International Marketing and Product Management. Dr. Kirmani's research focuses on online consumer behavior and sustainable and responsible consumption, topics that are highly relevant and important in the digital age. He has published multiple research articles in prestigious journals and received an Emerald Literati Award for his paper on consumer empowerment. He also collaborates with industry partners and academic peers to conduct market research and data analysis projects. He aims to contribute to the advancement of knowledge and practice in marketing and to inspire his students and colleagues with his enthusiasm and expertise.

Abdullah received his B.Tech. in Computer Science and Engineering from Deenbandhu Chhotu Ram University of Science and Technology (DCRUST), Murthal (Sonepat), Haryana, India, and his M.Tech. in Nanoscience from Jawaharlal Nehru University (JNU), New Delhi, India. He is currently pursuing a Ph.D. in Electrical Engineering at the Indian Institute of Technology Jodhpur (IIT Jodhpur), Rajasthan, India (342030). His research experience includes materials synthesis and characterization, AlGaN/GaN-based HEMT devices, and multiphysics simulation using COMSOL Multiphysics. His current work focuses on the design and optimization of micro gas chromatography (μGC) columns, including chemical mixture separation and mixing analysis in microfluidic systems. His research interests include MEMS, microfluidics, microscale transport phenomena, and lab-on-chip devices.

Abu Bakar Abdul Hamid chose academia as his profession in 1992, beginning as a lecturer and later rising to a Professor of Marketing and Supply Chain Management. He holds a BBA and an MBA from Northrop University (USA) and a PhD from the University of Derby, UK. He has demonstrated an excellent record of teaching and supervision for more than 25 years in the academic field, at both undergraduate and postgraduate levels. Above all, his achievement in graduating more than 35 PhD candidates proves his ability, capability, and passion in postgraduate supervisions. He has also produced impactful research and publications which directly strengthen his expertise in his area of interest. In particular, he has published more than 300 articles in competitive international journals, proceedings, books, and book chapters. He also managed to secure several competitive national grants and consultancies for various projects. Such commitment is truly a landmark of an academician. His accolades, academic recognition, and leadership demonstrate his level of professorship. His notable contributions are recognized locally and internationally, as proven by the multiple invitations he has received to be an invited speaker, reviewer, editor in journals, external assessor, and internal or external examiner. With such calibre, he has much to contribute to any academic institution in the world.

Md Mahdi Hasan Ahid is a research practitioner in the field of business and management, with a strong focus on key areas such as supply chain management, strategic innovation, marketing, enterprise efficiency, and management information systems. His research explores how emerging technologies and data-driven approaches can optimize organizational processes, enhance marketing effectiveness, and support sustainable growth across business ecosystems. By aligning innovation with practical business needs, he addresses real-world challenges through applied and impactful research. Ahid's work bridges academic theory and professional practice, making significant contributions to the evolving landscape of business, management, and digital transformation.

Parvez Ahmad is an Assistant Professor at SRM University. His research focuses on consumer behaviour and supply Chain Management. Mr Ahmad holds a Master of Business Administration degree in Operations and Marketing Management and a Bachelor of Science in Physics (HONS) from Aligarh Muslim University. He has contributed to the Service Quality of Food Delivery Apps. Ahmad has published research papers in reputed journals, including ABDC-A, B, C, Scopus, and Wos Wos-indexed journals. Currently, he is conducting experimental research to understand the consumer behaviour towards packaging waste through augmented reality.

Salam Al-E'mari earned her Ph.D. in Cybersecurity from Universiti Sains Malaysia (USM) in 2022. She is the Chair of the Information Security Department and an Assistant Professor at the University of Petra (UoP). With expertise in Blockchain, Deep Learning, and Network Security, she has contributed significantly to cybersecurity research. She previously earned her Bachelor's and Master's in Computer Science from Yarmouk University, Jordan, shaping her strong foundation in security and technology.

Shiney Chib is a distinguished academic leader currently serving as the Dean – Academics at Datta Meghe Institute of Management Studies, Nagpur, Maharashtra. In this leadership role, she is responsible for overseeing academic planning, curriculum development, and the effective implementation of teaching–learning processes across management programs. With rich experience in higher education and academic administration, Dr. Chib plays a key role in strengthening institutional academic frameworks and ensuring alignment with regulatory, accreditation, and quality assurance standards. She actively contributes to outcome-based education, academic audits, and continuous improvement initiatives. Dr. Shiney Chib is deeply committed to promoting academic excellence, student-centric learning, and faculty development. She encourages innovative pedagogical practices, interdisciplinary learning, and research-oriented academic culture within the institution. Through her visionary leadership and academic stewardship, Dr. Shiney Chib continues to significantly contribute to the growth and academic reputation of Datta Meghe Institute of Management Studies and to the development of future management professionals.

Md Mehedi Hasan Emon is a research practitioner in Business and Management, with specialized in Supply Chain Management, Digital Transformation, Marketing, Information Systems, and Educational Technology (Edutech). His work bridges a diverse range of domains including Artificial Intelligence in Business, Human-Computer Interaction, Cognitive Behaviour, E-commerce, and Smart Logistics. His research extensively explores the integration of emerging technologies in business ecosystems focusing on AI-driven innovation, behavioral responses to technology adoption, and digital marketing strategies. He has also contributed significantly to sustainability-focused fields such as GreenTech, Green Finance, Renewable Energy, and Blockchain-enabled financial innovation. Additionally, his work in Smart Cities and IoT adoption emphasizes the importance of user trust, security, and operational efficiency. Emon has authored numerous peer-reviewed publications on topics including AI adoption intention, supply chain visibility, digital learning acceptance, and crisis-resilient supply chains. Many of his studies adopt behavioral and cognitive perspectives to understand how professionals and consumers interact with technology highlighting the psychological and user-centric aspects of digital transformation. He has participated in several research initiatives funded by the University Grants Commission of Bangladesh and the European Union. His work aligns closely with the United Nations Sustainable Development Goals (SDGs), particularly in areas such as poverty reduction, access to quality education, clean and affordable energy, inclusive economic growth, sustainable industrialization, responsible consumption, climate resilience, and ocean sustainability. His work also reflects a commitment to reducing inequalities and fostering international partnerships for sustainable development. In addition to his research contributions, he serves as a peer reviewer for several high-impact academic journals and is widely recognized for promoting academic rigor and ethical scholarship. As a prolific author, he continues to shape the discourse on sustainability, innovation, and digital advancement through his research, writing, and knowledge dissemination.

Alijon Esanov is a faculty member in the Department of Uzbek Language and Literature at Termez University of Economics and Service, Termez, Uzbekistan. He is actively involved in teaching and academic activities related to Uzbek language, literature, and cultural studies, with an emphasis on linguistic heritage, literary analysis, and language education. His academic interests include Uzbek literary traditions, language pedagogy, and the promotion of national culture through higher education, and he contributes to curriculum development and scholarly initiatives aimed at enhancing language learning and literary appreciation.

Md Nafis Fuad is an accomplished researcher specializing in Business and Management, Digital Marketing, Human Resource Management (HRM), and Information Technology. His work emphasizes the integration of digital marketing analytics and the application of artificial intelligence in HR processes, with a particular focus on promoting sustainable business practices. Mr. Fuad has contributed numerous publications, earning recognition for his growing impact within the global academic and professional communities. His research bridges technology and management to address evolving challenges in modern business environments. With a clear vision to leverage artificial intelligence, Mr. Fuad strives to advance sustainability, improve operational efficiency, and foster innovation in digital marketing and HRM, thereby contributing to the transformation of contemporary business practices.

Dhananjay Kulkarni is a Senior Assistant Professor at the Balaji Institute of Management and Human Resource Development (BIMHRD), under Sri Balaji University, Pune. A seasoned academician and management professional, he brings a wealth of experience in teaching, training, and corporate interface. Prof. Kulkarni is known for his dynamic teaching style, practical approach to management education, and dedication to student development. His academic interests lie in the areas of management, leadership, and organizational behavior, where he continually bridges theory with real-world business practices. With a strong commitment to nurturing future leaders, Prof. Kulkarni contributes significantly to the institute's mission of excellence in management education and holistic student growth.

Tahsina Khan is serving as Deputy Director (Research) at the Centre for Higher Studies and Research in Bangladesh University of Professionals (BUP). In addition, she is also serving as the Assistant Editor of the BUP Journal. She is an Academician in Business Studies with more than 14 years of teaching, research & consulting experience in Higher Education Institutions. Over the years, she has successfully supervised multilateral academic programs in collaboration with the Government, NGOs, and Corporations from the Business sector. As a Visiting Lecturer, she has taught in the MBA program of the University of Gavle, Sweden. She has worked as Director of the research projects funded by the University Grants Commission (UGC) under the Ministry of Education. Her research papers were presented in National and International Conferences in Canada, France, Malaysia and Indonesia. As Session Chair, she presided over the conference organized by Higher Education and Innovation Group (HEAIG). She has also been invited as a resource speaker at the United Nations affiliated conference at the Yonsei University in Wonju, South Korea. She has published a number of peer-reviewed articles in reputed international journals and her policy brief paper on Rural Development has been included in the knowledge hub of the UN Task Force on SDG implementation. She is a member of International Sociological Association (ISA) which is associated with UNESCO, Economic & Social Council of the United Nations.

Mohammad Mofasserul Islam is an Assistant Professor and researcher at the College of Tourism and Hospitality Management, International University of Business Agriculture and Technology, Bangladesh. With a passion for advancing tourism and hospitality education, he specializes in areas such as sustainable tourism and innovative hospitality practices. Known for his commitment to academic excellence, he actively engages in research that bridges theory and practice, contributing to both local and global tourism discourse. His work emphasizes the integration of sustainability and innovation, aiming to enhance the industry's growth while addressing contemporary challenges.

P. Selvakumar is currently an Associate Professor in the Department of Science and Humanities at Nehru Institute of Technology, Coimbatore, Tamil Nadu, India. Prior to joining Nehru Institute of Technology, he held positions as an Assistant Professor in the Department of Science and Humanities various engineering colleges in Coimbatore, Tamil Nadu, India, spanning from 2011 to 2023. Dr.P. Selvakumar's academic and research interests lie primarily in the field of phytochemistry. He has made significant contributions to his field, with an impressive record that includes 30 journal publications, 12 patents, and 20 conference papers. Additionally, he has organized 5 seminars and conferences, further demonstrating his commitment to academic and scientific exchange. Throughout his career, Dr. P.Selvakumar has been recognized for his dedication and excellence in teaching, having been honored with several awards, including the Best Teacher Awards. He holds a prominent position in the academic community, contributing actively to research.

Ravikumar R. Natarajan is an experienced academician with over 12+ years of teaching and research expertise across institutions in India, the UAE, and the Maldives. He currently serves as an Assistant Professor at Marwadi University, Rajkot, specializing in Machine Learning, Recommender Systems, and AI-driven applications in healthcare and security. He holds a Ph.D. in Machine Learning and Recommender Systems from Amity University, Jaipur, a Master of Engineering in CSE from VMRF University, Salem, and a Bachelor of Engineering in CSE from Anna University. He also has a MiniMBA from the Swiss eLearning Institute. Dr. Ravikumar has authored more than 8+ multiple SCIE/Scopus-indexed journal articles, 25+ IEEE/Springer conference papers, and co-authored a book on Artificial Intelligence. He has also published 9 patents and contributed 10+ book chapters in emerging domains such as Federated Learning, Blockchain, and Digital Twins for IGI Global, Wiley and Springer publisher. He actively mentors students through initiatives like the Research Activities Club (RAC) and Student Research Internship Training (SRIT), promoting innovation and research culture.

Md. Adnan Rahman is an Associate Professor of Digital Marketing and MIS at Uttara University, Dhaka, Bangladesh. Additionally, he is the Director of the Office of Brand & Communication and Public Relations of this university. Dr. Adnan is a postdoctoral researcher at Infrastructure University Kuala Lumpur (IUKL), Malaysia. Dr. Adnan holds a PhD in Marketing from Putra Business School (AACSB-Accredited), UPM, Malaysia; an MSc in MIS; and an MA in IHRM from the University of Bedfordshire, United Kingdom.

Aarthi S is a dedicated Assistant Professor in Computer Science with over six years of teaching experience. She is currently pursuing her Ph.D. at Marwadi

University, Gujarat, and holds an M.Phil. and MCA from Bharathiar University, Tamil Nadu. Throughout her academic career, Aarthi has specialized in programming languages such as C++, Java, and C, and contributed to research in recommender systems and AI-related data privacy. She has published journal articles, contributed to book chapters, and actively participated in technical workshops. Known for her student mentorship and engagement in academic events, Aarthi remains committed to fostering innovation and excellence in computer science education.

Guru Basava Aradhya S. is a distinguished academic leader and Professor with 18 years of experience. Holding a PhD in Management and several international patents, his expertise encompasses HR analytics, AI-driven management, and strategic growth. He has published extensively in Scopus and ABDC journals and authored influential books on HR metrics and strategy . Currently, he serves as Professor in Dr DY Patil B School, Pune, Maharashtra.

Ansuman Samal is currently working as a Professor in the Faculty of Hospitality & Tourism Management at Siksha O Anusandhan Deemed to be University, Bhubaneswar, Odisha. He has more than 18 years of experience both in the field of marketing research and in academics. He has completed his graduation in Information Technology from Manipal Academy of Higher Education, MBA from KIIT Deemed to be University and PhD from Siksha O Anusandhan Deemed to be University. As an acclaimed scholar, he has received the Chancellor's Gold Medal from KIIT Deemed to be University for securing highest mark during the MBA programme. Before joining Siksha O Anusandhan, he was working as a senior researcher at IMRS Advisory Pvt. Ltd. In Bengaluru. As an academician, he has published more than 80 numbers of research articles in various National and International journals of repute. He has also authored 5 Books and has participated in more than 100 numbers of National and International Conferences, workshops, seminars / webinars and presented his research works. He has successfully guided 2 numbers of PhD students and another 4 students are currently continuing their research work under his guidance. His research interests include services marketing, hospitality & tourism management, consumer behavior, quality management, and strategic management.

Yousef K. Sanjalawe is an Assistant Professor specializing in Cybersecurity and Cloud Computing at the University of Jordan (JU), Jordan. He earned his PhD in Cloud Computing from Universiti Sains Malaysia (USM) in 2020, where his research focused on enhancing cloud service broker selection using optimization algorithms. Dr. Sanjalawe has extensive experience in academia, research, and professional training. He has supervised Ph.D. students in Cybersecurity, Cloud

Computing, IoT, Fog Computing, Optimization, and Artificial Intelligence (AI). From 2023 to 2024, he served as the Chair of the Cybersecurity Department at the American University of Madaba (AUM), Jordan, and from 2022 to 2024, he was an Assistant Professor in Cybersecurity at AUM.

Valisher Sapayev is a faculty member in the Department of General Professional Subjects at Mamun University, Khiva, Uzbekistan. He is actively engaged in undergraduate teaching and academic development, contributing to curriculum delivery and interdisciplinary learning across foundational professional subjects. His academic interests include higher education pedagogy, professional skill development, and the integration of contemporary instructional approaches to enhance student learning outcomes. Dr. Sapayev is involved in institutional academic activities and collaborations aimed at strengthening teaching quality and fostering a learner-centered educational environment.

Pamarthi Satyanarayana, specialize in Constitutional Law and Legal Order, focusing my research on the interface between individual rights and public policy, with a strong emphasis on civil liberties, social justice, and the right to privacy. Over the past 18 months, I have served as an Assistant Professor of Law at Vel Tech Rangarajan Dr. Sagunthala R&D Institute of Science and Technology in Chennai, Tamil Nadu. Here, I teach courses such as Constitutional Law, Legal Research and Writing, and both Civil and Criminal Law. My passion for teaching and in-depth subject knowledge have earned me recognition as a dedicated educator. In addition to my academic role, I actively engage with the community, partnering with legal clinics to provide pro bono services to underprivileged individuals. Looking forward, I aim to expand my research into emerging legal issues in the digital age, especially in privacy rights, while guiding aspiring law students and future legal scholars.

Achakkagari Shashidhar is pursuing a Ph.D. in the School of Management Studies at Hyderabad Central University. His research focuses on behavioural finance, sustainability, and public policy. Mr Achakkagari holds a Master of Business Administration degree in Business Analytics and a Bachelor of Commerce from Osmania University. Achakkagari has published research papers in reputed journals indexed in Scopus. Currently, he is working on Agricultural cash transfer schemes in Telugu states and also conducting experimental research to understand the consumer behaviour towards packaging waste through augmented reality

Zerin Tasnim is an Assistant Professor of Supply Chain Management at North South University, Dhaka, Bangladesh, where she also serves as the Course Coordinator for the MBA program. She holds a PhD in Management from Putra Business School, Universiti Putra Malaysia (UPM), and a BSc in Mechanical

Engineering from Bangladesh University of Engineering and Technology (BUET). Dr. Tasnim brings an interdisciplinary academic background and a global research perspective to her work, with research interests spanning digital supply chains, healthcare logistics, and sustainable and green operations.

Muhammad Usman is a Senior Lecturer in International Business. He is a member of the Ethics Review Panel (EPR) and Research Programme Appraisal (RPA) at UCLan. He teaches various modules at undergraduate and postgraduate level and supervises students' research projects. He is active in research and currently published various articles in high-ranking journals such as Environmental Science and Policy, International Journal of Finance and Economics and more. His research is in earnings management, corporate governance, environmental disclosure, and corporate finance.

P.S.Venkateswaran is currently working as a Professor in the Department of Management Studies, PSNA College of Engineering & Technology, Dindigul affiliated to Anna University, Chennai where he teaches courses in Advertising, marketing and Research Methods. He has served in various faculty positions from Assistant Professor to Professor in leading Arts & Colleges such as Cherran Arts and Science College, Kangeyam and Sree Saraswathi Thyagaraja College, Pollachi. He received MSc in Physics, an M.B.A., from Bharathiar University and MPhil from Alagappa University Karaikudi. He received his Ph.D in Business Administration from Madurai Kamaraj University, Madurai. He is having twenty two years of teaching and nine years of research & consultancy experience. His research activities include on Branding, Advertising and Digital marketing He conducted more than 90 Entrepreneurship Awareness Camps and trained around 8000 Engineering, Arts and Science College students and motivated them towards entrepreneurship. He also conducted 10 Faculty Development programmes, 10 EDP/WEDP programmes and 7 TEDP programmes. He trained more the 200 women entrepreneurs in Dindigul District.

Index

A

B

C

D

E

www.ingramcontent.com/pod-product-compliance
Lightning Source LLC
LaVergne TN
LVHW080900300926
849162LV00003B/490